On the Front Line

ON THE FRONT LINE

Organization of Work in the Information Economy

Stephen J. Frenkel
Marek Korczynski
Karen A. Shire
May Tam

ILR PRESS
AN IMPRINT OF
CORNELL UNIVERSITY PRESS
Ithaca and London

First published 1999 by Cornell University Press
First printing, Cornell Paperbacks, 1999

Cornell International Industrial and Labor Relations Report Number 35

Printed in the United States of America

Library of Congress Cataloging-in-Publication Data
On the front line: organization of work in the information economy /
    Stephen J. Frenkel . . . [et al.].
        p.   cm.
    Includes bibliographical references and index.
    ISBN 0-8014-3587-0 (cloth: alk. paper).—ISBN 0-8014-8567-3 (pbk: alk. paper)
    1. Work.   2. Production management.   3. Industrial sociology.
4. Service industries.   5. Workflow systems—Case studies.
I. Frenkel, Stephen.
HD4904.0487   1999
306.3'6—dc21   98-36539

Cornell University Press strives to use environmentally responsible suppliers and materials to the fullest extent possible in the publishing of its books. Such materials include vegetable-based, low-VOC inks and acid-free papers that are recycled, totally chlorine-free, or partly composed of nonwood fibers. Books that bear the logo of the FSC (Forest Stewardship Council) use paper taken from forests that have been inspected and certified as meeting the highest standards for environmental and social responsibility. For further information, visit our website at www.cornellpress.cornell.edu.

Cloth printing   10 9 8 7 6 5 4 3 2 1
Paperback printing   10 9 8 7 6 5 4 3 2 1

Contents

v

List of Figures

List of Tables

Preface

This book grew from a seed planted by Jane Hemstritch, a partner in Change Management Services, Andersen Consulting. She noted that consultants often gave customer-contact employees advice based on remarkably little solid research. This paradox sparked our interest in what we refer to as front-line work. Indeed, the unique and fruitful research partnership that developed merits comment since it has implications for project governance and the conduct of objective inquiry.

Most large-scale social science research projects are funded from the public purse and controlled by academic experts. This is changing, however, as governments restrict and channel funding in particular directions. Our project, supported mainly by Andersen Consulting, a private-sector organization, may therefore be seen as an emerging alternative.

The project was guided by two basic principles: cooperation and scientific integrity. A skeptic might wonder whether these principles are compatible with a project funded by a private-sector organization. The answer depends on one's personal values and what happens in practice. Clearly, a consulting organization is unlikely to support research that is fundamentally antithetical to its interests or those of its clients. Nevertheless, if these interests are sufficiently wide to encompass scientific research, then, in principle, there is no clash of interests. In exploring this issue before agreeing on a broad research agenda, we found common ground with Andersen Consulting. There were, however, two areas in which compromises had to be made.

The first was that Andersen Consulting wanted to ensure that the research findings would be converted into "knowledge capital" for use at client sites. To facilitate this knowledge transfer, we agreed to recruit an Andersen Consulting manager as a full-time researcher. He was selected by Steve Frenkel, the project director, in consultation with other team members, on the understanding that some of his time would be devoted to knowledge applications. In addition, Steve Frenkel agreed to participate in occasional public forums organized with Andersen Consulting for the purpose of disseminating knowledge to members of the organization and managers more generally.

The second compromise concerned administrative control of expenditures. To assure the donor that adequate control would be exercised over expenditures, we agreed to follow Andersen Consulting budgetary guidelines and to report regularly to an advisory committee that included two senior Andersen Consulting representatives. The committee met quarterly for three and half years and occasionally thereafter. Jane Hemstritch and Dexter Dunphy (previously executive director of the Centre for Corporate Change) were there from start to finish, while Anne De Lacy and Neil Perry traveled with us for much of the time. We thank them all.

Within these parameters, it was agreed that normal social scientific procedures would apply. In particular, recruitment and resource allocation, identification of the problems to be researched, and the methodology, interpretation, and publication of our findings were matters under the sole discretion of the research team leader in consultation with the team. In practice, this arrangement worked well. Leigh Donoghue, whom we recruited from Andersen Consulting, worked on the project for three years, contributing significantly to our ideas, to data collection, to mentoring of part-time research assistants, and to financial reporting. We extend our warmest thanks to him.

Generous funding encouraged us to broaden and deepen the research in ways that stretched our imaginations and stamina. Thus, our work covers fourteen case studies and a survey of more than one thousand employees working in Australia, Japan, and the United States. Simultaneously combining case study and survey work involved a great deal of iteration between different data sets, and synthesizing our findings while working as a virtual team distributed in three countries was not easy. Further, writing a book inevitably requires choices about what issues and data to include and exclude.

This book is about similarities and differences in work organization, specifically, the knowledge, skills, and creativity used in undertaking different kinds of customer-related—that is, front-line—work. It is not about differences in work organizations within similar work settings. We explore how authority relations (employment and control relations) and the lateral division of labor (co-worker and customer relations) vary in front-line service, sales, and knowledge work settings, including some employee consequences. Cross-national differences are a subsidiary theme. We compare Anglo-Saxon (Australian and U.S.) work organization with that of Japan.

Along the way we were helped by many people. Thanks to David Peetz and Roderick Martin (visiting from the United Kingdom) for commenting on a draft of our survey instrument. Data classification, coding, and other assistance were admirably executed by Steve Barnes, S. J. Chapman, Andrea Curr, Fiona Davies, Helen Fisher, Sylvia Kanavaros, Scott Kirkham, Julia Nathan, Keiko Numata, Gaby Pimstone, Sally Pittman, Barbara Potter, and Bill Sullivan. Cheryl Scott provided efficient administrative assistance, and Jean Rogers produced the figures in the book. The librarians at the Australian Graduate School of Management were always helpful in responding to our many requests.

In Japan, Bill Bramer, managing partner of Andersen Consulting, kindly facilitated introductions to leading Japanese firms. Professors Koya Azumi, Mire Koikari, Motohiro Morishima, and Kazuko Tanaka offered valuable comments on drafts of our survey. Nobuyuki Ota was especially helpful in negotiations with several Japanese companies. With Madoka Ota, he assisted in fieldwork and data coding.

In the United States, Susan Cohen gave us helpful advice on survey items. We would also like to thank Randy Hodson for his comments on several chapters and Harry Katz, who read and commented on the whole manuscript. Thanks too to Fran Benson, Erica Fox, and Candace Akins for their excellent editorial advice and assistance. Special thanks to Jane Hemstritch for her unflagging support, and to the workers and managers who cooperated so wholeheartedly with us.

Finally, we record our thanks to the Australian Research Council for establishing the Centre for Corporate Change which served as a congenial home for our project. The Council and the Matsushita International Foundation, directly supplemented our research funding, for which we are also grateful.

Abbreviations

ANOVA	One-way analysis of variance
B type (or B model)	Bureaucratic ideal type
CSR	Customer Service Representative
DOT	Dictionary of Occupational Titles
E type (or E model)	Entrepreneurial ideal type
ER	Employment Relations
HLC	Home Loan Consultant
HR	Human Resources
HRM	Human Resource Management
IT	Information Technology
KI type (or KI model)	Knowledge-Intensive ideal type
MM	Money Market
MNC	Multinational Corporation
OJT	On-the-Job Training
R & D	Research and Development
SD	Systems Developer
TQM	Total Quality Management
WO	Work Organization

Companies and Workflows

ABK	In top five financial services industry in Australia
ABKS	Sales workflow (home loans) in ABK
AIN	In top 15 percent financial services industry in Australia
AINSV	Service workflow (customer service representatives) in AIN
COMPUJ	In top ten in the world computer industry

COMPUJ SD	Knowledge workers (system developers) workflow in COMPUJ
JB	In top ten second-tier securities industry in Japan
JBSV	Service workflow (bond-ladies) in JB
JBS	Sales workflow (share salesmen) in JB
MBA	In top five US financial services industry
MBASV	Service workflow (customer service reps.) in Australian subsidiary of MBA
MBAS	Sales workflow (home loans) in Australian subsidiary of MBA
MFJ	In top ten in the world financial services industry
MFJSV	Service workflow (customer service reps.) in MFJ
TEL	In top five percent of Australia's communications industry
TELSV	Service workflow (customer service reps.) in TEL
TELSD	Knowledge worker (systems developers) workflow in TEL
UB	In top third in US financial services industry
UB1	Service workflow (customer service reps.) in UB
UB2	Second service workflow (as above) in UB
WB	In top ten in US financial services industry
WBMM	Knowledge workers (money market dealers) workflow in WB
WBSD	Second knowledge workers (systems developers) workflow in WB

Note: For further details on companies, see table 2.2, and on workflows, see table 2.3.

1 *Introduction*

IN the industrial era, scientific management was the handmaiden of mass production. Jobs were routinized and coordinated by large bureaucracies. In the informational economy, this is a no longer the case (Castells 1996; Kumar 1995). New forms of work organization are reshaping and replacing bureaucracies. To what extent are such changes fundamental rather than cosmetic? Is the death of the bureaucracy affecting work of varying complexity equally? Could it be that the transformation of work from bureaucracy to networks, shamrocks, and other new forms is too radical for most managers to implement?

Considerable evidence indicates that managers are adopting and discarding new forms of work organization at an unprecedented rate. Fads increase the sense of uncertainty among both managers and lower-level employees alike and, paradoxically, diminish the chances of success, which requires vision and strategy, and trust. Frequent tactical twists and turns undermine this process. In short, all employees are perplexed by the current changes occurring around them: they see substantial opportunities to improve productivity and satisfaction at work, but vision is blurred and trust is fragile. Solutions need to be found, but how?

The aim of this book is to contribute to the development of a more rigorous, analytical approach to identifying and implementing new models of work organization. In computing parlance, this process requires deep and systematic knowledge that will provide the platform for creating flexible applications.

As will become evident in more detail later, well-informed insights on appropriate forms of work organization do exist; however, these focus almost solely on production work—a shrinking part of the economy. Their relevance to the expanding service sector is questionable. Accordingly, we have located this study firmly in the service sector. Moreover, since concepts

1

developed to analyze production work are not likely to suit service work, forging new frameworks was necessary. Using extensive case study and survey materials, we focus on the work of front-line—that is, customer-oriented—employees whose tasks vary in complexity: from the relatively routine work of customer service representatives to the sometimes arcane activities of computer systems developers.

Our analysis is comparative in two respects: first, we explore how work organization varies among employees engaged in work of varying complexity; and, second, we compare work organization cross-nationally. For this purpose, we compare the United States and Australia—representing the Anglo-Saxon model of employment structure, on the one hand—and Japan—exemplifying an alternative, producer-oriented, postindustrial structure, on the other.[1] We show how variations in work complexity, regardless of national context, are associated with different forms of work organization, each resembling a particular ideal type (i.e., an internally consistent configuration that exists in theory but never perfectly in practice). We also demonstrate that, regardless of work complexity, the Japanese model of work organization is different from that of the Anglo-Saxon model and, contrary to findings in manufacturing, this difference is likely to impede economic performance.

As a prelude to our analysis, we shall briefly identify and consider the main trends and forces influencing work organization. This sets the scene for an appraisal of contemporary studies that have influenced the development of our theoretical framework. This discussion is followed by a summary of some of the issues and findings addressed in subsequent chapters of this book.

Trends and Forces Shaping Work Organization

Increasing market competition, customization of products, and technological change are altering the employment structure of the advanced societies. On the one hand, front-line service workers have become increasingly important, both as a proportion of the workforce and in strategic positions, at the interface of the organization and its customers. On the other hand, except for highly qualified employees, excess supply and market-strengthening government policies are generally weakening labor. Conse-

---

[1] In Australia and the United States there has been a long-term shift in employment from manufacturing to services, increasing considerably in producer services (e.g., financial services, consulting, accounting, and legal services). Simultaneously, relative employment growth occurred in personal and social service categories. The Japanese/German model differs in retaining sizable employment in manufacturing, and although these countries experienced significant growth in producer services, these tend to be within the manufacturing sector. As in the United States and Australia, Japan and Germany have undergone an increase in employment in personal and social services (Castells 1996: 211–16).

quently, the employment relationship has become more precarious and more pressured as management continuously search for ways to improve economic performance. This, in turn, has spurred both pessimistic and optimistic images of emerging forms of work organization.

Trend toward Service and Front-Line Work

High rates of labor-saving technological change in manufacturing, the growing demand for services, and the loss of lower-skilled production jobs to lower-wage countries, as a result of reductions in the barriers to international trade and foreign investment, have contributed to the relative decline of production jobs and the rise of service work. As Bell (1974) anti-cipated, the trend toward the growth of the service sector has continued. Thus, over the twenty-year period 1974–1994, service-sector employment increased by 9 percent, to 73 percent, in the United States, and by 13 percent, to 71 percent, in Australia. Service-sector employment also increased markedly during this period in Japan, from 50 percent to 60 percent, and employment in agriculture declined from 13 percent to 6 percent over this period (Organization for Economic Cooperation and Development [OECD] 1996a). In all these countries, the most rapid growth occurred in the financial and business service subsectors.[2] Indeed, projected estimates of employment in the twenty fastest-growing subsectors in the United States indicate that between 1994 and 2005 business services will expand the fastest, followed by personal services (U.S. Department of Labor 1996). The rise of the service sector is not reflected simply in employment figures, however. U.S. evidence indicates that the service sector accounts for four times more real value added than manufacturing.[3]

The notion that postindustrialism increasingly depends on theoretical knowledge (defined by Bell as the codification of knowledge into abstract systems of symbols having universal validity) also receives empirical support: witness the relative growth of brainpower industries, such as

[2] Between 1974 and 1994, this so-called producer service category increased from 7.4 percent to 11 percent of total employment in the United States and from 7.3 percent to 13 percent in Australia. For Japan, the increase was from 3.1 to 8.5 percent (OECD 1996b). Nevertheless, only about half the workers in the community, social, and personal services category, the largest of the four service categories in each of the three countries, are in the producer service category. In 1994, this category accounted for 34.5 percent of total U.S. employment. Corresponding figures for Australia and Japan are 26.1 percent and 22.8 percent respectively (OECD 1996b). Note that community and social services are funded mainly by governments. They are unlikely to grow substantially over the next decade.

[3] Cohen and Zysman (1987) have argued that manufacturing is a source of service activity. This dependence is not inevitable, however, particularly in a global economy, where the siting of economic activity depends on comparative advantage. See Lash and Urry 1994 for the view that services are relatively independent of manufacturing. For further details about the relative importance of services, see Quinn 1992: 17–21.

computers, telecommunications, and biotechnology (Thurow 1996). At the same time, economic dependence on "knowledge workers" (Drucker 1993) does not necessarily mean that these workers are so important that other employees should be ignored. Table 1.1 sheds light on contemporary occupational trends.

Notwithstanding differences in occupational definitions, table 1.1 shows that the percentages of professional workers in the United States, Australia, and Japan are growing relatively rapidly, as are those of technical, sales and marketing, and service workers.[4] By contrast, manual workers are in the three lowest categories in the table, are hardly growing at all, and represent much less than half the workforce in the three countries.

In short, these data suggest that the average level of knowledge and skills required in advanced societies is increasing, an inference supported by survey and other data (Gallie 1996; Szafran 1996). It is worth noting, however, that the employees who require the most theoretical knowledge— those in the professional specialty category—comprise less than 15 percent of total employment, and there is reason to believe these figures are inflated because of the inclusion of occupations designated professional so as to improve workers' status and earnings and to claim occupational jurisdiction (see Kumar 1978: 214–15). It would therefore be unnecessarily restrictive to confine our analysis to workers in these occupations. This conclusion is supported by leading management theorists (Drucker 1993; Quinn 1992) who suggest that the productivity and flexibility of both "knowledge workers" *and* "service workers" need to be addressed.

The rise of the front-line worker is conspicuous in its absence from the debate about future employment structures. Competitive pressures arising from globalization, product market deregulation, and privatization have encouraged organizational delayering and work restructuring, which has, in effect, made the front-line worker more important (Useem and Cappelli 1997:50–57; Littler et al. 1997). Product (and service) customization, attendant on rising customer incomes, market heterogeneity (hence the growth of teen and subteen markets), and company policy have further encouraged managers to place greater importance on customer relations and the contribution of front-line workers to customer satisfaction (Hage and Powers 1992).[5]

Increased competition also encourages stronger customer focus. The need

---

[4] Most noteworthy in this respect is Japan, where relatively few employees are classified as "executive and managerial" and relatively more are classified in functional categories. On average, it takes Japanese employees much longer to reach managerial positions than in Western countries.

[5] Affluent, more educated consumers—characteristic of those in most advanced societies— tend to be more knowledgeable and demanding, particularly since the more ready availability of information facilitated by information technology (IT) and legal requirements regarding more detailed product descriptions. Increased product awareness, sustained by advertising, also contributes to this trend.

Table 1.1. Changes in Employment and Employment by Major Occupational Category, United States, Australia, and Japan, Selected Periods

	United States		Australia		Japan	
	% change in employment per year 1979–1992	% of total workforce 1995	% change in employment per year 1988–1995	% of total workforce 1995	% change in employment per year 1980–1995	% of total workforce 1995
Executive and managerial	3.6	13.8	0.5	10.4	0.5	3.7
Professional speciality	3.1	14.5	3.4	14.1	5.0*	12.3*
Technicians and related support	4.1	3.1	6.4	5.8		
Sales and marketing	2.2	12.1	1.0	16.6	1.2	14.7
Clerical and administrative support	1.1	14.7	4.0	16.7	2.2	19.5
Service workers†	1.8	13.6	0.2	14.5	1.4	9.5
Precision production, craft, and repair	0.3	10.8	0.1	7.1	0.1	26.2
Operators, fabricators, and laborers	0.7	14.5	1.0	14.8	1.9	8.5
Agriculture, forestry, fishing, and related jobs	-0.4	2.9			-2.3	5.6

Note: It is not possible to compare over similar periods because of changes in the definitions of occupational categories.
* Includes "technicians and related support"; † Includes "sales and marketing" category.
Sources: United States: Commission on the Future of Worker Management Relations 1994; U.S. Bureau of the Census 1996. Australia: Australian Bureau of Statistics 1996c. Japan: Statistics Bureau 1997.

to "keep close to the customer," to "delight the customer," and to "make the moment of truth an unforgettable experience" are just a few of the slogans reflecting this rise in customer sovereignty. This trend is also reflected in the growth of total quality management (TQM), with its focus on buyers and clients, whether external or internal to the organization (Cole 1995; National Research Council 1994: 183–84; Useem and Cappelli 1997:42).[6]

IT has also played a significant role in transforming the workplace. New technology enables techniques such as TQM to be implemented more effectively. By embedding technology with informating properties— the capacity to provide relevant information and generate analytically based knowledge—IT encourages the development of computer, social, and analytical skills and hence contributes both to the emergence of new occupations (e.g., web designer) and worker empowerment (Zuboff 1988). IT may also alter management-employee relations by permitting a combination of decentralized decision making (including remote working) and centralized management control (Tapscott 1996: 92–93). In addition, IT fosters collaboration among colleagues, across time and space, and hence is viewed as a key enabler of new forms of work organization (Nohria and Berkley 1994). IT also has the potential to improve service quality (product presentation, speed of worker response to the customer, and so forth).[7] Finally, IT promotes the growth of new firms and new products, both of which tend to generate more front-line work. Outsourcing is facilitated since IT reduces the transaction costs associated with contracting, while providing a basis for developing new products, such as virtual reality games and Internet search engines.

To summarize, as a result of the forces noted above, the front-line worker has become a central figure in the workplace of contemporary capitalism. In what ways is this significant? And to what if any extent does empirical evidence support this observation?

Significance of Front-Line Work

Front-line work is different from production and back-office work. Since production work constitutes the basis for thinking about work organization, any new framework needs to take into account the distinguishing features and implications of front-line work. These features and their implications are touched on briefly below.

[6] In 1995, 37 percent of Australian workplaces with twenty or more employees and 69 percent of the largest workplaces (employing five hundred or more employees) reported that they pursued a TQM philosophy (Moorehead et al. 1997: 188).
[7] IT permits the rapid dissemination of information and knowledge to customers. This assists front-line workers in clarifying requirements and in advising and selling to customers. For example, banks provide information and knowledge via the Internet or through groupware products, such as Lotus Notes (National Research Council 1994: 182).

- Front-line work is people-oriented. Employees are required to interact constantly with customers in ways that are advantageous to the organization's goals. Workers are "on stage" undertaking tasks that involve emotional labor (Hochschild 1983).
- Front-line work is rarely completely routinized. Because social interaction is part of the product or service being supplied, workers are usually given some discretion to tailor their behavior to customer requirements.
- Front-line work is especially sensitive to changes in internal and external organizational environments. Variations in demand for products (e.g., additional cross-currency transactions arising from a change in exchange rates) and in supply (e.g., product unavailability, incorrect information supplied to customers) often affect front-line employees strongly and unpredictably. These employees are expected to "go with the flow," to display emotional resilience and flexibility. There are usually no buffers to protect workers from these "spikes."
- Front-line work is often strategically important. This reflects the position of front-line employees at the organization-public interface. As boundary spanners, front-line workers are often required to generate revenue through selling and to perform an intelligence-gathering role, in effect, helping to develop a customer knowledge base for future innovation.

Three pieces of evidence suggest the growing significance of front-line work. The first relates to the rapid expansion of telephone-related services. Although stated in terms of value rather than employment, this change implies strong growth in front-line work, as our research testifies. According to a technology consultancy, the 1996 sales of call-center systems in North America were valued at $3 billion. This represents a tenfold increase since 1991 and a twofold increase since 1994. Annual growth rates of 17 percent are expected to the year 2000 ("Please Hold" 1997: 74).

The second indicator comes from a survey of U.S. establishment-level managers. Bearing in mind that front-line workers comprise a critical service link between customers and organizations, respondents reported that, on average, compared to cost-based competition, service-based competition is more than twice as important and quality competition around two thirds more important (Osterman 1997: 105).

The third piece of evidence is based on projected occupational growth statistics for the United States, Australia, and Japan. These show that the increase in the percentage of professionals, technical employees, and service and sales workers—who are mainly front-liners and front-line support personnel—is likely to be higher than average (U.S. Department of Labor 1996; Department of Employment and Training 1991; Castells 1996: 227). Figure 1.1 shows the projected absolute growth of employees between 1994 and 2005 in sixty-eight U.S. occupations categorized according to major occupational category and work positioning—that is, whether

Figure 1.1. Projected Absolute Job Growth by Categories of Workers and Occupational Categories, United States, 1994–2005

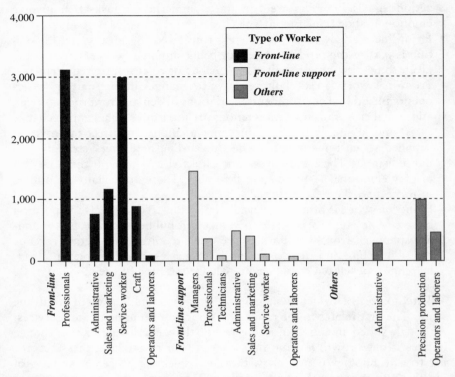

Source: Based on data taken from U.S. Bureau of the Census 1996: table 638, 408.

incumbents in the occupations work directly with customers (front-line), support front-line workers (front-line support), or work in the back office of organizations or as direct or indirect manual employees.

Figure 1.1 shows that most new jobs in the near future will tend to be front-line positions in professional and service occupations. Front-line positions and front-line support management positions in sales and marketing are also anticipated to provide substantial job opportunities. An analysis of the thirty fastest-growing minor (i.e., more detailed) occupational categories in the United States and Australia provides a similar picture (see U.S. Department of Labor 1995; Department of Employment and Training 1991). The fastest expansion is in the professional and services categories, and in both countries front-liners hold at least seventeen of the thirty fastest-growing minor occupations in these categories.

In sum, work in many rapidly growing occupations in advanced societies appears to be service related and people centered. Although the work is apparently based on theoretical knowledge, there is considerable variation; thus, some subsectors and occupations that do not require theoretical knowledge and have lower skill levels are nonetheless growing relatively rapidly. These trends provide a useful guide in selecting prototypical kinds of workers for research.

Implications of Changes for Work Organization

The structural changes fostering the trend toward front-line work has implications with respect to various aspects of work organization. Work tasks are likely to require customer-related knowledge and skills. In line with the frequent changes in products, procedures, and processes, employers are likely to value workers' willingness and ability to learn. Management will tend to develop policies that enhance employee knowledge and the skills necessary to ensure good customer relations; however, this will not eliminate the variation in work complexity noted earlier and may in turn encourage variations in work organization.

Workers' power is likely to increase in relation to management. Having discretion and the ability to influence customers means that customers and hence revenue are directly related to employee behavior; however, this influence needs to be viewed in the context of the generalized weak labor market position of most, though not all, employees. Finally, the shared experience of having regular interactions with customers is likely to influence relations among workers. It may encourage isolation (because workers have little time or incentive to work with colleagues), competition (because customer relations constitute the basis for earnings and status differences), or cohesion (because workers with specialized skills work together to solve customer problems).

More intense market competition fueled by globalization and other factors encourage management continuously to reduce costs, provide better service, or improve quality. These are not mutually exclusive goals (Quinn 1992: chap. 4; Moorehead et al. 1997: 242). The pressures on workers are more intense because large international institutional investors do not simply rely on selling or buying shares. Rather, they frequently try to influence corporate policy directly, and occasionally vote against company directors (Useem and Cappelli 1997: 35). This results in employment restructuring and changes in work regimes, including demands for more worker flexibility and greater employee commitment.[8]

Evidence of the reorganization of employment and work regimes comes from survey and official data. Increasing numerical and temporal flexibility is indicated by the recent growth of nonstandard employment, particu-

---

[8] Flexibility may assume a variety of forms, including numerical (varying the number of employees depending on demand), temporal (nonstandard work schedules), financial (contingent pay), and functional (skill upgrading or broadening).

Table 1.2. Nonstandard Forms of Employment, United States, Australia, and Japan, 1973 and 1993

Country	Self-employment as % of total employment in nonagricultural sectors		Part-time employment as % of total employment		Involuntary part-timers as % of total part-time employees 1993	Women as % of total part-time employees 1993
	1973	1993	1973	1993		
United States	6.7	17.5	15.6	17.5	30.7	66.2
Australia	9.5	12.9	11.9	23.9	32.9	75.3
Japan	14.0	10.3	13.9	21.1	9.2	67.7

Source: Based on data taken from International Labour Organization 1996: table 2.6, 26.

larly part-time employment and self-employment. Relevant data are presented in table 1.2.

Table 1.2 shows that the relative size of the self-employed sector in the United States more than doubled between 1973 and 1993. This is similar to the slightly lower rate of growth of part-time employment in Australia and Japan. Increasingly, companies are substituting these nonstandard forms of employment for full-time employment in order to reduce costs and more precisely match the demand and supply of labor (Katz 1997a: 75). This process is facilitated where the law permits self-employed and part-time workers to receive lower pro rata social security and health insurance benefits and where the latter are more easily dismissed (Houseman 1995). The tendency for the workforce to be characterized by a stable core and a relatively enlarged, disposable group at the periphery is a common feature of advanced societies.

Table 1.2 shows that about one-third of the part-time employees in the United States and Australia would prefer to have full-time jobs. The much lower underemployment rate in Japan is explained by the limited oppor--tunities for full-time work available to married women with children. This, together with tradition, reduces women's expectations, thereby making part-time work acceptable (Berggren and Nomura 1997:78–84). This proposition is consistent with evidence that 85 percent of the Japanese part-time workforce are married women (Castells 1996: 271). Table 1.2 highlights a more general point: women comprise the bulk of part-time workers in all three countries—Australia, the United States, and Japan.

Changing the organization of the workplace and work practices often leads to greater flexibility. In 1995, nearly half (48 percent) the workplaces in the private sector of Australia with twenty or more employees reported having experienced recent restructuring, while 43 percent had undergone changes in work practices. The incidence of change was higher in workplaces facing import competition (Moorehead et al. 1997: 237–39). Restructuring tended to reduce employment levels, while changes in work practices probably led to increased work effort. Australian and U.S. survey data suggest that employees, particularly managers and highly qualified workers who tend to work longer hours, perceive themselves to be working harder and feeling under greater stress (Australian Bureau of Statistics [ABS] 1996b; International Survey Research Center [ISRC] 1996; Lette and Schor 1994; Cappelli 1997: 195–96).[9] Reflecting a more general increase in effort, average working hours in the United States and Australia have also been increasing (OECD 1996b), although this was not true of Japan, at least not until the early 1990s.[10]

The reduction in full-time employment and other changes mentioned above have resulted in both workers and managers feeling greater job insecurity, reduced organizational commitment, and declining satisfaction with senior management (Heckscher 1995; ISRC 1997; Littler et al. 1997; DIR 1995;1996).[11] Employers refer to there being a new psychological contract with employees, entailing reduced job security and limited opportunities for internal promotions. Knowledge and skill enhancement, which enable employees to compete more easily in the job market are supposed to be part of this contract.[12] The trend away from company support to self-help is not confined to Western countries; it is also evident in Japan, where the emphasis is increasingly on individual performance rather than seniority-related ability as a criterion for pay determination and promotion (Morishima 1995). Clearly, these are challenging times for most workers.

Against a backdrop of labor-saving technological change and government policies aimed less at reducing unemployment than at limiting inflation, restructuring strategies have contributed to continuing high levels of unem-

[9] In Australia, male managers and administrators, who worked an average of 51.5 hours a week in 1995, topped the list of employees who worked the longest hours; they were followed by male professionals (42.6 hours). Among females, women managers and administrators worked the longest hours—40.1 hours per week, followed by professionals (34.3 hours). These averages include part-time workers and so understate the average number of hours worked by full-time workers (Australian Bureau of Statistics 1996).

[10] This was mainly because of the onset of a recession, which reduced the aggregate average hours worked. Changes in social values and amendment of the Labour Standards Law in 1987 may also have had some effect. Nevertheless, Japanese workers continue to work relatively long hours. In May 1997, about two hundred *karoshi* (death from overwork) cases were reported to be subject to Japanese court proceedings ("Fatal Attraction" 1997).

[11] Australian survey evidence regarding the effects of various workplace changes on employees indicates occupational variation, so that managers and sales and personal service workers generally feel more positive than do professional and technical employees (see Moorehead et al. 1997:280). The survey probably overstates the positive effects because it excludes employees laid off as a result of the changes.

[12] A relatively new management concept, that of the "boundaryless career," celebrates the interorganizational mobility typical of professional workers and legitimates the decline in employer responsibility to provide employees with opportunities for internal promotions. See Hirsch and Stanley 1996.

Table 1.3. Union Density, Private Sector and Total, United States, Australia, and Japan, Selected Years

	Union density					
	1985		1990		1995	
	Private sector	*Total*	*Private sector*	*Total*	*Private sector*	*Total*
United States	14.3	18.0	11.9	16.1	10.3	14.9
Australia[a]	34.5	45.6	30.8	40.5	24.0	31.1
Japan	19.5	28.9	18.2	25.2	18.1	23.8

Note: Union density is the number of union members divided by the number of wage and salary earners (employees) multiplied by 100. For the U.S., annual averages are based on monthly figures for wage and salary workers. For Australia, the total includes all persons unions regard as members. For Japan, union density is membership divided by the number of employees multiplied by 100. Figures given are the estimated ratio of organization based on our calculations from union density and employment data. [a] Figures from 1986, 1990, 1996.

Sources: U.S. Bureau of the Census 1996; Australian Bureau of Statistics 1996d; Statistics Bureau 1996.

ployment and widening earnings inequalities (Thurow 1996; International Labour Organization [ILO] 1996: 69–77).[13] Together with structural changes in employment, the high levels of unemployment and widening earnings inequalities have weakened labor organization, as evident from table 1.3.

Reflecting a long-term tendency, table 1.3 shows that for the latest year available (1995) private-sector union density is less than 25 percent in the United States, Japan, and Australia. Japanese unionism is more resilient, mainly because it is part of an enterprise-based labor relations system. In striking contrast to the United States and Australia, unionism continues to be favored by the overwhelming majority of large Japanese employers. Outside manufacturing and parts of the public sector, however, unions have limited power.

Given the drop in private-sector unionism, one might conclude that changes in work organization are unlikely to reflect workers' interests, in either process or content. Two major exceptions are workplaces where

[13] In 1990–1994, the standardized average annual unemployment level for the United States, Australia, and Japan was 6.6 percent, 9.5 percent, and 2.3 percent respectively. Japanese unemployment rose to 3.4 percent in 1996, the highest in more than thirty years (OECD 1996c; 1997a). Corresponding figures for the United States and Australia were 5.4 percent and 8.6 percent respectively (OECD 1997b, 1998). Reich (1991) has suggested that the globalization of labor markets for highly qualified specialists such as systems developers, corporate bankers, lawyers, and tax specialists is leading to polarization between an international economic elite of "symbolic analysts" who owe little or no allegiance to any country and an expanding mass of relatively impoverished workers whose prospects are restricted to the local economy and subject to intense competition from employees in lower-wage countries.

workers are able to influence the changes, as a result of their labor market power, as in the case of highly qualified employees, such as systems developers, or, more rarely, where management encourages employee participation in decision making.

Emerging Forms of Work Organization

The pressure for higher performance, stemming from intense competition based on the proliferation of customized products and services, and the availability of inexpensive IT as a work medium are combining to encourage new forms of work organization among front-line workers. These new forms of work organization are grounded less in detailed empirical research than in the fears and aspirations of workers and managers.[14] On the one hand, pessimists view the current changes as complementing or even reinforcing traditional structures of inequality; on the other hand, optimists favor the construction of entirely new organizational forms based on enabling technology and creative intelligence (Bowen and Lawler 1995; Zuboff 1988). We refer to these forms of work organization, summarized in table 1.4, as *regimented and empowered.*

These contrasting images serve as a basic template for comparisons of particular elements of work organization (referred to in the left-hand column of the table) that are pursued in subsequent chapters. We will be exploring whether the empirical evidence tends to confirm one or the other of these dominant images with regard to several types of front-line workers described more fully in the next chapter. In the meantime, we briefly review academic research on work organization. This helps to distinguish our theoretical position from that on which previous work was based and explains the logic of our inquiry.

Approaches to the Transformation of Work and Organization

The three broad approaches to analyzing work and organization—Marxism and regulation theory, microsociology, and organizational analysis—differ in concepts, units of analysis, and research methods, for, although their domains overlap, they address different problems. The following brief review highlights these differences and the respective contributions of these approaches to our understanding of significant issues. Our choice of the problems to address and our framework and analytical strategy builds on the strengths of each of these approaches while seeking to avoid their limitations.

[14] There are exceptions to this statement. See, for example, Cunningham, Hyman, and Baldry (1996), whose research indicates that the practice of empowerment falls considerably short of its promise.

Table 1.4. Features of the Regimented versus the Empowered Work Organization

	Regimented organization	Empowered organization
Work relations	Work intensification; "harder and smarter"	Intrinsically rewarding, "a learning environment"
Employment relations	HRM facilitates labor flexibility and higher performance; "employability" means management abdication of responsibility	HRM rightly reflects performance; "employability" means new knowledge and skills for boundaryless career development
Control relations	Inculcation of performance norms backed by constant surveillance and discipline	Normative identification with management; individual and co-worker initiatives
Co-worker relations	Management-controlled teams with regimented learning processes	Opportunities for support and learning from co-workers; highly participative work teams
Customer-worker-management relations	High level of dissatisfying emotional labor; possible incongruity between productivity requirements and customer satisfaction	Additional source of satisfaction and influence; a challenge balancing customer and other demands
Consequences	Work is coercive and regimented; threat of unemployment makes work tolerable	Work is enabling, competency-enhancing, and socially satisfying

Marxism and Regulation Theory

Marxism inspired the development of labor process theory and regulation theory, both of which analyze macro and micro structures and dynamics. The former assumes the existence of worker exploitation (in the Marxist sense), while the latter is more circumspect. The purpose of labor process theory is to reveal the dynamics of capitalist exploitation and worker resistance as structured by managerial and state strategies (Burawoy 1979).

In spite of contestable theoretical assumptions and a preoccupation with production workers, important concepts and insights based on empirical analyses have been generated from labor process theory, particularly relating to employment and control relations. Friedman (1977), for example, applied the contrasting notions of direct control and responsible autonomy to a variety of historical and contemporary work settings in the United Kingdom, while Edwards (1979) characterized the changing nature of management domination in the United States. Edwards saw this process as moving through three stages, from personal control, typical of small-firm, competitive capitalism, to technical control, in which machinery determined the nature and pace of work in larger factories. This was followed by bureaucratic control, in which large firms, encouraged by labor legislation and frequently in association with unions, developed procedures for containing and regulating conflict.

Burawoy (1983) formalized and extended the study of management domination by conceptualizing the role of the state and bringing the U.S. story up-to-date with the concept of hegemonic despotism. Thus, the hegemonic workplace regimes Edwards (1979) described as various forms of bureaucratic control give way under the pressure of international capital mobility and consequent intensified competition to state withdrawal of protective legislative support for labor including reduced unemployment and welfare benefits.

Under these conditions—which are similar to those described earlier—management, according to Burawoy (1983), tends to pursue a "hard" or "soft" control strategy. The former refers to a concerted attack on unions and workers' customs and practices, while the latter seeks to build consent based on such terms as greater flexibility and higher productivity and quality. The latter approach tends to be accompanied by new management techniques. In either case, hegemonic despotism refers to the threat posed by globalization to workplace survival and hence workers' jobs.

On the one hand, this characterization sets employment and control relations firmly within a political economic context, highlighting pressures on workers to accede to management requirements. On the other hand, Burawoy does not acknowledge that hard and soft management strategies are not mutually exclusive and that the growing interdependence of production coupled with microelectronic technology might encourage new forms of control. More fundamentally, this approach does not recognize that the rise of the front-line worker and the growing importance of knowledge work are likely to alter the character of domination. This point is acknowledged to some extent in more recent labor process research, which draws attention to internalized norms of service as a form of control (Knights and Sturdy 1990).

As part of their attempt to explain changing capitalist production arrangements, regulation theorists conceptualize changes in work arrangements. Firms and their relationships with suppliers (production organization) and employment relations (work execution, work organization, and management-employee relations), they argue, form a coherent system that is regulated by macro economic forces (international competition and state intervention). The contention is that a chronic crisis in profit accumulation is leading not to revolution but to the demise of Fordism and its replacement by new production systems that vary internationally according to different historical and institutional influences (Piore and Sabel 1984; Boyer 1997).

The new systems have several common denominators, however. These include programmable technology and skilled employees supported by loyalty-inducing and skill-enhancing human resource management (HRM) policies that permit the production of high-quality, low-cost, mass customized products. These characteristics may not extend to all workers. Gordon, Edwards, and Reich (1982) have drawn attention to the differentiated management strategies imposed on workers employed in different labor market segments. Thus, skilled, primary-segment workers (typically skilled men) enjoy superior conditions of employment compared, for example, with secondary-segment workers (often part-time women). The combination of functional and numerical flexibility is of course a feature of Toyotaism (i.e., lean production), which regulation theorists see as a variant of flexible production.[15]

Although regulation theory was developed mainly to account for changes in the manufacturing industry, Boyer (1997: 35–37) claims a double transition is currently under way in services. First, within traditional services (e.g., retailing and wholesaling, catering, etc.), an upskilling process is occurring based on the mastery of abstract knowledge via software systems and communications networks. Second, gaining in importance are the "modern and highly evolutionary services which demand a continual process of adaptation, such as legal services, architecture and software design" (Boyer 1997: 36). Boyer claims that organizational forms based on the new production principles also are emerging.[16]

An advantage of Marxist-inspired research, particularly regulation theory, is that it attempts to explain work and its organization from a multidisciplinary, systemic perspective. There are many interrelated hypotheses, however, few of which have been rigorously tested.[17] Thus, the applicability of the new production systems concept to service work remains only a claim at this stage, particularly since the upskilling process varies among subsectors and among different segments of the workforce. Moreover, it is important to distinguish between professional work that has traditionally been organized on a flexible, high-trust basis (Fox 1974; Friedson 1986: chap. 7), changes in this work and its organization, and the emergence of new types of work, such as software design. More generally, there is the related issue of whether the concept of a production system based on

[15] The Japanese model has become a source of inspiration to management theorists searching for a formula that works effectively under different institutional conditions. Hence the popular notion of "the flexible firm" (Atkinson 1984).

[16] Boyer (1997: 36) acknowledges the need for "a more substantial analysis that would doubtless emphasize the persistence of considerable heterogeneity across sectors." The presence of heterogeneity raises doubts, however, about the applicability of the new production system concept.

[17] The post-Fordist formulation gives an orderliness to production arrangements that is challenged by the proposition that advanced capitalism is "disorganized" and hence open to a variety of organizational forms. Lash and Urry (1987: 5–7) refer to the following features as sources of this "disorganization": flexible production in the context of growing international competition; deregulation of national markets; a decline in unionism and collective bargaining; and the concentration of labor in small workplaces.

product manufacture can adequately highlight features of service systems that vary considerably in work complexity (compare retail service clerks and surgeons) and that include customers as part of the process.

Microsociological Perspectives

Unlike Marxist and regulation school theorists, who view changes in work and work organization as part of a broader puzzle, microsociologists are concerned solely with the minutiae of how work is conceived, learned, accomplished, evaluated, and experienced over time (Becker 1963; Roy 1952, 1953). The impact of these changes on workers' identities is also viewed as important (Casey 1995; Du Gay 1996).[18] This concern has led to important insights and to controversy regarding the effects of emotional labor, defined as the conscious manipulation of workers' behavior to affect the feelings of others, typically customers (Wharton 1996; Morris and Feldman 1996).

Management uses various strategies to ensure that service is delivered efficiently and tailored to varying degrees to suit customers' requirements. Leidner (1993) identified two such strategies, each appropriate to different levels of work complexity. Fast-food service attendants followed relatively standardized work routines, and customer behavior was routinized (through the physical layout and instructions for ordering and queuing for food). Insurance salespeople, by contrast, were routinized by normative "transformation" (i.e., they were inculcated with a sense of responsibility by following the work routines management deemed superior). These routines had the effect of returning deviant prospective customers to normal customer status. An important implication of Leidner's analysis is that the front-line worker is part of a triangle of interests: there is inter-action with managers and customers, sometimes resulting in changing patterns of cooperation and conflict, although typically stabilizing around a pattern that is likely to differ between large and small customers (Lopez 1996).

Normative control, operating through corporate culture or specific management techniques that appeal to the notion of customer service, has received increasing attention in recent microsociological studies (Biggart 1987; Fuller and Smith 1991). As Kunda (1992) and Casey (1995) have shown, these control mechanisms lead workers to internalize tensions and contradictions. Similarly, Du Gay (1996: chap. 7) emphasizes that the implementation of management programs aimed at creating "enterprising subjects"—"individuals who calculate about themselves and work upon

---

[18] Of importance too are dilemmas of identity. For example, do workers see themselves as service workers or as servile subordinates? As cheerful robots or as authentic persons? This issue requires a psychological perspective and an individual level of empirical analysis that lies beyond the sociological approach adopted in this book.

themselves in order to better themselves" (145)—has ambiguous effects, so that only some workers conform to management expectations. In short, these studies provide a picture of limited organizational commitment, of worker accommodation to, rather than strong endorsement of, management values and norms.

In the spirit of the Chicago school (Hughes 1959), microsociological research has begun to focus on technical work. As noted earlier, this is a relatively large and growing occupational category covering workers who are expected continuously to combine contextual knowledge and a limited amount of theory to stay abreast of technological change. How technical workers learn and the efficacy of their practices are important issues, the answers to which may be generalizable to other occupations. Thus, in a study of photocopy machine repairpersons, Orr suggests that these workers act as *bricoleurs*, who piece together an understanding of the problem at hand, including alternative ways to resolve it (1996:11). In this process, manuals, which management provides and emphasizes as the key source of learning, are only one of several resources. Learning is mainly by doing, in consultation with colleagues and, to a more limited extent, with customers. The key to successful learning appears to be the "community of practice" (Lave and Wenger 1991).

Microsociological studies, typically based on ethnography, are valuable for their insights into work processes, including interactions among managers, workers, and customers. Such research stimulates the development of hypotheses, particularly concerning the dynamics of order and conflict and comparisons of social relationships in different work settings. Nevertheless, there are drawbacks: establishing the validity and typicality of accounts and interpreting the impact of multiple and complex causal variables remain serious problems. In addition, confining attention to the minutiae of working detracts from the nested nature of work (within business units, organizations, industries, countries, and so forth) and the impact of wider social forces.

Organizational Perspectives: Management, Sociology, and Industrial Relations

According to Hage and Powers (1992), *complexification*, the process whereby workers' levels of education rise and increasingly sophisticated technology is geared to research and development, is superseding *rationalization*, manifested in economies of scale, deskilling, and mass production. Researchers have claimed that higher-skilled work is increasingly undertaken in organic-professional network forms of organization. Unlike bureaucracies, authority in networks tends to be based more on personal knowledge, expertise, and social connections, rather than on position. Information and decisions tend to be negotiated across the network—via a lateral logic—rather than according to the top-down vertical logic characteristic of a bureaucracy.[19]

Leading social theorist Castells (1996: chap. 3) sees the network as the archetypal form of organization in the emerging informational economy. He claims that networks can handle knowledge and information more efficiently than bureaucracies and are able to respond to changing stimuli more rapidly and constructively, a proposition other management scholars have also argued (Mintzberg 1983; Lawler 1992; Daft and Lewin 1993). Blackler (1995: 1029–30) has conceptualized this as a shift in the characteristics of organizations structured around different types of knowledge.[20]

Dissenters claim that networks are less desirable than hybrids, in which management control is combined with co-worker decision making in teams (Applegate 1996). Nonaka and Takeuchi (1995) speak of "the hypertext organization," which overlays structures of lateral communication (across organizational units) on structures of hierarchical control. Other observers claim that market-mimicking forms within hierarchies are desirable and are becoming common (Ghoshal and Bartlett 1995; Halal 1994a; Pinchot and Pinchot 1993). By requiring business units to compete with outsourcing companies (e.g., for data processing or payroll administration), the market promotes entrepreneurialism in large bureaucracies. At the same time, specialist outsourcing organizations are encouraged to adopt entrepreneurial forms of work organization that win business away from the internal departments of large companies.

Some observers argue that networks are far less common than is often claimed (Eccles and Nohria 1992). Evidence summarized below suggests a flattening of the traditional bureaucracy, but whether this constitutes a tendency toward networks is much less clear. Thus, Cappelli and O'Shaunessy (cited in Useem and Cappelli 1997: 47–51) reported hierarchical flattening and widening of the spans of control in eleven insurance companies. A study of 140 major U.S. companies by the same authors indicates that between 1986 and 1992 the average number of employees in supervisory and management categories declined by 6 percent while the number of exempt nonsupervisory employees increased by an average of 22 percent (Useem and Cappelli 1997: 50–51). A national U.S. survey suggests that those organi-

---

[19] This observation is echoed in Barley's hypothesis concerning the ascendancy of the horizontal or occupational principle of organization and the corresponding decline of the vertical (hierarchical) principle (see Zabusky and Barley 1996: 188–92).

[20] In essence, dependence on knowledge-routinized organizations (based on knowledge embodied in technology) and on expert-dependent organizations (based on knowledge embodied in skilled workers) is being superseded by symbolic/analyst-dependent knowledge organizations ("embrained in" an elite of highly qualified personnel) and communications-intensive organizations (based on encultured knowledge or the norms and understandings developed through collaboration by knowledge workers). Whereas the two former types of organization focus on familiar problems, the latter two forms are geared to solving novel problems.

zations that are less bureaucratic (lower levels of formalization, hierarchy, and departmentalization) are small and younger and hence may be growing relatively rapidly (Kalleberg et al. 1996: 107–9), a finding consistent with the decline in workplace size in all three countries.[21]

Industrial relations researchers focus mainly on the workplace rather than the organization, using the work system as the main unit of analysis. The concept of work system encompasses three main elements: management's production and human resource practices; the organization of work (how jobs are defined, including requisite skills and organization in teams or as individuals); and management-union relations (Appelbaum and Batt 1994). Research indicates that a variety of new systems—which assume different forms according to varying historical and institutional conditions—have been emerging in recent years. Examples include lean production in Japan and flexible specialization in Italy. Multinational companies have become conduits for best practices, so that work systems are beginning to lose their national specificity. Thus, examples of lean production, in various hybrid forms, are evident worldwide, particularly in the auto industry (Elger and Smith 1994; Graham 1995; Macduffie 1995, 1997).

Work systems in large, globally competitive auto companies are unlikely to be typical of companies in other sectors. Broader U.S. and Australian evidence indicates that changes in work systems have typically been restricted to amending existing work systems rather than making qualitative breaks with the past. Thus, there has been modest adoption of one or more of the following innovations: job rotation, job redesign, employee problem-solving groups, TQM, self-directed work teams, and, in Australia, forms of joint consultation (Ichniowski et al. 1996: 325; Osterman 1997; Moorehead et al. 1997: 187–89; 236–41). Correlates of the new forms of work organization include higher-skilled, more autonomous jobs; quality-based competition, particularly in international markets; management support for employee-centered values; and employee training (Osterman 1997: 100–107). Evidence suggests that the changes in Japan have also been limited, focusing on increasing flexibility among permanent employees and introducing appraisal and reward systems with stronger merit components (Morishima 1995; Kawakita 1997; Lincoln and Nakata 1997).

U.S. research on work organization has tended to neglect service work in favor of production work. There are several reasons for this, including the perception that workplace change has been slower and less innovative

---

[21] According to Wriston (1992: 32), "The average U.S. factory employed fifty-one people in 1937 but only thirty-five people in 1982." In Australia, the size of the average workplace (those with twenty or more employees were included in the national survey on which these data are based) declined from 109 to 98 employees. Note, however, that in some sectors the size increased. Examples include finance and insurance, property and business services, and personal and other services (Moorehead et al. 1997: 29–30).

in service occupations (Appelbaum and Batt 1994: 102).[22] This is corroborated by Kalleberg et al. (1996: 120–22), who show that smaller establishments and those in the service sector are significantly less likely to have high-performance work systems characterized by decentralized decision making, internal labor markets, high levels of training, or performance-based reward systems.

A noteworthy exception is a recent study by Herzenberg and Wial (1998), who developed a taxonomy based on work, management, and labor market variables. They distinguish four types of work systems. The first "tightly constrained" type applies to workers undertaking highly routinized work under tight managerial control. Examples include fast-food workers and check proofers.

The second "semi-autonomous type" encompasses workers who have some job discretion (e.g., clerks and customer service representatives). Under this work system, applicants are carefully screened, task supervision is moderate, and internal job ladders exist.

The third "unrationalized labor-intensive type" is distinctive in that the work has not been rationalized by technology and the supervision is loose. Examples include truck drivers and child care workers.

Finally, the fourth "high-skill autonomous type" is characterized by low-volume, customized work requiring workers with high qualifications and skills. These workers are better paid and circulate in external occupational labor markets. Included in this group are a high proportion of workers in the professional, technical, and craft categories.

Herzenberg and Wial (1998) estimate that in 1996 only 4 percent of the U.S. service sector workforce worked in a tightly constrained system. This compared with 29 percent in the semi-autonomous system, 26 percent in the unrationalized labor-intensive system, and 40 percent in the high-skill autonomous system.

Herzenberg and Wial (1998) argue that between 1979 and 1996 technical and organizational change contributed to a slight decrease in the proportion of the U.S. workforce in tightly constrained work systems and a rather steeper decline in the proportion working in semi-autonomous arrangements. The proportion of workers in the unrationalized labor-intensive category stayed relatively stable (though there are expectations of future growth), while the proportion in the high-skill autonomous work

---

[22] Three further reasons for the neglect of service work, particularly front-line, private-sector work, are (1) the low union density, so that these workers have not presented major problems to management or the state; (2) until recently, the customer-worker interface has not been seen as problematic and worthy of serious analysis; and (3) less complex service work has often been undertaken by relatively low-paid women. As interest in the relationship between gender and work has increased, more attention has been paid to front-line service work (Hochschild 1983; Filby 1992; Smith 1994).

system expanded. There is a tendency toward rationalization under the semi-autonomous system—an observation supported by empirical evidence from the telecommunications industry[23]—in marked contrast to the continued vibrancy of the high-skill autonomous system. This is reflected in the emergence of the contradictory forms of work organization, described earlier.

Effects of changes in work organization. Limited U.S. evidence suggests that firms that have instituted "bundles" of related management and work practices perform better than their less innovative counterparts (Ichniowski et al. 1996: 321–22; Pfeffer 1998). Bundling also contributes to job satisfaction and organizational commitment.[24] This is supported by comparative research that contrasts Western Fordism with Japanese "welfare corporatism" (comprising employment security, internal labor markets, comprehensive welfare benefits, job enlargement and job rotation, and extensive consultation and union representation) (Dore 1973; Cole 1979; Lincoln and Kalleberg 1990). As noted earlier, however, comparatively few U.S. or Australian workplaces have introduced these bundles.

Although the trend toward higher-skilled jobs and high-skill, autonomous work systems encourages greater job satisfaction, other aspects of work—job security, effort, and promotion opportunities—have not kept pace with expectations. In addition, pay raises are rarely commensurate with increased job requirements, particularly in jobs in which women predominate (Baran 1987; Appelbaum 1993). Finally, inequalities in earnings only add to worker dissatisfaction (Baron and Pfeffer 1994).

One advantage of the industrial relations perspective is its framework. A work systems approach incorporates a focus on work activity, its broader organization, and its consequences, all of which are viewed as interdependent parts. This approach also includes concepts and research methods drawn from a variety of disciplines. Substantively, industrial

---

[23] Researchers have noted the growth in nonunion employment systems and increased variation in work systems within the unionized sector in many countries (Katz 1997b). Workers in major telecommunications companies in Australia and the United States have experienced contradictory tendencies as management seeks both economies of scale from the introduction of centralized technology, thereby perpetuating hierarchy and job specialization, while promoting customer responsiveness and employee involvement through TQM schemes (Bamber, Shadur, and Simmons 1997; Keefe and Batt 1997). According to Keefe and Batt (1997: 67), the former approach is dominant, a conclusion that also applies to Australia. In Japan, the telecommunications industry is moving away from a more rigid public-sector bureaucratic system to a more flexible system typical of Japanese private-sector companies (Nakamura and Hiraki 1997: 261).

[24] Aspects of task structure, such as greater complexity and higher intrinsic rewards, contribute to job satisfaction and organizational commitment, as do work values, which differ between American and Japanese workers (Lincoln and Kalleberg 1990). Other important variables include participation in job-level decision making, more positive management-employee relations, the presence of regular internal promotion procedures, the use of merit criteria for pay raises and promotions, and positive co-worker relations (Kalleberg et al. 1996: 314–19; Batt and Appelbaum 1995).

relations research provides evidence of the direction and nature of change at work. Its weaknesses include a preoccupation with production work, as noted earlier, and, where service work has been extensively analyzed, as in Herzenberg and Wial (1998), theoretical and empirical limitations.[25]

Overview of work organization theory and practice. This brief review suggests that a work organization should be viewed as a dynamic system operating within the workplace and comprising various elements that are related to the organization and society in which the work organization is embedded. Understanding these elements and their relationships suggests a research strategy informed by a multidisciplinary approach that provides empirical data that are both detailed and sufficiently wide in coverage to permit qualified generalization. The three approaches draw attention to a set of key issues—variations in employment and control relations; management, worker, and customer dynamics; work and learning processes; and differences and changes in work organization, including their consequences. We address these issues in subsequent chapters. In addition, we are interested in the future. Regulation theorists and management scholars emphasize *convergence* on the empowered, network form, arguing that the regimented bureaucracy is in terminal decline. By contrast, sociologists and industrial relations researchers hold to a *continuity* view (i.e., changes in work organizations are variants of the regimented, bureaucratic form). Hence, there is little cause for celebration (Kumar 1995), although some scholars appear to favor Japanese "welfare corporatism," a bureaucratic form that includes enabling qualities, particularly in the sphere of learning and self-development, and that compensates workers for its coercive qualities (Dore 1973; Lincoln and Kalleberg 1990). Finally, proponents of the postmodern, "patternless change" perspective claim that, because of contradictory tendencies, elements of work organization combine in many different ways or in ways that are not readily predictable (Crook, Pukalski, and Waters 1992).

Which of these views is likely to prevail? We return to this issue in the concluding chapter.

Theoretical Framework and Ideal Types of Work Organization

Our general theoretical orientation combines an emphasis on understanding context and meaning—an interpretive approach usually employed by

[25] These include the following: (1) as a taxonomy, the variables that are combined in various specified ways lack theoretical coherence; (2) perhaps because the variables are difficult to operationalize, they are not measured rigorously; (3) the validity of the taxonomy is questionable since work systems that are ostensibly very different (e.g., physicians and electricians) are included in the same work system category; and employees in some occupations (e.g., sales workers) cannot easily be allocated to any single category that does justice to the work system in which they participate.

microsociologists—with a structuralist approach—favored by many organizational sociologists—that seeks to generalize through the use of valid, replicable measures and sampling techniques. Following Giddens (1976), an assumption of this structuration approach is that social organization is the product of meaningful action within contexts that are both constraining and facilitating in ways that may not be evident to the actors. These contexts reflect elements of the wider social structure. This approach calls for empirical research that facilitates understanding of social action from the standpoint of those involved and a close acquaintance with structural factors—markets, technology, labor market institutions—that enable regular or typical social action (social structure or organization) to be identified and analyzed. We exclude self-identity, since this would require a more micro-level emphasis and additional concepts from social psychology. We also exclude detailed analysis of macroeconomic and institutional variables, since this would take us too far in the other direction.

In applying structuration theory to work and its organization, we place the conduct of front-line work—what we call *work relations*—at the center of our analysis. Drawing on the work of interpretive microsociologists and labor process analysts, we describe and explain the key features of work in terms of two concepts: the medium of work—the characteristics of what is being worked on (e.g., materials, symbols, and so forth)—and the act of work—the knowledge, skills, and creativity being employed. Using these three act-of-work variables as criteria, we show how front-line work varies in complexity.

Following Littler (1982) and Sorge and Streeck (1988), we distinguish between vertical relations—the hierarchical division of labor—and lateral relations—the functional or horizontal division of labor. *Vertical relations* refers to two aspects of hierarchical power: employment relations and control relations. *Employment relations* describes the conditions of employment—pay, training, promotion systems, and so on. Employment relations vary according to national and regional laws, social customs, and economic circumstances. They constitute a general form of control (Edwards 1986: 79). *Control relations* refers to the various means by which managers exercise direct hierarchical power over workers (Etzioni 1961). This concept is analogous to Edwards's (1986) notion of detailed control, which can be mediated by technology or by other structures such as unions.

Lateral relations refers to the ties between front-line workers and their colleagues, or what we refer to as *co-worker relations*, and relationships between workers and customers, which often also involve or are structured by management. These we label *customer-worker relations*. Co-worker relations have two components: relationships between workers who work together—*immediate co-worker relations*—and relationships with employees in other sections of the organization with whom workers are in frequent contact—or *adjacent co-worker relations*. Immediate co-worker relations may vary from competitive individualism to cooperative teamwork. Adjacent co-worker relations may vary in frequency, the extent and nature of the dependence, and the degree of cooperation. These components depend mainly on management design and enforcement of the formal division of labor.

The extent and nature of the collaboration that takes place between immediate co-workers vary according to the work complexity, management's human resource (HR) strategy, and the organizational and national culture (Dunphy and Bryant 1996; Lam 1996). The nature of co-worker relations is likely to have a significant effect on employees' satisfaction, relations with management, and learning processes (Batt and Keefe 1996; Orr 1996; Mathews 1994).

Relations between front-line workers and customers tend to be contradictory since the workers are required, on the one hand, to satisfy individual customers' requirements (to varying degrees), while, on the other hand, to project a positive image of the organization. The former invites less management control, while the latter encourages closer management attention. As noted above, tensions arising from contradictory behavior and other differences in interests are played out and resolved among workers, management, and customers resulting in distinctive patterns of relationships.

Figure 1.2 illustrates the elements of work organization.

As indicated in the above discussion, work comprises various media and activities that determine vertical and lateral relations. The *consequences* or *outcomes* of this organization (shown in figure 1.2.) affect customers, management, and workers. In the absence of standardized measures of customer satisfaction and economic performance relating to work organization, we concentrate on two attitudinal constructs—job satisfaction and organizational commitment—and three secondary variables—work stress, the quality of management-employee relations, and discretionary work effort (i.e., the extent to which workers are prepared to put more effort into their work without additional compensation).

Although not highlighted in figure 1.2, the conditions that structure work organization are also noteworthy. These include such internal factors as management policy and practice, technology, and the structure and culture of the wider organization of which the work organization may be a part. Among the external organizational factors of importance are the product and factor markets, political and labor institutions, and the availability of new technology.

Our goals in this volume are threefold: first, to analyze and test hypotheses derived from our qualitative research that relate to each element of work

Figure 1.2. Elements of Work Organization

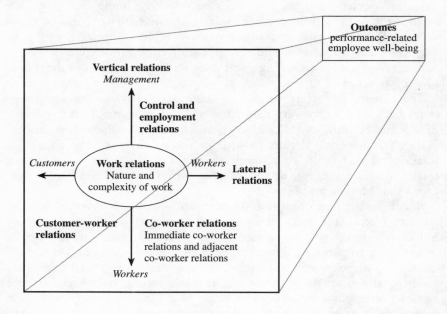

organization identified above; second, to examine the extent to which these elements are associated with one another, thereby forming distinct work organization patterns; and third, to explore some of the consequences of work organization in terms of the outcome variables mentioned above. Underlying these issues are two comparative primary and secondary themes: to explain the work organization of front-line service, sales, and knowledge workers and to explore differences in the work organizations of Japan and the United States and Australia.

Structure of the Empirical Research

It has been argued that the level of work uncertainty strongly influences the nature of work organization (Pava 1983; Stinchcombe 1990). Since uncertainty is related to work complexity, we anticipated that more routine service work would be amenable to a *bureaucratic* (B) form of organization, while more complex sales work would more likely be organized according to the *entrepreneurial* (E) model. By contrast, we anticipated that knowledge work—the most complex type of work we studied—would tend to be organized along network lines, or in what we prefer to call a *knowledge-intensive* (KI) arrangement. Since these three ideal types are mentioned throughout the book, they warrant a brief explanation.

We have developed these three ideal types so as to provide a lens through which we may examine similarities and differences in the forms of work organization revealed in our empirical analysis. These conceptual constructions act as benchmarks for exploring variations in the elements of work organization alluded to above and examined in detail in subsequent chapters. The ideal types are derived from an inferencing process grounded in our empirical data and are deduced from theory relating to the relative costs and benefits of various forms of work organization under varying conditions of work complexity. If there is any consensus in the disparate work organization literature, it is that the changes occurring in the workplace are undermining the effectiveness of bureaucratic organizations.

The essentials of our argument are as follows. Work is becoming more complex, in part because of customization and in part because high labor costs and IT in combination are reducing the demand for lower-skilled jobs and increasing the demand for jobs with higher-level competencies. As we have argued, workers are encouraged to become more customer focused under conditions of intense market competition. Employers cannot simply rely on standardized work processes and direct control by supervisors. In addition, uncertain product markets and the survival of firms in their current form (as a result of mergers and acquisition activity) make it difficult for employers to guarantee employment security and career progression. In short, as environmental instability and innovation have become central features of advanced societies, the costs of bureaucratic organization no longer justify the means. Thus, as Mintzberg (1983) and Heckscher and Donnellon (1994) have argued, these combinations of influences encourage the growth of alternative organizational structures.

As noted earlier, one such alternative is the network structure. Organizations with this structure are labeled as knowledge-intensive because the creation or processing of knowledge is a central activity. At the work organization level, the emphasis is on occupational specialization and lateral relations. Peer interaction occurs in teams characterized by divergent and convergent cycles of knowledge creation and shared understandings and norms (Mankin, Cohen, and Bikson 1996; Mohrman, Mohrman, and Cohen 1995; Piore et al. 1994). Longer-term relationships with clients are of critical importance in developing feasible and acceptable solutions. Trust and commitment among colleagues, clients, and managers, rather than short-term contracting or hierarchical control, are the basis for goal achievement (Fox 1974).

The network structure has relatively permeable boundaries as resources are mixed and matched, often in the form of temporary projects, with the aim of resolving diverse problems. Individual and organizational learning assume significance as innovation requires rapid, continuous, and systematic extensions and diffusion of current knowledge and skills in order to successfully meet, or indeed preempt, emerging market developments (Nonaka and Takeuchi 1995).

In the ideal KI organization, management relies on the knowledge and competencies of individuals as collectivities, as in Mintzberg's (1983) adhocracy and Blackler's (1995: 1030) communication-intensive organization. Because individuals are the main strategic resource and are not easily substitutable (given their particular combination of contextual and theoretical knowledge and normative orientation), employees in KI organizations receive favorable treatment in the form of high salaries and career opportunities that may take the form of mobility into management or movement into more challenging and prestigious projects.

Because knowledge workers are highly motivated by intrinsic considerations, they are not wedded to particular organizations; they may be keen to change organizations to participate in exciting projects. Knowledge and expertise become marketable commodities. These "expert professionals" (Brint 1994: 203–6) in effect are at the center of both organizational and occupational labor markets.

The B and KI ideal types are seen in work settings at opposite ends of the complexity spectrum. The work is neither of middle-range complexity nor mixed, involving both more and less complex tasks. One form of work organization appropriate to this middle range (in which we include mixed cases) is the entrepreneurial type. We use the term "entrepreneurial" here to suggest that the basic rationale for this organizational structure is to rejuvenate the organization by facilitating risk-taking behavior in accordance with corporate objectives and to minimize overhead costs under fluctuating market conditions (Ghoshal and Bartlett 1995; Halal 1994; Pinchot and Pinchot 1993).

The entrepreneurial work organization was foreshadowed historically by various kinds of internal contracting utilizing skilled labor (Clawson 1980; Littler 1982). Contracting has also been a feature of particular occupations, such as bricklaying, carpentry, and direct sales (Austrin 1980; Frenkel and Coolican 1984; Biggart 1987). In addition, the flexible, self-employed worker is becoming more common, as full-time employment, including for professionals and managers, becomes more difficult to obtain (Castells 1996: 276–77).

A common feature that enables contracting to be considered a viable choice for organizations is that individual output (including quality) can be standardized and measured, thereby minimizing problems associated with worker opportunism (Kirsch 1996). The E-type organization may be facilitated or constrained by social values: currently in many Western countries but much less strongly in Japan, notions of "entrepreneurialism," "free enterprise, "economic rationalism," and the employee as "an enterprising self" are conducive to the diffusion of E-type practices.

In an E-type organization, a worker contracts to provide output of a specified kind according to an agreed-upon pay scale, so that pay varies with output. Ultimately, the market, which influences the terms of the contract, is the arbiter. The contract is negotiated periodically to take account of changes in market conditions, costs, and technology. The contract is not between equals, although this may be the legal fiction.

In spite of the inequality of the relationship, the worker in the entrepreneurial organization has considerable discretion over the way work is executed. Typically, work is undertaken on an individual basis. Since we are focusing on inside contracting with an elaborate division of labor, completing the work is likely to require the cooperation of other workers. But because the worker, qua contractor, is dependent on his or her own knowledge and competencies to obtain work, the dominant orientation toward the customer is an instrumental one, similar to the one that ties the worker to the management of the organization. This means that management cannot intervene directly with the customer but must rely on the worker, thus placing the latter in a complex relationship with the sources of both resources and revenue.

The three ideal types of work organization are summarized in table 1.5, in accordance with the five dimensions of work organization outlined earlier and explored in subsequent chapters.

Having drawn attention to the differences in work relations in the three types of work organization, table 1.5 highlights some further differences. Regarding vertical relations, the B type is characterized by hierarchical domination according to specific rules, while the E type effects control by legally enforceable contracts. The KI type, as Powell (1990) indicates, is based on normative relationships of reciprocity.

The employment relations associated with these three ideal types reflect their respective rationales. The B type requires dependable, diligent workers whose commitment is secured by offering employment security, reasonable pay, and internal progression. By contrast, the focus in the E type is more on securing work output and employment flexibility in response to changes in demand. Thus, contracts in E-type organizations are fashioned so as to provide incentives to adhere to the contract, and employment and pay reflect workers' performance. Finally, the KI type is based on intrinsic motivation aimed at encouraging creativity and innovation.

In subsequent chapters, we will demonstrate that, for each of the five dimensions of work organization referred to above, the patterns in frontline service, sales, and knowledge work resemble, to a greater or lesser extent, those of the three ideal types. The most significant departure relates to service work, where managers are forced to concede discretion to

Table 1.5. Features of the Three Ideal Types of Work Organization

	Bureaucratic	Entrepreneurial	Knowledge-intensive
Work Relations			
Basis of work roles	Defined positions	Defined by market requirements	Occupational specialization, fluid application
Competencies (knowledge, skills, and creativity)	Narrow; dependability, diligence, contextual knowledge, action-centered	Broader; seize market opportunities, self-discipline, contextual knowledge, social skills	Broad; problem solving, abstract and contextual knowledge, analytical and social skills
Vertical Relations			
Employment Relations			
Reward system	High fixed element, pay related to seniority	High variable element, pay related to performance	Moderately high variable element, pay related to performance
Career structuring	Internal labor market progression	Reliance on external labor market	Internal and external labor market provision
Control Relations			
Basis	Hierarchical rank	Unequal contract	Collegial networks
Employee discretion	Limited, constrained by job design and rules	High regarding work process	High regarding work process and some discretion regarding goal setting
Form of control	Mainly via direct and technical control	Mainly output related	Peer norms and self-control where working alone; professional/management observation
Lateral Relations			
Co-worker relations			
With immediate colleagues	Individualized, interdependent work; little provision for team work	Individualized work; little interdependence	Team-based; high interdependence
With workers in other sections	Stable jurisdictional boundaries; tasks "handed off" to other sections	Dependent on others for completing transactions; tension	Necessity for teamwork and cooperation across specialisms
Customer Relations			
Roles of worker	Affectively neutral; service provider	Affective/instrumental; sales and service provider	Affectively positive; interpreter/adviser/ salesperson
Triangular relations	Simple; management-directed encounter	Complex; worker has instrumental relations with customer and with manager	Complex; worker has relationships with client and with manager

employees in dealing with customer-related uncertainty. Under these conditions, we see some features of the KI type overlaid on a bureaucratic infrastructure.

Looking Forward

Chapter 2 describes our research strategy—the methods we used to obtain data, including the procedures we employed to minimize threats to data reliability and validity and to enhance comparability. We use workflow—defined as a structured set of tasks (work) leading to a specified output—as the unit of analysis.

Chapter 3 focuses on work relations. Here the background theme is pessimistic versus optimistic responses to work—work as a joyful challenge or as regimented drudgery. In the foreground is a typology that enables front-line work in the three types of workflows to be carefully described and compared. This yields two polarized ideal types of worker—the routine and the professional. Descriptions of selected front-line work roles are provided and, on the basis of survey data, a discriminant analysis upholds our classification of workers into service, sales, and knowledge categories.

Chapters 4 and 5 focus on vertical relations. As indicated earlier, these comprise employment relations, the subject of chapter 4, and control relations, explored in chapter 5. Chapter 4 looks closely at four main elements of employment relations (ER)—recruitment, training, career structures, and reward systems. We suggest that particular configurations of these elements cohere to form part of the larger three (B, E, and KI) ideal types outlined earlier. Our research shows that, in service workflows, the dominant pattern is the attenuated bureaucratic form; in sales workflows, an entrepreneurial pattern, with some elements of the knowledge-intensive form, is evident; and in knowledge work workflows, we see a hybrid containing elements of both the knowledge-intensive and the bureaucratic form.

We then consider the impact of national institutions on ER patterns, arguing that Japanese workflows, regardless of the type of workers involved, are likely to be more bureaucratized than their Australian or U.S. counterparts. Evidence is provided to support this contention, but, as will become clear later, our interpretation differs from the conventional welfare corporatist view. In addition, we argue that the alleged higher performance of workers under the welfare corporatist model does not seem to apply to knowledge workers or women employees working in service settings.

Unions are one institution whose impact on ER is sometimes profound. We found that active unions have positive effects on employee satisfaction regarding bread-and-butter issues but not on other matters of importance to workers. Examples include promotion opportunities and training. Our data show that the impact of unions on employee performance is neither consistently positive nor negative.

In chapter 5, we develop a typology that enables us to interpret the nature of control in service, sales, and knowledge work workflows. The extent to which employee participation varies is also explored. These issues relate to the wider question of whether worker cooperation is based on active consent or simply accommodation to superior power. Our analysis indicates that different forms of control operate in different types of workflows: service workers take computer-generated information about their performance seriously; sales workers are concerned about meeting their sales targets; and knowledge workers are concerned about their reputation among their peers and managers. Participation in service and knowledge work workflows is broadly consistent with our expectations. Thus, service workers have significantly less influence in decision making than do sales and knowledge workers (whose influence varies considerably among workflows). Sales workers are more of an anomaly—reporting significantly less influence than knowledge workers in matters at the task level and significantly more influence than service workers in issues above the task level.

Our data show that different systems of control and participation are related to different outcomes. Thus, service workers have significantly better relations with management than do sales workers but this is not reflected in significantly more discretionary effort. Knowledge workers report better management-employee relations than do sales workers and claim to give significantly more discretionary effort than both service and sales workers. Overall, socionormative control and associated high levels of employee influence result in the most favorable outcomes; however, as we shall see, this form of control is particularly fragile.

Overall, our analysis suggests that patterns of control and participation vary systematically across workflows and contain contradictions that make it difficult to agree with either the optimistic or the pessimistic images referred to earlier. Even organizations with knowledge work workflows have problems sustaining legitimacy, hence making knowledge work less attractive than optimists envisage.

Lateral relations are the focus of chapters 6 and 7. Chapter 6 concentrates on co-worker relations, while chapter 7 is devoted to the customer interface. The background theme in chapter 6 is the alleged rise of network organizations and the demise of bureaucracies. If this optimistic proposition is valid, co-worker relations are likely to be strong across the three kinds of workflows. Alternatively, this trend may be most evident in knowledge work workflows and least evident where bureaucratic elements linger—in service workflows. Nonetheless, we use the three kinds of workflows as the basis for assessing the following dimensions of co-worker relations: task and learning interdependencies, integration of informal relations into formal structures, and forms of teamwork. The workflows are shown to resemble the ideal types, so that network features (high task and learning interdependencies, integration of informal and formal relations, and egalitarian teams) predominate in knowledge work workflows and are least evident in sales work workflows. Despite being relegated to the informal sphere, co-worker relations in service workflows provide psychological support and facilitate learning. In sum, the evidence tends to favor the optimistic scenario but with major qualifications: sales workflows run contrary to the network notion, whereas in service workflows, co-worker relations remain secondary to control relations.

Chapter 6 has two further aims: to compare co-worker relations in Japanese work organizations with cases in the United States and Australia and to analyze the outcomes of the results on co-worker relations in terms of job satisfaction and learning. Contrary to the model for the Japanese hybrid, we do not find cooperation and learning to be superior in Japanese knowledge work workflows. Further, team cohesion is significantly lower in Japanese service workflows than in their Australian and U.S. counterparts. In all three types of workflows, positive co-worker relations contribute to job satisfaction and satisfaction with learning outcomes.

Chapter 7 begins by contrasting the pessimistic and optimistic views of the worker implicated in the customer-worker-management triangle. Pessimists view the worker as caught in the reinforcing or contradictory forces of customer and management requirements. Emotional labor is consequently seen as an additional burden. By contrast, optimists view interactions with customers as opportunities to experience intrinsic satisfaction and influence.

Following elaboration of the three ideal types of customer-worker relations summarized in table 1.5, we explore the empirical evidence. Customer relations in service workflows bear out the expectations established in our discussion of the bureaucratic ideal type. Customer relations are informed by a routinizing logic, characterized by workers who relate to customers in narrow ways, and management who seek to routinize customer behavior. Our data diverge from the model, however, in revealing that considerable affectivity is demanded of, and expressed by, workers toward customers. This empathy encourages an optimistic view of the front-line worker; however, it conflicts with the routinizing logic of service workflows. Consequently, service workers are limited in the extent of satisfaction they can achieve from their interactions with customers.

Customer-worker relations most closely resemble those of the ideal type in sales workflows. Management establishes goals but leaves the process of how these goals are to be met largely up to the workers. Workers are expected to be proactive and to show affectivity toward customers, although this aim is mixed with instrumental motives. The customer is the dominant party. We also saw strong similarities in customer relations in our knowledge work workflows and in the KI ideal type. Having considerable discretion, knowledge workers seek to integrate their knowledge with those of the customer in ongoing efforts to define and solve complex problems. The result is a high level of interdependence between these two groups.

Overall, there is more support for the optimistic than the pessimistic image of customer-worker relations. Further, positive customer relations are strongly associated with workers' reported propensity to provide additional effort, and with job satisfaction. This does not apply to knowledge workers, who place less value than service or sales workers on satisfaction with customers.

Chapter 8 explores some of the consequences or outcomes of work organization. We use the concept of employee dependence on management to derive both general and specific propositions regarding the determinants of job satisfaction and organizational commitment across the three types of workflows and cross-nationally. We argue that to the extent that service workflows more closely resemble the bureaucratic ideal type than do sales and knowledge work workflows, service employees are more dependent on management. Hence, the postulate that vertical relations are relatively more important in contributing to job satisfaction and organizational commitment among service employees than among sales and knowledge workers. A similar argument applies to Japanese work organizations, which, as we show, are more bureaucratic than their Western counterparts, regardless of their workflow pattern. In this case, however, we suggest that stronger bureaucratization is likely to lead to lower satisfaction and commitment.

Our findings are broadly in line with hypotheses derived from a theoretical consideration of employee dependence on employing organizations. Thus, we find that, although satisfaction with vertical relations contributes significantly to service employees' job satisfaction and commitment, the impact of this set of variables is significant in relation to the job satisfaction of knowledge and sales workers but has less impact on their organizational commitment. Also in line with our hypotheses, we find that Japanese service and knowledge workers are more dissatisfied and less committed than comparable Western employees. These results need to be understood with reference to the specific contexts of which they are a part and not used to support generalized arguments concerning institutional differences between Japan, on the one hand, and the United States and Australia, on the other.

Chapter 9 looks to the future. We summarize our main findings as the basis for exploring possible work organization trajectories. The discussion is situated in the context of convergence, continuity, and patternless perspectives on change. We conclude with some comments on the generalizability of our findings and provide some direction for further research.

2   *Research Strategy and Methodology*

SOCIAL research of the kind described in this book depends on soliciting and maintaining support from various groups, including sponsors (for continued funding), senior managers (for site access), middle- and junior-level managers (to secure company data), supervisors and workers (to obtain data on work dynamics and organization), and, last but not least, research teams (to undertake the work). Having briefly mentioned aspects of the political process in the preface, it is our intention here to emphasize the strategic and technical features of the project, in particular the research strategy and methods used to substantiate our work.

This chapter has three objectives. The first is to explain the relationship between our research strategy and research aims. The second is to describe the research methods we employed, particularly the ways we minimized bias and threats to internal validity and reliability. The third objective is to provide readers with background information to help them understand the research context and the data and analyses presented in subsequent chapters. Each of the three objectives is considered in turn, concluding with a brief discussion of how we address the issues of causal analysis and generalizability in our research.

Research Strategy

As we noted in chapter 1, social scientists have done comparatively little research on front-line employees, although they represent a significant part of the workforce in advanced societies. Our project was designed to remedy this deficiency through a comparative analysis of the elements, patterns, and consequences of work organization, as described in chapter 1. Given the occupational diversity of front-line work and the methodological requirements of structuration theory, how could this be accomplished? The first challenge was to choose an appropriate unit of analysis; the second was to identify the criteria and select the sites to be studied, including the industries and companies in which they are situated. These two concerns are discussed in turn.

Unit of Analysis

In the research referred to in the previous chapter, organizations or workplaces (establishments) were the main units of analysis. As other scholars (Osterman 1984; Mintzberg 1983; Pava 1983) have noted, these structures often include multiple forms of work organization. In addition, size and complexity frequently make it difficult to adequately understand social action and to cover more than a handful of units in a single research project. These problems prompted us to choose the workflow as the main unit of analysis. By workflow, we mean a structured set of tasks (work) leading to a specified output (defined to include services) oriented toward a particular market (see National Research Council 1994: 139). Workflows are structured according to vertical and lateral relations; the relevant workers are also employed under particular terms and conditions of employment.

Workflows, as relatively small-scale units of analysis, have three methodological advantages over workplaces and organizations. First, using workflows as the unit of analysis makes obtaining an adequate understanding of social action easier, thereby limiting threats to internal validity. Second, their small scale and relatively specific features provide opportunities to replicate research in comparable workflows, hence increasing the reliability of the findings. Third, conducting multiple cases based on a theoretically guided selection of workflows provides a broader base for generating hypotheses and building theories.

Selection of Workflows and Research Methods

Workflows are nested in three contexts: companies, industries, and countries. Analytical relevance was the chief criterion used to decide which companies and what kinds of workflows we wanted to study. Relevance refers to several structural trends in advanced societies highlighted in the previous chapter. These, in turn, generated a set of criteria as explained below.

The first trend we noted was the continued expansion of service employment, particularly in the financial and business service categories. One criterion for selecting a site, therefore, was that it be in the leading industries within these subsectors. These included financial services, communications, and computer services, all three of which are central to the infrastructures of advanced economies.[1]

The second trend we observed was the remarkable growth in front-line work, especially among highly qualified knowledge workers and less qualified service workers, bearing in mind a general tendency toward upskilling in advanced societies. This suggested that we concentrate on front-line workers as part of a complex division of labor.

The third trend we noticed was that the application of information technology was resulting in an ongoing transformation of work. This pointed to the use of computer technology as a criterion for selecting companies and, if possible, workflows.

Fourth, and finally, directions in work organization (WO) patterns suggested that we examine leading companies. Hence, another criterion for selection was that the companies had to exhibit strong competitive performance and innovative employment relations strategies.

In choosing the countries in which to conduct our research, we recognized the importance of forces for both continuity—the weight of existing institutions and norms—and change, particularly tendencies toward globalization and customization. Since these forces vary among countries, we decided to focus on multiple countries. In making our final selection, we followed Castells (1996: 229), who distinguishes between two types of emerging industrial and occupational structures: the "service industry model" in the Anglo-Saxon countries—the United States, Canada, Australia, and the United Kingdom—and the "industrial production model," exemplified by companies in Japan and Germany. This suggested that we focus on the differences in companies and sites in countries representing each of these postindustrial models. Subsequently, we decided on Australia and the United States to represent the service industry model and Japan to represent the industrial production model.[2]

Two additional interrelated strategic decisions concerned the choice of research methods and the number of workflows to be studied. Our research methods are discussed in more detail in the following section. In essence, multiple case studies were complemented with a restricted survey analysis (Kalleberg et al. 1996) in a form of triangulation (Neuman 1997: 151). The value of comparative case studies lies in the detailed information afforded by the close acquaintance with the data, the insights into causal processes, and, as alluded to above, the chance for partial testing, includ-

[1] We agree with Castells (1996: 211–12) that producer services (i.e., financial and business service subsectors) are strategically crucial in advanced economies. As noted in chapter 1, this category comprises many of the fastest-growing industries in the advanced societies.
[2] The United States and Japan are the largest economies representing the two models. Australia was chosen primarily because the research team was based there. It is noteworthy that little is known about Japanese front-line workers and associated management systems. Evidence suggests that there is no counterpart to just-in-time production systems (Katz 1997b: 4–5; Shapira 1995).

ing further refinement of hypotheses as a contribution to theory building (Ragin 1987).

There were four reasons for complementing our qualitative information with survey data. First, providing standardized data across workflows facilitated comparative analysis. Second, and related, the survey provided data that were not easily captured in the fieldwork (e.g., workforce demographics, work values, levels of work satisfaction, and other consequences of WO). Third, the survey data acted as a check on the reliability of fieldwork-based findings, which, by their nature, were selective. Fourth, and finally, the survey data enabled us to test hypotheses generated mainly, but not exclusively, from the case studies.[3]

Emerging research findings showed that the level of service customization was associated with variations in the work complexity of front-line jobs. This insight enabled us to distinguish among three types of workflows: mass customized service, sales, and knowledge work. In subsequent chapters these are often referred to by the dominant type of front-line workers in the workflow. By way of introduction, details about each workflow are summarized in table 2.1.

Mass customized service workflows (hereafter *service workflows*) provide large volumes of customers with simple products that are customized to only a limited extent. An example of the relevant front-line worker in an organization with such a workflow is the retail bank customer service representative. A good deal of knowledge is embedded in IT systems, and hence front-line and other workers share a high level of shared dependence on technology. When workers encounter difficult problems, they typically contact their team leaders or supervisors. For the most part, however, these workers' contact is with customers.

Sales workflows provide a more complex and more customized product, such as home loans and other financial products sold by home loan consultants. Sales workers require social skills to build credibility, customer confidence, and trust. Knowledge tends to be embodied in the person (Blackler 1995). Sales workers depend on others in a sequential manner. They depend on referrers, who can be thought of as indirect customers—persons who refer clients to the loan consultants—and on "back-office" personnel (mainly credit analysts) to approve and process applications.

Knowledge work workflows are distinguished by a high level of customization and work complexity. To identify and help define problems, contacts between front-line workers and clients tend to be close and to extend over relatively long periods. For example, systems developers depend

---

[3] Hypotheses were also derived from inspection and analysis of the survey data and from relevant literature, for example, on the impact of technology on workers' perceptions of the nature of work, the influence of job values on work satisfaction, and the relationship between length of working hours and stress.

Table 2.1. Three Types of Workflows and Associated Characteristics

Workflow type	Level of customization	Work complexity of front-line worker	Task characteristics of front-line worker	Interdependence
Mass customized service n = 7 (e.g., customer service representative)	Low; many customers	Low; routinized mainly through embedded knowledge	Service (e.g., answering queries, effecting transactions)	Pooled and sequential; high supervisor and customer dependence
Sales n = 3 (e.g., home loan consultant)	Medium; buyers require trust	Medium-variable; some embodied routinization	Sales and service (e.g., selling and advising clients)	Mainly sequential; high dependence on indirect customers and on other workers
Knowledge work n = 4 (e.g., computer systems developer)	High; solutions tailored to the client	High; problem solving; limited routinization; embrained and encultured knowledge	Client relations; problem identification, analysis, and resolution	Reciprocal interdependence on colleagues, client, and management

mainly on their own knowledge and that of their colleagues—referred to as embrained and encultured knowledge respectively (Blackler 1995)—to analyze and resolve problems. Thus, management depends on knowledge workers to solve problems, while knowledge workers rely on management for resources and support. Accordingly, the relationship is characterized by reciprocal interdependence (Thompson 1967).

We began our research by studying service workflows in Australia. Efforts to gain access to workflows characterized by higher product customization and more complex work led to research on sales workflows in the same organizations. Simultaneously, attempts were made to gain access to similar types of workflows in similar industries in Japan and the United States and to study knowledge work sites in the three countries. This was a time-consuming process[4] and it led to several sites being rejected that did not meet our criteria. Finding organizations with comparable workflows was also made difficult by the limited presence of call centers (one of which we studied) and home loan salespeople in Japan. Consequently, we identified and pursued typological equivalents (i.e., Japanese workflows characterized by varying levels of service customization and work complexity). This did not necessarily lead to our selecting similar industries to those in Australia and the United States. For example, the Japanese communications industry is not known for its innovation, having only recently instituted technological and other changes; it is therefore more similar to other large, conservative, private-sector companies (Nakamura and Hiraki 1997). Thus, in seeking access to organizations with knowledge work workflows in Japan, we concentrated on the computer industry instead of on communications.

Since none of the members of the research team was a U.S. resident, access to companies in that country was also limited. In the case of the single knowledge work workflow we studied, a merger resulted in the company suspending work for several months on the project on which we were focusing. Since we could not wait, we terminated the research at the company.

Although it would have been desirable to obtain symmetry in the distribution of cases according to workflow type and country, access, timing, and resource difficulties made this impossible. Following Collier (1991), we nevertheless pursued a well-established method of case selection that combined a "most similar systems" and a "most different systems" approach. This was accomplished by comparing the variables comprising WO *within* each of the three different types of workflows and comparing *across* the

---

[4] Compared with their Australian and U.S. counterparts, Japanese managers required more meetings and a higher level of detail in our requests and presentations seeking company access. This had to do with our lack of corporate sponsorship and our "outsider" status (both with regard to the company and to Japan). Entree to knowledge work workflows was also time-consuming, in part because high-value products (e.g., systems development) were involved and ensuring customer security (e.g., in money market dealing) was a priority.

Figure 2.1. Implementation of Research Strategy as a Sequence of Methodological Tasks

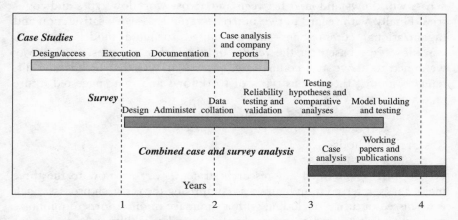

workflow types. This is consistent with Strauss's (1998: 185) observation that "establishing typologies (or similarities) may be the first step toward explaining differences."

Overview

Our research strategy entailed four major tasks: define the research problems, execute the case studies, administer the survey, and combine case and survey analysis into research outputs. The first task was discussed in the first chapter, so we shall concentrate on the remaining three. These are illustrated in figure 2.1.

The survey was designed in light of emerging case study findings relating to the WO framework and project goals. Management cooperation and the comparatively high response rate by employees owed a great deal to contacts established during the course of the case studies.[5]

Comparative analysis, including writing up the study, commenced after the case study and survey data became available, with the intention being to integrate and analyze the material thematically. Integration was achieved successively: by analyzing each of the cases in turn and then identifying attributes and processes common to each type of workflow. Themes—operationalized in terms of the various elements of WO and future tendencies, as outlined in chapter 1—were based on the WO framework.

---

[5] Management cooperation included permitting employees to take time off to complete the survey and, in some instances, providing researchers with lists of employees from which samples could be drawn. The only opposition came from senior management in two U.S. companies containing three workflows. In one company, there was sensitivity over trade union issues, and in the other company, pay levels were a private matter. In these workflows, the surveys omitted the sensitive items.

The themes were pursued through the case study and workflow analyses. Comparisons were made at various stages of the analysis: between and across workflows and later between and across workflow types and countries. Finally, with regard to two outcome variables—work satisfaction and organizational commitment—we attempted to build models for each workflow type based on the results of our earlier analyses. In this way we aimed to arrive at a comparative picture of WO that highlighted differences among the various types of workflows and that suggested future tendencies.

Research Methods

Having briefly described our research strategy, we turn now to the three major tasks, referred to in figure 2.1, comprising the research process. Each is discussed in turn, concluding with a summary of our efforts to minimize problems of research bias, internal validity, and reliability.

Case Studies

Design, access, and fieldwork. The case study design was based on the emerging WO framework and associated research issues, including the preferred research methods. Two designs were used. Most workflows that are designed to accomplish work that is broadly repeatable were studied in a "continuous presence" fashion for a finite period of time. Where work was organized on a project basis, we adopted a "slice-in-time" approach. In other words, rather than continuously immersing themselves in the workflow, researchers conducted fieldwork at strategic intervals depending on "deliverable dates" (i.e., dates when project outputs were expected). Differences in these methods (e.g., their bias toward continuity and change respectively) were taken into account in analyzing the data.

Before conducting the fourteen case studies, data were collected from management on a variety of issues included on a checklist. These covered the organization's structure, its human resource policy and practice, technological change affecting the workflow, and relevant position descriptions, as well as the distribution of employees by position in the workflow. In addition, interview schedules for line managers, staff managers, supervisors, and employees were drawn up. Included in each interview were semistructured questions that facilitated comparisons among workflows while, at the same time, permitting workflow-specific issues to be explored in depth. Early in the project we also agreed on a common approach to note taking vis-à-vis style and level of detail required. This issue was revisited in light of the special requirements of each case.

Following presentations to senior management, we identified the relevant workflows for research. The basic arrangement was that in exchange for guaranteeing confidentiality and providing management with a report of our findings, management would not interfere with our research.

With the exception of two Japanese cases for which resources were limited, two or three researchers worked together on each case. This had two advantages: it enabled us to conduct the research in reasonable depth in a relatively short period of time; and it facilitated relatively comprehensive coverage of relationships and issues. All managers associated with the workflow were sought for interviews, and selected supervisors and staff were interviewed prior to observation. Interviews were also conducted after the observation period, and, when interviewees were not representative of the total workflow workforce, we attempted to interview more widely— for example, if we had interviewed only full-timers and not any part-timers. Interviews were reviewed soon after completion. If necessary, discussions were continued with interviewees, thereby enabling us to sharpen our understanding; this approach also aided us when documenting our findings.

During the process of observation, we sat next to service workers and accompanied sales workers on their customer and office visits for an average of five hours per observed participant. We also attended team meetings and selected management meetings. The estimated duration of fieldwork for each case was about thirty person-days, usually spread over a two-month period. Care was taken not to bias our observations by observing workers with particular characteristics (e.g., the highest performers). In the case of two knowledge work workflows characterized by a project form of management, the observation period was more than six months.

Employees in call centers invariably agreed to our listening to their interchanges with customers. Headphones were used for this purpose, and notes were made as calls came in. Where necessary, clarification was sought from relevant employees. Some sales workers and knowledge workers denied our requests to accompany them to meetings with clients; others were agreeable.

In the course of each case study, the researchers regularly discussed and compared their observations. Ambiguities and differences in interpretation were clarified or shown to require further exploration. Midterm progress reviews were undertaken so that the researchers could check for gaps in research coverage and pursue major issues prior to completion of the fieldwork.

As mentioned earlier, management received confidential reports on individual case research, usually in the form of a presentation and a request that information be made available to employees. This feedback proved useful in three ways. First, it provided us with an opportunity to air ideas based on the research; second, it offered us an occasion to gather more data, particularly on recent developments in WO; and third, it was a way to encourage management to seek less conventional solutions to problems associated with the organization of work.

Case documentation and analysis. Basic company and workflow data were summarized according to a template. Coded data were handwritten in notebooks, which were then converted into computer-based soft copy according to a detailed set of categories indicated by the WO framework. The categories and rules for transcription were initially determined on an experimental basis but were subsequently refined and finalized. Research assistants, hired to transcribe the field notes, were systematically inducted into the project and their work checked regularly for accuracy, consistency, and intercoder reliability. Researchers who had undertaken specific case studies answered queries and guided research assistants in the transcription process. Completed cases were reviewed by a relevant fieldwork researcher in the course of which queries and categorizing problems were rectified.

Sensitive to differences between Japanese and English terminology, we addressed the lexicon equivalence issue (Neuman 1997: 411) in part by having the research in Japan supervised by a bilingual member of the research team who lived in Japan. She also guided the Japanese research assistants in documenting the research and played a leading role in translating the material.

Presentations of our findings were usually made to management immediately following completion of the documentation stage of the research, based on preliminary analysis of the combined case study and survey findings pertaining to the workflow in question. The analysis stage was then completed by integrating the company-specific data, management responses to our presentation, and survey data used to test hypotheses. Each case analysis was written by a fieldwork researcher, in accordance with an agreed-upon template informed by our research framework. Analyses were reviewed by a second fieldwork researcher. This helped to highlight gaps where data had not been fully utilized; it also assisted in making sense of the data. Where differences in interpretation remained, they were recorded in the final, reviewed analysis of the case. The case analyses served as one of the two bases for aggregating our workflow-level findings to the level of workflow types. The other source was the employee survey.

Employee Survey

Design and testing. The survey was designed for distribution to front-line employees and their immediate supervisors in the fourteen case study workflows and at four additional sites. The survey covered the various WO elements described in the previous chapter, particularly the following themes: job characteristics: job values and job satisfaction; technology; knowledge, skills, information, and learning; relations with colleagues; management, participation, and organizational commitment; and demographic details. Each survey reflected the wording for concepts used by the workers in the workflow being studied. To minimize problems of lexicon equivalence in Japan (Neuman 1997: 410), the survey was translated by a professional company and checked by several bilingual survey experts.[6] As a defense against unreliable measures, where possible, we used sets of items that had proved reliable in previous studies. In addition, the survey was piloted among sixty-two respondents, many of whom were employed in workflows subsequently included in the study. Reliability tests were conducted on responses to sets of questions measuring particular concepts. To ensure conceptual equivalence (Neuman 1997: 411–12) with regard to the Japanese workers, the survey was piloted among twenty-three front-line clerical staff at a Japanese university. Drafts of the survey were also circulated to academics and managers for comment. In addition, focus groups drawn from the pilot respondents helped to improve the clarity of the questions. These presurvey procedures contributed to an improved final instrument. Tests indicated that our measures were generally reliable and that they were equivalent cross-nationally (see appendix 2).

Administration and data collation. At ten workflows, a researcher supervised and ensured confidential administration of the survey. In nine cases, where this was not possible, confidential off-site administration methods were used (a collection box or self-addressed envelopes).[7] In fifteen of the total eighteen workflows, all workers and supervisors were asked to complete the questionnaire. In the remaining three workflows, senior managers, for various reasons, were unwilling to give the survey to the whole population. In these cases, one in two persons was sampled randomly from lists supplied by management. Analysis showed that these samples were not significantly different in age, sex, and employment status (full time versus part time) from those in which the sample included the total employee population in the workflow.

The overall survey response rate was 81 percent. The response rate for the questionnaires administered off site was 89 percent, mainly because fewer workflows were sampled and it was therefore easier to follow up with reluctant respondents and, if necessary, make substitutions.[8]

Data analysis and reporting conventions. Hypotheses were tested in the course of analyzing each case. The workflow typology described earlier,

[6] Lincoln and Kalleberg (1990: 50–51) suggest that Japanese people may tend to avoid extreme responses. Hence, they used a seven- rather than a five-item scale for their attitude questions. We disagree with this view. First, other survey analysts (e.g., Kosaka, 1994) do not see this as a particularly Japanese problem, and, second, our pilot study did not indicate any significant tendency among Japanese employees to choose the midpoint in the scale or to choose "don't know" in their answers to survey questions.

[7] In one workflow, both methods were used. The latter method was used for employees working outside the main location. Thus, the total number of workflows appears to be nineteen rather than eighteen.

[8] The dataset is available at the Social Science Data Archives, Australian National University (http://w.w.w.ssda.anu.edu.au/).

based on case study data, was validated through discriminant analysis of the survey data. This is described in chapter 3. One-way analysis of variance (ANOVA) is used throughout the book to identify the extent of similarities and differences among front-line workers in the three types of workflows. In addition, ANOVA is used to explore intra-workflow comparisons, for example, whether workers in workflows of the same type but in different countries have similar characteristics. Summary details of the factors and items we examined are included in subsequent chapters; further information is found in appendix 2. Pearson correlation tests were used to estimate the direction and magnitude of relationships between variables. In chapter 8, ordinary least squares regression is used to explore the relative impact of WO variables on two dependent variables: front-line workers' job satisfaction and their discretionary work effort. One-tail significance tests, reported on in subsequent chapters, refer to the confidence we have in generalizing survey results to front-line workers in the workflows being studied. Unless otherwise stated, probability levels were set at 0.05 for all estimates. This is in line with current convention, given the relatively small samples of sales and knowledge workers.

Synthesis and Overview

Guided by the WO framework, case study and survey data were combined in an iterative, bricoleur fashion, juxtaposing various pieces of data, exploring many different conjectures, moving in a spiral-like fashion from divergent discussion to convergent conclusions and back again on various themes. Arising from these processes, we developed the ideal types that structure the discussions in subsequent chapters. Along the way we developed papers that became the basis for this book and produced other papers, some of which have been published (Frenkel et al. 1995; Korczynski et al. 1996; Korczynski, Frenkel, and Tam, in press; Tam, Frenkel, and Korczynski, 1999). This activity helped clarify our thoughts and generate new interpretations that gave rise to further analysis. Writing proceeded in a dialogical fashion, with each chapter being thoroughly debated and reviewed before being finalized.

During all facets of the research process we were concerned with minimizing problems that might lead to unjustifiable conclusions. These had to do with the related issues of researcher bias, incomplete or incorrect understanding of social relations in the workflows, and the use of unreliable research methods. We believe that the triangulation of the research instruments and the participation of two or more researchers in each case study, when possible, limited biases in collecting, analyzing, and drawing conclusions from the data. Furthermore, undertaking in-depth case studies and collecting data with the help of systematic procedures reduced the probability of misunderstanding or obtaining incomplete perspectives on social relations in the workflows. Case studies, as noted earlier, are also an indispensable bridge between practice and theory formation.

With regard to reliability, we developed clear concepts according to the WO framework and fashioned a case study methodology that was replicated across the workflows, except in project-dominated workflows, where appropriate amendments were made. The use of standardized measures and statistical techniques based on a carefully tested survey, together with formal procedures for analyzing and writing up our research, helped in our general quest for reliability.

Research Organizations and Workflows

The fourteen case studies were undertaken in nine companies. Table 2.2 provides relevant details. To preserve confidentiality, the companies are referred to by acronyms. The country of majority ownership is usually indicated as follows: A = Australia, J = Japan, and U = United States. In the interests of brevity, this convention is not always followed. The industry sector is suggested by the following letters: B = banking, F = financial services, COMPU = computers, INS = insurance, and TEL = telecommunications. SV designates a service workflow; S, a sales workflow; and SD, a systems development (knowledge worker) workflow. The acronyms are shown in the left-hand column of table 2.2. Five of the companies are multinationals. Since undertaking this project, two of these companies were involved in mergers with corporations not included in our study. Thus, the estimated employment levels given for ABK and UB1 and UB2 are substantially lower than current levels. Also noteworthy, the Japanese financial service company is closely associated with one of Japan's, and indeed the world's, largest financial institutions.

As indicated in the table, all the companies we selected were high performers, and most claimed to be using advanced technology and paying their employees well above the average. Acquaintance with the industries and discussions with senior managers in other companies generally supported these claims. In short, our research sites are successful, mainly multinational companies in the heartland of informational, postindustrial economies. One would expect these firms to offer insights into emerging forms of work organization among front-line workers.

Although most of the firms listed in table 2.2 operate in the financial services sector, they tend to specialize in particular markets. Several companies are prominent in retail banking, one firm is a leading insurance company, and two specialize in wholesale banking. These markets, together with the computer industry and communications, are characterized by their intense competition, arising mainly from deregulation (especially financial services and communications) and rapid technological change

Table 2.2. Selected Characteristics of Companies Participating in the Study, 1995

Company	No. and type of workflow	Nationality of owner	No. of employees	Sector	Corporate ranking and key features
ABK	1 sales	Australia	2,409	Financial services	Top five financial services firms in return on net assets;[*] consumer-oriented; regional; positioning for merger
UB	2 service	U.S.	18,000	Financial services	Top third in U.S. financial services industry;[†] positioning for merger
WB	2 knowledge work	U.S.	14,000	Financial services	Top ten in U.S. financial services industry;[†] corporate and organizational restructuring
MBA	1 service; 1 sales	U.S.	85,300	Financial services	Top five in U.S. financial services industry;[†] corporate and organizational restructuring; cost reduction
MFJ	1 service	Multinational	85,000	Financial services	Top ten in world financial services industry[†] corporate and organizational restructuring; cost reduction
COMPUJ	1 knowledge work	Japan	41,078	Computers/ communications	Top ten in world computer industry;[‡] strategic and organizational change
AIN	1 service	Australia	4,352	Financial services	Top 15 percent in Australia; quality award winner; 1995 corporate and organizational restructuring; cost reduction
TEL	1 service; 1 knowledge work	Australia	32,000	Communications	Top 5 percent in Australia;[§] product and service improvement; downsizing
JB	1 service; 1 sales	Japan	4,200	Financial services	Top ten of second-tier security companies;[‖] improving customer confidence; cost reduction

Note: Ranking relates to revenue unless otherwise stated. [*] KPMG 1996; [†] Fortune 500 industry ranking; [‡] "Fortune Global 500"; [§] Dun and Bradstreet 1996–97; [‖] *Nihon Kezai Shimbun*, Inc. 1996.
Source: Company documents; Dun and Bradstreet 1996–97; "The Fortune 500" and "The Fortune Global 500" (1996).

(especially the computer industry). Deregulation has encouraged competition from new entrants, typically multinationals hastening the trend toward globalization. This has led to a blurring of industry boundaries (e.g., between insurance and banking and between communications and computers).

Table 2.2 also suggests that corporate responses to intense competition have varied. In some cases, companies have been looking to merge and have tended to pursue an approach that seeks incremental product and process innovation with an emphasis on cost limitation. As mentioned earlier, two firms announced mergers soon after the research was completed. Restructuring of senior management and of the organization more generally occurred in three other firms. Two of these restructurings involved substantial retrenchment; the other was aimed at integrating and utilizing the expertise of successful business units that had hitherto been relatively autonomous. Some other firms in the study had been through similar reorganizations in the recent past and were seeking to improve their products and services while continuing to reduce staff. In the computer-communications industry firm, management was emphasizing the company's ability to supply customers with software and consulting services, enabling firms to use a combination of the company's new products and existing equipment. Finally, senior managers in all the firms in the study were concerned about controlling costs.

Characteristics of the Workflows

As mentioned earlier, the choice of workflows for research was negotiated with senior management at each organization. Each management, of course, had its own agenda, so that our criteria never solely guided which workflows we studied.[9] Table 2.3 summarizes data on the principal characteristics of the workflows.[10] The workflows are referred to by slightly elaborated acronyms (used in table 2.2) that refer to the companies of which they are a part.

By way of further clarification, we offer some comments based mainly, but not exclusively, on the data in table 2.3. This is followed by a brief introduction to front-line workers in atypical workflows. We also provide

[9] In some cases, management wanted to learn how its company compared with other so-called leading-edge companies; in other cases, management wanted a deeper understanding of current problems. At one firm, the person supporting the research wanted us to reveal the need for organizational change and so enhance his position as an internal change agent. At another, some managers anticipated that our study would highlight the weaknesses of current decision-making processes concerning the use of technology and so contribute to changes these managers favored. In a third case, management was interested to learn how we conducted the research so that it might consider doing similar research in the future.

[10] In some instances, the case studies were conducted in a typical section of a workflow. Thus, the figure given for the size of the workflow does not necessarily mean that all the employees in a workflow were included in the case study.

Table 2.3. Selected Structural and Demographic Characteristics of Case Study Workflows

Workflow name/type	Front-line occupation	No. of employees in workflow	Features	% female	Average age in years	% with qualifications above high school	Average duration in position, in years	Average earnings in $U.S.§	Union density‖
Service type									
UB1	CSR	134*	Call center relocated nine months earlier; in the midst of rapid change and growth; many new managers; advanced HR practices.	59.6	30.8	78.0	1.7	23,750	—
UB2	CSR	136	Two-year-old call center; some distance from UB1, the main call center, but similar in many respects; less change than in UB1.	68.9	30.4	80.3	1.4	23,750	3.3
MBASV	CSR	70	Established call center that had high management turnover and many problems caused by other departments; customer problems adversely affected staff.	61.2	29.5	52.0	0.7	23,750	1.5
MFJSV	CSR	71†	Call center in Japan; work and employment practices tended to follow those of parent company.	76.3	30.8	90.0	2.7	46,067	<2

AINSV	CSR	128	Call center established one year earlier in a region far from headquarters; new managers and staff.	65.0	26.6	63.0	0.6	21,250	13.3
TELSV	CSR	73	Call center handling queries about accounts and services; located outside major city center; low management and employee turnover.	86.8	34.3	24.0	2.6	21,250	37.7
JBSV	"Bond-lady"	14	Mainly temporary female workforce employed to advise married women regarding reinvestment of bonds and other simple financial products; direct contact with customers through phone and home visits.	83.3	26.0	91.7	4.2	31,250	100.0
Sales type									
ABKS	HLC	18	Two-year-old experiment in entrepreneurial loan sales through a separate business unit controlled by a strongly task-/profit-oriented manager.	18.5	38.5	48.0	3.2	26,250	7.7

Table 2.3. Continued

Workflow name/type	Front-line occupation	No. of employees in workflow	Features	% female	Average age in years	% with qualifications above high school	Average duration in position, in years	Average earnings in $U.S.§	Union density‖
MBAS	HLC	41	Well-established loan sales unit that targeted higher-income earners; some experimentation with telephone sales; low technology compared to ABKS.	16.7	40.0	71.1	3.3	33,750	4.5
JBS	"Share salesman"	40	Long-standing business involving identification and persuasion of medium-sized companies to engage JBS as their main share sales agent. The share salesmen each visit about seventy companies to solicit business; limited use of IT.	—	44.4	82.6	3.7	82,500	23.3

Knowledge work type

		Description						
WBSD SD	150	Three main groups: corporate IT infrastructure developers; network maintenance/repair experts; and applications developers. The latter worked closely with internal business units. Qualitative research focused on the broker applications project.	23.1	31.7	94.0	2.6	75,000	0.9
WBMM Money market dealer	38	Stable, highly profitable, discrete group or "desk" of front-line dealers, traders, and structured deal analysts supported by processing staff (middle and back-office). Research focused mainly on distributors responsible for buying and selling financial instruments to large organizations.	14.3	29.3	86.0	2.4	95,000	5.0
COMPUJ SD	40‡	New business unit in which personnel with sales and engineering backgrounds combined in pursuit of client-focused systems consulting and implementation.	3.7	31.1	100.0	2.6	52,500	70.4

Table 2.3. Continued

Workflow name/type	Front-line occupation	No. of employees in workflow	Features	% female	Average age in years	% with qualifications above high school	Average duration in position, in years	Average earnings in $U.S.[§]	Union density[‖]
TELSD	SD	13	Located within a large, bureaucratic corporation; specialized business unit aimed at providing and managing communications technology. Research focused on a project introducing an electronic communications system into a large organization.	20.0	42.4	100.0	3.5	31,250	20.0

Note: CSR = customer service representative, HLC = home loan consultant, and SD = systems developer. * Excludes development and delivery personnel. [†] Excludes eighteen staff on consignment from another company. [‡] Based on company list; elsewhere figure given as 57. [§] Figures are for midpoint in a salary range provided in the employee survey. All conversions were made using the following exchange rates (means for 1995): Japanese yen to U.S. cents = 0.9725 (*Source:* OECD 1996c). Australian dollars to U.S. dollars = 0.7394 (*Source:* Australian Bureau of Statistics 1996b). [‖] Union density is the number of union members in the workflow as a percentage of the workflow workforce. Estimates are based mainly on survey data.

Sources: Company documents, official statistics, and survey data.

summary details of additional workflows that were not part of our case studies but were included in our survey.

Service workflows tend to employ the largest number of employees. Of the varied and broad occupational categories occupied by front-line workers, this book concentrates mainly on customer service representatives (CSRs), home loan consultants (HLCs), systems developers (SDs), and money market dealers (MM dealers). The first two types of workers represent service and sales workers respectively. Knowledge workers are represented by SDs and MM dealers; the former can be regarded mainly as project-oriented, while MM dealers are process-oriented.[11] We were able to locate CSRs in Japan at a multinational financial service company. Consequently, as noted earlier, we sought Japanese workers employed in analogous service occupations. MM dealers, and, more specifically, distributors (see chapter 3), were chosen because they undertook complex work tailored to the requirements of fund managers. Like systems developers, they helped these clients arrive at solutions.

Females are overrepresented in the lower-paid service occupations and underrepresented among higher-paid, front-line sales and knowledge workers. Workers in all three types of workflow tended to be relatively young; service workers were the youngest, and sales workers were the oldest.

A clearer picture emerges regarding education levels. Based on the responses to our employee survey, we estimated that an average of 84 percent of the knowledge workers (n = 159) had graduate or postgraduate degrees. This compared with 55 percent of the sales workers (n = 88) and 29 percent for the service workers (n = 600).

Two further points are worth noting. Some workflows (MBASV, TELSV, and ABKS) placed less emphasis than other workflows on formal qualifications in hiring, and, on the whole, Japanese employees were more highly qualified than their Australian or U.S. counterparts. This reflects Japan's relatively high educational standards.

Other relevant characteristics of the work settings include employees' job tenure, pay, workplace union density (as defined in the note to table 2.3), and job status (not shown in table 2.3). The job tenure profile is similar to that for age: service workers had the lowest relative job tenure, and sales workers had the highest. As hinted at earlier, pay varies by the type of workflow and occupation. Thus, on average, service workers were paid the least, while knowledge workers were paid the most. Note, however, midpoints are given, and converting to a common currency ignores large international differences in the cost of living.

---

[11] Project work usually involves interdependent teams that exist until the project is completed. Thereafter, new knowledge and skill combinations are constituted in accordance with the needs of new projects. By contrast, process work tends to be conducted more independently and to continue indefinitely.

Union density across the three types of workflows was generally low, even in service workflows, where one might have expected higher levels of unionization, given the larger units and more routine work. The average proportion of part-time employees in service workflows was 18 percent, compared with less than 2 percent in sales and knowledge workflows respectively. The largest relative part-time contingents were in the MB service workflows: 57 percent in Japan (where part-timers were all employed as temporary workers) and 25 percent in Australia. Staffing restrictions imposed by corporate management meant that managers at both subsidiaries were not allowed to hire full-time staff. In any case, management was keen to increase the proportion of part-timers (albeit to no more than about 20 percent) so as to match labor supply with changing demand. Consequently, part-timers were hired.

Only at MFJSV was a majority of the staff hired on a temporary basis. This was accomplished by insourcing through two companies that specialized in telecommunications. These firms employed bilingual staff proficient in basic telephone service work. In all other cases across the three types of workflows, at least 95 percent of the workers were permanent hires.

Atypical workflows. The atypical workflows in our sample were all in Japan. Among the service workflows, MBJ stands out as paying relatively high salaries. This is also true of JBS. The higher pay levels in these two workflows should not be taken at face value since they reflect the relative strength of the Japanese yen during 1995, when the research was conducted. This is not the whole story, however. Customer service representatives were in short supply at MFJSV because call-center work is rare in Japan and bilingual CSRs were scarce. This is reflected in the relatively high pay rates. In addition, as a foreign company and therefore not favored by the most successful entrants to the job market, MFJ was prepared to pay a premium to attract higher-caliber staff.

The workflow composed of the "bond-ladies," JBSV, differed from those of other service workers in several respects. First, the bond-ladies' work involved making mainly outgoing phone calls and some face-to-face contact with customers. The bond-lady's job was to advise mainly home-based customers—typically risk-averse married women and, to a lesser extent, male pensioners—on how to reinvest their savings. The bond-ladies were restricted to a range of fairly simple, low-risk financial products, the most important of which were government bonds. Their jobs combined sales and service, although much of their activity consisted of providing moral support and advice to customers. Bond-ladies had lists of customers whom they contacted when the latter's investments matured. Customers were urged to reinvest through the bond-ladies' company. With one exception (TELSV), the JBSV workflow had a higher proportion of female workers than other service workflows. But unlike TELSV, management discouraged the bond-ladies from continuing to work after they were married. The counterpart is that men were more highly concentrated in Japanese workflows consisting of sales (JBS) and knowledge workers (COMPUJ) than in corresponding workflows in U.S. and Australian companies. With enterprise unionism being one of the pillars of the traditional Japanese employment system, Japanese workflows tend to be more unionized than their U.S. and Australian counterparts.

The occupational title "share salesman" in the JBS workflow requires explanation. The task of the workers in this workflow was to identify medium-sized companies that were selling new shares. The aim was to persuade the managers at those companies that JB should act as their main sales agent. Each share salesman had about seventy companies he visited. As indicated in table 2.3, the share salesmen were older on average than their U.S. and Australian colleagues. Most significantly, the Japanese share salesmen had far more years of service with their companies. The average company tenure for salespersons in the other two sales workflows was slightly more than two years (ABKS) and four years (MBAS) respectively, versus about twenty-one years for JBS's salesmen.

Since pay in Japan is strongly related to seniority, the relatively high pay that the share salespersons earned was not simply a function of exchange rates. It was high relative to that of the bond-ladies and the COMPUJ systems developers because of the share salesmen's relatively long tenures with their companies.[12]

Our final point concerns the salaries of the knowledge workers. The high salaries paid to WB money market dealers and systems developers compared with their counterpart knowledge workers speaks to two characteristics of WB: its position as a leading financial institution in a particular niche market and, related to this, management's strategy of positioning the company among the highest-paying firms in the industry. In addition, the knowledge and skills of the persons in the relevant occupations were and continue to be in short supply. Why then is the pay of SDs at TEL relatively low? The main reason is that their pay was negotiated based on pay ranges set by unions that represented a wide variety of workers. The unsuitability of these pay ranges for SDs was a problem (see chapter 4), but altering pay relativities proved difficult to achieve in a complex internal labor market environment.

Survey data from the fourteen case study workflows was supplemented by information from four additional workflows. These covered service workers and were located in Australia. Three were owned by the telecommunications company and, except for their union density, were similar to the TEL service workflow. The TEL workflows were more heavily

---

[12] For example, the average company tenure of the bond-ladies was nearly five years (considerably more than their counterparts in service workflows), while it was eight years for the systems developers at COMPUJ.

unionized: the least organized of the three workflows had a density of nearly two-thirds (61.3 percent). The fourth workflow was owned by AIN and was similar to other service workflows in the financial service sector, except that it also had a relatively high union density (44.3 percent). In short, by adding these four workflows, we were able to explore the impact of unions on employment relations (see chapter 4). Furthermore, the addition of service workflows in the communications industry meant that the survey sample was more evenly distributed across an important part of the service sector.

Conclusion

Our research was designed to explicate the nature and dynamics of work organization among the increasingly significant category of the workforce we refer to as front-line workers. Our preferred research strategy included a concern for relevance or breadth, with an emphasis on depth—that is, our goal was to understand at an adequate level and as systematically as possible the structures, processes, and consequences of work organization. This entailed conducting multiple case studies and an employee survey. We also submitted our work to continuous collective scrutiny. These processes were combined, with the intention of minimizing problems of research bias, internal validity, and reliability.

In common with other so-called small N studies, our research design makes it difficult to develop adequate causal explanations at the workflow level. We cannot, for example, confidently answer the following question: what are the determinants of work organization? This is because the number of causal variables far exceeds the number of cases (Ragin 1987; Lieberson 1991). As befits exploratory research, we can describe, classify, and interpret in an informed manner, leading to new concepts and hypotheses relating to work organization. This does not mean abandoning causal analysis, however. It does mean, on the one hand, being aware that an interpretive yet critical approach, such as our own, provides a deeper, more holistic, if less precise account of cause-and-effect relationships than do positivist alternatives. On the other hand, in chapter 8 we attempt to conduct a multivariate causal analysis in relation to two carefully delineated outcome variables, while other outcome variables are analyzed as sets of bivariate relationships. We avoid the problem of the small size of our N by taking the individual worker as the unit of analysis, while recognizing that this may limit sociological explanations.

One final point directed at the issue of generalizability. Case-based research involves a trade-off that favors data integrity over enumerative generalizability. Nevertheless, we have expanded the generalizability of our research by examining a wide range of front-line workers across a relatively large number of cases in three countries. As mentioned earlier, this gives a broader base to our hypotheses and conclusions, and contributes to the generation of more robust theory. We also anticipate that our research findings will confirm readers' experience, thereby constituting a form of "naturalistic generalizability" (Morrill and Fine 1997: 441).

3   Work Relations

THE dominant views of work can be summed up in two contrasting images, that of "the electronic sweatshop," suggesting automation and regimentation, and that of "the intelligent, human-centered workplace," implying organizational and technological support for worker empowerment (Winslow and Bramer 1994; Quinn, Anderson, and Finkelstein 1996: 76). Which of these images more faithfully portrays contemporary reality? This chapter tries to answer this question by exploring the characteristics of front-line work in service, sales, and knowledge workflows respectively.

We begin by proposing that with respect to the constituents of work—knowledge, information, and people—front-line workers in the three types of workflows have much in common. Their tasks and roles, however, differ in both substance and complexity. Since conventional ways of classifying work are unsatisfactory for exploring these differences, the act-of-work framework is presented as an alternative. This enables us to distinguish between two ideal types of worker—the *routine* and the *professional*. Routine workers are typical of bureaucracies, while professional workers are associated with knowledge-intensive organizations (see table 1.5).

In the next section, we use the act-of-work framework to investigate the extent to which front-line workers in the three types of workflows resemble the ideal types and hence differ from one another. Based on qualitative data validated by quantitative analysis, we demonstrate differences in the work complexity of service, sales, and knowledge workers. This leads us to conclude that service workers most closely resemble the ideal type known as the routine worker.

Sales workers, like technical employees, are difficult to categorize (Barley and Orr 1997). They creatively combine considerable social skills with limited analytical skills, thereby constituting something of a mix of the two ideal types.

Knowledge workers undertake the most complex work of the three kinds of workers. This work is characterized by the use of theoretical knowledge and high levels of analytical and social skills applied creatively. These employees most closely resemble the professional ideal type.

In the third section, we present several hypotheses concerning the relationship between variations in work complexity and employees' work experience. Our focus is on four subjective aspects of work that are both theoretically important and significant to employees. These include workers' work values (what employees want out of work), their attitudes toward technology, the intrinsic satisfaction they derive from work, and their work-related stress. Similarities among the three kinds of workers are strongest in relation to work values. Contrary to the postmaterialist thesis, which suggests that intrinsic interests supplant extrinsic concerns (Inglehart and Abramson 1995), we found that workers valued pay and promotion most highly. Nevertheless, knowledge workers emphasized intrinsic aspects of their work more than did service and sales workers. Knowledge workers were also more satisfied with the technology they used and with the nature of their work; however, both they and sales workers reported being more frequently stressed than service workers. Overall, our findings suggest that work complexity influences the work experience substantially.

In the concluding section, we revisit the two images of the worker sketched above, arguing that the evidence suggests that workers are neither panoptic and regimented nor empowered. We complete the chapter by suggesting how variations in work complexity might influence other aspects of work organization, including control and coworker and customer relations.

Two caveats need to be addressed here. First, the terms *service*, *sales*, and *knowledge workers* respectively are used to refer to the predominant front-line workers in the three types of workflows outlined in chapter 1. Second, since the emphasis of this chapter is on comparing typical workers in the three types of workflows, we do not explore cross-national differences. These have been mentioned in chapter 2 and are discussed in more detail in chapter 8.

The Medium and the Act of Work

The medium of work refers to what is typically worked on in the course of completing tasks. This includes materials (as in traditional production work), people (as in personal service work), information (as in clerical work), or knowledge (as in scientific-professional work). The act of work refers to the activity or process whereby various media, knowledge, creativity, and skills are employed to complete the task.

In the industrial era, most work was closely related to manufacturing. Production—working directly on machines producing objects—was the centerpiece of the economy. In the postindustrial or informational economy, both the media employees work with—information, knowledge, and people (Porat 1977)—and the activities in which they are engaged are different. Serving, selling, and advising assume much greater significance.

Contemporary production workers and front-line employees share a common experience in having information technology as a key work medium. Ordered arrays of symbols are used to monitor and alter processes, create products, and provide services (Hirschhorn 1985; Zuboff 1988). Technology can be used in different ways, however. Automation often results in rationalization and standardization. Alternatively, IT can be used to inform and enrich workers' capabilities. Technology can enable workers to control their work more effectively and improve their communication with management, colleagues, customers, and suppliers (Tapscott 1996). IT also can be used as a means of centralizing management control over employees and limiting communication (Adler 1992).

Unlike production workers, front-line workers have regular interaction with customers. In other words, relations with customers—whose immediacy and poignancy have been referred to as "the moment of truth" (Carlzon 1987)—are important, since the front-line worker, qua organizational representative, is expected to intercede with the customer on behalf of the organization.

Beyond this, there are major differences among front-line workers in the work they undertake. No longer are traditional categories based on the way jobs are undertaken (e.g., manual/nonmanual, skilled/semiskilled) or the main purpose of work (managerial, sales, or, less abstractly, specific occupations) of much assistance.[1] In that front-line work is predominantly nonmanual, skills cannot be easily evaluated on the basis of traditional distinctions that emphasize formal qualifications and processes. Furthermore, as decision making becomes more decentralized, workers may undertake tasks that were previously the responsibility of supervisors. They also may work in teams and assume roles that are not specifically designated (Quinn 1992; Applegate 1994).[2]

As explained below, we combine two frameworks in order to locate

[1] Other distinctions, which suffer from the same limitation, are based on status (white/blue collar; exempt/nonexempt), demographic features ("gray" workers), temporal patterns (part time/full-time; permanent/temporary), and work location (office/home; formal/informal economy).

[2] In addition, new job titles have proliferated (examples from our research include "telephone banker" and "home loan consultant"). Further, even in broad jobs whose titles have remained the same, such as "business analyst" and "systems designer," substantial changes have occurred in work content over time.

service, sales, and knowledge workers theoretically and then compare them. The act-of-work perspective provides the concepts around which we can identify differences in the work complexity of these front-line workers and hence situate them among the ideal types of workers associated with bureaucratic and knowledge-intensive organizations. As we shall see, the work of sales employees can be organized on an internal contracting basis, consistent with the entrepreneurial-type work organization.

Components of the Act-of-Work Framework

The three components of the act-of-work framework are knowledge, skills, and creativity. We shall consider each component in turn before discussing them together in the context of the three ideal types of worker.

Knowledge. Knowledge has been used as a basis for distinguishing professional work from more routine white-collar work and skilled from semiskilled manual labor (Abbott 1988; Friedson 1986; Littler 1982). Professions such as medicine and engineering tend to require abstract, complex, scientific knowledge, while professions such as law and accountancy are based mainly on principles that include mastery and application of complex bodies of empirical information. In both cases, a body of theoretical knowledge consisting of codified concepts and principles is applied to a particular field or discipline. Requiring workers in the field to be familiar with this body of knowledge helps to maintain jurisdictional boundaries and limit occupational entry, thus contributing to employment on favorable terms and higher social status (Macdonald 1995).

By contrast, other fields require workers to have contextual knowledge— that is, knowledge of nongeneralizable policies or procedures ("know-how" or procedural knowledge) and task-objects ("know what" or declarative knowledge). Such knowledge may be formalized, as in documented service standards, or tacit, as in acceptable forms of dress. Contextual knowledge varies in particularity, from lower-order forms, such as company policies, to higher-order forms, such as industry trends. Contextual knowledge is less resistant than theoretical knowledge to routinized applications; it is more readily embedded in technology and hence can be made accessible for workers and customers.[3] Thus, persons working in occupations that use considerable theoretical knowledge are likely to work on more complex tasks than persons whose work is based largely on contextual knowledge.

[3] Expert systems can be used to routinize professional work, but for this to occur algorithms need to be developed that can be applied relatively unambiguously in particular instances (Blackler 1995). In addition, customers must trust the machines that embody this knowledge. According to Macdonald (1995: 172), professionals are more likely to apply the new technology to more routine activities, giving them more time for more complex work. Paraprofessionals, who work at the margins of a profession, are more likely to have their work automated.

It has become common for theorists to argue that knowledge creation, transfer, and application have become more critical than capital for competitive advantage (Drucker 1993; Quinn 1992). Such knowledge must be abstract in order to be generalized; however, it is unclear whether the rising importance of theoretical knowledge implies a decline in the significance of contextual knowledge, as Bell (1974) has argued, particularly for those highly qualified workers who are entrusted with its development and application. An alternative to this "theoretical knowledge as substitute" conjecture is the "theoretical knowledge as complement" hypothesis. According to this view, theoretical *and* contextual knowledge need to be expertly combined through an iterative process of diagnosis, inferencing, and application that has been demonstrated in software development and professional work more generally (Fincham et al. 1994; Beirne et al. 1998; Abbott 1991: 35–52). This process is especially likely to occur where innovation requires collaboration among different kinds of specialists, including customers. These alternative hypotheses are evaluated in the light of empirical evidence presented below.

Creativity. Workers use knowledge in various ways. Where work is algorithmic (has a clear, straightforward path to a solution), knowledge can be directly applied to accomplish tasks. Where work is heuristic (open-ended), the worker must improvise, using and creating knowledge. Note, however, that workers employed on algorithmic tasks often choose to work creatively, seeking to find quicker and more effective ways than those officially prescribed, hence the attempts by management, especially through quality circle and other direct forms of participation, to institutionalize this process.

Creativity is defined as a process of original problem solving—that is, an original, relevant, and complete solution is generated (Milgram 1990).[4] For our purposes, creativity can be thought of as a continuum ranging from high at one end to low at the other (Cattell and Bucher 1968; Hennessey and Amabile 1988).

Skills. Occupations and jobs vary in the skills required to execute typical tasks competently, and workers are usually hired to fit the appropriate job skill profiles. According to Stinchcombe (1990), the level of skills required varies with the uncertainties associated with different kinds of work. Work that is marked by higher levels of external and internal uncertainty is likely to require higher-level skills and vice versa.[5] Contrast, for example, soft-

---

[4] A high order of originality (e.g., a major creative breakthrough in science or the arts) involves not merely the extension or transformation of an existing paradigm but its replacement by a better one (Wertheimer 1945). Completeness refers to the extent to which the original insight is formulated, tested, and revised and the results developed comprehensively (MacKinnon 1962; Torrance 1988).

[5] Our approach distinguishes several elements of Stinchcombe's (1990) concept of skill, which he defines as "a set of routines . . . and many principles of decision which tell workers

ware designers (Beirne, Ramsay, and Panteli 1998), whose work is often highly customized and characterized by rapid technological change, with retail service workers, who serve a mass market and use technology to automate and simplify work tasks (Leidner 1993).

Nevertheless, individual workers in any particular occupation vary in their level of skill according to their formal training, on-the-job learning and experience, and personal aptitude and diligence. Three types of skill are readily identified: action-centered, analytical, and social. *Action-centered skills* (gross and fine motor skills that include manipulating physical objects) are associated with physical sensing and dexterity. In the IT era, computer navigation skills are especially important. According to Hirschhorn (1990: 90–91) and Zuboff (1988: 75–76), *analytical (or intellective) skills* involve reasoning based on abstract cues, explicit inference, synthesis, and systemic thinking. *Social skills* are purposeful actions oriented toward eliciting particular responses from others on a continuing basis. These cover a wide variety of activities, including helping, serving, advising, persuading, negotiating, mediating, and mentoring. Also relevant to our analysis are *self-management skills*, or the ability to organize time and tasks efficiently, and *personal adaptability*, the capacity to learn quickly and accomplish tasks in new ways.

Routine versus Professional Worker

Combinations of the three elements comprising the act of work— knowledge, creativity, and skills—give rise to work of varying complexity. Accordingly, two ideal types of front-line worker can be distinguished. These are identified in figure 3.1 as the *routine worker* and the *professional worker*, respectively. To simplify our theoretical analysis and reflecting the relative importance of these skills in undertaking front-line work, we restrict our attention to social and analytical skills.

As illustrated in figure 3.1, the routine worker uses little or no theoretical knowledge, is not creative, and does not apply analytical and social skills. This type of worker is associated with lower-level jobs in bureaucratic work organizations (see table 1.5) where employees are required to fit into defined positions and to take instructions from superordinates. By contrast, the professional worker relies on his or her theoretical knowledge, solves problems creatively, and has high levels of analytical and social skills. As indicated and discussed in relation to table 1.5, the professional worker is most appropriately located in knowledge-intensive organizations where

---

when to use one routine, when to use another" (33). He notes that skill levels are related to the complexity in the routine and to "the complexity outside the routine" (38). The latter refers to the stability or predictability of the context in which work is performed.

Figure 3.1. Workers as Ideal Types and as Located in the Three Types of Workflows

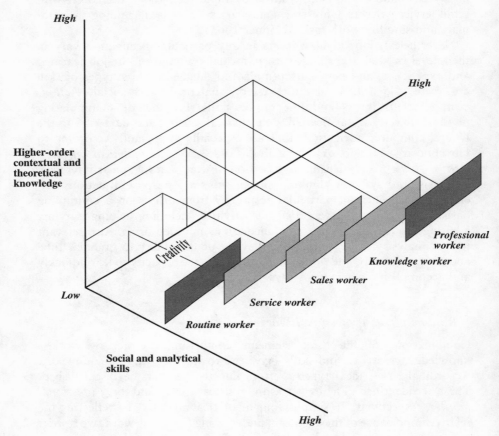

work roles are specialized yet fluid and complex problem solving is commonplace.

The Act of Work: Service, Sales and Knowledge Workers

Between the two ideal types of worker lie three empirical representations that broadly reflect our empirical findings. These are mass customized service workers, sales workers, and knowledge workers respectively. Several points are worth noting in relation to figure 3.1. First, because there are intra-occupational variations in work complexity, the empirical cases cannot be as readily distinguished from one another as the ideal types.[6] Hence, there are overlaps in the figure. Second, service workers and sales workers have more in common with respect to the complexity of their work than do sales workers and knowledge workers. This reflects the relatively large range of choice sales workers have in targeting customers. Third, there is no necessary connection between knowledge work and membership in a profession.[7]

Figure 3.1 helps us to anticipate the relationships among knowledge, creativity, and skills for the three empirical types of worker. Following Abbott (1988), our thesis is that, although contextual knowledge remains important for all three kinds of front-line worker, service workers rarely use theoretical and higher-order contextual knowledge, while sales workers and especially knowledge workers do. Workers use theoretical and contextual knowledge to identify, diagnose, and resolve problems, hence the distribution of ideal-type workers according to higher-order contextual knowledge and theoretical knowledge indicated in figure 3.1. This implies that the more complex and unique the problem, and the more workers are required to combine theoretical and contextual knowledge through analysis and inferencing, the greater the creativity required. This is suggested in figure 3.1.

All three types of worker use social skills. These differ in some respects and, as implied in figure 3.1, require differing levels of competency, as indicated in the somewhat outdated *Dictionary of Occupational Titles* (*DOT*) (U.S. Department of Labor 1991). For example, workers in service workflows need to respond rapidly to queries posed by customers. This requires summoning and conveying contextual knowledge of a declarative ("know-what") or procedural ("know-where") kind. Likewise, sales workers must be able to influence customers to purchase a product, which requires that they have a repertoire of reflexively constructed credibility- and trust-building practices. Social skills that include sales also involve answering queries. Thus, sales workers require a higher level of social skills than workers in service settings. Knowledge workers are required to have an even higher level of social skills so they can build and maintain trust, often with knowledgeable client experts, over a long period of time.

Workers in all three types of workflows use analytical skills. According to the U.S. Department of Labor, these are the three highest-level *DOT* categories that focus on data: "analyzing, coordinating and synthesizing" (1991: 1005). Service workers are expected to solve relatively simple prob-

[6] Parcel and Kaufman (1993) provide an extreme example of highly qualified chemists who undertook work requiring very limited creativity.

[7] There are three main reasons for this. Knowledge workers are employed in organizations whose prime aim is profit making rather than professional excellence. Furthermore, rapidly changing technology tends to undermine attempts at securing stable job jurisdictions and governments are reluctant to confer monopoly licensing on professional institutions that are likely to interfere with market forces.

lems, for which systems and rules apply to the great majority of cases. When there are system errors, or the rules are misapplied, problems arise. When these are repeated, as in the case of system errors (e.g., bank statements fail to be generated and mailed to customers), service workers typically consult with supervisors and develop interim coping strategies while experts resolve the problem.

In the case of sales workers, higher levels of customization and greater worker discretion mean that problems tend to be less standardized and analytical skills are more necessary on the job. Thus, a loan must be tailored to the particular circumstances of a customer whose financial position is only somewhat similar to others with whom the sales worker is familiar. At the same time, the sales worker must follow certain rules to establish the creditworthiness of the applicant and is limited by the products offered by the company.

In the case of the knowledge worker, the level of customization and extent of discretion are higher still. There are generally fewer constraints on finding a solution to what is more often a unique problem.

In the following discussion, we describe the work of service, sales, and knowledge workers in turn. Customer service representatives are taken as typical of service workers and home loan consultants as typical of sales workers. We have included two occupational categories of knowledge workers: systems developers and money market dealers. We did this to emphasize that some knowledge workers are employed as project workers—where goals and personnel are specific and have a finite life—while others work as process employees, characterized by greater continuity of objectives and employees.

Customer Service Representatives

The CSRs we observed work in cubicles, divided by shoulder-high partitions, in large, open-plan offices. Wearing headphones, they are connected to an integrated telephone/computer system. While speaking to customers on the telephone, they read and enter data into personal computers that are networked within the organization and often to other organizations such as credit rating companies and independent brokers. Colleagues occupy adjacent work stations. Although CSRs are expected to answer incoming calls for approximately 80 percent of their work time, they have access to colleagues, team leaders, and supervisors. CSRs are required to provide customers with detailed product and procedural information, to process customer transactions, and to attend to customer queries accurately and in a timely manner. Interactions with customers are expected to be in accordance with specified service standards. In addition, CSRs are increasingly encouraged to sell products.

Knowledge. CSRs use both lower- and higher-order contextual knowledge to accomplish their tasks. A limited amount of theoretical knowledge is useful, though not essential. The lower-order contextual knowledge in this case concerned company-specific products, procedures, software, practices, and people on whom the CSRs depended for information or assistance. Higher-level contextual knowledge included conceptual understanding—for example, the differences between fixed and variable rate loans and among various forms of car insurance—and knowledge of market or industry trends. Such knowledge enabled the CSRs to better understand customer concerns and increased their confidence in dealing with customers. As a CSR noted: *"The more you learn about how the products fit within the bank, that helps you help the customer—you can give a better explanation to customers."* A second CSR told a researcher: *"It helps that I know how money markets work because I can then better explain how interest rate changes affect customer loans."* A third CSR maintained that higher-level and theoretical knowledge, derived from a college education, were useful in conducting his work.[8]

Although some CSRs were eager to understand the logic behind various procedures, including industry developments more generally, they were not encouraged to pursue theoretical knowledge out of a fear that it would be used to extend their discretion with adverse consequences for the organization.[9] For example, the CSRs at MFJ were keen to understand how foreign exchange markets worked so they could better answer customer queries; however, management was reluctant for the CSRs to give advice that might be detrimental to customer-company relations and harm the company's reputation more generally.

Much of the knowledge CSRs use is embedded in print-based reference manuals and increasingly is available online. Locating information quickly is more problematic. Consequently, CSRs tend to rely on their memories or those of colleagues and supervisors. CSRs also learn whom to contact to progress or resolve queries. Experience in the position and in the company more generally helps in this regard.

Creativity. CSRs typically answer relatively routine inquiries and conduct simple transactions that nevertheless require attention to detail. As a CSR remarked, *"The main thing about this job is that you have to be methodical."* Creativity is required to resolve customer problems or to sell products.

In an effort to provide more customized service, the CSRs are given expanded levels of discretion, which provide greater opportunities to be creative. Thus, according to one CSR: *"Over the last two years we have a little*

[8] *"My business education has helped me a lot. The accounting—the way you set up accounts. And sales techniques learned at college are handy. So is the computer training, which helps me to solve problems."*

[9] There were some exceptions. These included companies in which "senior" or "executive" CSRs received higher-level training that included theoretical knowledge.

more scope to change customers' types of accounts, cross-selling, and do business referrals to other parts of the bank. We can also waive fees up to a certain amount. . . . So you can be creative in the way you deal with customers, compromise with them."

As an example of the use of creativity in a sales context, a customer called and asked a customer service representative at TEL for information about a particular product that might reduce telephone costs given a certain pattern of telephone use. The CSR questioned the customer about her phone use and, in light of this new information and her knowledge of the company's products, offered a more appropriate product. The customer readily accepted the recommendation, and the transaction was effected.

In some organizations, selected CSRs have opportunities to do off-line project work. This might involve preparing reports, or serving on special-purpose teams dealing with such activities as updating reference systems, resolving employee problems, changing selection procedures, or advising on the practicalities of introducing new technology. Although project work rarely takes more than 10 percent of a CSR's work time, such work nonetheless affords opportunities for creativity.

Skills. Action-centered computer skills, such as inputting, word processing, and an understanding of navigating systems, are essential but received little comment except when software impeded customer service. Social skills—used mainly in relation to customers and to a lesser extent other employees with whom the CSRs came into regular contact—were generally deemed most important. These included a range of "emotional labor" capabilities (Noon and Blyton 1996), such as the ability to remain calm amid the pressure of responding to a continuous stream of customer calls and the ability to maintain a friendly, positive, and tactful attitude while simultaneously remaining disengaged psychologically as protection from abusive customers. The CSRs emphasized the importance of having "a thick skin" and "dealing with the situation rather than the person."

Active listening (i.e., being attentive to the explicit and implicit cues given by customers) is also required. For example, a CSR related how she could pick up from the tone and rhythm of a customer's voice whether the customer was likely to be telling the truth regarding credit card ownership.

Patience and empathy were viewed as positive attributes, particularly when customers were upset. Being able to quickly clarify and identify customers' requirements—"to be able to quickly go to the heart of the matter"—was also admired. Managers valued the sales aspect of the CSR role. The CSRs were more ambivalent.

CSRs also have to have strong self-management skills so they can locate relevant information quickly and thereby resolve customers' queries and problems in a timely manner. They have to be able to analyze and help resolve relatively simple problems raised by customers. Finally, they are required to unlearn and learn quickly in order to cope with rapid changes in products, procedures, and systems.

In summary, in their dependence on lower-order contextual knowledge, the CSRs we observed resembled the ideal type referred to as the routine worker. However, they demonstrated creativity, social skills, and organizational skills in executing more complex tasks. Other than estimating and calculating, the CSRs rarely used analytical skills. Thus, although their work may have been routine compared with that of sales and knowledge workers, it was not as routine and uncreative as sometimes depicted (Menzies 1996). A similar conclusion applies to front-line service workers whose work was not computer mediated to the same extent. The JB bond-ladies we studied relied mainly on face-to-face interactions with customers. Although the financial products they sold were relatively simple, they used social and self-management skills, too.[10]

Home Loan Consultants

The HLCs we observed are front-line sales workers who sell primarily home mortgages, as well as other products such as insurance and credit cards. Their customers include employees, self-employed persons, and small business proprietors. These HLCs usually visit prospective customers in their homes or places of business. Equipped with a cell phone, and increasingly with a notebook computer, they are prototypical "teleworkers" (Halal 1996). They have online connections to credit rating agencies and to their own organization and tend to work at all hours. Management provides guidelines on job territories and sets quarterly sales targets.

The HLCs we studied had considerable autonomy, although loans had to meet management-established criteria. Remuneration was strongly performance related, usually based on the number or value of loans and other products that were sold. These employees typically worked through three channels—a referral network composed of professional intermediaries (accountants, solicitors, and real estate agents) who assisted their clients in obtaining mortgages; phone leads, arising from marketing campaigns; and direct customer contact, either previous clients or through applicants investigating loan options for themselves. In short, HLCs have two faces: that of the entrepreneur and that of the employee. Like entrepreneurs, they need

---

[10] Since the bond-ladies visited their mainly women customers in their homes, social interaction assumed a more intimate tone, involving discussion about family and personal matters. Financial regulation meant that competition over interest rates and other financial matters was very limited, hence requiring the women to gain their customers' trust to generate repeat business. With regard to self-management skills, the bond-ladies examined the financial newspapers and company databases regularly so that they could advise customers on the merits of various financial products. The bond-ladies shared financial knowledge with one another, thereby building up a more informed, collective position regarding their evaluation of markets and products. Chapter 7 discusses learning in more detail.

to be self-reliant, both in building and maintaining referral networks and in selling to customers. In addition, much of their success (or failure) reflects their own efforts. They are dependent on their employing organization for the maintenance of product quality and delivery, assistance in obtaining sales leads, loans processing, and ultimately their employment.

Knowledge. Like CSRs, HLCs need lower-order contextual knowledge about the company's products, credit assessment criteria, and the procedures to be followed in submitting a loan for approval. However, they also need a higher-order contextual knowledge base. Knowledge of the details of competitors' products and of trends in the housing market enabled the HLCs to gain rapport and subsequent loan applicants through referrals. Financial knowledge is also useful. According to one HLC, *"Having a financial background is important for understanding how things work and in selling. If you know your products and have this kind of background, you can answer client questions and offer different options. You can get clients to trust you."*

Understanding economics is also useful. HLCs need to appear authoritative in discussions with clients and referrers regarding the loan payment implications of likely changes in interest rates and taxes. Note that changes in products and procedures, markets, and laws mean that HLCs, like CSRs, must continually update their knowledge.

HLCs also benefit from applying theoretical knowledge relating to accounting and finance. This enables them to understand customers' financial needs in greater depth and hence to make a more informed assessment of a customer's economic capacity and options.

Creativity. The HLCs we studied had a range of choices in undertaking their role. In broad terms, they could follow a routinized strategy, relying primarily on selling relatively simple first-home mortgages, or they could choose to be more creative by specializing in self-employed professionals and small business proprietors who were seeking second mortgages or loans for investment purposes.

Social creativity was required to develop and sustain referral networks and to understand the needs of special categories of clients (e.g., doctors or lawyers). This required building and maintaining a successful reputation, which in turn necessitated applying the various kinds of knowledge discussed above and the skills discussed below.

Social creativity of a similar kind was deployed in developing relationships with clients so that personal rapport and trust were carefully constructed. Another form of creativity related to analytical competency is also noteworthy. This refers to the constructive tailoring of loan options, ensuring through discussion that the loan is acceptable to the client and meets the organization's lending criteria. In the words of an HLC, *"A [loan] situation can be approached in a number of different ways. You have to persuade the customer that your way is the better way for them in the long run.*" To do this, HLCs use their accounting and financial knowledge to explore ways to help a prospective client meet the lending criteria. This may include reducing the cost of a loan (within company guidelines) and minimizing the tax burden on a client.[11] Such creative accounting is described variously as "ferreting out" or "leaving no stone unturned in looking at a client's revenue and costs." HLCs warn that creativity should not involve entering into illicit or illegal arrangements that credit analysts are likely to reject downstream or that might jeopardize the reputation of the HLC in the long run. Finally, HLCs can be creative by proposing new products to management.

Skills. As indicated in the following comments by two HLCs, social skills are paramount in building relationships with referrers and customers.

> HLC 1: *The challenge in our job is to influence people. Be a good social networker; make people feel comfortable; exude confidence to enhance belief in the product; be able to turn people around and close the deal.*

> HLC 2: *Our business is not lending. It is relationship building. You need to be able to persuade people into something that they believe is good for them. You must be convincing without being too pushy.*

HLCs frequently employ two forms of discourse or tactics—personalization and professionalism—to build and sustain credibility and trust (see Oakes 1990; Prus 1989). These help to ascertain an applicant's capacity to pay and, if this is verified, to influence the customer to buy the product. Personalization tactics are aimed at reducing the psychological distance between the HLC and the customer, enabling the applicant to identify with the HLC. Such tactics include joking, "putting yourself out for the customer," and providing reassurance through proffering more general advice regarding taxation and loan options, for example. Not surprisingly, HLCs see themselves as being in the business of serving and selling. As an HLC commented, *"You won't get sales without service."*

In practice, personalization tactics overlap with professionalism tactics, or the means by which an HLC influences a customer by appealing to the image and rational discourse of the expert. These include appropriate modes of dress and demeanor, persuasive communication of knowledge and advice, and the exercise of skills in developing loan options. Personalization and professionalism come together in managing prospective customers'

---

[11] Two HLCs provided examples of how they are creative in selling loans: (1) "If a customer has two properties and wants a large loan, it may be preferable to seek two loans for the same total amount, applying for one now and the other later or taking both out now. Fees can be reduced to make it worthwhile doing it this way." (2) "If a customer doesn't like the $300 application fee [for a loan], then I encourage the person to take out a credit card, which gives them instant credit. Later the person can decide whether or not to keep the card."

expectations. Thus, prospective customers whose financial positions may not warrant loans at the level requested need to be handled delicately and offered alternative options.

Although social skills are important, the HLCs we observed emphasized the need for two other competencies: strong determination and self-reliance. These were commonly described as the need to be "highly motivated" and "results-oriented." The HLCs believed it was important to "be able to keep going in the face of rejection."

The HLCs also thought self-management skills were important. As an HLC observed, *"You have to be able to keep several balls in the air at once,"* or able to pursue several sales leads simultaneously, to ensure a high loan approval rate and hence high earnings. Another HLC noted that time management is particularly important: *"I don't waste any time. I only go [to see a customer] if I know it's a deal. I use the phone to test interest. I'm also careful to do the deal and then get out."*

The ability to use creative analytical skills to "package" attractive options for loan applicants differentiated the high earners from their colleagues. Although the HLCs used software embodied in notebook computers to demonstrate various options and scenarios, technology was rarely emphasized. Rather, it was seen as complementary to other sources of information.

In sum, the HLCs made use of lower- and higher-order contextual knowledge and a limited amount of theoretical knowledge. Some employed considerable social and analytical creativity. Social and self-management competencies also were important. The HLCs used a wider range of social skills than the CSRs, and there were greater demands on the HLCs' time. Superior analytical skills contributed to success. Thus, as indicated by the work complexity represented diagrammatically in figure 3.1, HLCs, as typical sales workers, lie between, and overlap with, service and knowledge workers.

Information Technology Systems Developers

Systems developers build IT systems in accordance with specifications agreed upon with clients. The work usually consists of defining a problem, specifying a solution, and then designing, constructing, testing, and implementing a system. Systems development is typically executed on a project basis using a structured methodology. Depending on the novelty of the problem, management requirements, and the disposition of the employees, the methodology might involve a highly formalized, linear model (waterfall methodology) or a more iterative, parallel-processing model (spiral methodology).

A generally high level of uncertainty prevails in systems development work. This stems from two related features: the rapid technological progress in the tools used for design and implementation and the problems associated with project resourcing, particularly the shortages of employees with specialized expertise. These characteristics contribute to difficulties in successfully implementing IT projects (Fincham et al. 1994).

Systems development involves complex problem solving that often requires knowledge held by different specialists. Expertise in business analysis, data analysis, programming, testing, database administration, and project management may all be required. All systems development work requires knowledge about contemporary computing in general and particular aspects in detail. Software, including such elements as codes, languages, and programs, are both tools for accomplishing work and, when developed and combined in particular ways, the product of such endeavors. The achievement of project goals requires collaboration among specialists. Problems vary in their uniqueness, which determines the extent of the creativity required. Uniqueness is more common in the earlier phases of projects. A process of pattern discovery, often involving various specialists in "brainstorming" (characterized by intense debate), tends to precede iteration. This often proceeds along a convergent path leading to pattern recognition, problem identification, and resolution. In later phases, problems tend to be more tractable, enabling convergence to occur earlier. Although methodologies and case tools threaten to standardize and deskill the work of systems developers, high levels of customization and interaction with clients ensure that the work (often undertaken at clients' sites) remains complex. In addition, the dynamic nature of the IT industry requires system developers to constantly update and apply new knowledge. As Fincham (1994: 48) has noted, these workers enjoy discretion and trust, a point that can be extended to relations with clients.

Knowledge. Based on electronics and engineering and employing a variety of methodologies, the SD's theoretical knowledge is highly valued for imagining and experimenting with alternative solutions to business problems. Theoretical knowledge is regarded as valuable for several reasons:

- It permits generalization and common work norms.
- It promotes dialogue and hence learning and collaboration among specialists.
- It enables conceptualization of a total system—a language for understanding the larger picture and how the parts are supposed to fit and work together, including translation of client requirements into technical specifications.
- It assists in transforming tacit knowledge, a very significant part of the SD's knowledge stock, into explicit knowledge (Nonaka and Takeuchi 1995).
- It facilitates learning by encouraging pattern recognition and hence problem solving.

- It increases individuals' professional status and labor market opportunities by adding to specialists' stock of knowledge.

At the same time, changes in technology facilitate the envisioning of alternative scenarios and the application of new analytical frameworks and methodologies. These developments have the unintended effect of encouraging conflict among SDs.[12]

For SDs, theoretical knowledge and higher-order contextual knowledge are closely related. Thus, a decision to use an object-oriented design (which entails a different analytical perspective) requires an appropriate programming language.[13] Much technical learning is on the job, and SDs liken their activity to a craft rather than a science. Lower-order contextual knowledge is also essential since building credibility with clients requires firsthand acquaintance with specific systems working in situ, particularly when these involve a combination of various types of software and hardware. Experiential understanding of technology in relation to specific client requirements provides the basis for integrating new and old technology and evaluating technological innovations that can be applied to new projects. Where SDs are responsible for generating sales, they must also be closely acquainted with clients' technical and business needs.

Creativity. The image of SDs as "geeks"—somewhat eccentric, highly intelligent introverts—stems from their association with creative endeavors and the discretion they are given to solve problems without undue emphasis on cost. These experts tend to draw inspiration from the challenge of working with new technology. In the words of one SD: *"There is a fascination with technology itself—what's the latest whiz-bang. Windows 95 needs . . . which needs . . . which needs . . . We keep looking for the next one [technology] to solve problems."*

Not all the SD's problem solving involves new technology. On the contrary, creativity is required to combine the old with the new and to deal with the unexpected. As another SD stated: *"Matching compatibility with the company's [existing] technology is the most difficult part. Sometimes the whole system doesn't work due to incompatibility, which, according to the plan, was not considered to be a problem."*

In the early stage of a project, technical options are offered in an attempt to meet the clients' needs with respect to functionality and costs. An SD

---

[12] A current controversy to which Beirne, Ramsay, and Panteli (1998) refer concerns the wider issue of systems configuration: whether to follow Microsoft in favoring decentralized, individually networked personal computing or to adopt Oracle's network computing model, which points toward centralization of management control.

[13] As an SD commented: *"Building objects in COBOL [the standard programming language used in the organization] is equivalent to trying to do calculus with roman numerals."* A decision to discontinue with COBOL in effect opened up a new debate: whether to program using a more appropriate language such as JAVA or to rely on Microsoft to produce relevant tools and therefore program in Microsoft Visual Basic.

commented: *"You've got to be creative when writing a program. You're concerned about memory and speed. There are things that need to be reduced—e.g., time to be ready to the hard disk. You have to figure out how. You break it into subprocesses, and look at their order and reduce overall time."* The SDs we met often referred to the need to conceptualize alternative solutions for customers in the proposal stage and to solve and adjust to whatever problems arose in attempts to harmonize new and old computer systems.

Problems may not be foreseen and must later be resolved; and when they do occur, they may be equivocal (Weick 1969: 40)—that is, subject to a variety of interpretations and hence require a method of resolution that implies initial equivocality but subsequent convergence on a solution. Experimentation, debate, and judgment are critical to this process. In describing his work in solving computer network problems, an SD suggested that *"quite a few things can knock out a network, which allows you to brainstorm what might be wrong. So you must be creative."* He likened the process to "a detective situation" in which there must be a constant search for clues placed within a framework of knowledge that often remains tacit. Not all problems have workable solutions; finding ways to minimize adverse effects might be the best one can do. There is also the more general challenge of translating designs into real systems clients find acceptable.

In each specialist domain, creativity is required to solve technical problems. Although some work is accomplished alone, much of the creativity arises from working with colleagues, a feature, as the following comment indicates, that is typically highly valued: *The best aspect of the job is learning new things, working with my group. I love the challenge of making things work that people think will not work."* Much is learned by experimentation informed by debate.

SDs vary in their knowledge and skills, and some assignments are more routine than others. Thus, an SD commented: *"I'd say 60 percent of my work is creative—it doesn't involve 'cut-and-dried situations'"* (i.e., there are easily identifiable solutions).

Skills. Analytical skills are most important, for these are essential for design and technical problem solving in complex environments. Some SD jobs require the application of "what you know rather than coming up with something new." Other SD work addresses unique problems that require the SDs to develop systems that will enable a business to replace older software with faster, user-friendlier systems.

In defining problems and developing solutions, SDs work closely with client representatives and other specialists. This requires social skills, including the capacity to communicate clearly, to generate and promote continuing support and enthusiasm among various stakeholders for project goals, and, for project leaders, the ability to broker different interests. This latter skill is especially important when experts and users have different views of what is both desirable and feasible.[14] SDs tend to downplay the significance of social skills, however, in favor of their analytical abilities.

SDs also are expected to be adaptable, able to learn new tasks or how to undertake current tasks in different ways. One SD commented: *"If you aren't learning, then you are not getting anything out of the job."* Personal adaptability and a will to succeed are essential to project work, in which being familiar with changes in technology may offer new, more effective solutions. At the same time, employees frequently move from one project to another, sometimes in different industries and often in different companies. It is therefore necessary to be able to work harmoniously with a diverse range of people.

Money Market Dealers

Money market dealers buy and sell money market products (bonds, promissory notes, bills of exchange, short-dated securities, and cash) to corporate and institutional fund managers. Buying and selling high-volume, low-margin debt is viewed as a basis for providing market information and developing relationships with a small number of clients representing major institutional investors. This in turn enables the dealers to sell "structured products" (derivatives and swaps) to clients, who are charged substantial fees for this activity. By reducing risk, these dealers aim to provide clients with a more predictable return on their investments.

Dealers work in distinctive environments, commonly referred to as "desks." Each desk focuses on a particular part of the investment banking market and includes about twenty-five people, who work in a large, open-plan room occupied by a total of about one hundred employees and characterized by considerable noise. The money markets desk that we observed included other specialists (a price maker, traders, balance sheet specialists, and structured deal analysts), all of whom worked alongside one another. Each workstation consisted of a phone and a personal computer. Dealers had access to overhead screens that provided updates on market trends and related information. Dealers depended on various specialist colleagues for information on buying and selling prices and for advice on devising complex deals and developing technology to create and maintain client databases and software tools to make rapid, complex calculations.

Knowledge. Dealers use theoretical knowledge as a platform for interpreting and weaving together higher- and lower-order forms of contextual

---

[14] Users are often concerned with finding fast and intuitively simple applications. Systems designers may differ in defining the most appropriate software. Such differences are fueled by rivalries among software vendors and the proclivities of individual experts, whose familiarity with different software varies and whose visions of computing in the future may be different.

knowledge. Formal training in macroeconomics, particularly finance, and marketing helps the dealers conceptualize market developments and present arguments to clients. The dealers, however, emphasized their broader contextual knowledge of particular markets and factors underlying their movements. This knowledge was based less on economic theory than on the capacity to "see" past patterns in present movements and thereby make market predictions.

Lower-order contextual knowledge is also important. This takes the form of detailed information and interpretation of the client company, the personal characteristics of the fund manager, and the prime motives behind his/her trading strategy. Because dealers are responsible for large-scale movements of funds, they are required to follow company rules and procedures, which in turn requires considerable lower-order contextual knowledge.

Creativity. Dealers seek to differentiate themselves from competitors by providing advice based on more timely and more plausible interpretations of unfolding market developments. For this, they rely on information from economic specialists and discussions with colleagues. Creativity is also demonstrated in the process of eliciting client objectives and concerns regarding investment options, influencing clients' perceptions, and customizing products to meet clients' expectations. Dealers also display "lateral vision" in suggesting novel ways to structure deals subsequently explored in more detail by structured deal analysts. Comparing a novice to an experienced expert, a dealer explained: *"Like chess, an experienced person can see openings and ways of structuring [a deal] that a less experienced person might miss."*

Skills. Social skills, such as listening, joking, and tactfulness, are important in building rapport with clients and colleagues. Flexibility in relation to clients' values and personalities, combined with analytical skills and the provision of appropriate products, form the basis for ongoing relationships.[15] Dealers also emphasized the importance of self-management skills: theirs is a high-discretion role that requires priority setting and time management to ensure that service and sales are expertly combined in ways that successfully maintain relationships with clients.

Mathematical aptitude and a knowledge of markets facilitate understanding, analysis, and the promotion of structured products. Analytical skills are also necessary to interpret market movements. Two further key skills include being "street smart"—that is, able to see an advantageous situation and act quickly to capitalize on it—and "having six pairs of eyes and ears." As a dealer explained, *"You learn to hear what is important. . . . New people complain they are not getting the information, but it is a*

---

[15] One of the female dealers argued that such flexibility in dealing with male clients could compromise her integrity. She therefore set limits on how far she would adapt to a client's personality.

matter of knowing how to listen. Got to keep open to what is happening, screen out the noise, that's very important."

Finally, dealers are becoming more reliant on IT for accessing data, building databases, and making complex calculations. Basic computer skills are therefore necessary.

Our conclusion regarding systems developers and money market dealers is that they make greater use of higher-order contextual knowledge than theoretical knowledge; nevertheless, the latter, as well as their use of creativity and high-level analytical and social skills, is important in distinguishing these workers from sales and service workers. Thus, systems developers and money market dealers are closer to the professional ideal type than are home loan managers or customer service representatives. Note, however, that the work of SDs and MM dealers involves practical problem solving, characterized by considerable cooperation with colleagues and customers whose knowledge and expertise are complementary rather than similar to theirs. These features serve to differentiate these workers from the professional ideal type, who has a monopoly of expertise and consults with customers only to better diagnose problems.

Differences in Work Complexity among Front-Line Workers

Our qualitative data point to systematic differences in the work complexity of service, sales, and knowledge workers. Can this threefold categorization be sustained across the fourteen workflows included in our study? Discriminant analysis, a technique used to assess classification schemes statistically (Klecka 1980), helps to answer this question. We propose that our categorization is validated if two conditions are met: (1) the results summarized in table 3.1 (and detailed in appendix 1) are consistent with the vignettes sketched above of front-line employees typical of the three types of workflows; and (2) the variables predict the allocation of a high proportion of workers in the three different kinds of workflows ("actual workflow" in table 3.1) to the correct three categories ("predicted workflow" in the same table). "High" is defined as greater than 66.6 percent.

Table 3.1 shows that about seven in ten respondents are correctly allocated to one of the three workflows. This finding meets our first validity criterion. The "fit" is highest for service workers (74.1 %) and lowest for sales workers (50.5%). We anticipated these results, particularly the higher misclassification of sales workers, based on our fieldwork experience.

There are three main reasons workers were misclassified. The first is because of the "heterogeneity effect," which is most applicable to sales workers. "Heterogeneity" refers to the fact that some workers in each type of workflow do different kinds of work than their colleagues. For example,

Table 3.1. Predicted Membership in Service, Sales, and
Knowledge Work Workflows, in Percent

Actual workflow	Predicted workflow membership in %		
	Service	Sales	Knowledge work
Service	74.1	19.7	6.2
Sales	38.5	50.5	11.0
Knowledge Work	17.4	14.3	68.3

Note: N workflows 14; respondents 867.
Source: Employee survey.

among the sales respondents, fourteen out of thirty-nine focused on simple transactions via the telephone, while their colleagues undertook more
complex loan assignments and worked directly with loan applicants. The
work of the former group can be described as mass customization with a
sales emphasis. This is consistent with the results reported in table 3.1,
which indicate that most of the misclassifications are toward the service
worker category.

The second reason workers were misclassified is because of what we call
the "role-taking" effect. This refers to variations in competency that lead
some employees, usually with management's consent or encouragement,
to undertake more challenging and, in some cases, less challenging tasks.
For example, some CSRs became part-time trainers and hence did more
problem solving and creative work than other service workers. Again, this
is consistent with the results reported in table 3.1, which show that about
a quarter of the CSRs answered relevant questions in a way that led to their
classification as sales or knowledge workers. Likewise, other CSRs dealt
with credit and debit cards rather than more general banking products,
reflecting their less challenging tasks.

The third reason workers were misclassified, though more restricted in
its application, was because some employees were unable to meet management's expectations in new roles. In one case, IT engineers who focused on
sales were unaccustomed to the complexity of the technology and therefore
concentrated on developing rapport with customers, which required less
knowledge, creativity, and skills.

We also investigated a fourth reason, which we labeled the "novice"
effect. The argument in its support is that workers with limited experience
are likely to perceive work as more complex and creative than more experienced workers do. This was not supported by regression analysis, which
indicated that length of time in an occupation had no significant effect on
respondents' self-reported levels of creativity and use of analytical skills,
after taking into account variations across workflows. Accordingly, we con-

cluded that, having met the second criterion outlined above, our classification based on the act-of-work variables was valid.[16]

In sum, based on qualitative evidence, our threefold categorization of front-line workers is validated by survey data across the fourteen workflows, using the act-of-work variables as discriminators. We noted, however, that service work was somewhat less routine than suggested by the bureaucratic ideal type and that sales work varied in complexity, occasionally overlapping with service work and knowledge work.

Whether theoretical knowledge is a substitute for contextual knowledge or a complement to it at higher levels of work complexity can be gleaned from our qualitative research findings on knowledge workers. These pointed to the continuing importance of contextual knowledge in front-line work. This supports the "theoretical knowledge as complement hypothesis." Thus, it was vital that systems developers understood the context, both technical and political, as a basis for developing viable technological solutions. Money market dealers combined an understanding of company policies regarding transactions (narrow contextual knowledge), movements in the markets (broader contextual knowledge), knowledge of clients' personalities and priorities (a mixture of theoretical and contextual knowledge), and knowledge of finance (mainly theoretical knowledge) to undertake their work successfully.

Work Complexity and Work Experience

We turn now to the effects of variations in work complexity on service, sales, and knowledge workers. The emphasis here is on four aspects of theoretical importance and relevance: work values; workers' perceptions of, and satisfaction with, IT; the extent to which workers derive intrinsic satisfaction from work; and work-related stress. Note that all references to ANOVA are one-way and based on data we obtained from our employee survey.

Hypotheses

Kalleberg defines work values as "the conceptions of what is desirable that individuals hold with respect to their work activity" (1977: 129). Accord-

---

[16] According to the analysis, the following are significant discriminating variables: knowledge of company policies and products, customers' needs, markets and their trends, competitors' products, and principles and techniques specific to the occupations. Creativity was a significant discriminating variable for employees in service workflows reporting the lowest level of creativity, followed by sales employees and knowledge workers respectively. Social, analytical, and self-management skills were also significant discriminators.

ing to the postmaterialism thesis (Inglehart and Abramson 1995), workers in advanced societies are likely to be increasingly concerned with intrinsic rather than extrinsic (pay and working conditions) aspects of work. This thesis is supported in part by cross-national studies, which have noted a shift toward work orientations that emphasize self-actualization through more interesting and challenging work (Yankelovitch 1983; Jowell 1993). The following hypothesis can be derived from this theory:

Hypothesis 1a: *The work values of service, sales, and knowledge workers are likely to resemble rather than differ from one another, focusing more on intrinsic rather than on extrinsic, features.*

Proponents of another theory view variations in the nature and conditions of work as a key influence on workers' work values (Kohn and Schooler 1983; Kanter 1976; Tam, Frenkel, and Korczynski, 1999). According to the theory's proponents, workers who are employed in jobs that offer opportunities to use knowledge and skills creatively and that provide possibilities for advancement will be more likely to value the intrinsic features of their jobs than workers in jobs in which these features are absent. This leads to the following hypothesis:

Hypothesis 1b: *Knowledge workers (who have more opportunities to derive intrinsic rewards) are more likely than service workers to value the intrinsic elements of their work. Sales workers are likely to occupy the middle ground, since they experience autonomy and challenge but their work is more restricted by procedures than that of knowledge workers.*

Perceptions of and satisfaction with technology. IT has been widely used to execute tasks and has been the subject of considerable research (Child and Loveridge 1990; Adler 1992). Following Adler (1992), technology enhances employees' effectiveness and enablement. With greater effectiveness, workers are better able to achieve their operational goals, while with greater enablement, workers can control technology, rather than the other way around. Because knowledge workers use technology as a tool for problem solving rather than being an appendage to it, we would expect the following to be true:

Hypothesis 2: *Technology is likely to be both effective and enabling for knowledge workers. Accordingly, these workers will be more satisfied with technology than service or sales workers. Service and sales workers are unlikely to differ significantly in their satisfaction with technology because, in the former case, technology is often a source of frustration and, in the latter case, it is not seen as critical to work performance.*

Satisfaction with the nature of work. According to job design and sociotechnical systems theorists (Davis and Taylor 1976; Hackman and Oldham 1980), the more opportunities there are to derive intrinsic satisfaction from work, the more likely workers are to be satisfied. Based on evidence presented earlier, this suggests the following conjecture:

Hypothesis 3a: *Knowledge workers and sales workers are likely to be significantly more satisfied with their work than service workers.*

This is because the jobs held by knowledge workers and sales workers offer considerably more opportunities for challenge, variety, and opportunities to learn and experiment than do the jobs of service workers.

An alternative theory argues that workers' job values vary and significantly affect employees' expectations (Kalleberg 1977; Knoop 1994). The additive variant of this theory suggests that where workers have become accustomed to not experiencing a particular facet in their jobs, they will lower their expectations of this facet, making them more satisfied than they would otherwise have been in the absence of the added-value effect. According to this argument, because intrinsic facets are less available in service work, compared with sales and knowledge work, service workers will tend to deemphasize the intrinsic facets of their jobs. Hence, contra the hypothesis derived from job design theory:

Hypothesis 3b: *Service workers will not be significantly less satisfied with the nature of their work than knowledge and sales workers.*

Work-related stress. As noted in chapter 1, work-related stress appears to be increasing. Indeed, Keefe and Batt (1997: 78) suggest that customer service representatives, our typical service worker, are the most stressed of U.S. telecommunications employees. This contention does not sit easily with the proposition that jobs offering more autonomy and longer working hours tend to be the most stressful(Spector et al. 1988). Similarly, Karasek and Theorell (1990) argue that the greater the "decision latitude" or opportunities to use skills, exercise initiative, and control working conditions, the more likely workers are to experience higher levels of stress. Since knowledge workers and sales workers have been shown to use their knowledge, skills, and creativity more than their service worker counterparts, we hypothesize the following, contra Keefe and Batt:

Hypothesis 4a: *Knowledge workers and sales workers will experience stress more frequently than will service employees.*

Empirical Evidence

Work values. Table 3.2 presents data on the work values of the service, sales, and knowledge workers we studied. Respondents were asked to select

Table 3.2. Relative Value Accorded Five Highest-Ranked Features of Jobs, by Workflow Type

Job feature	Service N = 608	Sales N = 90	Knowledge work N = 160	Relative importance
Extrinsic				
Pay	1st	1st	1st	n.s.
Promotion prospects	2d	2d	3rd	n.s.
Job security	3rd	3rd		More important for service and sales workers than for knowledge workers
Intrinsic				
Nature of work	4th	4th	2nd	More important for knowledge workers than for other workers
Influence over work-related decisions		(6th)	5th	More important for knowledge and sales workers than for service workers
Social				
Relations among colleagues	5th		4th	Less important for sales workers than for knowledge and service workers
Customer relations		5th		More important for sales than for knowledge and service workers

Note: n.s. = not statistically significant at $p < 0.05$.
Source: Employee survey.

and rank-order five work values out of a list of fourteen that they considered most important.[17] Average aggregate rankings are shown in the table. Significant differences in the relative importance of the average scores for respondents in each of the three types of workflows, based on ANOVA, are shown in the right-hand column of the table.

In that respondents prioritized only seven of fourteen available items, we concluded that *service, sales, and knowledge workers share similar broad priorities*, a view reinforced by evidence that the workers in all three groups tend to value extrinsic more than intrinsic or social facets of work. Indeed, on two of the items—pay and promotion prospects—there were no significant differences across the three groups. Thus, although the evidence supports the first part of the first values-related hypothesis (1a), it contradicts the second part, which posited that there would be a convergence on postmaterialist values. Indeed, our findings suggest that, rather than favoring

[17] The other items were capability and efficiency of management, flexibility of working hours, workload, training provision, technology at work, the way job performance is measured, amount of leisure time left by the job, and relations with customers.

self-expressive values, *workers seem to be shifting toward more materialist values.* This suggests that as organizational and technological changes have given rise to uncertainty, workers have tended to focus more on the extrinsic facets of their jobs.

Among knowledge workers, the trend toward materialist values seems to reflect the increased application of performance-related pay. Pay levels are a badge of self-esteem and may also become a status symbol where information on individual pay levels is publicly available, either officially or through informal channels.

The comments in the right-hand column of table 3.2, which summarize our ANOVA results, support our second hypothesis (1b), that knowledge workers value intrinsic facets of work more highly than do sales and service workers. Also noteworthy are the findings reported in the table on the social facets of work. On the one hand, the significantly lower importance sales workers accord to coworker relations reflects the individualistic nature of sales work noted earlier. On the other hand, as table 3.2 also shows, for the instrumental reasons mentioned earlier, sales workers view customer relations as especially important.

Perceptions and satisfaction with technology. In outlining our hypotheses, we identified two aspects of technology: effectiveness and enablement. These concepts were operationalized with moderate success.[18] In line with our hypothesis (2), ANOVA showed that the knowledge workers perceived technology as both more effective and more enabling than did the sales and service workers (for effectiveness $F (2,850) = 36.36$, $p < 0.001$; for enablement $F (2,850) = 31.67$, $p < 0.001$).

Did this lead to knowledge workers reporting higher satisfaction with technology than sales and service workers, as hypothesized earlier? Based on our analysis of variance, the answer is yes. Our findings were consistent with the evidence: compared with service and knowledge workers, sales workers made less use of IT and were more ambivalent about its usefulness. Thus, ANOVA results show that the salespersons in our study spent significantly less time using computers than did the service and knowledge workers ($F (2,860) = 339.16$, $p < 0.001$).

Salespersons told our researchers that, although notebook computers and expert systems impressed customers and hastened the loan-qualifying process, this technology had two major drawbacks: it interfered with the trust-building process, and it tended to increase salespersons' administrative workload. Illustrative comments include the following:

HLC 1: *I don't use the computer with experienced borrowers (second/third home buyer) because it restricts the flow of the interview when you are trying to build rapport with the customer.*

---

[18] Appendix 2 contains operational definitions of effectiveness and enablement.

HLC 2: *[The expert system] means more work is put on us—we [HLCs] have to do the approval letters. And because the loan clerks don't have copies of the paperwork, because it's all online, they don't help us. So, in effect, it's a way of giving us more work.*

Compared with the sales and knowledge workers, the service workers depended more heavily on technology and complained about it more frequently. The major criticisms related to four issues: the complexity of the systems resulting from new software being overlaid on old systems; its limited functionality with respect to customer requirements; slow system speed, particularly while changing screens; and the consequences of system malfunctions, such as customers venting their frustration at front-line service workers. The following quotations are relevant in this regard:

CSR 1: *Our systems aren't smart or user friendly. . . . Newcomers find the systems too difficult—there are so many of them and so many screens—you need a Ph.D. to use it!*

CSR 2: *[The software] runs too slowly, and there is no information on how to use it.*

Manager: *Generally [CSRs] want to do a good job for customers, but they are often constrained by systems, particularly due to a mismatch of systems for provisioning, for billing, and for product information.*

CSR 3: *Systems problems cause customers to get angry and they take it out on us.*

A final point concerns the relationship between the relevant factors—effectiveness and enablement—and workers' satisfaction with technology. With one exception, we found that workers' satisfaction with technology was significantly associated with its effectiveness but had no significant relationship with enablement.[19] These relationships were stronger for service workers, suggesting that knowledge workers may take technology for granted and feel less dependent on it to complete their work successfully. More generally, the results indicate that, to workers, *the effectiveness of technology is more important than the extent to which they are able to control it.* This suggests that workers are conditioned by their past experiences not to expect to exert control over technology but that technology will help them to work more effectively. Hence, they value the effectiveness of technology over its enablement. An alternative interpretation is that even where workers control technology, the means to which it is put lies beyond the workers' discretion. Thus, they place less value on its emancipatory role

---

[19] The details are as follows. Correlations between effectiveness and satisfaction with technology were as follows: service workers ($r = 0.63$; $p < 0.001$; $n = 601$); sales workers ($r = 0.71$; $p < 0.001$; $n = 88$), and knowledge workers (r = not statistically significant).

than on its instrumental capacity to help get work done. This perspective is consistent with Derber's (1982: 172–80) argument that, insofar as professionals increasingly work in organizational settings managed by corporate managers, these employees enjoy task control but not ideological control. In short, these professionals lose control over the product of their labor and how it is sold in the market.

Satisfaction with the nature of work. ANOVA results show that in line with hypothesis 3a, the knowledge and sales workers in our study were significantly more satisfied with the nature of their work (defined as "work which is challenging and has variety and opportunities to learn") than the service workers ($F_{(2,858)} = 34.50$, $p < 0.001$).[20] Knowledge and sales workers emphasized the autonomy and satisfaction they felt from achieving their goals. Sales workers liked providing a service to customers; knowledge workers were more inclined to emphasize technology and learning, and, partly for this reason, they enjoyed being in close touch with competent colleagues. The following quotes illustrate these points:

SD 1: *I like working with new technology so you keep up with what is happening. I also like moving around on projects that are breaking new ground—it's challenging work.*

SD 2: *It's the continuous learning [that I like] and the satisfaction of knowing you are achieving what no one else has done.*

Dealer 1: *It's the wide exposure to markets and products [that I like]; the learning curve is high. And we can run with good ideas. There's opportunity for innovation, and a fair degree of flexibility.*

Dealer 2: *You learn new things all the time. I like that. Also, the team is a good working environment. It's a good team. We are successful and have a good reputation.*

Dealer 3: *It feels like you are working for yourself in the comfort of a desk that knows what they are doing.*

In contrast, service workers emphasized the extrinsic and social aspects of their jobs. Some liked the routine nature of the work, while others experienced this as monotony once the introductory period had passed. For example:

CSR 1: *One of the best things about this job is the hours. I like the flexibility it gives me.*

CSR 2: *The best part of the job is the customers, the things you can do for them, rapport with them. Most of them are nice.*

[20] We have taken this item to signify the intrinsic aspects rather than, or in addition to, "influence over work-related decisions" because it reflects this concept more clearly. Workers' influence is discussed in chapter 5.

CSR 3: *I like work being routine, helping customers when you can. It's a good environment, a good spirit here.*

CSR 4: *I'm bored. It's a monotonous job. You have to follow the systems, so there's not much control, which is a pain. I like the people, though.*

Since the findings are no different when differences in work values are taken into account, these results appear to support the hypothesis derived from job design and sociotechnical theory that work characteristics strongly influence work values. Matters may not be that simple, however, for, as indicated earlier, service workers do value interesting and challenging work (albeit less than sales and knowledge workers), arguably leading them to expect work to be intrinsically satisfying. Consequently, their expectations are not strongly dampened, and, because their work has less to offer in these respects, they are less satisfied with the nature of their work than are sales and knowledge workers. Their satisfaction with the nature of their work contributes more to their overall satisfaction with work ($r = 0.62$, $p < 0.05$) than is true for knowledge workers ($r = 0.44$, $p < 0.05$). This suggests that, because service workers derive less satisfaction from the nature of their work than do knowledge workers and derive less satisfaction than expected in relation to pay and promotion opportunities,[21] the satisfaction service workers do experience is especially important to them.

Work stress. An analysis of variance based on survey data supports hypothesis 4a that the knowledge workers and sales workers experienced stress significantly more frequently than the service workers ($F(2,848) = 54.31$, $p < 0.001$) and reported less satisfaction with the amount of leisure time available as a result of their jobs ($F(2,859) = 28.92$, $p < 0.001$). These findings are in line with an interpretation that emphasizes worker responsibility for critical outcomes (e.g., project results on which innovation depends, in the case of SDs, or deals involving large amounts of money, in the case of dealers), which often entail long work hours. The pervasiveness of responsibility-induced stress, which is not confined to knowledge workers, is exemplified in the following quotations:

SD 1: *Just before a deliverable, I'll work twelve-hour days. Here we are still in the early stage [of the project], so I work normal hours of nine to five or six.*

SD 2: *We feel overwhelmed by the increasing need for technical knowledge of systems as we enter into higher value-added consulting sales [of computer systems].*

[21] Only 52 percent of service workers claimed to be "very satisfied" or "satisfied" with their pay, and 36 percent gave similar responses regarding their prospects for promotion ($n = 615$). As noted earlier, these were two of the highest-ranked work values service workers mentioned.

Dealer 1: *Losing money tears you apart; you feel you are not doing your job. It puts doubts in your mind, makes you feel like a loser all round. . . . You can't help take it personally.*

Dealer 2: *Everyone here is a market junkie. The traders have computers at home and trade from home [at night]. They tend to be chained to the desk at work. Most meetings are held when the markets are closed, like at lunchtime. We have meetings three times a week in the evenings, and most staff would lose four to five Saturdays a year.*

HLC 1: *It's difficult to sustain a normal lifestyle. I work sixty hours a week, six days a week. You need to be flexible. . . . You can't afford to leave the phone, because we depend on it for business.*

HLC 2: *This job threatens marriage and family life. Being on the end of a mobile phone [i.e., a cell phone] means we are "never truly relaxed." Time becomes continuous—night/day, work/ nonwork distinctions disappear in the [HLC] job.*

Our interpretation is further supported by the negative and significant association between satisfaction with amount of leisure time and stress ($r = -0.41$; $p < 0.001$; $n = 161$ for knowledge workers; $r = -0.45$; $p < 0.001$; $n = 90$ for sales workers; and $r = -0.27$; $p < 0.001$; $n = 599$ for service workers).

In sum, the evidence presented above supports several propositions. First, there are more similarities than differences in the work values of service, sales, and knowledge workers. Second, contrary to postmaterialist value theory—which implies convergence on the relative salience of intrinsic work values—our data point to an emphasis on extrinsic work values.[22] Third, in spite of what is noted above, there were significant differences among the knowledge workers and the sales and service workers. The knowledge workers value the intrinsic facets of their jobs more than the service and sales workers do; the knowledge workers perceive technology to be more effective and more enabling; and, not surprisingly, they reported higher satisfaction with technology. Fourth, although we were unable to disconfirm the job values hypothesis with regard to satisfaction with the nature of work, the data were consistent with job design theory, which posits a universal positive psychological response to variety, challenge, discretion, and opportunities for learning at work. Thus, knowledge and sales workers

[22] First, uncertainty concerning job security is likely to encourage concern with current and future earnings; second, as work becomes more complex and demanding, workers expect improved earnings, particularly where other terms of employment are stable or declining (e.g., developmental training and promotion opportunities). Third, for knowledge workers especially, but also for other workers regulated by pay-for-performance reward systems, the level of earnings serves both as a badge of management endorsement (social worth) and a basis for self-identity and status at work.

reported significantly higher satisfaction with their work than did service workers. At the same time, sales and knowledge workers were significantly more stressed than service workers, a finding consistent with arguments that posit job responsibility and long working hours as key causes of stress.

Overall, our findings suggest that variations in the act of work, which define work complexity, exert a substantial influence on employees' work experiences. This is most striking when comparisons are made between knowledge workers (employed in the most complex work) and service workers (employed in the least complex work). In this connection, it is noteworthy that the rewards for knowledge workers are not consistently higher. Thus, although knowledge workers report higher intrinsic satisfaction with their work than service workers, knowledge workers are no more satisfied with their work overall and service workers feel more secure in their jobs and experience less job-related stress.

Conclusion

This chapter began by contrasting the regimented, overworked worker with the empowered knowledge worker. The evidence presented in this chapter suggests the need for a more complex picture that varies according to the type of workflow in which the worker is employed. Thus, although it is true that the service workers we observed performed more routine tasks, were less satisfied with their work, and had less control over technology than their knowledge and sales worker counterparts, service workers did have opportunities to use their social and organizational skills creatively. In addition, they experienced stress less frequently than anticipated. In short, the service workers in our study did not fit the stereotype image of the technologically incarcerated, regimented front-line employee. Nevertheless, their profile more closely fits that of the ideal type known as the routine worker than that of the professional employee.

The sales and knowledge workers were highly stressed, but they enjoyed considerable autonomy from management in undertaking their work. As we have shown, these workers used higher-order contextual and theoretical knowledge than the service workers and used more demanding social and analytical skills that could not easily be routinized. Thus, the sales and knowledge employees could be considered "empowered." Evidence presented in chapter 6, however, indicates that the sales workers were constrained by other workers charged with upholding company rules. Knowledge workers also were subject to control by employees: their immediate colleagues maintained norms that were integral to collaborative work. Furthermore, both groups of workers experienced stress more frequently than did the service workers and were no more satisfied than the service workers with their jobs overall. In sum, the knowledge workers we observed do not experience work as nirvana, even though they resemble the professional ideal type in many ways.

The contention, supported by our data, that work complexity shapes several key aspects of the work experience suggests the possibility that this influence extends beyond the realm of work relations to other elements of work organization. For example, we anticipate that service, sales, and knowledge workers will occupy different labor markets and that these workers' employment relations will differ accordingly. Thus, we would expect service workers to be employed in the highly structured internal labor markets one associates with bureaucratic organizations, while the labor market for sales and knowledge workers would likely be as much occupational (with high mobility between firms) as organizational. Nevertheless, we expect managers to have substantial discretion to offer additional rewards to high-performing employees in order to retain their services. We also anticipate that control relations will differ among the three types of workflows. The greater creativity and skills displayed by knowledge and sales workers imply more independence from management than service workers enjoy and hence greater task-level influence.

We would also expect co-worker relations to be different in the three workflows. We saw that service work is mainly customer oriented, requiring limited collaboration with colleagues. This is also the case in sales work, which, as noted earlier, is frequently conducted one on one with individual customers outside the workplace. By contrast, most knowledge work is collaborative. Hence, the frequency and nature of the relations with colleagues are likely to differ among the three groups of workers. Finally, customer relations also tend to vary with work complexity. Service workers are likely to have brief encounters with customers; sales workers will have longer, mainly instrumental relationships; and knowledge workers will tend to have the most complex, long-term involvement with clients. These issues are addressed in subsequent chapters.

4 *Employment Relations*

THIS chapter concentrates on employment relations—the procedures and practices governing relationships between workers and their employers. Our first objective is to evaluate differences in contemporary ER as these relate to front-line service, sales, and knowledge workflows respectively. Osterman (1984) has suggested that such differences exist, as has more recent work that highlights the significance of the demise of internal labor markets and the corresponding rise of occupational labor markets, the greater emphasis on individual performance, and the increase in worker flexibility (Zabusky and Barley 1996: 189–91; Osterman ed. 1996). Proponents of the regimented WO perspective view these tendencies as assertions of management power aimed at raising worker productivity. Empowerment adherents interpret this trend more positively, as a means of rewarding individual differences in competency while simultaneously freeing up internal labor markets to competition from workers outside the firm.

Our second objective is to investigate the impact of various external institutions on ER patterns. This is done in two ways. The first way is by analyzing intercountry variations to determine whether ER systems regulating front-line workers in Japan differ from those in Australia and the United States. Such differences appear to be substantial, both in their patterns and effects, with the result that Japanese "welfare corporatism" displays superiority over Western neo-Fordism (Dore 1973; Lincoln and Kalleberg 1990; Womack, Jones, and Roos 1990; MacDuffie 1995). This literature is restricted, however, mainly to permanent male workers in production settings.

The second way to examine the impact of external institutions is to analyze the impact of a particular institution while minimizing the influence of other factors. Because their impact on management-employee relations and firm performance is so controversial, we have chosen to look at trade unions (Freeman and Medoff 1984; Cooke 1994; Standing 1992). Our analysis is confined to service workflows in Australia and the United States, where the labor markets are more similar to each other than they are in either country to that in Japan. This approach also minimizes differences in workers' attitudes to unions arising from variations in work complexity and ER arrangements. Service workflows are also sufficiently numerous and diverse with regard to union strength to make quantitative analysis possible.

In the first section of this chapter, we distinguish among bureaucratic, entrepreneurial, and knowledge-intensive forms of employment relations. This taxonomy provides the basis for developing several hypotheses that relate our empirical evidence on ER patterns to service, sales, and knowledge work workflows. The second section provides empirical evidence that supports our hypothesis that service workflows are structured along weak bureaucratic lines, while sales workflows are more entrepreneurial, in that they are relatively unstructured and dominated by external market mechanisms (see Osterman 1984; Strauss 1990). Knowledge work workflows are hybrids comprising features of the knowledge-intensive and bureaucratic types that may vary over time (Bacharach, Bamberger, and Conley 1991; Ackroyd 1996: 616–17).

In the third section we address institutional issues by outlining several hypotheses premised on comparisons between Japanese and Australian/ U.S. ER systems, including their effects. Hypotheses relating to the impact of unions are also summarized. Using matched pairs of cases, we explore the supposed differences between Japanese and Australian/U.S. forms of employment relations and the alleged superiority of the former in terms of employees' orientation to ER and to work performance. Our findings challenge the conventional wisdom by pointing out that the Japanese large-company ER system comprises two bureaucratic patterns, one the familiar welfare corporatist model designed for permanent male workers, the other, its meaner, flexible, shadow, which applies mainly to females.

For our analysis of the effect of trade unions on ER patterns, we compare workers' attitudes toward work performance in highly unionized and low unionized/nonunion service sites in Australian and U.S. business units. Our findings indicate that, compared with their colleagues in workflows in which unions are inactive or absent, workers in workflows in which unions are active are better off in some respects and worse off in others. Overall, these workers are more satisfied but no less likely to perform effectively than workers in nonunionized workflows or those in which the union is inactive. In the concluding section we discuss some of the more important implications of our analysis for management-employee relations.

Structuring Employment Relations

Decisions about how to structure ER typically center on hiring, training, retaining, and rewarding employees (Osterman 1987; 1988; Batt 1996). Hiring issues include the skills and knowledge required of relevant employees; characteristics of the recruitment process, particularly whether workers are hired from outside or inside the organization; and criteria used in the hiring process. Training decisions relate to the predominant sources (internal or external to the organization) and nature of the training. Staff retention concerns employment security, which is related to whether career opportunities exist within or external to the organization. Finally, rewards encompass such issues as the features of the payment system, particularly the extent to which pay is fixed or variable and based on performance or other criteria.

Structuring decisions are typically influenced by prevailing legal and social norms, including the influence of such labor market institutions as unions and professional associations (Baron et al. 1986; Dore 1987; Gordon, Edwards, and Reich 1982; Frenkel and Coolican 1984; Friedson 1986). Other important considerations include labor scarcity, organizational size, and use of technology (Kalleberg et al. 1996; Cappelli et al. 1997). Using our own terminology but following Osterman (1984), three types of ER can be identified in relation to the ideal types of workflows outlined in chapter 1. These are summarized in table 4.1 according to the four influences on structuring decisions referred to above.

Bureaucratic Forms of Employment Relations

Bureaucratic forms of ER are associated with semiroutinized work, although in Japan knowledge workers are often found in such settings. Bureaucratic forms of ER may be unilaterally regulated by management or jointly regulated through collective agreements with unions (Edwards 1979; Jacoby 1985; Morishima 1994). Usually, a bureaucratic form of ER is imposed on clerical workers in large companies. Externally recruited novices occupy positions at the base of the job ladder, and subsequent positions are filled internally according to formalized rules. Employees are expected to be dependable and committed to the organization's goals. Because they are role takers, these workers are also expected to become thoroughly familiar with the company's rules, norms, and work procedures. The company provides formal training, focusing on job proficiency and potential career progression. By establishing career ladders, the company offers employees opportunities for promotion and employment security. Semiroutine work is usually part of an interdependent process involving large numbers of employees. Payment usually depends on seniority or experience rather than on individual performance.

Table 4.1. Features of Employment Relations in Bureaucratic, Entrepreneurial, and Knowledge-Intensive Workflows

	Bureaucratic	Entrepreneurial	Knowledge-intensive
Recruitment			
Basis	External at ports of entry, thereafter internal	External; no differentiating levels	External at ports of entry and at higher levels
Criteria	Dependability, commitment	Dependability and conformity to established management norms	Qualifications, experience, creativity, organizational congruence
Training			
Main source	Organization	Minimal	Professional institutions
Features	Formal training programs aimed at job proficiency and employee development supplemented by OJT	OJT	Courses and OJT
Career opportunities			
Internal versus external	Mainly internal	None	Mainly external
Employment security	High	Limited	Variable; depends on external labor market
Reward system			
Fixed versus variable pay	High fixed element	Fixed—time or closely related to performance	High variable element; explicit skill acquisition
Criteria for raises	Seniority, Experience/tacit skill acquisition	External labor market or performance	Performance

Source: Adapted from Osterman 1984.

Entrepreneurial Forms of Employment Relations

Entrepreneurial forms of employment relations are associated with work in which the incentive for employers to train workers is limited. Two conditions under which entrepreneurial forms might occur are when the work is routine and employees are therefore interchangeable and when the competencies required to undertake the work are less significant than the personal attributes of the applicants. Thus, as indicated in chapter 3 and discussed more fully in chapter 7, salespeople depend on their social skills and network of contacts to obtain leads. Management considers these to be important attributes but also features that facilitate worker mobility between firms. Accordingly, management decisions reflect movements or anticipated movements in the external labor market. Recruitment is solely via the external labor market, and, since hiring criteria are quite straightforward, hiring is usually a relatively simple process. There are no internal job ladders, and there is no employment security. Pay is either time related, in which case pay rises relative to the time spent at work, or is closely tied to individual output, as in piecework or payment-by-results systems.

Knowledge-Intensive Forms of Employment Relations

Knowledge-intensive forms of ER emphasize lateral rather than vertical ties and are associated with jobs involving complex tasks based on the application of specialized, transferable knowledge and skills. Legally regulated professionals, such as doctors and architects, typically work in such settings. Theoretical knowledge and appropriate techniques are imparted through training provided by specialized institutions responsible for maintaining standards. Learning is ongoing, however, since workers are required to utilize new technology and solve new problems. Recruitment is not confined to novices. Employers are concerned mainly with qualifications and experience. In addition, personal attributes, including creativity, values, and norms acceptable to management, are likely to be important. The knowledge-intensive form of ER offers opportunities for achievement—moving to more challenging projects carrying greater prestige, either with the same employer or with a different organization. If the external labor market is strong, as is frequently the case, employment security is neither sought nor provided. Individual contributions can often be identified, and employers typically want to retain high-performing employees and disengage from low performers. Accordingly, pay systems include relatively large, variable, performance-related elements.

Employment Relations Elements Common to the Three Types of Workflows

Several ER-related features tend to be common across our three types of workflows, although, as we shall see, their consequences may vary. Two features bureaucratic organizations have in common, for example, are that they tend to be large and to have multiple sites. Another common feature is that they operate in markets characterized by intense product market competition. Pressures vary, however, assuming different forms with different effects. Thus, in most of the IT-intensive service workflows we studied, technology provided a cost advantage over conventional (branch) service delivery and hence led to rapid growth in employment. Devising ways to improve service and increase revenue was a challenge for management. Cost containment was a lower priority. Similarly, there was less pressure to reduce unit costs in knowledge work workflows, where increased competition meant delivering more innovative, higher-quality solutions on time and, only if possible, at lower cost. By contrast, in the sales workflows in Australia, price continued to be an important element of the purchasing decision. This needs to be understood against the backdrop of the recently deregulated banking industry, in which mortgage originators and insurance companies have entered the home loan market. Consequently, cost pressures were strongest in these workflows, exacerbated by the threat of alternative forms of delivery (by telephone and via the Internet in the future), from within the organization, and by competitors. Management was therefore keen to convert fixed costs to variable costs as much as possible and to tie the latter as closely as possible to revenue generation.

Since front-line work varies in complexity, service, sales, and knowledge workers circulate in different labor markets. The service and sales labor markets we observed were characterized by apparent excess supply, evidenced by the large applicants-to-vacancy ratio reported by our informants. Yet managers complained that applicants lacked relevant competencies. The labor market for knowledge workers was much tighter.[1] Nevertheless, managers widely acknowledged that prospective employees were also likely to differ in performance and to be rewarded accordingly.

Regardless of workflow type, we expected to find more evidence of the bureaucratic form of ER in large Japanese companies than in their Australian or U.S. counterparts (Dore 1987; Lincoln and Kalleberg 1990; Morishima 1995). The welfare corporatist variant is based on there being employment security for male workers, career paths centered on internal promotion, seniority-based pay, and enterprise unionism. Although changes have occurred in light of intensified market competition, labor shortages of some highly qualified employees, and opposition by women, the Japanese employment system remains largely intact (Berggren and Nomura 1997; Sako and Sato 1997).

Unions have historically favored bureaucratic and knowledge-intensive forms of ER, depending on whether they represented workers engaged in routine or skilled work. Among our case study participants, there was little

---

[1] Tran (1997) provides evidence that the labor market for systems developers is "hot" in the United States in an article aptly titled "The Geek Shall Inherit the Earth." Survey data provided by a consulting firm in Australia covering salary trends in forty-four large companies in the financial services industry show that between May 1995 and May 1996 the salaries of customer service representatives increased by 7.1 percent, while that of senior systems programmers increased by 8.5 percent. The salary of money market managers (the closest available job category to dealers) increased by 25.1 percent, when the industry average was 4.9 percent. Over the same period, the estimated average annual salary increase for all Australian private-sector occupations, excluding banking, in establishments covered by federal enterprise agreements was 4.6 percent (Department of Industrial Relations 1997: 63).

evidence of unionism among either the sales workers or the knowledge workers, with the exception of the workers at TELSD and COMPUJ. In the former case, the unions had long sought and then gained a bureaucratic form of ER; the same was true at COMPUJ, as might be expected in a large Japanese company with an enterprise union.[2] Our focus, therefore, is on unionized service workflows. Nevertheless, the impact of these unions may be difficult to discern. This is partly because the current environment is inhospitable to unions since changes in Australian labor law (Deery, Plowman, and Walsh 1997: 9.24–9.34) have resulted in a more decentralized, legally regulated labor market system similar to that of the United States (Commission on the Future of Worker Management Relations 1994). In addition, the declining union density in the three countries has put unions on the defensive. Unions may have members at the workflow level, but this does not necessarily make a difference to employees' working lives.

Hypotheses

With the above discussion in mind, and beginning with service workflows, we advance three hypotheses.

Hypothesis 1: *Employment relations in service workflows are likely to reflect an attenuated bureaucratic form.*

Product market competition based on mass customization encourages management to recruit selectively and to train workers to service customers more effectively. The high firm-specific, contextual knowledge workers need to have with respect to products, procedures, and systems means that management needs to invest relatively heavily in initial training. The hope is that management will recoup this investment by retaining competent workers. Accordingly, management will make some effort to ensure internal mobility and employment security for competent employees.

The reward system is likely to have a relatively large fixed element to reward dependability but also a small variable element to reward superior performance, again with the intention of retaining the most effective workers. At the same time, technology and management practices aimed at routinizing the work reduce management dependence on front-line workers' discretion. Customers, in effect, take on more product selection functions by using more effective information systems. This tendency appeals to management's predilection for exercising control over the work process and

---

[2] At COMPUJ, all workers below a particular salary level who were not temporary transferees from other subsidiaries or associated companies were required to be union members. This contrasted with TELSD, where the workers were not union members, although their terms and conditions of employment were regulated by a contract that was largely the product of management-union negotiations.

costs. It implies less need for selectivity in recruitment, very limited training and career opportunities, and a reward system that encourages dependability rather than initiative. This tendency toward the development of entrepreneurial ER will not be welcomed by workers whose values—high pay, promotion prospects, job security, and intrinsically satisfying work—incline them to favor a modified bureaucratic pattern. The unstable outcome is likely to be a weak form of bureaucratic ER.

> Hypothesis 2: *Employment relations in sales workflows will in most respects resemble the entrepreneurial form; in a limited number of other respects, these arrangements will tend toward the knowledge-intensive form.*

The entrepreneurial form of ER offers distinct advantages to employers of sales workers intent on controlling costs. Little investment is required in selection and training, and with no career ladders or entitlements to employment security, administration and labor costs are kept to a minimum. A highly flexible performance-related reward system is used to motivate employees. If rewards are high enough and targets are achievable, workers will be motivated to sell more products and to stay with the organization. Having contracted to the organization on the basis of the extant reward system, workers who consistently fail to sell according to target will be encouraged to leave or will be fired. In effect, labor costs, being largely composed of variable costs, vary with revenue. When sales are slow, employees can be expected to resist threats to employment and income security, as they would under the entrepreneurial pattern of employment relations.

There are two points of tension in the employee-management relationship, related to training and internal career opportunities. Because workers are employed as entrepreneur-employees does not mean they are uninterested in employment security and careers within their current organizations. Indeed, because sales workers are likely to view training as an investment in their future effectiveness, many are likely to be dissatisfied with the very limited training they receive. Moreover, as bearers of the new entrepreneurialism in what remain essentially bureaucratic organizations, workers are likely to have strong expectations about internal career opportunities, a point on which we presented evidence in the previous chapter. Consequently, despite their preference for independence from management and support for elements of the entrepreneurial ER pattern, sales workers are likely to seek training and career opportunities more typical of the knowledge-intensive form. The extent of their success in doing so is an empirical matter.

> Hypothesis 3: *Employment relations in knowledge work workflows are likely to include a mix of elements drawn from knowledge-intensive and bureaucratic forms of ER.*

We anticipate seeing elements of the bureaucratic ER pattern in what is basically an occupational form. Most employees are likely to endorse this as it offers advantages for their future dealings with their current employer without limiting alternative job opportunities.

Knowledge workers tend to be highly qualified, having obtained their credentials from institutions external to the employing organization. They enjoy the advantage of tight labor markets and are recruited largely on the basis of their qualifications and experience. Knowledge workers tend to be occupationally stable and organizationally mobile. Theoretical knowledge facilitates mobility across firms, and management hires at both the novice and expert levels. To reflect market forces and differences in competence, rewards tend to be flexible and there is likely to be an emphasis on systematic training and career planning, together with a participative management culture (Alvesson 1995; Casey 1995; Kunda 1992). This analysis suggests that, except in Japanese companies, the knowledge-intensive form is likely to prevail.

Knowledge workers are expected, however, to meet professional (maintain up-to-date knowledge and technical mastery) and organizational objectives (contribute to profit-generating innovations). In turn, employers face the challenge of developing employment systems that foster professional and organizational commitment, thereby retaining the most effective workers. Two basic strategies are available: complete substitution of the knowledge-intensive form by the bureaucratic form or hybridization (i.e., effecting partial supplementation by combining specific elements of the knowledge-intensive form with aspects of the bureaucratic form that knowledge workers value and that are likely to secure their organizational attachment). Since the latter is more feasible and likely to yield more benefits to management, we anticipate that management would foster elements of the bureaucratic form in knowledge work workflows. This would tend to relieve, though not eliminate, the tension between workers pursuing primarily knowledge-intensive interests (i.e., professionals) and employers whose emphasis is on organizational goals (Derber, Schwartz, and Magrass 1990; Brewer 1996). As explained later, Japanese companies have developed a hybrid ER structure that combines elements of knowledge-intensive and bureaucratic forms.

Employment Relations in Service, Sales, and Knowledge Work Workflows

Now that we have identified the four elements that distinguish the three ideal types of employment relations, we can turn to our comparison of ER patterns in service, sales, and knowledge work workflows. Because acronyms are used to identify workflows and companies, readers are advised to refer to chapter 2 (tables 2.2 and 2.3). Japanese workflows are excluded because they are considered in a later section. Note that job characteristics are not discussed in detail except when they were not covered in the previous chapter.

Service Workflows

Job characteristics. Front-line service jobs combine routine and nonroutine tasks. In the latter case, these are usually accompanied by management guidelines that circumscribe employee discretion. Nevertheless, we observed opportunities to demonstrate initiative regarding problem solving and selling, and some managers encouraged employee participation in project work, with double-edged effects. On the one hand, participating in projects relieved employees of routine tasks and provided a means of self-development. On the other hand, successful projects demonstrated employee effectiveness and heightened workers' career expectations, which their current employers may not have been able to meet.

Hiring. Management went to considerable lengths, including conducting two or three personal interviews and an over-the-phone assessment, to recruit suitable staff. Less than 20 percent of those who were interviewed were hired, and in some cases the figure went below 10 percent. Often this was because candidates lacked the necessary person profile. Further, hiring focused on relatively inexperienced applicants. With the trend toward keeping workplaces open twenty-four hours a day, part-timers were favored.[3] At some sites, part-timers were expected to work different shifts than full-time staff, but typically the wages and conditions for part-timers were the same as those of their permanent colleagues.

Standard management requirements were high secondary school grade qualifications and at least one year's experience in a customer service role, preferably in business services. Although a source of contention, university graduates were also hired in most service workflows. Particular personality attributes and orientations were emphasized since most managers agreed that *"it is easier to train to knowledge and skills and hire to self-images, traits, and motives because these aspects tend to be more difficult to develop or train"* (manager, UB1). Among these traits and orientations were *"dedication, loyalty, high performance, and initiative"* (TELSV) and *"self-discipline, trustworthiness, credibility, and professionalism"* (MBASV). UB1 and UB2 advertisements referred to the need for *"strong bureaucratic skills, initiative, and a positive, service-driven attitude and the presence of mind to work well under pressure, coupled with polished communications skills and a strong detail orientation."*

[3] Survey data (n = 862) reveal that nearly 19 percent of the service workers were part-timers, compared with only 1 percent in the sales and knowledge work workflows.

Managers at some companies emphasized employee initiative. For example, a manager at MFJSV stated that *"to change our culture we need a new type of staff, those with energy and initiative. The new employees have to take ownership. They have to understand our strategy and then understand how to work by themselves."* This tendency was associated with sales becoming an integral part of the front-line worker's role. In most cases, however, sales experience was not yet a mandatory requirement.

In sum, recruitment practices pointed toward a diluted bureaucratic pattern of employment relations in which hiring was largely at the base of the organization. Management emphasized that hiring decisions were critical in securing committed, competent workers. External hiring for positions above entry level suggested that management was prepared to compromise internal career opportunities to obtain high-quality labor.

Training. Companies typically allocated about 5 percent of their total business unit budgets to training. This included one full-time trainer for approximately fifty customer service representatives. In addition, experienced CSRs trained new recruits as part of their role.

All new recruits to call-center work were required to take training courses, most of which lasted for between four and six weeks. Training was largely aimed at providing employees with the knowledge and skills to work effectively in the shortest possible time. Consequently, the emphasis was mainly on narrow contextual knowledge—company products, systems, procedures—and customer-related skills.

More experienced workers tended to receive training only when there were major changes in technology, products, or procedures.[4] In three companies—MFJ, UB, and AIN—more experienced workers received advanced training as part of an employee development strategy. Two other companies were considering introducing competency-based training systems, which would have given employees who passed a qualifications test higher pay and enhanced status. As indicated by the following remark, however, management tended to be overwhelmed by the demand for training of new hires: *"It's difficult to do anything other than new CSR training or product training. There's so much demand for this kind of thing."* (MBASV)

Survey data indicate that service employees regarded training courses as the most important source of knowledge and skills, followed by learning from immediate colleagues and from supervisors/team leaders. Statistical analysis indicates that service workers were significantly more likely than sales and knowledge workers to report that formal training programs were their main source of learning ($F_{(2,695)} = 40.74$, $p < 0.001$). Furthermore,

[4] CSRs were expected to learn in an ongoing, incremental fashion from their supervisors or from e-mail sent to them by management during the course of the day. Employees often preferred to rely on immediate colleagues. This additional learning was sometimes felt to be a burden since CSRs had little time for this activity outside team meetings.

service workers were significantly more satisfied with the companies' training provisions than workers in sales and knowledge work workflows (F $(2,758) = 10.16$, $p < 0.001$).

Several methods were typically combined in formal training courses, as indicated in the following quotation from a trainer at TEL: *"I do a lot of practice, role plays, doing what they learn. So, after we've done some formal training, then there's a lot of reinforcement by discussion and practice. There's a lot of peer sharing of knowledge so they are not just dependent on the trainer."* She went on to explain that learning and practice were combined. Practice was done through "buddying"—in which novices sat with and learned from experienced CSRs. She continued: *"Here they learn and practice—so it's train, then practice, then train, then out [to work]."* At UB, a trainer explained that *"our philosophy is learning by doing; only a small amount of time is showing and telling as compared to doing. We have a lot of role plays and exercises and interaction between the new hires."* The trainer explained further that *"training is mainly classroom based, which involves listening-in to real [phone] calls [with customers]. In the last week the new hires sit next to a part-time trainer [experienced CSR] and have daily meetings with that person."* At most of the call centers, supervisors or team leaders also used silent monitoring and side-by-side coaching to ensure ongoing training. This form of on-the-job training is discussed further in chapter 5.

In sum, consistent with what might be anticipated in service workflows with bureaucratic employment relations, company-provided, formal training was paramount. This training focused almost exclusively on ensuring immediate job proficiency, however. Very little training was aimed at employee development and career progression.

Career structuring. Supervisors and/or managers conducted systematic annual appraisals of individual employees in all the service workflows we studied. The main purpose of these appraisals was to provide employees with information and advice on their performance, rather than to plan and develop employee competencies. Management also relied on the appraisals in making decisions about promotions and selecting employees for project work.

All the service workflows had informal career ladders. Novices progressed to the status of experienced worker (sometimes involving more complex work) and then to team leader or supervisor. Two points are worth noting about this "line track." First, team leader and supervisor positions were open to candidates from outside the company, although only after internal applicants had been considered. Second, the track was truncated. Managerial positions were typically advertised externally. In some workflows, however, management emphasized that participation in the workflow was a "good stepping-stone" to jobs in other parts of the organization. But at only one company—UB—where there was some coordination across departments on this issue—was this a reality. Even there, large-scale organizational change and an impending merger limited employee opportunities for advancement.

Two additional initiatives had been introduced in some workflows. At UB1, UB2, MFJSV, and AINSV, there was a "staff track," which offered experienced workers the possibility of becoming trainers. These employees generally undertook a short train-the-trainer course and went on to train new workers. These reassignments were made at periodic intervals when new workers were recruited. In the meantime, these employees were expected to answer novices' queries and to provide general support for inexperienced workers. These network trainers, as they were sometimes called, received additional pay at the discretion of management. Opportunities for further promotion were restricted, however, by the limited number of full-time training positions available.

The second initiative, adopted in two workflows (MBASV and MFJSV), entailed the creation of a new, higher-status position that effectively gave formal status to a minority of experienced employees. At MBASV "senior CSRs," as they were called, were on the roster for a "help line" through which they assisted other workers with queries. There were plans to raise their pay commensurate with their new status. At MFJSV, "executive CSRs" were entrusted with dealing with customers whose assets exceeded a certain amount. In the latter case, these workers received additional training and pay and were expected to demonstrate exemplary initiative, particularly in selling.

Survey data revealed that most of the service workers retained a bureaucratic career orientation but were dissatisfied with their prospects. Thus, 60 percent of the full-time service workers who responded (n = 372) viewed their career prospects as better with their current employers than with another employer (11 percent), while nearly 21 percent believed their prospects were limited and a further 8 percent claimed to be uninterested in a career.

The service workers had similar expectations as the sales workers concerning their chances of being promoted internally (57 percent of sales workers [n = 85] expected to be promoted internally) but lower expectations than the knowledge workers (76.8 percent [n = 155] expected internal promotions). Only 38 percent of full-time service employees reported being very satisfied or satisfied with their career prospects, compared with 31 percent who claimed to be neither satisfied nor dissatisfied and another 31 percent who said they were dissatisfied or very dissatisfied.

Perceptions that their career opportunities were limited were not accompanied by job insecurity, however. Demand for service jobs was expanding, and although part-time work was becoming more common, management saw the part-timers as complementary to, not substitutes for, the full-time employees. Consequently, the full-timers did not feel threatened by the part-timers.[5]

To summarize, internal career ladders existed for service workers, but they were not underpinned by formal rules and were limited in range. Thus, on the one hand, employment security was more firmly in line with what one would expect in a company with bureaucratic employment relations. On the other hand, this security had no formal backing; it would last only as long as demand expanded and there was high turnover among experienced staff.

Reward systems. The reward systems combined position-related features with performance-related criteria. The CSR position was typically situated in a salary band that reflected the qualifications and competencies required to undertake the job. Supervisors and managers could be in the same salary grade (where grades were wide) or, more frequently, they were in higher grades. A worker's position in the salary grade was initially determined by the employee's attractiveness to the organization (labor market position); subsequently, it depended on the employee's annual appraisals.

In recent years there had been pressure on managers to limit salary raises, so that even high performers had not been rewarded very much. For example, as part of a recent annual salary review, UB—reputed to be a good employer—awarded a 6 percent increase to employees with "above-average" ratings and up to 10 percent to those rated "exceptional." MBA awarded a 3 percent annual increase to "average" performers and 7 percent to workers who performed "above average."

Performance-related prizes for excellent service—usually given in response to letters from customers—and rewards for outstanding sales were common. They were paid in cash or in kind (gift vouchers or restaurant outings) and were sometimes based on a team's performance. The monetary returns were usually small, however. For example, workers at UB complained that the company's prize for sales leaders was only $400 a quarter, arguing that it was not commensurate with the effort expended. Management tended to view these schemes from the perspective of the recognition and status they conferred on employees. As noted in chapter 3, employees in service workflows were generally dissatisfied with their rewards.

To summarize, the reward system for service workers was associated with the bureaucratic pattern of ER. This system was supplemented, however, by pay raises and other rewards, including promotion based on individual performance—an element associated with knowledge-intensive ER. This observation, together with our previous findings, supports hypothesis 1

[5] Statistical analysis reveals that the service workers in our study (full time and part time) were significantly more satisfied with their job security than the sales and knowledge workers $(F_{(1,757)} = 48.67, p < 0.001)$. In effect, the service workers remained relatively protected by bureaucratic procedures compared with their sales and knowledge work colleagues, for whom consistent failure to perform was more likely to evoke a punitive response.

that employment relations in service workflows are characterized by an attenuated bureaucratic form of ER.

Sales Workflows

Job characteristics. As noted in chapter 3, compared with customer service representatives, home loan consultants draw on higher-level contextual knowledge and a wider repertoire of social skills. Once learned and mastered, these competencies are transferable across organizations in the financial services sector. Since sales requires developing credibility with customers, buttressed by a favorable image of one's product, salespersons must also be knowledgeable about their competitors' products. Thus, employers tend to believe that experienced salespersons will require little training and can, in most respects, be employed according to the entrepreneurial ER model.

Recruitment. The managers at the companies we visited had attempted to recruit salespersons internally but were largely unsuccessful in their efforts. The paucity of applicants spoke to differences in the cultures of entrepreneurial and bureaucratic organizations. Thus, the entrepreneurial workflows were more customer focused, and rewards were reflected in individual performance. By contrast, in the bureaucratic workflows, there was more interaction among colleagues, so that individual performance was less visible and less consequential. There were also differences in work habits. As a manager opined: *"I'd like to see more of our people in [the organization] do this type of work, but it's longer hours, harder, more pressure, and the work hours are out of the ordinary."*

Managers recruited externally, seeking employees with at least three years' sales experience, preferably in the financial services sector.[6] This is reflected in survey data, which show that the sales workers had been in their current occupation for longer (on average, nine years) than their service (nearly six years) and knowledge worker counterparts (about eight years).

Management regarded recruiting as an important activity. After placing advertisements and conducting a first round of screening, managers normally held two sets of interviews before making a job offer. Managers looked for particular competencies (e.g., evidence of longstanding customer relations, marketing and service skills, problem solving/lateral thinking, and time management) and personality attributes (motivation to succeed, tenacity/resilience, independence, and a high level of integrity). The difficulties the company had in finding suitable employees was evident in the claim by one manager that he had made only three job offers from a field

---

[6] ABKS was experimenting with having employees on temporary assignment from other departments to see whether there was a mutually agreeable "fit" between the person and the work role.

of sixteen interviewees. High labor turnover compounded the recruitment problem.[7]

In sum, new salespersons were hired from the external labor market according to criteria that prioritized experience, competencies, and personality attributes that could not easily be substituted for other features. As we shall see, salespersons had no career ladders. This meant that recruitment most closely followed the entrepreneurial pattern, although the importance accorded to the process was more characteristic of ER in its more knowledge-intensive form.

Training. Management assumed that new recruits were competent, and consequently they received less than two weeks of what was often unsystematic training. For example, a home loan consultant told a researcher that *"it depends when you are recruited. If there are some courses on [i.e., being run by the training department for other sections of the organization] that will help you, then you can probably attend these. If there aren't any courses, well, that's it."* Some managers guided new recruits for several weeks, including assigning them to "buddy" with more experienced salespeople. Such practices were not institutionalized, however; they depended on individual managers providing support.

Although there was increasing emphasis on formal training, managers continued to believe that the most appropriate way to train salespeople was by giving them on-the-job experience.[8] HLCs tended to agree: *"The key to learning is the hands-on approach—talking to customers, reading material in the office, the manual on products, and asking colleagues,"* said one HLC. A colleague added: *"I've learned a lot from [an experienced HLC]. He's one of the best, and he knows all there is to know."* Survey data corroborate these views. When asked to rank various sources of learning, HLCs ranked learning from immediate colleagues as most important. This was followed by learning from other employees (probably credit analysts who analyze and endorse loan applications)[9] and from team leaders (man-

---

[7] At ABKS, eighteen of the original twenty-five HLCs we studied had left their positions within twelve months. On the one hand, two-thirds of these had not been meeting their targets. On the other hand, of the five top performers, only one was still with the company.

[8] Two factors, however, encouraged management to devote greater attention to formal training. The first was that there had been problems with loan submissions, mostly in the form of inadequate or incorrect documentation. Problems increased when salespeople found it difficult to attain their sales targets. This led to higher administrative costs and reduced customer satisfaction. The second factor was that in one workflow (ABKS) new technology had been introduced (presentation and analysis software) and in another (MBASV), new management systems (total quality management). Training needs in these two workflows were provided mainly through short courses. The emphasis was on job competency rather than on employee development.

[9] HLCs learned from credit analysts in three ways. The first way was through passive experience. Loans were submitted, some were endorsed for settlement, others were rejected outright or returned with a request for additional information or clarification. Telephone discussions between the customer and the credit analyst, in which the analyst explained the status of the request, were often relayed to the HLC by the customer. The second way HLCs

agers who had knowledge of loan procedures). By contrast, training courses were ranked sixth.[10]

In sum, since the company strove to hire experienced salespeople, company-provided training was very limited. This may change in the future, but at the time the research was undertaken both managers and salespeople tended to favor on-the-job training. These findings suggest an entrepreneurial approach to ER in this area.

Career structuring. Because attaining monthly sales targets was the paramount goal, salespeople and their managers were usually in contact at least twice a week, usually by telephone. They also had weekly small-group meetings to discuss progress. Both managers and employees tended to regard the less frequent one-on-one appraisal meeting as something of a formality. These appraisals encompassed broader issues, such as ways employees could expand their referral networks and develop better customer service. These appraisals also served as opportunities to set broad goals for the next period. Career development issues, such as opportunities to advance and training requirements, received little or no attention.

These findings are consistent with situations in which there are no career ladders. Opportunities for promotion into a position as a loan sales manager were limited, and the salary was unattractive compared with what a successful salesperson could earn. The same logic applied to other positions in the organization. In short, there were few internal positions that highly paid, entrepreneurial workers would find attractive, despite company rhetoric that emphasized organizational flexibility and customer responsiveness.

The sales workers in our study appeared to believe the corporate rhetoric, perceiving greater career opportunities within their organizations than with other employers.[11] Moreover, reflecting their ambitiousness, salespeople ranked their prospects for promotion as second most important (after pay) out of fourteen work-related items. Statistical analysis of relevant survey data shows that these workers were not significantly more dissatis-

---

learned was in conflict situations. HLCs routinely argued with credit analysts about company criteria for assessing loans. The third way they learned was through constructive dialogue. HLCs would contact a credit analyst and seek advice on how a particular aspect of a loan might best be handled. This enabled the HLC to assess whether the loan was worth pursuing. According to an ANOVA analysis of survey data, salespeople were significantly more likely to emphasize learning from customers than were the workers in either service or knowledge work workflows (F $(2,771)$ = 9.39, p < 0.001). Salespeople ranked learning from customers fourth out of ten possible sources of learning.

[10] HLCs regarded company-provided training as "very ordinary" or "not very useful." When asked how satisfied they were with the training, only 35 percent of the salespeople (n = 66) claimed to be very satisfied or satisfied, versus 33 percent who said they were dissatisfied or very dissatisfied; the remainder claimed to be neither satisfied nor dissatisfied.

[11] Nevertheless, significantly more salespeople believed that their career prospects were better with another employer (34 percent). By contrast, only 12 percent of the service workers and 15 percent of the knowledge workers felt this way.

fied with their promotion prospects than service workers or knowledge workers.

The level of rewards and employment security among the salespeople depended on whether they attained sales targets. The influence of factors beyond their control (changes in interest rates and marketing decisions within the organization), combined with the intense product market competition, tended to make these workers relatively insecure. This is evident in statistical analysis, which shows that salespeople were significantly more dissatisfied with their employment security than service workers but not compared with knowledge workers.

To summarize, the absence of career ladders and lack of employment security reflected a management strategy that created uneasiness among the salespeople. Despite their proclivity to be entrepreneurial, these workers sought internal promotions and protection from the vagaries of the external market.

Reward systems. Typically, the salespeople received a base salary, various allowances—a car allowance, for example—and, most important, a commission based on sales of loans and other financial products. Management set monthly sales targets for individuals, which often varied according to the salesperson's experience. If employees failed to achieve a minimum sales level over several consecutive months, they not only received substantially less pay but also were advised to resign. Most did so to avoid having their contracts formally terminated.

For high performers, commissions represented about twice their fixed salary (base rate and allowances). Our survey shows that 35 percent of the salespeople earned more than 40 percent of their fixed salary in commission. This compares with less than 1 percent of service workers. No reliable data are available for knowledge workers.

Management frequently adjusted payment-by-results systems to suit its own requirements and sometimes those of employees. At ABK, for example, a new system was introduced, in response to intense competition and slower sales, that increased the base pay rate and slightly reduced the rate of commission on loan sales. Later that year, management offered HLCs who had met or exceeded sales targets over the previous six months the option of a company car in lieu of increasing their commission.

MBA also changed its payment system. This was in response to an attempt by senior management to reduce costs and increase customer demand, combined with pressure from HLCs to increase their base rate. The base rate was raised and the commission rate reduced only for those HLCs who qualified as top performers.[12] Some high-performing HLCs believed that their earnings would be reduced as a result of the change and

[12] Top performers were defined as HLCs who had recorded the highest value of sales over the past two years and who had "been committed to training/coaching other [HLCs]." The goal, however, was to encourage knowledge transfer, not sales, although no audit was done to ensure that learning or coaching took place.

bitterly opposed this scheme. A compromise was eventually reached that addressed these workers' concerns.

In some companies, salespeople received awards for high individual performance, often on a monthly and annual basis. Some companies also rewarded team performance. Employees had a say in determining the nature of these awards, and awards were not always given solely for top performance. For example, at MBA, there was a "most improved salesperson's award." Awards were usually accompanied by considerable celebration, designed to express a "work hard, play hard" ethos and to engender solidarity among employees.

In conclusion, reward systems in the sales workflows included a high variable element and were structured to encourage and reflect individual performance. This is more typically found in knowledge-intensive rather than bureaucratic settings. Nevertheless, in most other respects, ER more closely resembled the entrepreneurial form, as suggested by the hypothesis 2 advanced earlier.

Knowledge Work Workflows

Job characteristics. The effectiveness of knowledge work depends on the ability to combine theoretical and contextual knowledge (Derber, Schwartz, and Magrass 1990; Quinn, Anderson, and Finkelstein 1996), as well as to share understandings with different kinds of specialists (Mohrman, Mohrman, and Cohen 1995). In addition, the conduciveness of the social context for realizing intrinsic work goals—especially learning and mastering new knowledge and skills—is an important aspect of the job.

Recruitment. Hiring is especially important since organizations often rely on the exploitation of knowledge to achieve competitive advantage and the difference between hiring an average and a high-potential candidate can significantly affect an organization's reputation and profitability.

Graduates were hired on an annual basis, while experienced persons were recruited when vacancies arose. The emphasis in the workflows we studied was on hiring for immediate organizational requirements, so that, compared with the number of "experienced hires," there were relatively few recent graduates. Positions requiring experienced employees were typically advertised both internally and externally, and specialist employment agencies handled initial screenings of external candidates. Thereafter, candidates were brought in for at least three sets of formal interviews, which in some organizations included psychological tests. These were not used at TELSV and WBMM but were at WBSD, where such a test had recently been instituted.[13]

---

[13] According to several managers, the motives for developing and applying this test arose out of a consultant's report written in response to the company's high turnover rate among its systems developers. The report concluded that improved hiring processes were necessary. The test—which took four hours to complete—was specially constructed by a consultant based on a profile of eight of the subsidiary's most competent SDs.

The selection process was usually undertaken by line managers with relevant knowledge, assisted by the most competent employees (who possessed relevant skills). Hiring criteria were closely followed. TEL was in some ways an exception with respect to hiring and other human resource practices, since these were regulated by procedures negotiated with the unions that represented lower-level TEL technicians and other workers.

Selection was based on qualifications, experience, reputation (sometimes of the educational institution the person attended), and personal attributes. The latter was emphasized (see Granovetter 1992: chap. 9). For example, at TEL, managers preferred to hire people with whom they had worked before, and at WBMM a manager remarked that *"we rarely hire sight unseen, cold. People on the team keep their feelers out. We keep track of the good people in the industry."* Previous or current colleagues were often asked about prospective employees, sometimes through third parties.[14] The importance attached to personality and work style is an acknowledgment that knowledge work is characterized by high levels of discretion, trust, and teamwork, features that can be enhanced or impaired by personal attributes.

Such hiring situations are two-way streets, however: candidates need to be made familiar with the prevailing work culture to make informed choices about whether to accept a job. Thus, the emphasis given to personal attributes is best seen as a process of discovering whether there is actual or potential alignment of values and norms between candidates and their prospective managers and colleagues. The following extract from an interview with a money market dealer indicates the way management values—in this case, the desire to succeed in obtaining the position—significantly influenced candidate selection.

I wasn't part of a graduate interview process. The [manager] didn't find anyone he wanted [through that process], so when I applied I was lucky. [The manager] was looking via an agency. He wanted one or two suitable people. I applied and got an interview. [A manager] and a [senior dealer] interviewed me. They told the agency they would probably leave it. I was really depressed, so I got their phone number but, meanwhile, I spoke to the agent. He said he would ring [them] rather than me. They said: "OK, we'll give you another interview." They set it at 7 A.M. [The senior manager] was really offhand to me; he was very short, cut me off a lot. Then he said: "I am going to get [the

---

[14] A case in point was a money market dealer who had recently joined WB and who was able to talk authoritatively about someone who joined the company several months later. The dealer commented: *"I was instrumental in getting Judy. I knew she would fit in."* Similarly, a dealer commented: *"I got a call from someone at WB. It was a good offer. It was a good reason to leave [his current organization] and come here. WB is seen as the market leader."* A further example: *"There was a vacancy on the desk. Five people here have worked for [a specific organization]. They knew me, so they phoned me and asked me if I was interested. I came."*

*team leader] to talk to you." [The team leader] said, "Tell me in one minute
what your attributes are and why you are suitable." I did it all in a few minutes.
Next day they phoned to say I got the job. After I joined, [one of the
managers] said the fact that you rang back showed more about you than the
interview.*

The senior manager referred to above expanded on his belief that it was
important to assess the character of prospective employees as part of the
interview process.

*I give 'em a real hard time in the interview process to get behind the bullshit.
Find out the real character. I don't believe in psych testing. It is a very subjective process. I don't even have questions when I go in. Character is important so long as they have the basics, a reasonable academic record, etc. I hire
on character and personality. I am confident that our strategy and environment will deliver success provided the right personality is hired.*

In short, qualifications and experience are important criteria for recruitment, but they are only the baseline requirements. Also important are the
candidate's personality, work style, and values, particularly the congruence
between the norms and culture of the work organization and its management and those of the prospective employee. Together with the fact that
hiring is mainly through the external labor market, these criteria point to
a tendency for ER in knowledge work workflows to resemble a modified
form of the knowledge-intensive pattern.

Training. The managers in the knowledge work workflows we studied
were ambivalent about the value of training. It was regarded as important
for developing novel solutions or new products that might give the company
a competitive edge, but it was also seen as an expense (of time rather than
money) that had to be measured against the achievement of short-term
goals. A common solution to this conundrum was for managers to justify
training related to the achievement of current work assignments and to
restrict broader training to inexperienced recruits. Thus, a systems developer at WB remarked: *"I go to courses by going to my project manager
and arguing that there is a need in relation to my current project. I've never
pushed for anything that was not immediately task related. That would be
futile."*

At WBMM, new graduates were expected to participate in courses
run by the relevant professional body, the Securities Institute.[15] By contrast,

---

[15] These courses were considered complementary to on-the-job learning. Graduates who
joined the desk were usually placed in the middle office, where deals were checked before
being finalized. Here, they learned about various financial instruments and application of
policy and were exposed to different front-office roles, such as trading, selling, price making,
and deal structuring. After several months, they were moved to the balance sheet area, where
they gained a perspective on the flow of funds into and out of the organization. They would

experienced dealers attended a course in computing arranged by the desk's technology support team. At TELSD, knowledge workers did not attend any courses during the six-month period of our research.

Survey evidence indicates that knowledge workers viewed their immediate colleagues as the main source of learning, followed by manuals and reference guides. In third place were publications and research materials. Statistical analysis indicates that knowledge workers were significantly more likely to refer to publications and research findings than service or sales workers ($F (2,695) = 114.03$, $p < 0.001$). These results reflect the relative importance knowledge workers accord theoretical knowledge and new techniques. The knowledge workers disconfirmed the importance of external courses as ongoing sources of learning, drawing attention, rather, to the importance of learning from colleagues through on-the-job training (OJT).

Money budgeted for training knowledge workers tended to be underspent. This reflected managers' concerns with meeting short-term targets and workers' commitment to their immediate projects. Workers also shared the view that "courses are only good if you follow them immediately with practice." At WBSD, knowledge limitations (regarding computing architectures) and skill shortages (especially in relation to emerging programming languages) encouraged management to adopt a more proactive approach to training. Consequently, a skills matrix, mapping the current reservoir of skills, had been documented. Periodic assessments were planned to compare skill requirements to available skills. Training decisions would be made accordingly.

Our survey data support the contention that the unstructured nature of OJT from expert colleagues coupled with the limited amount of time available for postemployment formal training is likely to cause dissatisfaction among knowledge workers. Thus, only 39 percent of respondents (n = 134) claimed to be very satisfied or satisfied with the training provided at their workplaces, 33 percent said they were neither satisfied nor dissatisfied, and 28 percent said they were dissatisfied or very dissatisfied.

To summarize, the evidence points to the greater emphasis among knowledge workers on OJT rather than on training provided by professional institutions. This is less true of training of new hires, although OJT still underpins formal training. Nonetheless, knowledge workers were encouraged to attend courses, often provided in-house, that catered to the immediate needs of their current assignments. These features suggest that knowledge workers learn in a similar way to technical workers—on the basis of communities of practice—albeit building on a theoretical base and with some reference to formal documentation (Orr 1996). This is consis-

---

understudy and progressively undertake various tasks until management assigned them a position on the front desk. This could take up to three years.

tent with Abbott's (1988) observation that the essence of professional work lies in diagnosis, inference, and treatment (i.e., application), processes that involve a fusion of theoretical and contextual knowledge. Our analysis thus suggests a mixture of the characteristics of the knowledge-intensive ideal type, with its emphasis on formalized, institutionalized training, and the entrepreneurial form of employment relations, which emphasizes on-the-job learning.

Career structuring. The managers of knowledge workers whom we studied did not use appraisals as vehicles for developing employees. As a manager observed, *"The focus of management is on winning customers and getting on with the job, rather than looking at individual needs."* Career opportunities were also limited. A senior manager at WBSD noted:

> *I don't know what a career in technology means in 1996. Some people still want to be a project manager. I don't agree with that as an automatic aim. It takes away [from direct work] those with initiative and creativity. There isn't a specific career path, and I don't think there should be one, not like a bureaucracy. . . . As long as a manager is finding opportunities [i.e., challenging and creative work] for his employees, there won't be a problem.*

The same manager affirmed that WBSD valued its highly expert workers: *"Three of our top SDs receive large bonuses and have the title of AGM [assistant general manager] even though they have no employees reporting to them."* A senior colleague in WBMM also observed that careers within that organization were limited: *"Most people here have nowhere to go in the organization. There's space for 15 percent, but for the rest, they need to look outside."*[16]

In TEL, there was a career structure of sorts, which had been designed for another part of the organization. SDs were in grades well below those of executives, with the result that a gap existed between these employees and those in the managerial grades. Furthermore, there was no additional pay or status attached to excellence as a technical specialist. To retain the most competent SDs, management promoted employees into executive positions. This required managing people, and it contributed to "executive creep." Attempts at filling the grade gap with employees in technical positions requiring higher competencies were apparently opposed by the unions, which sought to participate in determining criteria for promotion.

In spite of the limited opportunities, knowledge workers expected to remain with their current employers. Thus, of the 91 percent of the full-time knowledge workers who were pursuing careers, 84 percent stated that their career opportunities were better with their current employers than

---

[16] HR managers were more sympathetic. They argued that helping employees plan their careers was necessary to maintain morale and retain employees. This was a process that they intended to encourage in the near future.

with other employers. Nonetheless, given the bleak picture painted above, it is not surprising that only 38 percent of relevant survey respondents (n = 134) said that they were very satisfied or satisfied with their prospects for promotion. Thirty-seven percent claimed to be neither satisfied nor dissatisfied, and 25 percent said they were very dissatisfied or dissatisfied.

Further, given the uncertainty arising from the increased emphasis on meeting performance targets in the context of fierce product market competition, organizational restructuring, and technological changes, it is not surprising that knowledge workers (and sales workers) were significantly less satisfied than service workers with their job security. Nevertheless, nearly two-thirds (66 percent) of the knowledge workers who responded to our survey (n = 134) claimed to be very satisfied or satisfied with their job security, versus 24 percent who reported being neither satisfied nor dissatisfied and 10 percent who said they were very dissatisfied or dissatisfied.

Set against a backdrop of favorable opportunities for interfirm mobility, these findings suggest that knowledge workers seek the advantages of both knowledge-intensive and bureaucratic forms of employment relations. This is consistent with the survey finding that only 13 percent of knowledge workers were members of a professional association. Thus, without unilateral jurisdiction over a clearly demarcated, related set of occupations, these workers hedged against the risk of a market downturn by attempting to carve out careers in their current organizations.

Reward systems. Except for employees in Japanese companies and in TELSD, where pay was based largely on seniority, the knowledge workers we studied derived relatively large proportions of their pay from performance-related bonuses. Thus, at WBSD, which, in contrast to WBMM, did not generate revenue, bonuses were restricted to an upper limit of about 50 percent of salary. In other workflows, such as WBMM, where pay was directly related to revenue generated, bonuses were as high as twice the salaries.[17]

Performance-based reward systems operated according to two quite different social principles—market worth, determined periodically by surveys of relevant labor markets, and performance. These criteria were highly subjective, involving periodic consultation and bargaining among managers to arrive at each employee's remuneration.[18] Performance-based systems

[17] The variable element was rewarded in a variety of forms, including as investments, low-interest loans, insurance payments, motor car leasing, and child care payments.

[18] For example, in WBMM there were formal discussions among the managers of various desks, followed by further discussions with the senior manager responsible for all the desks. He/she would have consulted with the senior management committee and received some advice regarding the funds available for bonuses. More informal discussions between the managers of each desk and the senior manager would follow regarding individual bonuses, eventually concluding with agreement on what each employee would receive that year. There was no formal appeals procedure, but rare cases of apparent gross injustice were reconsidered.

applied to groups and individuals separately or jointly depending on management and, to some extent, employee preference. Criteria for determining performance-based bonuses tended to be centralized and governed by a few simple rules, which meant that the system could be easily understood and executed by line managers, who retained discretion to substantially adjust pay according to individual performance.

Where reward systems were based on occupational grading, providing little flexibility to reward more competent employees differentially, managers tended to bend the rules and/or seek to reform the system so as to retain and motivate employees. In TELSD, salaries were graded according to formal position, and progression up the salary grade depended on years of service. Promotion was inhibited by the "grade gap" mentioned above, and the reward system was twisted to suit management's needs. Thus, employees were reclassified into higher grades without much justification. Project managers were classified as higher-grade "communications consultants," for example, enabling senior management to pay these employees more than if they were classified as IT specialists.

Another manager at TEL cited a project in which management was forced to upgrade technical specialists to executive positions in order to retain them, even though this resulted in some specialists earning more than managers. As mentioned earlier, TEL management had tried to insert new grades into the pay structure but had met with resistance from the unions.

With performance-related pay systems, the assumption is that individual performance can be measured relatively easily and pay adjusted accordingly. As a brief comparison between WBMM and WBSD indicates, this was not always possible. In contrast to WBMM, where there was no mention of changing the reward system, the reward system at WBSD was regarded as a major source of unintended adverse consequences. For example, a senior manager at WBMM suggested that *"each year there are guys who will bitch about not getting enough money. I'd say 50 percent go out [of the process] satisfied, 25 percent are happy, and 10 percent are unhappy."* By contrast, at WBSD, a senior manager observed that *"you [also] get one upmanship, people putting each other down, infighting."* A colleague added that *"it [bonuses] forces results-based behavior. Maybe that's OK for money market traders, but not so for techos, where there are a lot of intangibles [i.e., unforeseen problems]. We're trying to show that we are recognizing intangibles [i.e., not building systems that appear to work at first but result in many problems downstream]. That's [building systems with no operating problems] bloody hard to do."*

These contrasting assessments are based on four differences between these two workflows. First, at WBMM, the measurement of performance was relatively straightforward. It consisted of revenue from deals and trading profits, taking into account employee experience and individual and team effort. At WBSD, the criteria for judging employee performance were more subjective. As a systems developer remarked: *"It's very arbitrary. A lot depends on how your manager feels about you. It's not a good system."*

Bearing in mind that bonuses were dispensed to individuals rather than teams, the second difference was that at WBMM most employees worked as individuals, albeit with team support, making assessment of individual performance easier. By contrast, at WBSD, SDs were typically organized in project teams characterized by a high degree of interdependence, making assessment of individual contributions more difficult.

The third difference made bonus setting easier at WBMM: managers worked more closely with employees in the workflow, spending at least two-thirds of their time on the desk. By contrast, at WBSD, managers responsible for setting bonuses were physically removed from many IT projects and relied on summary reports by project managers, including some about leading-edge technology projects that were difficult to evaluate.

Fourth, and finally, managers at WBMM placed a higher priority on bonus setting and devoted considerably more time to it than did their counterparts at WBSD. We did not overhear any remarks in WBMM about the way the bonus process was managed, whereas it was not uncommon in WBSD to hear remarks like the following: *"I think we're not managing it [the bonus system] well. If we could figure out what behavior we want to reinforce, that would be a start. At present there's no real measures. The problem is that even where measures exist, . . . they can be manipulated."*

To summarize, reward systems in knowledge work workflows tend to have relatively large variable performance-based elements, consistent with the knowledge-intensive ideal. Where rewards are inflexible, because pay raises are based on seniority, age, or some other status-related factor, such systems are surreptitiously subverted, as occurred in TELSD, or the intent is to reform them, as occurred in COMPUJ. More generally, our discussion confirms hypothesis 3 advanced earlier that employment relations in knowledge work workflows are likely to represent a hybrid of elements common in knowledge-intensive and bureaucratic forms.

Overview

We have shown that ER patterns vary according to the type of workflow in which these patterns develop. Service workflows are characterized by attenuated bureaucratic patterns of ER; sales workflows, in most respects, resemble the entrepreneurial form; and knowledge work workflows evidence a combination of knowledge-intensive and bureaucratic elements in a hybrid pattern. We contend that these differences are associated with variations in the complexity of the work. Thus, relatively routine service work lends itself to standardization and hierarchical control, whereas sales work, which involves more worker discretion and measurable outputs, is conducive to entrepreneurialism. By contrast, highly complex work, characterized by considerable reciprocal interdependence with customers and co-workers, encourages structuring in a manner that combines employee autonomy with organizational control. This is the essence of the hybrid form. Finally, it is necessary, in this connection, to remind readers that institutions also influence employment relations patterns.

We have focused on the differences in ER systems across the three types of workflows; however, several common elements are worth noting. These include the significance of contextual knowledge as it relates to job characteristics, the importance of personality attributes in the hiring process, and the limited emphasis given to training for employee development. Our analysis also indicates that workers are dissatisfied with their limited opportunities to advance within their companies and feel insecure about their long-term employment prospects with their current employers.

Institutional Contexts as Sources of Variation in Employment Relations

In this section we outline hypotheses and provide supporting evidence regarding the impact of institutional variations on ER patterns and employees' attitudes toward performance. Two themes will be developed: the differences between Japanese and Western (Australian/U.S.) ER patterns and whether the presence of so-called active unions makes a difference in these patterns and in workers' attitudes toward performance. We omit discussion of ER in the one Japanese sales workflow, because the ER systems in both sales and knowledge work workflows in Japan were the same and it is thus sufficient to focus solely on the knowledge work case.

According to our first hypothesis:

Hypothesis 4: *Regardless of workflow type, the bureaucratic form of ER will be more prominent in Japanese workflows than in Australian/U.S. workflows.*

The rationale for this proposition is as follows. Although the bureaucratic form has been common in large, multisite U.S. (Kalleberg et al. 1996: 98–99) and Australian firms, evidence presented in chapter 1 suggests that with more emphasis on performance and the consequent increase in downsizing, outsourcing, and flattened hierarchies, fewer organizations may be bureaucratic in form (Hecksher 1995; Osterman 1996). Deregulation has been a feature of both Australian and U.S. environments. Likewise, companies have promoted the values of entrepreneurialism and innovation, against a background of basically similar cultural values (Hickson and Pugh 1995: 12–70). By contrast, several historical and institutional factors have encouraged large Japanese companies to support a more bureaucratic ER system. These include the welfare corporatist pattern of providing employment security and seniority-based pay and merit-based promotions, which are part of a complex internal labor market system within a broadly egalitarian earnings hierarchy. Direct employee involvement and worker representation through enterprise unionism are additional important features of the Japanese system.

Within large Japanese corporations in which this bureaucratic system predominates, there is a second ER subsystem that emphasizes numerical rather than functional flexibility. Covered under this subsystem are mainly non-career-track, primarily female employees working in relatively routine jobs. As we shall see, this is the arrangement under which our Japanese service workers were employed.

Compared with the United States and Australia, market liberalization and deregulation have been limited in Japan. Longer-term relationships with large-scale financial institutions have contributed to the continuity of its dualistic system, which is underpinned by longstanding cultural values favoring collectivism, consensus, and gender role differentiation. In spite of some changes, particularly vis-à-vis managers and higher-qualified white-collar workers, these have not been significant enough to warrant altering the hypothesis advanced above (Shapira 1995; Sato 1997; Morishima 1995).

The following two hypotheses, in combination, assert that social institutions tend to shape existing forms of employment relations and influence employees' attitudes toward performance.

Hypothesis 5: *Permanent male workers in Japanese workflows will have a higher performance orientation than their colleagues in similar Australian/U.S. workflows.*

Hypothesis 6: *Female workers in Japanese workflows will have a lower performance orientation than their counterparts working in similar Australian/U.S. workflows.*

By performance orientation, we mean a combination of organizational commitment and discretionary work effort (effort the worker claims will be forthcoming without any change in rewards or sanctions). *Ceteris paribus*, both variables contribute to greater effort and application and hence to higher work performance. Consequently, the higher the values of these two variables, the higher the worker's performance orientation.[19]

Given that Japanese welfare corporatism is restricted to permanent male workers in large companies and most female workers are employed under alternative arrangements (Brinton 1993; Wakisaka 1997), we submit, following Lincoln and Kalleberg (1990), that the Japanese bureaucratic system

---

[19] When operationalized, these concepts are internally reliable and positively related ($r = 0.33$; $p < 0.05$; $n = 857$). Details of the items comprising the two concepts and their reliability are given in appendix 2.

evokes a higher performance orientation among permanent Japanese male workers than among their U.S. or Australian peers. The reasons are likely to be a combination of loyalty encouraged by the paternalistic features of the system and pragmatic accommodation, given the limited, acceptable employment alternatives. The opposite logic applies to temporary women workers, who hold job values that are similar to those of their non-Japanese counterparts.[20] One would expect that the absence of supporting ER structures for women, coexisting with their presence for permanent male workers, would be likely to foster greater dissatisfaction among Japanese women than among their non-Japanese counterparts engaged in similar work.

Japanese versus Australian/U.S. Service Workflows

This section summarizes employment relations at JBSV, including, where relevant, commonalities and differences between the JBSV bond-ladies and the MBASV women customer service representatives. There are three grounds for choosing MBASV as an appropriate workflow for comparison. First, like JBSV, MBASV is a service workflow within a financial services firm. Second, MBASV had also experienced considerable customer dissatisfaction, although the causes in the two workflows were different.[21] Third, MBASV typifies the combination of strong control (of systems) and strong support (for employees) typical of management practice in Australian and U.S. service workflows. We focus on female workers because more than 80 percent of the employees at JBSV are female. By concentrating on women workers at MBASV and JBSV, we are, in effect, controlling for gender.

Job characteristics. The workflow JBSV, composed of bond-ladies, was confined to women who were between twenty and twenty-nine years of age. They were employed to service and sell mainly to female customers responsible for investing family savings. The bond-ladies sold a variety of simple savings products, on which they provided information and advice through regular visits to customers in their homes. Only a limited amount of business was transacted on the phone. The women's work consisted mainly of ascertaining when their clients' investments were maturing and advising

[20] Analysis of variance on relevant survey data shows that there is no significant difference between JBSV female workers and their MBASV counterparts with regard to the value they placed on pay, job security, and training. JBSV front-ladies did accord significantly lower importance to promotion prospects, however, than MBASV female workers (F $(1,47) = 3.70$, $p < 0.1$).

[21] At MBA, the problems occurred because personnel in other departments made errors that customers subsequently raised with the CSRs. At JB, the issue was a wider one of reduced confidence in the firm stemming from customer criticism of the financial services industry in the wake of losses suffered following the 1992 stock market crash and persistent scandals in the banking industry.

them to reinvest in the same or similar products sold by the company. The knowledge, skills, and creativity requirements of the job were not noticeably different from those of other service workers described in this and other chapters.

Recruitment. The bond-ladies worked in regional offices and at company headquarters. Following attendance at a company seminar and two sets of interviews with different levels of management, candidates were hired from outside the company on a regional basis. This system was different than for male candidates, who were hired for career tracks by the corporate HR department.

To qualify for a second interview, the bond-ladies had to pass a basic knowledge test. The bond-ladies we observed ranged from high school graduates through junior college attendees to university graduates. Management favored particular personal attributes, including determination to succeed, cheerfulness in the face of adversity, and adaptability. The women worked independently and hence needed to be both sympathetic and confident in relating to customers. In short, unlike the requirements in an organization with bureaucratic employment relations, but similar to those of customer service representatives, management sought dependable and committed employees.

Training. The bond-ladies received limited training, some of which was specifically designed for women. They underwent a four-day induction program (compared with about three months for male employees), which focused on social and communication skills. The women then entered the workplace and engaged in self-study and training by peers and supervisors. This was followed by a four-day training seminar designed to assist the women in passing the bond exam, required to sell bonds, given by the Ministry of Finance. Thereafter, the bond-ladies continued with OJT. Further training was gender-oriented (e.g., in social etiquette).

In contrast to male workers, the bond-ladies received no training in computer systems and sales. Statistical analysis based on relevant survey data shows that more experienced bond-ladies (i.e., those with more than one year's job tenure) received significantly less training than their counterparts at MBASV and were significantly less satisfied with the training they received ($F (1,49) = 4.34$, $p < 0.05$).

In sum, management invested less in training bond-ladies in Japan than it did in counterpart Australian (and, by implication, U.S.) workflows. Further, the women received less training than their Japanese male counterparts.[22] Training took place mainly, though not exclusively, on the job. In addition, some training was specifically designed for women.

---

[22] Male securities staff spent several months in courses and subsequently were assigned to different branches for the first five years of their employment. Thereafter, they were rotated into company headquarters. The bond-ladies did not participate in any job-rotation program.

Career opportunities. The bond-ladies were *ippan-shoku*—noncareer-track personnel—whereas their male counterparts were *sogo-shuku*—career-track employees. In 1989, it became possible for bond-ladies to transfer to *sogo-shuku* status. This depends on employee preference and individual performance. At the time of our study, management did not encourage such transfers, and women expected to marry and leave the workforce, both of which made transfers uncommon.

On joining the organization, the bond-ladies usually started at one of two grades (depending on their educational qualifications and market worth) in a six-level grading structure. Progression depended on experience. High-performing women could progress faster, and some reached the top of their grades in four years. There was no progression beyond this grade, however, except to transfer to the career track or become a supervisor, but, given that men held all the management positions, there were very limited opportunities to be promoted.

The traditional view in Japan is that young women beyond a certain age should not be full-time employees, so management offered very limited career progression beyond a six- or seven-year period. Many of the bond-ladies encountered difficulties in dealing with customers, because they were insufficiently trained, and consequently there was a high turnover (about 25 percent a year) among those with less than three years' service.

The evidence presented above suggests that the bond-ladies had more limited career opportunities and less employment security than the service workers described earlier. This is supported by statistical analyses that indicate that the bond-ladies were significantly less satisfied with both their prospects for promotion and their job security than MBASV workers (for promotion prospects, $F_{(1,49)} = 3.24$, $p < 0.1$; for job security, $F_{(1,49)} = 5.57$, $p < 0.05$).

Reward system. The bond-ladies' salaries included a base salary (based on their educational qualifications and pay levels at comparable companies), a monthly allowance, and a bonus. Increases in base salary depended on the firm's profitability and years of service (seniority). Faster progression, which was rare, could also lead to raises based on superior performance appraisals. As Endo (1994) has observed, the *satei* system depends a good deal on the supervisor's opinion. Monthly allowances, which represented about 7 percent of total salary, varied according to grade and years of service. Bonuses, paid every six months, averaged about 15 percent of total salary. The bonus level depended largely on company profitability, although some adjustments were made (amounting to less than 5 percent) for individual performance. Bonuses were reduced in 1996 compared with the previous year by an average of 16 percent. The bond-ladies also received prizes for outstanding performance. These were more honorific than providing monetary value.

Although some elements of the reward system were meant to reflect differences in individual performance, its most basic feature was the connection between reward and seniority. In this respect the reward system for the bond-ladies differed from that of the company's other service workers, which placed more emphasis on individual performance. Statistical analysis of relevant survey data indicates that the bond-ladies were significantly less satisfied with their pay than were their MBASV counterparts (F $(1,49)$ $= 28.39$, $p < 0.001$).

To summarize, in their job characteristics and the recruitment procedures used, the bond-ladies were not easily distinguishable from comparable Australian or U.S. service workers. The Japanese women's training was less formal and systematic, however, and was not geared to progression within the company. Career opportunities were more truncated, and employment security was not assured beyond about six years. The reward system was also less performance-oriented and more seniority-based. In short, employment relations represented a secondary labor market variant or female shadow of the welfare corporatist, bureaucratic form characteristic of large Japanese corporations. Not surprisingly, the bond-ladies were significantly less satisfied than their MBASV counterparts. Nevertheless, the enterprise union did support their requests. At the time of our study, for example, the union was pressing management to introduce an ability-based reward system that included the use of more objective criteria in performance appraisals.

Japanese versus Australian/U.S. Knowledge Work Workflows

For this comparison, we focused on what was referred to as the 5SI workflow at COMPUJ, a Japanese multinational, and a workflow in Australia composed of systems applications developers who worked for WB, a U.S. multinational. The latter workflow was chosen because the work of its employees most closely resembled that of the SDs at COMPUJ.[23]

Job characteristics. COMPUJ SDs solicited, negotiated, and implemented new computer systems in customers' firms. Much of this work involved customized integration (i.e., creating computing systems that built on the clients' current hardware and software, adding new elements, and achieving overall superior performance through more effective integration of the total systems). Thus, the SDs required theoretical knowledge to conceptualize the integration but also considerable contextual knowledge, including the ability to combine current and new software in creative ways. This was clearly knowledge work, though the degree of creativity involved varied with the complexity of extant systems and clients' goals.

Recruitment. COMPUJ followed the conventional Japanese practice of

[23] These employees wrote programs and provided broader technological support for the money market dealers. The SDs reported to the money market business managers; the money market dealers were, in effect, their customers. The work of the SDs involved integrating new and old systems in a broadly comparable way to COMPUJ SDs.

annually hiring graduates with appropriate personality characteristics from reputable universities. After an induction period, the HR department, in consultation with line management, assigned the new recruits to various divisions and departments. In the case of the SDs, nearly 60 percent had degrees in engineering. Usually professors known to senior management recommended these employees. Reflecting slow economic growth and increasing competition in the Japanese computing industry, the company reduced the number of new recruits in 1996 by 20 percent compared with the previous year. There had been a tendency in recent years to recruit more experienced employees through the external labor market, but their numbers have remained small. Recruitment to above-entry positions was virtually all by internal promotion, consistent with a bureaucratic pattern of employment relations.

Training. Graduates normally undertook ten months of induction training, which included a series of courses on general business and on such specific issues as accounting, costing, and information security. During this period, supervisors in the division to which the graduates were temporarily attached gave them specific assignments. In addition, graduates sat with *senpai* (slightly older employees), from whom they could learn.

In contrast to induction training, which was organized by the HR department but administered by a training center, postinduction training was mainly decentralized to the business divisions. It included further courses in general management and in specialized technical topics. Employees were expected to pass the intermediate stage of an internally certified systems engineering course within five years of employment. Management also encouraged employees to take external courses and to participate in public correspondence courses that provided advanced certification.

Formal learning was supplemented by what was referred to as OJD (on-the-job-development), which aimed to enable employees to contribute to the company independently as soon as possible. A manager defined this as *"being able to sell, make the system, and give technical support with cost [considerations] in mind."*

OJD was conducted at essentially two levels: *kachos* (supervisors) assisting *shunin* (employees), and the latter advising *tantos* (inexperienced employees). The importance attached to learning is indicated in the fact that effectiveness at mentoring was included in employees' annual appraisals.

Learning also took place through job rotation. Employees were transferred to different departments in the company, on average, once every five years. They could also be transferred to subsidiaries or to other companies on a permanent or temporary basis, in which case they were termed *shukko*. As discussed further in chapter 6, job rotation entailed making new contacts, adopting new perspectives, and mastering new tasks. In short, training at COMPUJ included learning through a variety of management-controlled channels consistent with the company's bureaucratic pattern of employment relations.[24]

Career opportunities. At the time of our study, COMPUJ had recently introduced achievement-based appraisals. The aim was to enhance the validity of what had traditionally been a subjective, hierarchical process through the use of a management-by-objectives approach. Thus, appraisals encouraged self-development through further training and higher performance.

Appraisals formed the basis for promotion (from tanto to shunin), which generally occurred about seven years after entry into the organization. In the past, about 10 percent of an age cohort had traditionally been selected for faster promotion; however, over the past five years, this had been reduced to less than 4 percent. Thus, promotion was becoming more difficult and a higher proportion of eligible employees occupied lower-ranking positions. The traditional age range for promotion to kacho, for example, was thirty-four to forty years; this had increased to between thirty-six and forty-eight. Promotion to *bucho* (manager) was even more difficult. Accordingly, a new position—*sennin bucho*—had been introduced to "promote" older kachos who had not progressed in the traditional way.

Our survey data confirm that an overwhelming majority (92 percent) of COMPUJ SDs anticipated continuing their careers with the company rather than with other employers. Consistent with a bureaucratic form of ER, this figure was higher than for employees at WBSD (78 percent). Low levels of satisfaction with prospects for promotion are likely to reflect more limited career prospects, as mentioned above. This is confirmed by survey data that indicate that only 19 percent of COMPUJ respondents claimed to be very satisfied or satisfied with their career prospects. This compares with 50 percent who said they were neither satisfied nor dissatisfied and 31 percent who claimed to be dissatisfied or very dissatisfied. Statistical analysis based on this survey item indicates that the attitudes of WB SDS were not significantly different in this respect (F $(1,75)$ = 0.02, p = 0.88).

Yet, although it was reducing the number of new recruits, delaying promotions, and seeking to improve company performance, COMPUJ showed no signs of reducing employment security. As a result, on the one hand, we would expect COMPUJ employees to report a higher level of satisfaction with employment security than comparable employees at WBSD. On the other hand, the strong external labor market position of WB SDs might have encouraged them to view their prospects more positively, even though they had no formal job security. These arguments pointed to an alternative conjecture: there was not much difference in workers' perceptions of their

[24] Interestingly, statistical analysis based on relevant survey data indicates that more experienced COMPUJ respondents (with more than one year's job tenure) did not receive significantly more training than their WBSD counterparts. Nor were they significantly more satisfied with the training they received (F $(1,76)$ = 0.87, p = 0.35).

employment security in the two companies. Analysis of variance with respect to satisfaction with the job security item confirmed this conjecture ($F_{(1,75)} = 1.57$, $p = 0.21$).

In sum, in spite of the reduced career prospects, COMPUJ retained the vestiges of career ladders and employment security, reflecting its endorsement of a more bureaucratic form of ER than at its Australian /U.S. counterpart.

Reward system. Recently graduated SDs at COMPUJ started at the entry pay level. This reflected market worth as established by enterprise-level collective bargaining in the annual *shunto* (Sako and Sato 1997). Pay comprised two main elements: basic pay (including special allowances depending on the number of dependents the employee had and the amount of time spent working away from home) and bonus. Basic pay raises varied with age, educational qualifications, rank, and performance. Age or seniority (which is the same thing when employees of similar age are recruited at entry level) continued to be the most important determinant of pay. By contrast, bonuses depended mainly on company profitability with some adjustment for individual performance. In recent years, increases in the bonus had been curtailed; however, the company and the union still negotiated basic pay and bonuses annually. Management had introduced a larger element of performance-based pay into managers' salary determinations, and, following an agreement with the union, an experiment with a similar system was under way among a group of nonmanagement employees. This experiment enabled the union to assess the desirability of departing from a seniority-based system. As a prelude to introducing the new scheme among the SD staff, management had removed time clocks and given employees more discretion over their use of time.

Survey data suggest that COMPUJ workers were dissatisfied with their pay; only 13 percent claimed to be very satisfied or satisfied, and 53 percent stated they were very dissatisfied or dissatisfied. Statistical analysis based on this survey item shows that COMPUJ workers were significantly more dissatisfied than their WBSD counterparts ($F_{(1,76)} = 26.70$, $p < 0.001$). In short, having a conventional Japanese reward system consistent with a bureaucratic form of ER is not necessarily a source of satisfaction. COMPUJ management was clearly following wider trends in emphasizing performance as a criterion for pay increases, and it continued to be the main criterion for promotion.

Based on the above analysis, we conclude that employment relations at COMPUJ constitute a variant of the bureaucratic pattern. This contrasts with the hybrid occupational/organizational form characteristic of Australian/U.S. knowledge work workflows described earlier. In sum, the evidence supports hypothesis 4 to the effect that *regardless of the type of workflow, the bureaucratic form is more prominent in Japan than in the United States/Australia.*

Institutions, Gender, and Workers' Performance Orientations

We turn now to our hypotheses on the impact of external institutions on gender and on indicators of workers' performance. Our analysis is based on similar comparisons to those used above.

In line with the hypothesis advanced earlier, statistical analysis shows that women employees in MBASV scored significantly higher for both organizational commitment and discretionary effort (for organizational commitment, $F(1,49) = 14.58$, $p < 0.005$; for discretionary effort, $F(1,49) = 21.84$, $p < 0.001$). Statistical analysis indicates that COMPUJ SDs had a significantly lower performance orientation than WBSD workers (for organizational commitment, $F(1,75) = 36.95$, $p < 0.001$; for discretionary effort, $F(1,76) = 4.45$, $p < 0.05$). This is contrary to the hypothesis. This finding can be explained, however, as follows. The role of the SD at COMPUJ was relatively new. There was uncertainty concerning the employees' ability to combine technical and sales functions and hence to perform satisfactorily. As noted above, the SDs were also dissatisfied with their training, believing it to be insufficiently tailored to their current needs. In the meantime, bonuses had been reduced and sales prospects were limited given the recessionary economy. There was also uncertainty about the likely introduction of a new performance-based pay system. For all these reasons, morale at COMPUJ was low, as reflected in their survey responses.

In sum, our findings contradict the conventional view that Japanese ER systems have uniformly superior effects on employees' attitudes toward performance. This view was developed on the basis of international comparisons of production workers; their relevance to knowledge workers or to the majority of noncareer-track women employees is questionable. Further, comparative evidence on the performance orientation of sales workers suggests that, although the above conclusion applies to these employees, the results are less persuasive than assumed.[25]

Institutions and Employment Relations: Is There a Union Effect?

Based on the work of Freeman and Medoff (1984), two hypotheses can be advanced concerning the impact of unions on ER and on employees' performance orientation. The first hypothesis is as follows:

Hypothesis 5a: *ER structures in workflows in which unions have a significant presence will be characterized by higher wages and greater "voice" or worker participation than similar types of workflows with little or no union presence.*

---

[25] We compared a matched pair of sales work workflows, JBS and ABKS, in Japan and Australia respectively. ABK sales workers reported significantly higher levels of discretionary effort than JB employees, but there was no significant difference regarding organizational commitment (for discretionary effort, $F(1,48) = 12.93$, $p < 0.001$).

The second hypothesis is as follows:

Hypothesis 5b: Employees' performance orientation is likely to be higher in workflows in which unions have a significant presence than in workflows in which unions have little or no presence.

According to Freeman and Medoff (1984), unions have two main effects: a monopoly effect, which tends to drive wages and conditions higher than the market rate, and a voice effect, which enables workers to participate in some management decisions. These propositions are included in the first hypothesis above. Freeman and Medoff argue further that both effects sharpen management efficiency and that, as a result of constructive participation in their union, under conditions of trust between management and unions, employees will demonstrate greater commitment to work and their employing organization. This is the basis of the second hypothesis.

Our analysis is restricted to service workflows in which there are sufficient data for comparisons to be made with workflows in which union influence is likely to vary substantially. We distinguish between workflows with *active* and *inactive* unions. In active union workflows, at least 35 percent of the workers are unionized (n workflows = 5; n survey respondents = 325). In inactive workflows, union density is less than 35 percent (n workflows = 4; n respondents = 240). This cutoff point has been chosen because about one-third union density in Australia is sufficient for employees to feel that joining and participating in the union is a legitimate activity accepted by management. The average union density for active and inactive union workflows is 59 percent and 5 percent respectively. All sites are situated in Australia (n = 7, five active and two inactive sites) and in the United States (two inactive union sites).

ER in active and inactive union workflows. In so-called active union workflows, unions tend to influence work practices, employee evaluation processes, training, opportunity and reward systems, and the grievance process. This influence may be achieved through joint consultation and collective bargaining above the workflow level. Common issues include use of full-time rather than part-time employees; employee participation in determining working hours and involvement in work teams; control over individual performance data; introduction of new training, rewards, and promotional structures; and representation in grievance procedures.

To what extent did workers benefit from union attempts to regulate ER? Results based on statistical analysis of relevant survey data can be summarized as follows. In three out of five areas—satisfaction with pay, hours of work, and job security—workers in active union workflows had significantly higher scores than their counterparts in inactive union workflows (for satisfaction with pay, $F_{(1,560)} = 5.76$, $p < 0.05$; for satisfaction with working hours, $F_{(1,559)} = 27.13$, $p < 0.001$); for satisfaction with job security, F $(1,560) = 22.38$, p < 0.001). In one area—influence in decision making—there was no difference. Finally, on items pertaining to satisfaction with training and promotion opportunities, the scores of workers in inactive union workflows were higher. Also noteworthy, overall, the work satisfaction scores of workers in active union workflows were significantly higher than those in inactive workflows (F $(1,528) = 22.39$, p < 0.001).

These findings provide only partial support for hypothesis 5a. Unions make a positive difference in traditional areas but that bargaining beyond the workflow level does not contribute to employees' perceptions that they have more influence. Moreover, nonunion firms, through carefully directed HR practices, can provide better training and promotion opportunities. Overall, however, unions give workers more than they take away. In particular, employees benefit from the sense of security that management did not project at any of the inactive Australian or U.S. sites.

With regard to the hypothesis relating to workers' performance orientation, an analysis of variance indicates no significant differences between the active and the inactive workflows in relation to the variables discretionary effort and organizational commitment (for discretionary effort, F $(1,558) = 1.62$, p $= 0.20$; for organizational commitment, F $(1,560) = 1.98$, p $= 0.16$). Hence, with reference to hypothesis 5b, we conclude that, although unions make a difference in ER by contributing to workers' satisfaction in various ways, they do not appear to foster a stronger performance orientation. This does not mean, however, that the data support the monopoly view of unionism. Much depends on the degree of trust that develops among management, unions, and employees, and in this regard there were no significant differences between workflows in which unions had an active versus an inactive presence.

Conclusion

Our empirical analysis indicates that employment relations, including recruitment, training, career structures, and reward systems, vary systematically. In the service workflows we studied, an attenuated form of bureaucratic ER existed; in the sales workflows, an entrepreneurial pattern with some elements of the knowledge-intensive form predominated; and in the knowledge work workflows, a hybrid consisting of elements of knowledge-intensive and bureaucratic patterns was evident. We argued that these variations were associated with differences in work complexity.

Our findings also point to institutions as important influences on ER. We argued that, regardless of workflow type, in Japanese workflows the institutional effect would result in a more pronounced form of bureaucratic employment relations. The empirical evidence supports this contention but not in a simple way. The evidence demonstrates that Japanese ER, at least

in service workflows, is dualistic, comprising a relatively benign bureaucratic form for overwhelmingly male career-track employees and a less
supportive, highly attenuated bureaucratic form for predominantly female
noncareer-track employees. Further analysis showed that the alleged
higher-performance orientation of Japanese employees did not appear to
be generalizable to knowledge workers or to women employed in service
settings.

Our evidence also shows that active unions can make a difference in ER.
Specifically, they were a positive influence on employee satisfaction with
bread-and-butter issues but not with other matters of importance to
workers—for example, opportunities for promotions and training. The
impact of unions on indicators of employee performance is neither
consistently positive nor negative. Further research is likely to show that
variations in union influence will depend on internal union resources and
dynamics and on union relationships with management.

The implications of our analysis for management-employee relations are
consistent with the findings on control patterns reported in chapter 5 but
need to be seen in the context of the detailed control strategies described
in that chapter. With this qualification, we can see how managers and
workers in service workflows are likely to hold ambivalent attitudes. On
the one hand, managers are under pressure to improve employee productivity and the quality of service and to generate sales revenue. On the other
hand, managers acknowledge the need to provide employees with support,
rewards, and career prospects that compensate them for their limited intrinsic satisfaction and ensure employee retention. Workers, for their part,
welcome the training they receive but are critical that it is not sustained
much beyond the trainee stage and that prospects for internal promotions
are limited. Because of this ambiguity, one would expect management-
employee relations to be a sensitive issue that management would constantly have to address so as to avoid events that would bring such
contradictions to the surface. As we shall see, by and large, first-line management provided this supportive role.

There is a stronger basis for employee-management conflict in Japanese
service workflows than in those in Australia or the United States. The
weight of social convention regarding women's roles tends to restrict overt
conflict, leading to high labor turnover. This is likely to change as women
become more educated, marry later, and oppose discrimination in employment, a practice the Equal Employment Opportunity Act of 1985 is legit-
imizing (Berggren and Nomura 1997: 78–84; Shire and Ota 1997).

Compared to the other two types of workflows and those outside Japan,
the management-employee relations in the sales workflows we studied were
based on a narrower monetary nexus. As noted above, management provided few resources for training and very limited career opportunities. The
quality of relations was likely to hinge on the construction and dynamics

of the reward system, including management's willingness to adjust the system to take into account changing employee requirements. In short, there is a greater risk of overt conflict in sales workflows, particularly when sales are slow. In addition, because they depend on being assertive, sales workers are likely to be more demanding than their service worker counterparts. As noted in the next chapter, it was only in a sales workflow that we came across what was in effect a strike.

In knowledge work workflows outside Japan, the employees in our study were more often in strong labor market positions. They tried to keep their options open vis-à-vis working for other employers or becoming self-employed, while simultaneously seeking to advance in their current organizations. Management responses varied with the scarcity value of the worker's expertise and individual talent. Employees differed in their perceptions of fair treatment. Where human resources were managed carefully and sensitively (as at WBMM), there was little overt conflict. Where these qualities were absent, there was considerable tension, often assuming lateral forms, such as factionalism and interdepartmental rivalries, and reflected in higher labor turnover (WBSD).

Such conflicts were less apparent in Japanese knowledge work workflows, in which a bureaucratic pattern of employment relations (and supporting decision-making methods) ensured strong company identification. This may not result in a high level of satisfaction, but the obligation to minimize overt conflict is well understood and rarely transgressed.

In sum, employment relations, conceived as a general form of control over labor, have a strong bearing on employees' attitudes toward work performance and on management-employee relations more generally. In the next chapter we explore variations in the strategies management uses to control and encourage worker involvement.

5 Control Relations

EARLIER, we argued that vertical relations encompass both employment relations and control relations, the former providing the general, contractual foundation for the exercise of detailed control, that is "the ability of ... managers to obtain desired work behavior from workers" (Edwards 1979: 17). Having analyzed employment relations, we now explore differences in management control and worker participation in decision making across sales, service, and knowledge work workflows, in the context of the two contrasting images of work organization sketched in chapter 1.

Specifically, we ask whether workers are subjected to continuous normative pressure to behave appropriately and constantly monitored and disciplined to that effect, or is normative consensus achieved through consultation and negotiation, implying that workers are trusted to comply with management intentions? This wider issue is examined first by analyzing the dominant forms of management control and then by assessing the extent to which employees participate in the control process. We are also interested in employee responses to different systems of control and participation.

The three primary contemporary forms of management control include measurement of behavior and output, and inculcation of norms either by clans (which may include managers and/or co-workers) or self-regulation (Kirsch 1996). In practice, self-control is influenced by prevailing norms, so we do not pursue this distinction any further. Regarding participation, we inquire whether workers in the three different types of workflows differ in the issues in which they are involved and the amount of influence they exercise (Strauss 1982). We anticipate that forms of control that permit workers more discretion and that provide opportunities to participate in decision making are more likely to foster employee cooperation and effort (Fox 1974; Miller and Monge 1986).

This chapter begins by sketching optimistic and pessimistic perspectives on the changing nature of control. The former emphasize the withering away of behavior-based control and its substitution by normative, peer-based control, while the latter emphasize the potential role of IT in caging employees electronically.

Empirical evidence is presented in the second part of the chapter. With some exceptions, our findings are broadly consistent with expectations. Service workflows are characterized by what is subsequently referred to as *info-normative control*: IT-generated information forms the basis for control but is complemented by normative control through the activities of facilitative supervisors (Frenkel et al. 1995). This differs from *output-procedural control*, which prevails in sales workflows. Here, output measurement based on customer decisions (to apply and qualify for loans) is complemented mainly by enforcement of company procedures. Finally, in the knowledge work workflows, in which co-workers' influence was expected to be the dominant variant of normative control, we find management and co-worker influences working simultaneously. As in the sales workflows, company procedures supplement normative control. We label this *socio-normative control*.

The third and fourth parts of the chapter focus on participation and employee responses respectively. Our discussion of participation is set in the context of differing views of this phenomenon in the contemporary workplace, and our hypotheses are based on the ideal types. With the exception of sales workers, whose reported profile of influence differs from expectations but is nevertheless comprehensible by referring to qualitative data, the findings support our conjecture that service workers are significantly less empowered than knowledge workers. In examining workers' responses to control relations, we concentrate on two aspects: *quality of management-employee relations* (which may range from highly conflictual to highly cooperative) and, related to this, *discretionary work effort*. This concept refers to the additional contribution employees are prepared to make because of their commitment rather than the immediate prospect of improved rewards. Hypotheses relating variations in these variables to the three types of workflows are tested and briefly discussed.

The chapter concludes by relating our findings to the contrasting perspectives on contemporary workplace control outlined at the beginning of the chapter. Since systematic variations in control relations exist and all three types of control are marked by contradictions, we caution against one-sided generalizations, arguing, nevertheless, that images of control serve the useful social function of suggesting desirable possibilities.

Management Control in Theory

In the optimistic vision of the postbureaucratic organization, management control relations have been supplanted by strong ties among co-workers

(Heckscher and Applegate 1994). Zabusky and Barley (1996: 189) argue: "Just as the vertical division of labor gradually overshadowed the horizontal [i.e., lateral] during the early twentieth century, it is conceivable that changing modes of production may occasion a resurgence of horizontally organized work. There is evidence that such a shift may have already begun." This tendency apparently signals the death knell of bureaucracy and foreshadows the emergence of the "empowered" worker." And in spite of survey evidence to the contrary (see chapter 1), there appears to be a trend toward normative control (Knights and Sturdy 1990; Kunda 1992), particularly in settings dominated by co-worker relations and participative management. More direct employee participation does not necessarily signal a significant decrease in management control, however. Indeed, there is some disquiet about "pseudo-participation" (Alvesson 1995) and the role of IT in giving management privileged access to and use of information for control purposes. Not surprisingly, the panopticon metaphor (suggesting a restrictive setting that permits continuous monitoring of behavior) has become more common, implying that workers cannot escape the continuous gaze of management (Sewell and Wilkinson 1992 Menzies 1996; Taylor 1998).

To adjudicate these different perspectives and structure empirical evidence requires an appropriate analytical framework. This framework should be sensitive to the way in which primary and secondary elements of control cohere as distinct forms in different settings. Following Ouchi (1979) and other organization theorists, our basic framework, summarized in figure 5.1, indicates that the form of control exhibited is related to two key factors: management's knowledge of the labor process and management's ability to measure output.

Figure 5.1 shows that different combinations of management knowledge of the labor process and ability to measure output yield different types of control. In reality, management's knowledge is never perfect, and its ability to measure output varies. Furthermore, as Eisenhardt (1985) has observed, costs associated with different forms of control and degrees of uncertainty also enter into management's calculus. Thus, in practice, we anticipated the presence of both primary and secondary elements of control, the latter making up for the deficiencies of the former. Taken together, these various combinations comprise distinct forms of control. These can be mapped to the three ideal types of work organization, facilitating the construction of hypotheses relating these forms of control to the three types of workflows.

Our analysis is sensitive to the way information and measurement vary depending on the form of control being imposed.[1] This is related to the role

---

[1] Information, in the form of employment or behavior measures, can be used in a simple top-down manner, as in a traditional hierarchy, or output targets can be negotiated among workers and management. It is also possible for information relating to control to be used in a bottom-up manner. Measures of behavior may be narrow or comprehensive; they may also

Figure 5.1. Four Types of Management Control

**Management's knowledge
of labor process**

		Perfect	Imperfect
	High	Behavior or output measurement (cell 1)	Output measurement (cell 2)
Management's ability to measure output			
	Low	Behavior measurement (cell 3)	Clan and/or self-control (cell 4)

of IT as a controlling medium. In addition, given the alleged trend toward customer sovereignty (Abercrombie 1991) and the increasingly blurred boundary between customers and workers (Hirschhorn 1985), the potential role of customers as sources of information for control is also addressed. We also acknowledge the potentially active role of workers in shaping forms of control and in participating in decision making, whether through resistance or active consent. In this way our analysis seeks to overcome the somewhat static, management-centered feature of the typology outlined in figure 5.1.[2]

Control Relations in the Ideal Types

With the above comments in mind, we turn now to table 5.1, which outlines our expectations regarding the different forms of control in the three ideal types of control situations.

Control in the bureaucratic ideal type. Under this situation, management is able to program much of the tasks workers undertake and to measure expected outputs. This points to behavior or output control as being the dominant control mechanism. In front-line settings, however, management's knowledge of the labor process and output measurement is imperfect. This stems from management uncertainty regarding customer-worker interactions, given that customers are not programmable and workers cannot

vary in their extent of subjectivity. Thus, more complex work—in which quality rather than productivity is more important—may be more difficult to measure objectively. More comprehensive measures are more likely to contain contradictions. For example, more output may mean that there is some compromise on quality and vice versa.

[2] This is consistent with recent analyses in the labor process tradition that emphasize the need to conceptualize the role of workers as active subjects of workplace control (see P. Thompson 1990; Willmott 1990).

Table 5.1. Control in the Three Ideal Types of Workflows

Ideal type	Bureaucracy	Entrepreneurial	Knowledge-intensive
Management's ability to measure outputs	High	High	Low
Management's knowledge of the labor process	High, imperfect	Low	Low
Form of control in figure 5.1	Behavior or output (cell 1)	Output (cell 2)	Clan supplemented by output and behavior (cell 4)
Customer and IT role in use of information	Information used to reinforce behavior or output control	Customer decisions main basis for control	Customer information plays some role in control
	Key role for IT	Limited role for IT	Limited role for IT
Use of information in control process	Hierarchical	Hierarchical	Negotiated

respond in entirely standardized fashions. The supervisor's presence is likely to affect customers' responses adversely, and there are likely to be too many customer-worker interactions for management to monitor. Measurement of the quality of the interactions is also problematic without customer information. This would require management intervention in customer-worker relations, with the possibility of adversely affecting outcomes, or eliciting information from customers through costly surveys.

These problems suggest that where IT is used extensively, it will be adapted to monitor worker behavior, or management will search for less intrusive, more effective ways of monitoring the quality of service provided. Another possibility is that customer responses, through surveys or mystery shopping (in which staff are employed to act as shoppers for the purpose of monitoring workers' behavior), will be used to evaluate service and to monitor and control behavior (see Fuller and Smith 1991; Leidner 1993; Van Maanen 1991). Since bureaucracies are grounded in the need for conformity to rules, we expect information about customer-worker interactions to be used in a hierarchical manner to reinforce company policies and procedures.

Control in the entrepreneurial ideal type. Workers in entrepreneurial settings have considerable discretion to undertake their work in conformity with management's output expectations. Management therefore has imperfect knowledge of the labor process, particularly if product markets and customer requirements are changing. Accordingly, management focuses on output measurement. In front-line settings, output measures are likely to be directly linked to customer decisions, particularly relating to product sales. As a result of this reliance on discretion in cus-tomer-worker interactions, output control may pose opportunism problems for management. Thus, sales targets may be achieved by means that jeop-ardize long-term company interests. Consequently, we anticipate that output control in the E ideal type may be supplemented by behavior control. As a medium of control, IT is likely to be used to record and update output results, and computers may play some role in generating information to monitor workers' behavior. Overall, however, IT is unlikely to feature as prominently as in the B ideal type. The role of the worker as a quasi-agent, at arm's length from management, suggests that output information in the E ideal type will be used in a hierarchical manner, essentially to encourage higher output.

Control in the knowledge-intensive ideal type. Management cannot program highly customized outputs, and because of the complex nature of knowledge work, which is designed to produce such outputs, attempts to tightly control worker behavior are likely to prove counterproductive. Complex work requires trust in the competence of one's workers (Fox 1974). Output control can also present other major problems. This is because outputs may change as a result of changes in customer require-ments, particularly in the context of changing technology and hence new technical opportunities. This ambiguity around output goals and associated costs poses problems for management in evaluating workers' performance. Nevertheless, management can be expected to use output control, especially information from customers, as a supplement to clan control.

Clan control is based on there being common values in workflows. These are propagated through the use of social mechanisms, such as careful selec-tion, and use of rituals that both induct and subsequently reinforce group norms. In the KI ideal type, the sources of these values and norms are the occupational community or profession (Friedson 1986; Abbott 1988), which has an interest in improving the techniques and status of the specialist occupation, and management, whose interest is in harnessing workers' creativity and skills for the pursuit of corporate objectives. Clan or normative control is paradoxical, for it is potentially the most powerful force in motivating employees yet also the most fragile. Where workers have common values and norms, they are highly motivated, but maintaining harmony between organizational and occupational interests is difficult under changing circumstances (Raelin 1986). Where consensus on common values and norms dissolve, there is likely to be political feuding and con-sequent disorder. Further, reestablishing the clan is usually difficult follow-ing periods of such conflict.

Creating and maintaining normative consensus among physically acces-sible co-workers depends on there being reciprocal social exchange through frequent personal contact. IT-generated information is unlikely to feature as a control mechanism, although it is likely to be used as a medium for clan support.

We are now able to anticipate the forms of control most likely to predominate in the three types of workflows. Control in service workflows is likely to be based primarily on behavior or output measures. Where applicable, IT will be a feature of such control. Sales workflows, by contrast, will be dominated by output controls supplemented by behavior controls. Finally, in knowledge work workflows, the dominant feature will be the use of clan or normative control, supplemented by output control.

Management Control in Practice

An examination of the forms of control practiced in each of the three types of workflows reveals that these can be distinguished as info-normative, output-procedural, and socio-normative control respectively.

Info-normative Control in Service Workflows

In the service workflows, management had considerable but imperfect knowledge of the labor process, and its ability to measure outputs was limited insofar as service work encompasses aspects of quality in addition to productivity. Consequently, management tended to rely primarily on measurement and control of worker behavior. This included inculcating appropriate behavioral norms (Frenkel et al. 1995). Output control was considered a supplementary control mechanism.

It is worth noting in passing that it is difficult to distinguish between behavior and output in front-line work, since behavior is an aspect of service output. As explained below, IT played a pivotal role in behavioral control. IT-generated data permitted the partial substitution of electronic for direct forms of behavioral control, enabling management to concentrate on developing workers' commitment to their role.[3] This approach was pursued mainly by supervisors adopting a facilitative rather than a directive style.

In most workflows, supervisors had been promoted from front-line roles on the basis of their superior performance. Furthermore, a key part of their role as supervisor was dealing with more complex customer calls that service workers passed to them. Consequently, supervisors and their immediate managers were closely acquainted with the labor process. This was confirmed by survey evidence, which showed that more than 77 percent of service workers considered their immediate supervisors knowledgeable

---

[3] IT tends to lower the ratio of supervisors to employees. In IT-intensive service workflows, the average ratio was 1 : 14, versus 1 : 12 for salespeople and 1:7 for knowledge workers.

about the work tasks of their subordinates (n = 611). As indicated in our discussion of control in the B ideal type, this did not mean that supervisors could easily observe employees working. This problem was partially overcome in call centers by the use of phone-call monitoring, in which the supervisor listened into a call and subsequently evaluated the quality of the interaction between worker and customer. Call monitoring, discussed below, covered an average of only five calls per worker in any one week, out of about three hundred calls that workers dealt with in an average week. At three of the workflows (UB1, UB2, and MBASV), management told workers that all phone calls were tape-recorded. This was done more for security reasons—to provide legal evidence when there was a dispute between the organization and a customer—than to control worker behavior.[4]

Management's ability to measure output was limited to sales data, however, although sales were not yet a central aspect of call-center activity. Quantitative measures, such as the number of customers dealt with and the average duration of calls, were relatively easy to compile and to use, especially given workers' reliance on IT and the informating (i.e., abstract information and knowledge-generating) capacity of the technology.

Thus, management relied on IT to supply behavior-related measurements. In addition to those measures mentioned above, these included the time workers took to answer calls and time spent off the phone, supposedly on call-related work. Reflecting a general skepticism about the extent and meaning of these controls, an interviewee aptly remarked: *"You get measured on how many times you scratch your shoulder."* However, these measures conveyed little about customers' perception of the quality of service they received, which was vital to limiting cost increases (through scale economies) and generating revenue (through the provision of services and sales).

The pervasiveness of these controls is acknowledged in survey data. These show that of the 87 percent of service workers who claimed that technology generated performance data (n = 609), 80 percent agreed with the statement "information generated by the technology is used frequently" (n = 535) and 74 percent agreed that it is "a key measure of my work performance" (n = 535). The term *pervasiveness* above refers not only to the scope of the measures used but also to their transparency and frequency. Thus, the computer system at several workflows provided a real-time display of the work status of *all* front-line workers in the call center.

At a majority of the service workflows, an IT manager monitored the work status of front-line workers. This fulfilled two main functions. First, it provided data on the demand and supply of calls, which was useful in

---

[4] Nevertheless, workers criticized this practice. For example, at MBASV, where the official acronym for the recording of the calls was OSCAR, an interviewee claimed that this stood for "Oh, Shit, Calls Are Recorded."

planning labor requirements, including allocating part-time workers and rest periods. Second, it indicated worker productivity: which workers were on and off the phone and, if the latter, for how long they were off duty. At some workflows, this information was made available in real time to supervisors. In either case, supervisors could "see" when work was not being undertaken, and workers were aware of the constant gaze of the computer system.[5] If a supervisor thought a worker was not following rules, the supervisor would "have a quiet word" with the worker involved.[6] In addition, performance data in the form of reports were usually made available to supervisors both daily and weekly. These covered individuals who comprised the various "teams" to which workers were assigned.

The pervasiveness of IT-generated data did not necessarily mean that workers viewed themselves as trapped in an electronic panopticon. Whether this was the case depended on how the information was used (Kidwell and Bennett 1994). In addition to facilitative supervision, two other mechanisms restricted workers' perceptions of being trapped. One was the limited relevance of the data. For example, at MBASV, supervisors viewed the measures and criteria of adequate performance as something over which they had little control. Customer problems that adversely affected these measures, such as the number of calls taken and their average duration, reflected the inefficiencies of other departments, while performance criteria were viewed as imposed by regional managers who were seemingly out of touch with local problems.

The other mechanism at work was management laxity. Not all of the behavior measures at the call centers were translated into financial data, so that senior corporate management did not take them seriously. Although call-center managers did refer to these operational data regularly, they were rarely considered part of a call center's key performance indicators. In addition, because these managers were well aware of the contradictions in various measures, they used the measures as broad indicators of performance trends rather than as specific targets.[7] This meant that lower down the line, supervisors and workers paid attention to the data but did not ascribe overwhelming significance to them.

[5] At UB1, an IT workflow officer who was alerted by the IT system to workers who were off duty for extended times would pick up a pair of binoculars to peer at workers on the other side of the large office. He and his colleagues claimed that this was a comment on the massive size of the new workspace. Workers, however, complained to management that personnel were "spying" on them.

[6] At some workflows, the role of the IT manager qua employee monitor created problems with supervisors, because, in the absence of the supervisor (who may have been off the office floor at meetings or undertaking administrative duties), these managers either contacted workers directly or asked team leaders to undertake what was seen as disciplinary action. Workers and team leaders resented this, and supervisors opposed the action.

[7] The most noteworthy contradiction was between productivity and quality. Taking more calls and keeping calls shorter, on average, in duration were likely to run counter to better customer service.

Digressing for a moment, at JBSV, the Japanese workflow in which phone work and the use of IT were less common than face-to-face interactions with customers, direct supervisory control of worker behavior prevailed. Women workers were expected to behave differently from their male counterparts. Monitoring by male supervisors focused on immediate job tasks, such as handling small errors. By contrast, evaluations of male workers focused on key criteria for promotion to management grades, including the ability to take on new work assignments. Further, in the category of general work behaviors, women were evaluated on their grooming and temperament, while men were evaluated on their decision-making abilities and analytical style.

Service quality, call monitoring, and worker behavior. As mentioned earlier, the quality of customer service could not be measured automatically. In a minority of workflows (TELSV and UB1), management undertook customer surveys and investigated using mystery callers (paid by the company). The survey data were used to ascertain trends in customer sentiment, but the data were not automatically made available to supervisors or employees for the purpose of improving workers' behavior. Instead, complaints concerning individual workers were usually investigated and acted upon.[8] Although this procedure set important limits on how workers interacted with customers, such complaints were rare, particularly since workers were not obliged to give their names to customers. Rather, customer service was assessed through the widespread practice of call monitoring.

With the exception of JBSV, supervisors were expected to monitor a sample of calls that their team members answered.[9] This was done in two nonmutually exclusive ways: by what were commonly referred to as remote and side-by-side monitoring. With remote monitoring, a supervisor "tapped" into the line at his/her own desk, usually without the worker or customer's knowledge. With the side-by-side method, a supervisor also listened in on a separate phone, sitting alongside individual workers.

Call monitoring presumes that if workers are not monitored, they will not execute their tasks appropriately. This apparent lack of trust can be viewed differently, however (Fox 1974). Management claimed that call monitoring could be a vehicle for employees to learn and develop and that it served to transfer "correct" behavior and associated norms from superior workers (supervisors and team leaders) to employees, particularly new

---

[8] In some workflows, management also encouraged individual workers who received letters of praise from customers. At MBASV, for example, managers read such letters at staff meetings. This was received enthusiastically by employees. At UB, as mentioned in chapter 4, positive customer feedback was reflected in service prizes.

[9] The existence of IT makes call monitoring possible. It is not, however, inevitable. Thus, current research at two call centers in Germany suggests that a combination of an influential works council and an attitude on the part of management that such control is inappropriate for relatively highly qualified employees has resulted in an agreement not to undertake call monitoring. More research is needed to establish whether this is a common response.

hires. Thus, call monitoring had two objectives: discipline and development. Which was more prominent depended a great deal on management's behavior, particularly the role played by supervisors.

When a supervisor listened in on a call, he/she assessed the worker's behavior against set criteria. After several calls had been monitored and recorded, the supervisor met with the individual worker to analyze performance. This meeting usually took place relatively soon after the monitoring in private in a meeting room or the supervisor's office. The calls, which had been tape-recorded, were played back and evaluated in the context of the assessment made by the supervisor. Two features of the several sessions we attended were noteworthy. First, supervisors frequently referred to the implications of workers' behavior vis-à-vis customer satisfaction. Workers were asked to put themselves "in the customer's shoes," which helped to persuade workers of the reasonableness of the criteria used to evaluate their calls and the usefulness of the monitoring. Second, employees were often harsher judges of their behavior than their supervisors, indicating that the relevant behavioral norms had been internalized. Employees were given call-related objectives, formally recorded in employee development plans, for the next period. This served to legitimize monitoring by emphasizing its "employee development" component.

In spite of these procedures, not all employees had high regard for call monitoring.[10] The following comments made by workers at TELSV reflect their sensitivity to the practice:

I hate the idea of being listened in by a supervisor. It's very different from helping out, or coaching another worker.

It is stressful. Because you're aware of it, you feel you're being false, trying to cover everything.[11]

Other workers in TELSV, however, saw benefits in call monitoring:

It's good; the supervisor praises you, and I go away in high spirits.

It's a good idea. I wanted an earlier assessment"

By and large, workers in the workflows we studied viewed call monitoring positively. This was evident from the way workers referred to it as "call coaching." Workers also emphasized its developmental aspects, an obser-

---

[10] Chapter 6 discusses the resistance that occurred among workers at several workflows when management attempted to combine call monitoring with elements of co-worker control.

[11] The TELSV workflow was exceptional in that workers were notified before their calls were monitored. This had been negotiated by the union as a protection against arbitrary, intrusive supervision. At a supervisors meeting, a supervisor commented: *"I'm back into call coaching. . . . Boy, they improve and shoot through the calls when they know [I'm listening]."*

vation supported by survey data. Thus, 48 percent of the service workers (n = 611) claimed to be satisfied or very satisfied with the way their job performance was measured, compared with 19 percent who stated that they were very dissatisfied or dissatisfied. The remaining respondents expressed indifference.

In short, call monitoring was a key instrument in the daily "toolbox" of supervisors and managers in the call centers. This was also evident in formal performance appraisals, discussed below.

Facilitative supervision. In addition to call monitoring, management sought to foster employee commitment through performance appraisals, usually conducted annually. Like call-monitoring sessions, these were participative in structure and substance. The structure promoted dialogue between the supervisor and the worker, and the goal was to avoid making the process appear to be a one-way, hierarchically ordered disciplinary exercise.

In addition to sections in which the supervisor wrote his/her comments, the performance appraisal form contained a section in which workers were asked to voice their opinions. Usually there was also a section requesting an agreed-upon statement on performance aims calibrated in terms of the measures used by the company.

Our survey indicates that service workers were favorably disposed to performance appraisals. Seventy one percent of our respondents who had been appraised at their current workplaces agreed that the appraisal process helped them to work better (n = 445); 80 per cent said it was conducted appropriately (n = 449); 65 percent agreed that it was based on facts rather than on management opinion (n = 445); and 67 percent agreed that the criteria were clear to them well ahead of the appraisal itself (n = 444). Thus, although participation in performance appraisals, as in call monitoring, was limited and managerially structured, it played a key role in encouraging management-favored behavior and norms, including acceptance of performance monitoring and associated measures.[12]

In summary, supervisors adopted a facilitative role in which coaching was central to monitoring and performance appraisal (Korczynski et al. 1996). In this, they were assisted by the power of information technology to provide performance data. Gender was also a noteworthy factor. Thus, excluding JBSV, women comprised an estimated 61 percent of the supervisors in the service workflows and about a third of the managers. Survey and qualitative evidence suggests that female supervisors were seen to be

---

[12] By "managerially structured," we mean that management solely determined the format and performance measures. Note that the format for conducting an appraisal, in which a worker meets with his/her supervisor or manager alone, is likely to be more threatening to workers than a format that involves one's co-workers.

more facilitative than their male counterparts.[13] Normative consent to managerial requirements, encouraged by facilitative management, was central to workers' qualified support for the way in which their work was measured and controlled.

Output-Procedural Control in Sales Workflows

In the sales workflows, work was structured so that management could measure output but had imperfect knowledge of the labor process. This led to an output-based form of control supplemented mainly by procedures. This form is broadly consistent with the entrepreneurial ideal type.

In contrast to the tentative and participative way in which measures were used in the service workflows, output measures in the sales workflows were explicitly stated and conveyed to workers in a hierarchical manner. The measures were tied to a commission system, which, as we noted in chapter 4, was based on the principle that more output (number of loans or sales revenue) meant higher earnings and greater job security. This summary is incomplete, however, for reliance on output control presumes that the workers have the means available to produce the desired output without jeopardizing the long-term interests of the firm. This assumption is questionable, for, as pointed out in the discussion of the E ideal type, workers could have made sales to customers whose probability of defaulting was high. Illegal means could also be used to generate sales, thereby exposing the organization to costly litigation. As we shall see, these behavioral problems are likely to be exacerbated when rewards and job security are closely tied to achieving sales goals. In sum, output control comes to be supplemented by other mechanisms. Most important, a separate group of employees (credit analysts) enforced procedural rules.

In the case of home loan consultants, these rules consisted of criteria and customer assessment procedures for granting loans, and loan approvals were typically conditional on meeting these requirements. As a salesperson explained, *"The boss doesn't care [how and when you do your work] as long as you work to the guidelines [i.e., company procedures] and work to the figures in your budget."* At ABKS, where expert systems were used to assess customers' financial status and creditworthiness, these rules were built into the software, making it impossible for salespersons to seek loan approvals for clients who clearly did not qualify. Inevitably, there were mar-

---

[13] Evidence comes from a comparison of mean weighted factor scores based on evaluations by service worker of their supervisors. The latter were divided into men and women. Female supervisors scored significantly higher on questions related to knowledge and supportiveness and on two other factors over which supervisors had considerable influence—team effectiveness and team cohesion. Customer service representatives working under women supervisors also scored significantly higher on an item in which they were asked to rank their satisfaction with management. See appendix 3.

ginal cases and cases in which salespersons were seen to be "stretching" the criteria. This led to strained relationships between salespersons and credit analysts, discussed more fully in chapter 7.

Managers at ABK conducted spot checks on loan requests to see that salespeople were following company procedures. At MBAS, management had introduced a form of mystery shopping that led to reports on individual sales workers' behavior. Following requests from managers, referrers (e.g., estate agents, accountants, and solicitors who refer customers to salespeople) also reported on employees' behavior. Evaluating sales performance in relation to sales targets and making salespeople sensitive to both their failures and successes in achieving targets were also used to encourage normative compliance. At MBAS, for example, collective (team or area) output was displayed and discussed at weekly meetings.

In contrast to the service workflows, first-line management (the equivalent of supervisors) had little detailed knowledge of the behavior of individual salespersons. Indeed, at ABKS, "Executive Consultants," as they were formally known, were not even recruited from the ranks of front-line workers. The role of these managers and their counterparts at MBAS (known as "Development Managers") was threefold: to scout for new business by contacting new referrers and maintaining established contacts;[14] to develop new products; and to ensure that sales targets were being met. Supervisors coached new recruits, and salespersons who failed to meet their targets for two or more successive months were required to report on required visits to referrers. In addition to monitoring sales workers' behavior, managers occasionally adjudicated conflicts between salespersons and credit analysts regarding approval of specific loans.

The geographical separation of managers from their mobile sales force made knowledge of the labor process more problematic. It is perhaps not surprising, therefore, that statistical analysis indicates that salespersons rated their supervisors as having significantly less knowledge of their labor process than did service workers ($F_{(2,857)} = 10.64$, $p < 0.001$). In addition, unlike the situation at the call centers, management was unable to observe customer-worker interactions unobtrusively.

As noted earlier, management relied mainly on output measures.[15] These related to sales revenue or the number of loans issued and the value of other financial products sold within a specified period. Thus, output could be relatively unambiguously measured, and the measures were less widely dis-

[14] These managers sometimes attended sales meetings, especially at JB, where it was customary at a certain stage in negotiations with a client firm for the salesperson to invite his/her manager to attend a meeting with the customer. Management reported that observing how the customer representatives interacted with the worker provided crucial information on the salesperson's performance.

[15] At JBS, this was not so straightforward. Negotiations with customers could go on for months, making it difficult to have clear, meaningful, quantifiable output measures. Hence, management relied on behavioral measures.

tributed than in the service workflows. IT was used mainly to facilitate loan approvals and processing, rather than to monitor performance, for, as we noted in chapter 3, there was relatively little IT investment in front-line work and hence the informating potential for use as part of a control system was limited.[16]

In contrast to the service workflows, management in the sales workflows gave low priority to performance appraisals. With a few exceptions, workers and managers tended to view the appraisal process as a bureaucratic imposition taking time away from the main goal of increasing sales revenue. This is noteworthy, because formally the appraisal process included goals other than output; at MBAS, for example, the assessment included items on the quality of relations with colleagues and referrers.

As discussed in chapter 4, sales workers at ABKS and MBAS received a base salary and a commission on sales of financial products. Management also set monthly sales targets for individuals, which usually varied according to experience. The intent of this reward system was to provide strong incentives for employees to sell loans and other products and to ensure that company costs varied closely with revenue generation. The contradiction of this system, however, is that it operated mainly through a narrow performance-related scheme, leading to low trust among employees.

Prior to the adoption of an entrepreneurial form of work organization at ABKS and MBAS, sales managers (as they were called) received salaries and little or no performance-related pay. Up to a limit, they were entrusted to approve their own sales of loan products. The entrepreneurial system changed this by encouraging a greater emphasis on sales and at the same time increasing the risk of "bad loans." As a manager remarked, *"With the commission system, you develop mercenaries."* Another worker said that *"the commission system provides an incentive, but it causes problems around honesty."* In an effort to avoid these problems, management decided to reduce the salespersons' discretion, in effect transferring the credit analysis function to a different group of employees. As discussed in chapter 6, this led to continuing tension between front- and back-office staff. In addition, as noted above, management at ABKS and MBAS introduced supplementary techniques to monitor sales workers' behavior.

In short, dependence on a performance-based reward system in the sales workflows undermined reliance on output control, encouraging greater emphasis on rule-based behavior control (i.e., the application of output procedural control). In addition, management reduced the sales workers' discretion, leading to significantly lower trust in management than among service and knowledge workers ($F (2,861) = 9.77$, $p < 0.001$). This senti-

---

[16] IT was used to record loan approvals and settlements and sales of other financial products. These data were presented for individual salespersons and for "teams" in relation to the budget and past experience. Trend graphs were also generated. These data were made available to all ABKS and MBAS managers on a weekly basis.

ment is nicely captured in this comment made by a salesperson: *"Most people use the place, because they [the company] use us."*

Socio-normative Control in Knowledge Work Workflows

The control system in knowledge work workflows rested on a combination of management-inspired norms, the imperfect measurement of project or team outputs, and peer norms. In practice, peer control was less significant than in the knowledge-intensive ideal, and of the three forms of control, the socio-normative kind appeared to be the least stable, tending toward worker anomie in at least two of our four workflows. This results, we contend, from an overreliance on a single form of control, rather than, as in the service and sales workflows, dependence on a system in which a primary form of control was supplemented by secondary mechanisms.

In most of the knowledge work workflows—which, in three cases, covered systems developers broadly defined and, in another, money market dealers—the degree of occupational specialization required meant that most first-line managers did not have detailed knowledge of the workers' labor process. For example, a project manager at WBSD said: *"Ten years ago you could be a jack of all trades, but today things are specialized. You see this in adverts: there are separate adverts for business analysts and programmers, whereas in the old days these were combined in a single job ad."* Similarly, in money market dealing, a trader could not usually substitute for a distributor and vice versa.

Knowledge obsolescence was also a concern. For example, unless project managers worked with new software and distributors worked with structured deal experts to develop new derivatives, it was difficult to keep abreast of the rapid changes occurring in these fields. Thus, statistical analysis, derived from qualitative research, confirmed our hypothesis that knowledge workers perceived their immediate managers as significantly less knowledgeable about the labor process than did respondents in service workflows ($F_{(2,859)} = 10.64$, $p < 0.001$). This finding is consistent with the profile of the KI ideal type, in which knowledge workers and their immediate managers are more likely to exchange information and negotiate in setting goals than are service or sales workers. This hypothesis was also confirmed by statistical analysis, which showed that knowledge workers perceived that they had significantly greater direct influence and involvement in setting goals for their teams than did service and sales workers ($F_{(2,859)} = 80.85$, $p < 0.001$).

Having limited acquaintance with emerging technologies and products, managers tended to rely on informal behavioral measures. Conversations with other employees and customers, though imprecise, were the main basis for judgment. Thus, at WBSD, managers emphasized the importance of constantly "getting a feel" for the work of individuals by walking around and talking to their immediate managers, colleagues, and customers/users. At WBMM, the open-plan, congested, "goldfish-bowl" nature of the money market desk meant that managers could hear and see individual workers making deals. In addition, managers at WBMM kept in contact with some of its larger clients and in this way obtained information about the behavior of particular workers.

At COMPUJ, management mainly gathered information on the behavior of more junior workers and trusted more experienced workers. As a manager put it: *"My subordinates have been working under me for five years now, so I know the extent of their productivity and capabilities. All I do is listen to their broad project plan and give them direction. After that, they're on their own."* For a number of managers at COMPUJ, information from customers was a key basis for control. One manager remarked that *"the customer evaluates the employee."*

Despite a keen interest in outputs, management in the knowledge work workflows found measuring and hence drawing conclusions about employee effectiveness difficult. Distinguishing individual output in the context of highly interdependent project work and assessing teamwork output where project goals, technology, or methodologies were changing during the course of the project were just some of the challenges.[17] Nevertheless, output control was not impossible. In WBMM, a key part of the control system was that performance-related pay in the form of a bonus was related to team performance. Backed by data on each individual and close acquaintance with employees, managers claimed that, on average, fewer than 10 percent of employees each year felt aggrieved at the outcome of their appraisals and related bonus earnings. Interviews with workers following receipt of their annual bonuses corroborated this opinion.

Management at COMPUJ also measured outputs reasonably precisely, but employees contested their meaning and hence their relevance. As in the sales workflows, output was related to purchasing decisions made by customers. Each worker had sales targets, and evaluations of performance were partly related to performance against these targets. In addition, customers would inform management of their satisfaction with projects. Although the central HR department favored using sales figures as the sole criterion for judging performance, all the supervisors and managers we interviewed opposed this approach and emphasized the importance of adopting a longer-term, wider perspective on performance. This clash was essentially between those favoring the output-oriented logic associated with the E type of work organization and those favoring the less precise, normative logic of the KI ideal type.

---

[17] In TELSD, employees failed to deliver a project to a client on time and, consequently, the company involved was liable for financial penalties. Management argued that the project had not failed, because it could be used to generate further business with the client and hence would boost the longer-term profitability of the organization considerably.

A lack of management consensus on business unit goals opens the door to contestation over means. Thus, at COMPUJ, senior line managers maintained two very different conceptions of integration of the sales and design engineers. Some managers believed it meant combining engineering and sales roles at the individual level, while others emphasized sharing knowledge and working together collectively. This tendency toward anomie threatened team cohesion and limited the effectiveness of project teams.

By contrast, WBMM practiced a modified yet effective form of clan control. The following four features supported consensus around values and norms: (1) favorable antecedent conditions in the form of especially tailored personnel selection and induction procedures and a team-based performance-related reward system; (2) the presence of effective, cooperative worker-managers (i.e., technically superior managers who continued to work closely with other team members in fulfilling team goals); (3) a team with a successful reputation to defend; (4) clearly articulated objectives at the individual and team level; and (5) secondary mechanisms supporting the maintenance of normative consensus.

Managers on the WBMM team spent most of their time on the desk, interacting informally with employees: As one of the managers remarked, *"I only do an hour or two managing; the downside is that sometimes things don't get done—things that should be put on paper, but overall this is the best way."* Team members saw the three managers as highly competent but "tough." Other team members shared this opinion, as indicated by the following remark: *"Near enough is not good enough here. You must be good, and you have to work hard, without support. It's a tough environment and a lot is expected of you."*[18] The MM desk had been the most successful in the dealing room over the past two years. This status was seen to need continual defense in the face of members of other desks who "want[ed] to knock us off our perch."

There was one common denominator regarding objectives, however: the goal was to make money. How this was done was a matter of "looking, listening, and learning." As a dealer explained, *"The deals we are doing today are quite different from last year. . . . It's a rapidly changing industry and you have to keep on top of it all the time."*

Among the supporting mechanisms managers used to reinforce team cohesion was relocating back-office employees responsible for checking transactions to an area in close physical proximity to front-line employees. This reduced the status gap between front-line and processing staff and highlighted management's desire to encourage adherence to company policies and procedures in deal making.

---

[18] One of the women dealers remarked that *"Once I was upset, I was crying. I got dragged into a room and was told not to cry at work."* She maintained that the managers were not interested in knowing her as a person, only as a co-worker. She lamented: *"There's this no personal contact attitude."*

Strong team cohesion based on common norms was evident from remarks gathered in the course of our research. The following are some examples:

Everyone is so focused and hard working, you feel you are letting the team down if you go home early one night.

You need to weigh pros and cons of time spent with different customers, as long as you can convince your peers. If you don't do well on something, they will tell you.

If you have a problem, you can sort it out with [the manager]. Or, more generally, we debate and sort it out in our meeting.

In TELSD and WBSD, several of the five conditions noted above were absent. In TELSD, as indicated in chapter 4, the recruitment and reward procedures reflected the larger and more bureaucratic organization of which TELSD was a small part. Managers worked closely with employees on projects; however, they were not effective in conveying clear objectives, especially relating to project methodology. Indeed, in spite of a formal water-fall methodology, in which each stage of a project followed in a planned sequence, the group used more of an iterative, spiral approach, in which various aspects of the project progressed simultaneously as a series of experiments (Mankin, Cohen, and Bikson 1996: chap. 8).

The use of this methodology was an unintended consequence of several factors, including limited management experience with a new type of project and the *laissez-faire* style of the project manager. Difficulties also arose in managing relationships between workers who had little experience working together and specialist networking software engineers employed by a contractor who was formally accountable to the project manager but not responsible for the software engineers' behavior. Individuals had considerable discretion to work on issues that did not appear to be part of the critical path of the overall project. Although the workers enjoyed this high level of discretion, management was criticized for its "lack of direction" and "disorganization." As one worker remarked: "[The project managers] lack project management skills—they underestimated the time to complete tasks and worry about technical issues but neglect other issues. . . . They don't understand the business environment." The project manager remarked that he wanted to be seen as part of the team rather than as the team leader. One consequence was that occasions for cultivating common norms were underutilized. Project team meetings were not held on a regular schedule, were relatively unstructured, and were dominated by discussions of technical issues. Strategic and methodological matters were largely neglected.

The *laissez-faire* management style also resulted in an absence of formal control mechanisms, which might have substituted for the lack of higher-level normative consensus. For example, during the early phase of the project there were no formal quality assurance reviews or risk management processes established. Only when the project was endangered by the possibility of litigation for failing to complete the work by an agreed-upon deadline was a new manager put in charge. This resulted in a more structured approach consistent with the original intention.

In contrast to TELSD, WBSD was situated within a broader organizational context that favored decentralized, action-oriented management. This was partly reflected in the presence of a performance-related bonus system, based on individual contributions.[19] Unlike the situation at WBMM, this scheme was managed in a way that focused on individual performance. There was little emphasis on the contribution of individuals to project (collective) success. This was especially the case as the bonus period approached. A manager remarked that *"the bonus is a sickness. It causes dysfunctional behavior around the end of the year. Managers use it as a crutch instead of relying on good management principles [to manage employees]."* The project manager's expertise was problematic. He had considerable project management experience but admitted to knowing little about the new object-oriented design technology that was initially used on the project. Further, the workers on the project had only occasionally worked together in the past, so there was no collective reputation to defend. The major problem, however, was similar to one at TELSD: the lack of consensus among those involved in the project. The implications were even more serious than at TELSD, since the lack of consensus affected goals and means.

To elaborate, one of the main projects being undertaken at WBSD concerned the design and introduction of new software for financial brokers. At the same time, the corporate IT group had been pressing senior management to introduce a new subsidiary-wide, object-oriented, design-based systems architecture. The aim was to increase flexibility in reconfiguring elements for specific business applications, while speeding up the use of new technology and hence improving service productivity and quality. The design engineers who dominated the corporate IT group saw the broker applications project as a vehicle for introducing the new architecture, since the project was small in scale and nonstrategic from a business standpoint.

Senior management's decision to experiment with object-oriented design had two broad organizational implications. First, it signaled the company's intention to adopt a controversial new technology with which many systems

[19] Contra the KI ideal type and similar to the approach used at WBSD, management used this information to make hierarchical rather than negotiated decisions. Other managers reasonably familiar with the work of individual employees were consulted before decisions about relative performance and bonuses were made. These comments were conveyed directly to the individual workers involved. With rare exceptions, there were no subsequent negotiations with employees.

developers were as yet unfamiliar; and, second, it implied the adoption of a more centralized approach to systems development, a tendency the computer specialists responsible for business application projects fiercely resisted. The upshot was described as akin to "religious wars" fought with passion, faith, and proselytizing zeal. More details are provided in the following chapter. Here our focus is on the control-related consequences in the broker applications project.

The first consequence was that the project manager lost control, mainly because he was unacquainted with the new technology. As a result, leading corporate IT managers were given an opportunity to "hijack" the project. In the words of one senior manager, *"We didn't allow [the project manager] to manage it. He was pushed around by [the senior IT manager]."*

The second consequence was that the workers on the project were ambivalent: they were eager to learn and apply object-oriented design (through experimentation and attendance in special courses); however, they criticized "the guru" (representing corporate IT) for mystifying the nature and implementation of this technology in an untried financial services environment (see chapter 7). The structured techniques (data flow diagrams and data models) that comprised the waterfall methodology initially envisaged for the project were dispensed with in favor of a spiral approach involving continuous experimentation and testing. Lack of progress and considerable intramanagement conflict eventually resulted in a decision to revert back to a modified waterfall approach (which incorporated some parallel writing and prototype testing) and to sever the link with the new architecture. Thus, some six months later, the project manager resumed control and employees reported being much more satisfied.[20]

In summary, the experience in WBMM shows that normative control can be effective, whereas the experiences in TELSD and WBSD highlight its fragility and hence the potential for anomie and consequent loss of control. When order is restored, it appears to be accompanied by more formal, rule-based methodologies, which supplement normative control. This was the case at WBMM, where management developed secondary control mechanisms, alongside and to reinforce normative controls. Contrary to the KI ideal type, which emphasizes the role of co-workers as a source of normative control, their influence varied, from significant at WBMM to less important than the role of management at the other knowledge work workflows, including COMPUJ.[21]

---

[20] The project manager of the broker applications project conceptualized the change in two dimensions: the stability of the business problem and the stability of technology. The connection between the project and the architecture led to an unstable business problem, while the object-oriented design technology was unstable. In his view this was a "recipe for disaster." The resulting problems led management to reposition the project into the stable business problem/stable technology cell of the two-by-two matrix.

[21] At COMPUJ, normative control emanated mainly from management rather than from employees. Hierarchically structured performance appraisals—in which workers had no access

In line with what one would expect in a workflow approximating the KI ideal type, the roles of the customer and of IT were not especially important. In WBMM, managers occasionally consulted key customers, and IT was increasingly used to monitor market information and in constructing complex deals. In TELSD, the customer was important at the preresearch bid stage of the project but less so in the implementation stage, when our research was undertaken. The situation was similar in COMPUJ, where close consultation between clients and sales engineers was aimed at securing feasible solutions. In WBSD, the business manager, in the role of internal customer, left implementation in the hands of the systems developers. As a medium for the exchange of information and team problem solving, IT was less important than face-to-face relations at the three workflows mentioned above.[22]

Two reasons can be advanced for the relative weakness of co-worker influence in the knowledge work workflows we studied. One is that these workflows were in profit-oriented organizations, where management-inspired organizational values and norms are most likely to dominate. The other reason is that, unlike the established professions, such as medicine and law, the occupations we are analyzing are not buttressed by powerful professional organizations. Consequently, occupational identities are weak. This was especially the case at COMPUJ, where the assumption of long-term, if not lifetime, employment prevails.

Overview of control in the three types of workflows

Our evidence indicates that different forms of control are exhibited in the three types of workflows. *Info-normative control*, characterized by the use of pervasive IT-generated data and facilitative management, predominated in the service workflows. This form of control departs from the B ideal type in three main ways: (1) the extent to which normative elements were invoked; (2) the facilitative rather than directive nature of the supervision; and, (3) insofar as behavior and output control can be distinguished, the extent to which these appeared to be complementary rather than substitutes for each other.

Output procedural control, in which the control of sales targets was the primary element of control, was a feature of the sales workflows. Output measures encouraged sales volume. These were complemented by policies and procedures and management practices aimed at containing opportunistic behavior. These measures only served to reinforce the low trust

---

to their evaluations and had only a sense of their outcome from subsequent promotion decisions—were taken seriously at COMPUJ. This control was supplemented by output controls—sales targets set unilaterally by management.

[22] This does not mean that knowledge work cannot be accomplished through the medium of IT. Indeed, "virtual teams," working in different locations, are becoming more common (Oravec 1996). They were not a feature of our sample, however.

between management and salespeople. The only exception was the sales force at the Japanese workflow JBS. Here there was less emphasis on output control, greater earnings stability, and higher employment security, resulting in more trusting relationships. Overall, however, the control mechanisms used in the sales workflows closely resembled those used in the E ideal type.

Knowledge workers were subject to some monitoring of their behavior and some output measuring, but, because of the problems associated with such mechanisms, management relied mainly on *socio-normative control*. This resembled the clan control found in the KI ideal type, except that in the latter no distinction was made between co-workers and management as potentially competing sources of norms and values. Our analysis indicated that not only changing circumstances threatened normative consensus but the existence of different goals and interests. Thus, anomie is an ever-present threat to efficiency in knowledge work workflows.

Worker Participation in Theory

Our analysis of control suggests that differences in the extent of worker participation in decision making in the three types of workflows may be less clear-cut than one would expect based on the ideal types. Nevertheless, there is something of a linear trend so that service workers participate least in decision making, knowledge workers participate most, and sales workers occupy the middle ground. These findings are at odds with some pessimistic and optimistic visions of contemporary control relations and consistent with analyses that emphasize continuity rather than change in this area (Ichniowski et al. 1996; Brewer 1996; Nonaka and Takeuchi 1995).

Contra the pessimists, the service workers in our study had opportunities to participate in work-related decision making, mainly through discretion in how they accomplished their tasks; involvement in off-line project work; and discussions in team meetings. Similarly, there is little evidence that the labor of knowledge workers is becoming routinized and subject to significant bureaucratic control. Contra the optimists, front-line service workers have not really been "empowered," if this is taken to mean having substantial discretion to make job-related decisions (Davidow and Uttal 1989; Davidow and Malone 1992; Quinn 1992; Schlesinger and Heskett 1992). Although sales workers have more discretion than service workers, as we have noted, they too are restricted by company policies and procedures. Knowledge workers have considerable job and, where relevant, project-related autonomy; however, they do not appear to exercise much influence in wider workplace or organizational matters. These impressions will be examined more carefully below.

Before outlining the level of participation we expected in each of the three types of workflows, two conceptual distinctions need to made. First, *scope*

Table 5.2. Worker Participation in the Three Ideal Types of Workflows

Ideal type	Bureaucratic	Entrepreneurial	Knowledge-intensive
Influence at task level	Low—tasks programmed and hence limited worker discretion	High—management is output-focused; workers decide how tasks should be arranged	High—task complexity and goal ambiguity permit high task discretion
Influence above task level	Low—workers are recipients of directives and information	Low—workers act as quasi-agents at arm's length from management	Medium-high—outputs are negotiated

of participation refers to the nature of the issues in which workers participate. These may be mainly operational or work related, and/or strategic and organizational. Second, the *amount of influence* may range from the regular receipt of information where influence is minimal to having a major say in decision making where influence is clearly significant.

Participation in the Ideal Types

Table 5.2 summarizes our expectations regarding participation in the three ideal types of workflows. Consistent with a factor analysis that helps to delineate the scope of participation, we distinguish between the amount of influence at the task level (over job-related matters) and above task level (over workplace and wider organizational issues), respectively.

Bureaucratic ideal type. In the B ideal-type workflow, participation is low, at, and above task level. Given predictable markets, management is able to program tasks to limit worker discretion. Because the logic of a bureaucracy implies that there are commands and a flow of information from the apex to the base of the organization, participation in decision making is also low above the task level. Accordingly, worker influence is severely restricted.

Entrepreneurial ideal type. In the E ideal-type workflow, participation is high at the task level and low at workplace and organizational levels. Product market uncertainty in particular means that tasks cannot be programmed. Thus, workers are granted high discretion in undertaking their work. Participation above the task level, however, is low because workers are effectively recruited as quasi-agents within a contractual framework determined by management in anticipation of projected costs and revenue.

Knowledge-intensive ideal type. In the KI ideal-type workflow, participation is high at and above task level. This is largely because of work and output uncertainty. Complex work cannot be programmed, and outputs are difficult to precisely define, bearing in mind that the work is often innovative, highly customized, and liable to change during the course of execution. The expectation of high levels of employee influence at both task and above-task (project) levels finds wide empirical support (Derber, Schwartz, and Magrass 1990; Ramsay, Panteli, and Beirne 1998; Partnoy 1997).

Participation in policy-level decisions is most likely among groups that hold strategic power. SDs who control technology in large organizations tend to fall into this category, whereas money market dealers usually do not (Eccles and Crane 1988)[23] Thus, referring to systems developers, Fincham et al. suggest that "strategic practices themselves are less a top-down initiative, and more a part of the decision making process around IT, as expert groups themselves define the strategic context via their knowledge of the organization and wider technological environment" (1994: 6). This does not mean that these knowledge workers are likely to dominate, for, as we noted earlier in discussing WBSD, experts are not always united in their views, and typically several user groups are involved in decisions that senior management must broker.

Worker Participation in Practice

We examine participation mainly though not exclusively through the results of our employee survey. Respondents were asked how much direct influence and involvement they had in decision making in nine work-related areas. A factor analysis yielded two distinct factors broadly corresponding to task-level and above-task-level decisions, respectively (see appendix 2 for details).

Participation in Service Workflows

From our discussion of participation in the three ideal types of workflows, we expected that service workers would have significantly less influence at task and above-task levels than sales or knowledge workers. ANOVA confirms this hypothesis at the task level (F $(2,853) = 236.93$, p < 0.001). Qualitative research findings also support this finding. Thus, in all the service workflows, management carefully delineated jobs using job descriptions. These tended to standardize worker behavior, although, as noted in chapter 3, they allowed some task participation consistent with the flexibility required to deal with customers. Where task participation was formally encouraged, it was tightly controlled. Thus, at AINSV, workers were allo-

---

[23] This is because money market dealers are usually only one group in an investment banking institution consisting of other important functions.

cated different levels of authority to effect transactions. For example, the most junior workers, at level one, were not permitted to change a customer's address on the IT system. Any attempt to do so was automatically blocked by the system. By contrast, workers at level two were allowed to make such changes.

Although task participation was low, the presence of levels of authority in this workflow and similar developments at other service workflows indicated a trend toward increased task participation. At MBASV, for instance, workers had recently been given what management termed "empowerment." "Empowerment" involved giving workers authority to increase customer credit limits within certain tightly defined boundaries. These transactions were rigorously monitored and enforced. Thus, at MBASV when staff made an error in extending credit limits, they faced the prospect of "disempowerment," which entailed a reprimand by the call center manager and the possibility of dismissal if the error was made again. In team meetings and in informal discussions with their supervisors, workers opposed this devolution of authority. Management subsequently toned down the emphasis on punishment for noncompliance, in effect bringing procedures in line with practices at most comparable companies.

As we anticipated, based on the theoretical literature and our survey data, ANOVA confirmed that the service workers experienced significantly lower levels of influence above the task level compared with their sales and knowledge worker counterparts ($F (2,856) = 165.22$, $p < 0.001$). This was in spite of the presence of various direct participation mechanisms, such as process-improvement groups at AINSV and MBASV. At UB1 and UB2, a workplace consultative council spanned both workflows. At TELSV, a trade union was the main channel of influence. Unions were recognized at three of the workflows but had an important impact on decision making only at TEL, where senior management and the leaders of the national union had recently embarked on a "participative" approach. This involved seeking union influence in qualitative issues that had traditionally been regarded as under management prerogative. Union influence was clearly visible in some areas—in the (limited) use and (favorable) treatment of part-time workers; the controlled use of call monitoring; (fair) performance development reviews; and (restricted) use of individual performance data—but not discernible in other matters (IT design, the introduction of new forms of teams, and skill-based pay). Nonetheless, survey responses and interviews indicated that workers at TELSV *did not perceive themselves* as having strong "direct influence and involvement" above the task level.

Participation in Sales Workflows

We expected sales workers to report relatively high task participation, on a par with knowledge workers. Although their influence was significantly greater than that of service workers, it was also significantly *lower* than that of knowledge workers. One explanation for this difference is that the sales workers had less influence in determining their goals (sales targets) than the knowledge workers, who usually controlled their relationships with clients (money market dealers) and the way projects were undertaken (systems developers). Furthermore, in the case of the sales workers, management was concerned about the possibility of opportunistic behavior. Hence, as explained earlier, the sales workers were subject to various procedural and behavioral controls. Nevertheless, within these constraints, salespeople had substantial autonomy. For example, a leading salesman at ABKS had created a tight network of referrers (financial advisers, accountants, and solicitors) who would refer clients to one another. A key part of maintaining this network and facilitating mutual support was the weekly game of golf. Another salesman, at MBAS, used his Italian background to create a web of contacts in the community that helped him find customers.

With regard to influence above the task level, ANOVA analysis showed a pattern similar to the one for task-level participation. This contradicted our expectations, which pointed to a low level of influence similar to that of service workers but different from that of knowledge workers. How can this be explained?

Qualitative evidence indicates that, although they were hired as quasi-agents, the sales workers in our study did exercise some influence on management policy. For example, when management at MBAS revised the commission system—effectively lowering the rates for higher-paid salespeople—the salespeople refused to work until the policy was reversed. Subsequently, a compromise was reached. Furthermore, these consistently successful salespeople were regularly asked for their input on new advertising and marketing strategies. These "high fliers" were also more successful at using their management contacts to obtain authorization for loans that credit analysts initially opposed. Indeed, in one case at ABKS, the most successful salesperson persuaded senior management to change the bank's policy on extending mortgages when two or more applicants would be splitting the mortgage payments. Finally, some salespeople also claimed to have a significant influence over product development.

In short, on the one hand, contrary to the E ideal type, the salespeople in our study were less autonomous in undertaking their tasks than anticipated. On the other hand, there were more opportunities for influence above the task level than expected.

Participation in Knowledge Work Workflows

Evidence referred to earlier indicates that employee influence was significantly higher among knowledge workers than service and sales workers, both at task and above-task levels. This is in line with what we expected based on our discussion of the KI ideal type. By referring to qualitative data, this picture can be fleshed out more fully, revealing variations in intersite influence.

WBSD was typical in that knowledge workers were granted substantial autonomy at the task level. The project manager made no attempt to narrowly define how tasks were to be completed. Rather, he viewed his role as creating a consensus around the project's general goals and methodology. The degree of task-level autonomy knowledge workers were given was highlighted when one of the workers left the company. The rest of the team subsequently found out that he left a "black hole" in the project, as a result of insufficient ongoing integration by the project manager and limited communication among team members. This reflects a more general tendency evident at TELSD for projects based on high levels of worker autonomy to spin out of control.

The integration issue was part of a wider project management problem at WBSD. As noted earlier, the broker applications manager lost control of the project in its initial stages because other IT experts were keen to use the project as a vehicle to introduce object-oriented design technology more widely. Although this decision might have opened up the new architecture to worker influence, this did not occur, for three main reasons. First, systems developers preferred to immerse themselves in project technicalities than to engage in "religious wars" conducted at high levels of abstraction. Second, most SDs had very limited knowledge about and expertise in the new technology, particularly in relation to the development of a new architecture. Hence, they were reluctant to become involved in what were often acrimonious and lengthy discussions. Third, past experiences in which workers were given limited influence had tended to breed apathy. For example, senior management had earlier encouraged participation above the task level through the creation of an online, Lotus notes-based discussion forum. Initially, the SDs had participated actively; however, a lack of senior management involvement, and hence limited use of the SDs' input as part of the IT decision-making process, led to the demise of the forum.

In common with other knowledge workers, WBMM dealers saw themselves as having substantial task-level influence. Together with strong coworker control, this had a paradoxical effect. On the one hand, the dealers were always seeking more innovative solutions to client problems, particularly in view of the prevailing norm that individual success should be celebrated and emulated. This encouraged experimentation. On the other hand, failure could lead to public humiliation by a team where "there is only room for the best." The net consequences of these opposing tendencies appeared to depend on the confidence and expertise of individual dealers. More successful dealers were much less concerned about failure than novices, an unintended positive outcome from an efficiency standpoint.

It would be wrong to exaggerate the extent of workers' above-task-level participation at WBMM. It was considerable, albeit limited largely to sectional, or desk-level, issues. For example, in addition to informal discussions about client and trading strategies among groups of front-desk workers, weekly meetings focused mainly on market and client trends, client strategy, training, IT upgrading for front-line support, and the relations among groups at various desks. These meetings were marked by considerable debate in which one or more of the three managers played a brokering role. Some individuals were more vocal than others, and some carried more influence. Overall, however, influence depended on expertise, based on current success and/or reputation, rather than formal position.

Of particular note was the limited discussion devoted to issues outside the direct interests of the desk. Consequently, issues of wider organizational significance were rarely discussed. When some dealers complained that management paid too little attention to conveying the broader picture, managers countered by arguing that the company was based on a federal structure in which success depended on the autonomy of the parts (desks and departments), which in turn depended on each team meeting or exceeding its goals.

Employee influence at the task level was also relatively high at COMPUJ, although its more hierarchical authority structure served to limit employee influence, particularly with regard to project-level decisions. Employees lacked influence above this level; however, unlike workers at the other knowledge work workflows, workers at COMPUJ were represented by an enterprise union. This institution had some influence on wider HR decisions, including the introduction of a new performance evaluation system and organizational restructuring.[24] Regardless of the limitations of enterprise unionism, this channel constituted a way for knowledge workers at COMPUJ to exert influence above the task level.

Overview

Participation in service and knowledge work workflows was found to be broadly consistent with what one would expect based on the ideal types: service workers had significantly less influence in decision making than sales and knowledge workers at both task and above-task levels. Sales workers were more of an anomaly. From the literature on the E ideal type, we anticipated that sales workers would have a level of influence at the task level

[24] The new system of performance evaluation was introduced first among managers. A trial was then agreed to so that the system could be tested and evaluated jointly with the union prior to its amendment and its wider introduction among staff. Regarding organizational restructuring, union officials were informed more than a year before the reorganization and were given more details several months before the change. Union officials proffered their views and, in the estimation of the full-time official, *"Management took some of our opinions and ignored others."*

similar to that of knowledge workers, as befits contractor-workers, but that their influence above the task level would be very limited (being that they are at arm's length from management) and hence more like that of service workers. Instead, sales workers had significantly less influence than knowledge workers in task-level matters and significantly more influence than service workers in above-task-level issues.

Qualitative data helped explain these unexpected differences. We concluded that, although some knowledge workers had significant influence above the task level, this varied considerably by workflow, a finding that might be added to the reasons given earlier for why there are no significant differences between sales workers and knowledge workers in their above-task-level influence.

Workers' Responses to Control and Opportunities for Participation

Having examined the nature of control and participation, we turn to their consequences, in particular, the quality of management-employee relations and discretionary effort. These so-called dependent variables will be addressed in turn.

Quality of Management-Employee Relations

The quality of management-employee relations is typically indicated by the extent of conflict or cooperation between the parties. Indicators of conflict, such as strikes, provide useful clues to the management-employee relationship; however, there are two main disadvantages to focusing on conflict: it can assume nondirected or covert forms and hence be difficult to detect, particularly in front-line work settings; and seemingly conflictual behavior (e.g., labor turnover) can reflect other motives, making it difficult to use these data as a basis for assessing the extent of conflict (Edwards and Scullion 1982). Indicators of cooperation, such as worker participation in quality circles and suggestion schemes share an interpretation problem: does such behavior reflect commitment or accommodation to management?

We have opted to use three indicators of the quality of management-employee relations. These are drawn from our employee survey and reflect workers' evaluations of management. They are as follows:

- supportiveness of immediate supervisors;
- capability and efficiency of management; and
- trustworthiness of senior [workplace] management.[25]

---

[25] For the operationalization of immediate supervisor support and the trustworthiness of senior [workplace] management, see appendix 2. Capability and efficiency of management is a single-item variable.

We hypothesize that *the quality of management-employee relations will be lower in the sales workflows than in the knowledge work and service workflows*. This hypothesis is based on the following reasoning. Other things being equal, the less influence workers have, the greater the likelihood of conflict. This leads to the conjecture that conflict will be greatest in the service workflows. Other things are not equal, however. Our analysis of control in the service and sales workflows showed considerable differences in the way management exercised control. Info-normative control was characterized by a range of management behaviors, from seeking the active consent of workers to the use and interpretation of IT-generated measures. This contrasted with the sales workflows, which were characterized by output-procedural control and in which workers strove to attain sales targets while adhering to behavioral rules. Thus, it could be argued that, in making little effort to foster consent, management was increasing the likelihood of conflict. This outcome underlines the tenuous legitimacy of first-line managers in sales workflows compared with their more respected service workflow counterparts.

Our findings confirmed the hypothesis. With respect to each of the three measures, the ANOVA results were similar: sales workers evaluated management significantly less favorably than did service or knowledge workers ($F_{(2,859)} = 6.75$, $p < 0.001$); there were no statistically significant differences between service and knowledge workers

Also relevant, over the ten years prior to our study, there had been only one "work stoppage" in the fourteen workflows we studied. Significantly, this "strike," referred to earlier in the context of management-initiated changes in the remuneration system, occurred at MBAS, a sales workflow.

Discretionary Work Effort

The concept of discretionary effort draws attention to the elasticity of the labor contract, as emphasized by Baldamus (1961) and labor process theorists (Knights 1990; P. Thompson 1990). This concept also suggests that different management control systems, including those that provide opportunities for participation, will vary in their impact on workers' attitudes and levels of discretionary effort (Bailey 1993). Given that knowledge workers have been shown to work under more benign systems of employment relations and, through their higher levels of participation, to enjoy more influence in decision making, we hypothesized that *knowledge workers will reciprocate by exerting higher discretionary effort than sales or service workers*.

To measure discretionary work effort, we used a three-item, internally reliable factor derived from the employee survey (see appendix 2). Results from statistical analysis indicated that the level of discretionary effort was highest among knowledge workers and significantly different from that of service workers (F $(2,855)$ = 12.49, p < 0.001). This supports our hypothesis. What we did not anticipate, however, was that the average level of discretionary effort among sales workers and knowledge workers would be similar. Why should this be so? A plausible reason is that sales workers and knowledge workers interpreted the survey question differently. Among the sales workers, all efforts to go beyond the targets set by management were rewarded in accordance with the output-related reward system. Thus, in effect, there was no way these workers could voluntarily exert additional effort without receiving immediate gain.

In summary, our research indicated, as we anticipated, that workers' responses varied systematically depending on the system of control and participation in place. Service workers had significantly better relations with management than sales workers, but this was not reflected in their exerting significantly more discretionary effort. This probably reflects the machine-paced nature of call-center work, which restricts the amount of additional voluntary effort workers can put forth. Sales workers had the least satisfactory relationships with management. This contrasted with the knowledge workers, who reported having better relations with management than did the sales workers and exerting significantly more discretionary effort than either the service or sales workers. Overall, socio-normative control and associated high levels of employee influence resulted in the most favorable outcomes, however, as noted earlier, this form of control is particularly fragile and may be less appropriate for use in service and sales settings.

Conclusion

This chapter related the patterns of control and participation in the three types of workflows to what we expected based on the literature on the ideal types. We also examined some important consequences of these patterns. Our intention in this final section is to examine our findings in the context of the optimistic and pessimistic images of control presented at the beginning of this chapter.

Optimists and pessimists agree that changes are taking place in the nature of organizational control, but, in seizing on elements that support their values, they ignore other elements that challenge their perspective. Our analysis indicates that patterns of control and participation not only vary systematically across the three types of workflows we studied, making generalization difficult, but that, because of contradictory tendencies, there was also space for local variables—the nature of workplace leadership, the texture of worker relations, and so forth—to substantially influence management-employee relations. Contradictory tendencies were most evident in the service and sales workflows. For example, info-normative control in the service workflows involved control through the use of both IT-generated numbers and facilitative management. Although the former is likely to provoke employee resistance, the latter encourages employees to expand their knowledge and skills and to participate in task-level decision making. Similarly, output-procedural control entails considerable task discretion and employee participation. This encourages positive management-employee relations; however, individually based, performance-related pay systems lead to uncertainty, limited cooperation among immediate co-workers, and conflict with adjacent workers. The imposition of behavioral rules and the monitoring of sales workers' behavior promote low trust in spite of the positive aspects of control referred to above.

Socio-normative control coupled with relatively high employee participation is the least contradictory pattern. Typically used in knowledge work workflows, this pattern encourages cooperative management-employee relations and significantly more discretionary work effort among employees than either output-procedural or info-normative control. Nevertheless, there are problems. Socio-normative control is rarely negotiated: workers influence prevailing norms, but management tends to be the dominant force. Normative control is in reality a site of competing interests that without careful management can easily degenerate into anomie. Moreover, although substantial employee job discretion and wider employee influence tend to accompany high levels of job responsibility, our cases indicate that influence above the task level is not assured. Long work hours and stress may also limit knowledge workers' organizational commitment.

In sum, the evidence is complex and contradictory. Accordingly, our research endorses neither the optimistic nor the pessimistic image of control except as a vision of what to strive for and what to avoid.

6   Co-worker Relations

WE now shift our emphasis from vertical relations to lateral relations. In this chapter we analyze co-worker relations in front-line work, and in the next chapter, customer-worker relations.

Literature on postbureaucratic work organizations suggests that the network is replacing the bureaucratic model in contemporary workplaces. In support of this argument, researchers point to the dense interactions among workers and the increasing functional interdependency. Using the image of the two types of workers discussed in chapter 1, workers in postbureaucratic settings are seen as empowered and highly dependent on each other for support and learning and are most likely to be organized into participative team arrangements. In contrast, workers in bureaucratic settings are dependent on their supervisors and managers rather than on co-workers, and whatever learning takes place tends to be regimented. Our research indicates that there is no convergence toward a network model of work organization, but that, based on evidence of important deviations from the regimented model, service workflows incorporate elements of the empowered model.

We would expect co-worker relations to be of least importance in organizations that resemble the B and E types and for co-worker interdependency to be highest among knowledge workers. In subsequent sections we contrast the ideal with our empirical evidence about co-worker relations and team working in service, sales, and knowledge work workflows.

We begin by examining learning and task interdependencies. Task interdependency refers to variations in the extent to which completing front-line work is dependent on co-workers' cooperation. Likewise, learning interdependency is present when on-the-job training involves co-workers, either as coaches or advisers, for example. These interdependencies are analyzed among both front-line co-workers (immediate co-workers) and between front-line and back-office staff (adjacent co-workers).

Qualitative data enable us to focus on informal as well as formal aspects of co-worker relations. Our findings are that co-worker relations are important in all three types of workflows, although the characteristics, as well as the contributions of these relations, vary according to workflow type.

Part of the analysis of interdependency in knowledge work workflows focuses on cross-national differences. Recent theories suggest that the hybrid Japanese knowledge work organization, which combines bureaucratic and network elements, yields considerable benefits, particularly in advancing learning. Our findings show, however, that, much like service workers, Japanese knowledge workers depend more on their supervisors for learning than do their Australian counterparts.

Our analysis turns next to team working in the three workflows and the extent to which this is dependent on there being interdependency in tasks and learning. We also consider variations in the delegation of authority to the team level (supervised versus more participative), as a way of analyzing whether intrateam relations foreground co-worker relations or supervisor-worker relations. We expect that even when there are teams in work settings that resemble B and E ideal types, they will more closely approximate supervisor-led work groups than actual co-working arrangements. We would expect to find team working only in knowledge work settings. We would also expect teams in work organizations that resemble the KI type to be egalitarian, except in Japan, where they are likely to be structured more hierarchically.

All of these expectations were supported. Observing team life cross-nationally and in the three types of workflows also yielded some important findings about teams as the context for co-worker relations. In the service workflows in particular, the teams were mainly a context for the development of supervisor-worker relations, although the hierarchical tone of these relations was mitigated in practice as supervisors took on more supportive roles, especially in regard to learning. Our observations also revealed that, although there were no formal teams in the sales workflows, team-like partnerships developed among some sales workers. Finally, for the knowledge work workflows, our cross-national comparison revealed that the teams in Japan were significantly less cohesive than those in Australia.

Following these analyses, we examine survey data, across the three types of workflows and cross-nationally, to determine how our findings on co-worker relations relate to job satisfaction and satisfaction with learning outcomes. Despite differences in the interdependencies and types of teams in the three types of workflows, in all three types co-worker relations were significantly related to job satisfaction and satisfaction with learning.

The Japanese workers, regardless of the type of workflow in which they worked, were less satisfied with their learning outcomes than were the Australian or U.S. workers, again suggesting that working in a more hierarchical organization has a negative impact on workers' job satisfaction overall.

We conclude that co-worker relations are an important dimension of working and learning for front-line workers, regardless of the type of workflow in which they work. These findings are especially important in regard to service work, in which, according to the bureaucratic model, co-worker relations play no role in work and may in fact interfere with efficiency and standardization of service. Our findings point to the positive contribution of co-worker relations, even when they are informal and contested by management, as they are in bureaucratic settings. But, despite our generally positive findings about the value of co-worker relations, we did not find evidence of a convergence toward the empowered worker model in the formal design of either service or sales work, which continues to be based on regimentation. In practice, however, we observed elements of the empowered worker model, suggesting a lag between formal work design and informal practice.

In the knowledge work workflows, the empowered worker model is the formal design. Nonetheless, analyses of co-worker relations revealed considerable problems in communication, especially among individuals with discrete specializations. Cross-national evidence indicates that the hybrid model, typically found in knowledge work workflows in Japan, is not associated with positive co-worker relations; thus, we found significantly lower satisfaction with co-worker relations in knowledge work workflows in that country than in the less hierarchically structured knowledge work workflows in Australia.

The Postbureaucracy Thesis and Co-worker Relations in the Three Types of Workflows

The changes occurring in bureaucratic work organizations have been variously described as transformations to "network organizations" (Lincoln 1982, Eccles and Crane 1988, Rockart and Short 1991), "interactive organizations" (Heckscher 1995), "collaborative organizations" (Mintzberg et al. 1996), and "horizontal coordination" (Aoki 1988). These concepts imply a shift to a more integrated, team-based, fluid form of organization. Unlike the old discussions of "organic" bureaucracies (Burns and Stalker 1961; Daft 1982), these new concepts are neither restricted to innovative work processes nor based specifically on contingency theory. Rather, they are based on a generalized assumption of a more complex, highly skilled division of labor (Hage and Powers 1992). Our KI ideal type is a variant of the postbureaucratic work organization.

The bureaucratic model is based on there being a functional division of labor and a vertical command structure. Coordination is top down. In contrast, postbureaucratic organization involves a fusion of the division of labor, and coordination is through informed consensus rather than hierarchy and authority (Barley and Orr 1997). People enter into relations that are determined by problems rather than predetermined by organizational structure (Heckscher 1995).

The entrepreneurial alternative to bureaucratic organization is altogether different from the innovations suggested by the postbureaucratic thesis; in fact, the entrepreneurial organization ("market model") has been called a false alternative to bureaucracy (Heckscher 1995). Ties among people are contractual in the entrepreneurial organization, and, like market exchanges, relations are unstable, short term, and characterized by low trust. Co-worker relations in the entrepreneurial organization are competitive by design. Each worker is dependent on the organization to complete his/her work, and the overall atmosphere is one of tension, implied by the low-trust, short-term nature of the worker-worker and worker-organization relationship.

The task interdependencies among immediate and adjacent co-workers in each of the ideal types of workflows, as well as other dimensions of co-worker relations, are outlined and compared in table 6.1. As depicted in the table, relations among immediate co-workers will involve low/no interdependency in B-type and E-type settings and high interdependency in KI-type settings. Relations among adjacent workers will be high in all three types of workflows; however, in knowledge work workflows, we would expect considerable integration of front-line specialists.

Learning on the Job

The literature on the postbureaucratic model does not directly discuss learning during the transition from bureaucratic to network forms of work organization. Our results, reported in chapter 4, indicate that in all three types of workflows workers named peers as important sources of learning, although the importance given to co-workers varied. Our results corroborate previous research in arguing that the role of on-the-job contextual learning is increasing in importance. For example, among various technicians in settings similar to our knowledge work workflows, "communities of practice," in which co-workers coached each other and learned by doing, were central to contextual learning on the job (Barley 1993, Orr 1996; Fincham et al. 1994). In contrast, in more bureaucratic

Table 6.1. Features of Co-worker Relations in the Bureaucratic, Entrepreneurial, and Knowledge-Intensive Ideal Types

	B ideal type	E ideal type	KI ideal type
Task interdependencies	Immediate: low adjacent: high	Immediate: absent adjacent: high	Immediate: high adjacent: integrated with immediate
Learning interdependencies	Immediate: low adjacent: absent	Immediate: absent adjacent: medium	Immediate: high adjacent: integrated with immediate
Integration of informal relations	Informal relations, but not integrated in formal WO	Informal relations absent, or contested by management	Informal/formal WO blurred and informal relations integrated in WO
Form of teamwork	Work groups	Absent	Egalitarian project teams and network designs

settings, such learning was generally not encouraged (Brown and Duguid 1991).

Referring again to table 6.1, we would expect co-worker learning to be strongest in the workflows that most closely resemble the KI ideal type and lowest in the most bureaucratic workflows. As discussed in chapter 4, workers in bureaucratic organizations depend mainly on their supervisors for learning. By contrast, workers in entrepreneurial settings tend to be more self-reliant (Biggart 1987) and to depend on adjacent co-workers (rather than immediate co-workers or supervisors) for learning (see chapter 4).

The aspects of co-worker relations discussed so far refer to the official design of work and learning. In practice, however, these relations unfold through informal as well as formal interactions in the course of the workday.[1] Thus, informal dimensions of co-worker relations are considered in the next section.

---

[1] Industrial sociologists and others have long recognized informal relations, as in relations not prescribed by the division of labor, as central to how work is accomplished (e.g., Roy 1953; Eccles and Nohria 1992; Lincoln 1982). Labor research has focused on co-worker relations outside formal work associations and on their importance to worker solidarity (Fantasia 1988). The human relations school also focused on the contributions of informal co-worker relations, in this case on their impact on workers' motivation (Roethlisberger and Dickson 1939). Recent work on postbureaucratic WOs has also distinguished between the role of informal relations in bureaucratic and postbureaucratic WOs. Heckscher (1994) argues that in B-type organizations, informal relations run counter to the formal organization and are typically forced underground, whereas in postbureaucratic WOs the contribution of informal co-worker networks are more widely recognized.

Informal Relations

The distinction between formal and informal spheres of co-worker relations is itself characteristic of the bureaucratic organization; the informal sphere is central to how work is accomplished but typically is contested by supervisors in their effort to monitor and control work (Ibarra 1992). In knowledge work organizations, the distinction between informal and formal working relations is blurred, and the informal dimension is formally recognized as the realm in which work is done most effectively. The implication is that in knowledge work organizations, in which there is less top-down coordination, supervisors are less likely to try to restrict informal co-worker relations. In bureaucratic settings, supervisors are more likely to judge such relations as interfering with the top-down coordination of work. Thus, formal and informal relations will hardly be distinguished in knowledge work settings, and, rather than limiting informal relations, we would expect managers to facilitate such interactions.

The logic of the entrepreneurial work organization is that competition overshadows cooperation. Co-worker relations are neither formal nor informal. As in the bureaucratic organization, we would expect managers to contest informal relations.

Hybrid Work Organizations

An important question as organizations make the transition from being bureaucratic to postbureaucratic networks concerns the future of hierarchical/authority relations. One position holds that work organizations that emphasize co-worker collaboration may be incompatible with the managerial hierarchies typical of bureaucracies (Heckscher 1995). This position holds that hierarchical authority relations interfere with the effectiveness of work that demands close co-worker cooperation (Mintzberg et al. 1996). The alternative position in favor of hybrid hierarchical/collaborative organizations has most forcibly been presented from the perspective of the Japanese work organization model (Nonaka and Takeuchi 1995; Nonaka 1988; Aoki 1988).[2] Based on this model, we would expect Japanese knowl-

---

[2] Nonaka and Takeuchi (1995) call the hybrid a "hypertext" organization because it lays horizontal forms of coordination and co-worker communication onto a vertical command and coordination structure. Nonaka's earlier work (1988) on "middle-up-down" management also suggests a particular management style that encourages co-worker collaboration while maintaining managerial control, especially through the use of task completion deadlines. Aoki (1988) labels his version of the hybrid organization a "horizontal hierarchy." Unlike vertical hierarchies, in which the members of the firm compete with each other for a limited set of promotional possibilities, the ranking system in large Japanese organizations sets few limits on the number of positions at the lowest and middle ranges of the managerial hierarchy. Most members of the firm can expect to move up to at least lower-management levels; thus, competition is delayed until middle-management ranks are attained. This structure provides incentives to collaborate. For a discussion of the American version of the hybrid WO, see Applegate 1996.

Figure 6.1. Types of Teams according to Level of Interdependency and Supervisor-Worker Relations

		Supervisor-Worker Relations	
		Hierarchical	*Participative*

Co-worker Interdependency	*Low*	• Work groups
		• Parallel teams/
		  quality circles
			• Self-managing
			  work teams

	High	• Supervised
		  project teams
			• Egalitarian
			  project teams
			• Network designs

edge work to differ from the Australian cases in the preservation of hierarchical control of both tasks and learning. The inclusion of a Japanese case enables us to assess the compatibility thesis: does the preservation of hierarchy in a hybrid organization interfere with co-worker relations in task completion and learning?

Co-worker Relations, Teams, and Networks

The presence of teams is typically considered an integral feature of postbureaucratic organizations (Donnellon and Scully 1994). We argue, however, that teams are not a unitary phenomenon (Dunphy and Bryant 1996) and thus expect that the form of teamwork will vary depending on the type of work organization we are examining.[3] This variation will depend on the interdependencies that exist among co-workers with respect to tasks and learning and on the structure of the authority relations in the team context. As figure 6.1 illustrates, we would expect teams to vary according to whether interdependencies are low or high and whether or not managerial hierarchies are carried into the team organization.

In work settings in which co-worker interdependencies are low and supervisor-worker relations are hierarchical, work groups may be called teams and quality circles may also be present, but team working involving denser

---

[3] Teams have long been recognized as the primary form of WO in complex, uncertain, and innovative work contexts (Cohen 1993; Stinchcombe 1990). In the last decade and a half, however, teams have also been recognized as important in the integration of direct and indirect work in blue-collar settings (Kochan, Katz, and McKersie 1986; Womack, Jones, and Roos 1990). Our research demonstrates that they are now quite common in service and other white-collar work contexts.

co-worker interactions and more participative styles of management are less likely. Although managers in such workplaces may use the term "team," we prefer, following Dunphy and Bryant (1996), to use the term "work group" for such cases. We would expect work groups to be associated with both bureaucratic and entrepreneurial organizations. We do not expect there to be differences in the form of the team, in that bureaucratic and entrepreneurial workflows share essentially low interdependency among immediate co-workers, although managers may make less use of the rhetoric of team working in entrepreneurial settings.

In bureaucratic settings, quality circles or other *parallel teams* (Cohen 1993) that are delegated specific tasks but have little authority or autonomy may also be present alongside work groups. Further, in some adapted bureaucratic organizations, we may expect to find *self-managed front-line teams* that have some discretionary authority.

As discussed above, high interdependency is characteristic of knowledge work workflows, and it is in these workflows that we expect to find more interactive forms of team working. Previous research on teams in complex work contexts distinguishes between *project teams* and *network designs* (Cohen 1993). Project teams involve temporary groups of specialists, sometimes from different organizations, who have different functional or technical backgrounds (Cohen 1993). Fincham et al. (1994), in their study of software engineers, distinguish between hierarchical and egalitarian project teams, arguing that hierarchical teams are suitable for more routine work and for meeting deadlines, while egalitarian teams are superior for finding solutions to complex problems and in situations of uncertainty. We expect project teams to be more egalitarian the more the work organization resembles the KI ideal type.

Network designs emerge out of informal co-worker relations and may exist alongside project teams in knowledge work settings. Knowledge work typically involves collaboration among co-workers with different specializations or functions. Consequently, the presence of network designs implies the presence of cross-departmental projects and hence diagonal career paths (Cohen 1993). Such paths are characteristic of Japanese work organizations (Nonaka and Takeuchi 1995). Thus, we would expect the Japanese variant of the KI ideal type, referred to above as the hybrid model, to include both project teams and a network design. As discussed above, this model is characterized by its hierarchical relations; thus, we would expect to find *supervised project teams* in the Japanese case rather than *egalitarian project teams*, as in Australia.

Interdependencies in Tasks and Learning

We will be discussing co-worker interdependencies along two dimensions—task interdependencies (do workers need to cooperate directly in completing tasks?) and learning interdependencies (does on-the-job training depend on peer training or informal learning opportunities?)—as they relate to relations among both immediate and adjacent co-workers. Drawing on the interdependencies in B, E, and KI ideal-type organizations, we would expect the most significant difference to be between service and sales workflows, where interdependencies are low, on the one hand, and knowledge work workflows, where interdependencies are high, on the other.

We would expect the distinction between relations with immediate and adjacent co-workers to be less relevant in knowledge work workflows. Further, we would expect the distinction between informal and formal relations in these settings to be blurred in comparison with the service and sales workflows, where supervisors and managers are likely to discourage informal relations. After analyzing the nature of the interdependencies in each of the three types of workflows, we examine the relationship between interworkflow differences in workers' valuation of and satisfaction with co-worker relations.

Service Workflows

Based on the B ideal type, we expect to see low task and learning interdependencies among immediate co-workers and low learning interdependencies among adjacent co-workers in service workplaces. We expect to find high task interdependency between front-line and adjacent co-workers, however, since bureaucratic ideal-type organizations involve a functional division of labor, in which front-line jobs are clearly demarcated and dependent on other functions in the workflow. Informal relations, to the extent they are possible given management's technical control of service work, will be relegated to an informal sphere and are likely to be contested by supervisors.

Our qualitative research points to two aspects of service work that constrain co-worker relations in the act of work: the standardization of tasks and the informating capacity of IT to regulate worker behavior. As noted in chapter 3, service workers are dependent on IT (rather than on each other) to respond to customers' inquiries. As discussed in chapter 5, supervisors are cast in dual roles: they are expected both to control and to coach workers. Further, behavioral control through the informating capacities of IT, whereby workers are evaluated according to how much time they spend on the phone, means there is little time available for communication among co-workers. As noted in the previous chapter, in the service workflows we studied, supervisors had complete knowledge of the work process. Thus, customer service representatives were most likely to turn for help and advice to their supervisors or other officially sanctioned resources rather than to each other.

In all the call centers, the physical arrangement underscored the expectation that employees would work independently, without peer interaction, in executing tasks. The typical office consisted of a desk with a computer, a phone system, and a headset, framed by a three-wall cubicle high enough to prevent easy communication between neighbors.[4] The major exception was the Japanese workplace JBSV, where desks were arranged, as is typical in Japan, in small islands. Here employees faced and bordered each other without physical barriers, and communication could flow freely. Nonetheless, by positioning themselves at the head of the island, facing in toward subordinates, supervisors could monitor co-worker communication. At JBSV, depending on co-workers for information or advice after completing the training phase was seen as a weakness rather than an example of collegial collaboration.

The use of IT also circumscribed rather than promoted interaction. In most of the workplaces where employees had access to e-mail, management thought it was used for "social purposes" unrelated to work (AINSV). In other workflows, after being introduced to e-mail, CSRs were restricted to receiving messages (TELSV and MBASV), thus transforming electronic communication into top-down communication. In one workflow, MFJSV, only managerial employees had access to e-mail. Thus, in none of the workplaces did the use of e-mail substitute for face-to-face communication among employees, and supervisors controlled the use of both forms of communication.

Nonetheless, despite the carrel walls and the pervasive measurements of time spent on customer business, co-workers developed close informal relations. Most important, "communities of coping" were formed wherein co-workers recounted stories of rude customers to alleviate stress. Employees used various workday contexts and opportunities to seek out mutual support. At TELSV, training sessions provided settings in which to recount customers' excuses for not paying their bills. At UB1, employees complained during team meetings about nasty customers, while at MFJSV employees wrote their thoughts in a notebook, begun as a tool for workers on the day shift to communicate with workers on the night shift about a caller who had repeatedly annoyed several of the CSRs. In some workflows, team meetings provided a context for creating and extending communities of coping, but no more or less so than other contexts and opportunities (training sessions, seating arrangements, social outings, and so forth).

Service employees readily referred to the support they counted on from co-workers, and in some workflows workers said their co-workers were the best part of the job. A CSR at MBASV said, *"I've never seen a group cooperate the way people do here,"* while another remarked, in tribute to his co-workers, *"It would be a great place if the jobs weren't so awful."*

[4] At only one of the Australian workplaces, TELSV, were the cubicle walls low enough for workers to communicate with their neighbors, but here as at MBASV, managers were worried about employees leaving their desks to talk with co-workers and sought ways to restrict such behavior.

Some CSRs made a connection between their relations with co-workers and their performance on the job: *"We try to cover for each other so the customer is satisfied."* While some supervisors, themselves former CSRs, well recognized the benefits of positive co-worker relations, the formal design of work, the emphasis on standardization of service (usually for quality control), and the pervasive use of IT measures of work behavior served as important constraints on co-worker interaction. Supervisors were instructed to evaluate employees in part on how efficiently they used their time. This was defined as time spent directly on customer calls and was measured automatically by an information system linked to the CSRs' telephones. The information gathered in this way was often used as an indicator of workplace efficiency. As an executive manager at MFJ explained, *"[MFJSV] is managed by the information system."* Thus, in most service workflows, supervisors were put in the organizational role (by their own managers) of limiting co-worker interactions.

Management attempted to regulate workers' coping practices by formally authorizing supervisors to handle customer complaints. At MFJSV, employees were instructed from the beginning to refer problematic customers directly to their supervisor. Trainers at AINSV instructed employees not to gossip about customers, and, if they needed to talk to someone after dealing with an abusive customer, to consult with a supervisor rather than a peer. When told this, one worker responded, echoing a more general feeling, *"If I've been told off, I want to talk about it."* At MBASV, CSRs sometimes "wandered about" in search of information when there were no supervisors around; this also alleviated boredom and stress. Managers targeted this practice in setting up alternative routes for communicating problems to senior CSRs, back-office staff, or supervisors. Although CSRs were often more than happy to pass off difficult customers to their supervisors, seeing their supervisors as supporting them in this way, employees in some workflows were instructed only to seek advice from peers designated by management as "senior" co-workers.

Qualitative data point to other ways in which management contested informal relations among co-workers. At JBSV, for example, a supervisor criticized employees when they spoke to each other in the strictly informal forms used to denote closeness in the Japanese language.

In sum, although informal relations were of importance to service employees, these relations were not integrated into the design of the work organization and at times were contested by management.

In the service workflows, learning interdependencies were stronger than task interdependencies. Management sanctioned co-worker relations during on-the-job training and typically encouraged their development in off-the-job induction training. At MFJSV, for example, the on-the-job training included a phase in which new recruits were assigned to experienced employees. At TELSV, the on-the-job training was more tightly controlled by the company's full-time trainers, who sat on the office floor with new recruits. At some point, however, in all six call centers, supervisors were expected to participate in the training through call monitoring. This expanding involvement in training was part of the trend from directive to more facilitative supervision (see chapter 5). As reported in Korczynski et al., a prime aspect of this new role involved "the facilitation of learning" (1996: 74).

Several factors tended to favor supervisors over peers as sources of learning in the service workflows: the physical barriers between workstations, which prohibited employees from interacting with each other; the formal procedures for raising queries, such as a support line at MBASV; the dominance of team leaders/supervisors at team meetings; and other management directives that confined workers to specified channels of learning (Korczynski et al. 1996). As discussed in chapter 5, supervisors in the service workflows were recruited from CSR positions on the basis of their expertise and were thus the best sources of information.

Nonetheless, co-workers did depend on each other for informal learning, especially during induction training. At UB2, an employee described the atmosphere as a *"great support system; ask the person next to you. People are very helpful—great thing about this job."* After 9 P.M., when there were no team leaders at work, workers reported that the relations among co-workers were close and supportive: *"We all helped everyone with knowledge, to help the customer, to be a team."* In the absence of official sanctioning of such initiatives, these "communities of practice," like the "communities of coping," were often relegated to the informal sphere of co-worker relations.

The workflows in all the service settings had clear divisions of labor such that most support functions, including operations, marketing, and in some cases treasury departments for the handling of customer business, were located in other departments, away from the front line. ANOVA analysis of responses to survey questions pertaining to co-worker interdependence shows that service workers were significantly more dependent on adjacent co-workers than were sales or knowledge workers: ($F_{(2,856)} = 5.68$, $p < 0.001$) The service workers reported, however, that the quality of their relations with members of other departments was negative. In many of the service workflows, workers had neither formal nor informal contact with employees in other departments. At the call centers, such contact was physically impossible given the amount of time CSRs were expected to spend on the phone. At MBASV, some employees had been at the call center for two years and still not met people in related departments. At AINSV, an employee in the claims department mistook one of our researchers for a call-center employee, although the two workplaces bordered each other and there was frequent contact by telephone.

Sales Workflows

Based on the characteristics of the E ideal type, we would not expect co-worker relations to be a feature of sales work since its official design assumes that each transaction is individually contracted and that competition exists among immediate co-workers. One would expect interpersonal relations among adjacent co-workers, however, since sales workers are dependent on the employing organization for processing their sales and for providing knowledge specific to organizational procedures and rules. Thus, if it follows the model for the E ideal type, there should be low interdependence between workers and their immediate co-workers but high interdependence between workers and adjacent co-workers. Informal relations are not likely, given the contractual nature of the work and the commission-based remuneration system.

As expected, the sales workers we observed were in competitive relations with each other, and individual sales records determined income. An exception was the Japanese workflow, where promotions rather than income were at stake. At JBS, sales workers did not receive commissions but faced intense competition for promotions.[5] At ABKS, where one manager described the competition as underpinning the mobile design of the sales workflow, a worker described his job as follows: *"Work by yourself, don't manage staff, live or fall by your own efforts except for approvers [credit analysts]."*

If sales workers offered each other leads, the reaction was usually one of suspicion: *"If someone rings with leads, something is wrong."* One worker described his co-workers as *"a bunch of rats."* *"Always someone here [is] stealing what you've got."* Another sales worker remarked that *"you trust nobody. You have no friends—probably the worst aspect of the job."*

The mobile nature of the work kept the sales workers relatively isolated from each other. One salesperson described the work as *"a loner's job."* There is *"little contact with fellow mobile lenders, . . . no one to talk to on Monday about the weekend—it's the worst aspect of the job."* Employees of MBAS generated some of their business by responding to phone inquiries. Consequently, they reported that they spent more time in the office and had more interaction with co-workers. By contrast, Japanese sales workers spent most of their time visiting clients, and, as a result, sales workers felt that they kept information from each other. Sales workers reported *"relying too much on private channels"* for information about prospective clients.

The nature of the employment relations in the Japanese versus the Australian sales workflows resulted in an important cross-national difference.

[5] The average age of the salespeople at JBS was forty-four, meaning that they were at the stage when promotions were most competitive and just a decade from facing the threat of company-enforced preretirement demotions if they did not attain executive management status.

As argued in chapter 4, employment relations in the Australian sales work-flows tended to be rather unstructured, which meant that the workers had no predictable career paths in their organizations. By contrast, employment relations in the Japanese sales workflow tended to be bureaucratic. Sales workers were recruited from within the organization and rotated throughout the branches and headquarters. As a byproduct of this system, they developed personal networks throughout the company. Thus, the workers could rely on both these personal networks as well as external sources for leads to prospective clients. One Japanese sales worker reported that, rather than depending on co-workers, he turned to *"the kacho" [section head] of general affairs, the kacho of the planning division in charge of purchasing supplies [in case they could use a client's product], the JBS computer subsidiary, the general manager of the sales division [in case the company wanted to invest in other companies' stocks],* and in some cases to the chairman of the company for support.

The sales workflow in Japan also differed from the ones in Australia in workers' reliance on supervisors. In Japan, supervisors doubled as referrers and had some knowledge of the sales process. The nature of Japanese sales practices also made sales workers dependent on their supervisors. By getting involved in sales efforts, higher-ranked managers demonstrated interest in, and commitment to, customers. One sales worker at JBS explained:

> However hard an effort a sales worker makes, it is difficult to meet key persons in a client organization without involving managers from [JB]. Only if a top manager visits a customer can [JB] be seen as worth considering. This is beyond the capacity of a sales worker-level employee. The relationship with the customer is made with board-level managers at [JB].

Australian sales workers were much more self-reliant; however, the competitive nature of their work led them to feel much more socially isolated.

The learning experiences of the sales workers in both countries also tended to be fraught with tension. In the Australian sales workflows, income was based in part on commissions, so that, in practice, workers were discouraged from taking time to train their peers. At MBAS, attempts were made to buddy new employees with experienced pros, but, without supervisors overseeing the process, training would have been neglected.

ABKS also had a mentor system, which required new recruits to split their commissions with their mentor-trainers. At the time of our research, ABKS's system was not in use, however, because the mentors objected to losing sales time and the trainees did not like paying half their commissions to their mentors.

At JBS, experienced sales workers were supposed to mentor less experienced employees, and supervisors were expected to ensure that the more seasoned employees cooperated. Workers tended to rely more on their "private channels" than on co-workers for learning. This was confirmed by an ANOVA analysis that indicated that the Japanese sales workers were significantly less likely than the Australian sales workers to name immediate co-workers as sources of learning ($F (1,62) = 6.51$, $p < 0.01$).

Overall, relations among immediate co-workers in the sales workflows were rather weak. At the most competitive site, ABKS, evidence of informal partnering, and an interest in extending such partnering, suggested that workers did not necessarily support competitive, individualized relations.

Sales workers depended especially on adjacent co-workers for task completion. In all the sales workflows, a transaction had to be "passed off" to a credit analyst, whose job it was to finalize the deal. At ABKS, this function had been part of the sales role in the past, but the move to a commission system had led to a separation of sales and analyst roles in order to minimize the risk of bad loans. Approved loans meant commissions for sales workers, and happy customers and referrers, so the sales workers' self-interest in getting approvals was clear. Credit analysts were also important sources of learning, however, and as part of their induction training, sales workers sat with credit analysts for two weeks. After the induction process was over, credit analysts tended to offer negative feedback, to point out mistakes in or to reject loan applications that did not follow company guidelines. In turn, sales workers at ABKS, for instance, complained that the lending guidelines were not transparent and were inconsistent.

The situation in the Japanese workflow JBS was similar. Once a client chose JBS as its lead manager for registering shares, the case would be passed to a team of financial specialists who would have access to the client's business records and give financial advice in advance of registration, as well as undertake the registration process on the client's behalf. After registration, JBS would be given stocks to sell on behalf of the client, and the sales workers were expected to take a role in promoting stock sales. Communicating with financial specialists about the client at that stage would constitute insider training. Nonetheless, before a client had been won over, sales workers often needed input from financial analysts. More contact would have helped in this regard.

Differences in work styles contributed to the generally poor relations at JBS between front-line and back-office staff. Specialists and analysts tended to give advice on the basis of rational and technical criteria, whereas sales workers used more subjective criteria in deciding clients' credit worthiness or their willingness to issue stock.

In the home loan sales workflows, sales workers complained that clients could not adequately communicate on loan forms their credit worthiness and analysts were reluctant to rely on sales workers' verbal assurances. In the Japanese workflow, sales work was rooted in the development of friendly personal relations, and only after these were established did client work involve business services such as providing financial advice and expertise. Thus, sales workers were seen as providing a "soft" service, while financial analysts viewed themselves as providing technical expertise.

Survey evidence presented in chapter 4 confirms the qualitative evidence outlined in this chapter that back-office staff are an important source of learning for sales workers, significantly more so than for either service or knowledge workers.[6] As a dimension of co-worker relations, however, relations between front-line sales workers and back-office credit analysts were marked by antagonism.

Knowledge Work Workflows

In this section we discuss interdependency in the three SD workflows and then the money market dealers workflow.

Interdependency among systems developers. Front-line SD work was carried out by project teams that included workers with different technical and adjacent specializations, so that distinctions between immediate and adjacent co-workers was of little relevance. Compared with service and sales workers, SD workers were highly dependent on co-workers for their specialized expertise. That all three SD workflows used spiral methodologies, in practice if not in theory, also contributed to the high level of interdependence among SD workers. We referred to this in our discussion of TELSD and WBSD in the previous chapter. At COMPUJ, engineers were involved in the sales phase, so that product development overlapped with sales activity.

In all three SD workflows—TELSD, WBSD, and COMPUJ—having overlapping functions was considered an innovative response to customer requirements. This strengthened the usual interdependencies among members of functionally mixed project teams and made the work more complex and uncertain.

In none of the SD workflows were relations among specialists smooth. Problems adjusting to the use of several different theoretical languages, as well as perceived differences in the collective personalities of members of different specializations, created tension. Relations among co-workers were a source of frustration for individuals having to work with different people as projects changed. Project leaders had to counter a tendency for workers to associate exclusively with colleagues in the same specialty.

At WBSD, the members of the broker applications team gave their frustration a name—"paralysis by analysis." Here the main interdependency

---

[6] This analysis is based on ANOVA techniques and a question on other employees as a source of learning ($F_{(2,771)} = 13.2$, $p < 0.005$).

was between corporate-level IT specialists, who developed system architecture at an abstract conceptual level, and business unit–level IT practitioners, who combined knowledge of the business unit with systems knowledge at an applications level. The "abstract specialists" were brought into the team as advisers, but the "applications specialists," including the project team leader, had difficulty understanding technical aspects of the architecture. In meetings meant to explain the architecture (a learning opportunity), corporate IT staff would *present it on a huge whiteboard with [a picture of] two hundred components, which made people feel stupid. This is arrogant. People can't understand it.*

Rather than facilitating learning, the presence of corporate IT staff created a culture of silence when something was not understood. Because of their status as consultants and the originators of the architecture, team members were obliged to follow the advice of corporate IT staff members, and local team members likened this to having *one thousand chiefs on this project. No one could understand the architecture, and the specialists didn't demystify it.* The consultants *have all the say and none of the responsibility.* In effect, because they had command of a language few others knew, the IT experts came to exert substantial informal influence on management. This remained unchecked because management had been promised that the new architecture would result in faster and more flexible business applications.

The TELSD project team included specialists in product development and operations, as well as software specialists from two subcontracted firms. The intention was that the design and operations staff would overlap and that the subcontractors would be full team members, but divisions persisted among the specialists and to some extent were exacerbated during the life of the project. One employee described these divisions as among people with *different mentalities. Operations people have ownership of their outputs, while development people build and walk away leaving operations to worry about things.*

Among the development staff, the work atmosphere was described as *everyone in their corners working on individual tasks,* whereas co-workers in operations had far more interaction. *All sit together and throw issues around* was the way one employee described their work situation. Another explained that there was a spirit of *the individual can't know everything* and *people need to rely on one another,* recognizing that *others have more skills than you.* In summary, interdependency among co-workers was high, but cohesion and learning were most evident among staff with the same specialization.

In contrast to the SD workflow in Australia, SD employees in Japan were organized into sections responsible for multiple projects, so that workers tended to belong to more than one project team. Most of the employees had a sales background, but young engineers were members of both SD projects and sales sections. A separate section composed of only engineers was also part of the front-line work organization. As a sales prospect developed, engineers from this section would be called on to join in product development work. As mentioned above, including product development engineers in a sales department project was an innovation in work organization on COMPUJ's part, but the integration was even less complete than in the Australian workflows.

As at TELSD, the engineers and salespeople at COMPUJ were described as having different personalities and incompatible work perspectives. One section head explained that each group of employees took pleasure in the completion of opposite phases of projects. For a salesperson, the time to celebrate was when a customer agreed to a contract; for the engineer, this was the beginning of his or her work.

The interdependencies between the sales and engineering staff were not balanced, so that the salespeople were becoming more dependent on having access to specialized systems knowledge to make their sales pitches, while the engineers believed they had relatively little to gain from working with salespeople. One young engineer said that he tried to avoid interacting with salespeople since they interrupted his work all the time if he got too close.

The motivation for the engineers at COMPUJ to contribute to the sales effort derived from the fact that sales managers did their performance evaluations, which was basically an element of hierarchical control. In the case of only one engineer was this forced cooperation between the engineers and the salespeople successful. The other engineers refused to cooperate in selling, though they provided salespeople with engineering knowledge when requested. One engineer managed to leave the sales section altogether and join the engineers-only section. Hierarchical control was thus not an effective way to inspire the engineers to participate fully in sales activities.

The Japanese workflow differed from the Australian workflows in the employees' dependence on their supervisors. An ANOVA analysis of survey results on sources of learning shows that the Japanese knowledge workers were more dependent on their supervisors for learning than were comparable Australian workers ($F_{(1,149)} = 24.05$, $p < 0.001$). In fact, immediate colleagues—the source of learning the Australian SDs considered the most important—was not even included in the Japanese knowledge workers' top five responses. Our observations of young Japanese employees tended to contradict this finding, however, since, rather than seeking advice from their supervisors, they turned to each other. Further, when young employees did consult their supervisors, their superiors tended to respond harshly. In response to one young employee's concerns about an upcoming meeting, his supervisor went through a list of phone calls and arrangements the employee should have thought to make and reprimanded him for not inviting a certain manager to the meeting, something a supervisor, not a lower-ranked employee, would be expected to do.

We concluded that supervisors were the most important source of learning in the Japanese knowledge work workflows but that the hierarchical structuring of the learning relationship did not encourage workers to consult them. As discussed in chapter 4, COMPUJ emphasized self-development among its SD workers, including encouraging workers to search for answers on their own. The effectiveness of learning in this context is considered in the final section of this chapter, in which we examine learning outcomes in the Japanese and Australian SD workflows. Based on our qualitative research, we expected to show that the hierarchical structure of learning in the Japanese hybrid knowledge work organization leads to less effective outcomes.

Interdependency among money market dealers. Rather than having discrete specializations, front-line workers in the WBMM workflow were involved in closely related work (see chapter 3). Interdependencies were based on the fact that workers specialized in different products and had varying levels of experience. Further, the interdependencies were more or less symmetrical. The integration of distributors, traders, price makers, and middle-office workers closely related to deal making was partly based on the need for contextual knowledge and was encouraged by the open "desk" layout. One worker joked that the workers knew each other's families, since it was impossible to have private phone conversations. The level of noise and activity was very high. One worker described the environment as characterized by the *"constant chatter on the phones and between the people next to one another."*

It was impossible for WBMM staff to know everything about their products and the markets in which they were trading, so they depended on rapid access to one another for information. As noted in chapter 4, WBMM dealers usually entered the workforce with some experience in financial services but also depended on their colleagues and their on-the-job experience to develop knowledge and skills. Oral communication on the job and listening to colleagues making deals were the key means of learning that we observed. Dealers were very explicit about the interdependencies among co-workers as the following comment illustrates: *"This is a very close environment. If one doesn't get on with others on the desk, it would be hard to last. It would be hard to be successful without the support of others. For example, we need structured analysts to formulate deals, while the latter need the former to get the client's interest. Dealers need price makers to advise what is potentially profitable to buy and sell."*

Unlike the SD workflows, however, the MM dealers were in organizations with differentiated products, and customers demanding services other than money market products (e.g., fixed-interest deposits, foreign exchange, trading) had to deal with other product "desks." Although the trend was toward one-stop service, in the meantime dealers were in competition with workers at adjacent desks, leading to tense relations and some of the same communication problems evident in the SD workflows. One manager likened the desks to warring "tribes."

Interdependencies Across the Workflows

In this section we compare our findings about interdependency with what we expected based on our knowledge of the B, E, and KI ideal-type organizations. Unexpected findings are highlighted, as well as the main differences and similarities.

Based on the B ideal type, we expected that task interdependency in the service workflows would be low among immediate co-workers but high among adjacent co-workers. This was confirmed by our qualitative and survey evidence. From our qualitative evidence, however, we concluded that, since there was little direct interaction among adjacent workers, relations would be limited. In fact, supervisors and managers mediated relations with workers in adjacent functional areas.

We also expected low learning interdependency among co-workers in service workflows and, instead, that supervisors would play central roles in on-the-job training. Although this was largely confirmed, co-workers clearly had prescribed roles in training, especially during the induction stage. Relations among co-workers were also evident and important in providing "communities of coping" and support in other aspects of task completion and learning. Primarily, however, vertical relations (worker-supervisor) were more in evidence in the service workflows.

The results for the sales workflows also generally conformed to our expectations, based on the E ideal type. Interdependency among co-workers was weak, and relations among adjacent co-workers were tense. Informal partnering had developed in one workflow, but the mobile nature of the job generally created a barrier to communication among co-workers. Also, management's preference for a competitive work environment discouraged workers from pursuing informal relations. Nonetheless, there was some evidence that the sales workers were interested in working together to alleviate the loneliness and isolation of their work.

As expected, given the complex and uncertain nature of knowledge work, there was high interdependency among co-workers. In practice, however, relations among workers with different specialties were not smooth. As the hybrid WO model predicts, the Japanese knowledge workers were more dependent on their supervisors than on their peers for on-the-job training, but the Japanese workers tended to consult their peers nonetheless. Relations were more positive among co-workers in the Australian MM dealers workflow. Here, the distinctions among workers with different specialties were less sharp.

In both the service and sales workflows, interdependency among immediate and adjacent co-workers was low with respect to task completion and learning. By management design, tasks were completed individually and communication among co-workers was discouraged. In some of the sales workflows, workers attempted to work together but were forced either to hide or to limit their interactions. As a consequence, relations among co-workers were mainly informal and were not seen as contributing to management goals. Informal relations were especially important in coping with stress. Further, in the service and sales workflows, co-worker relations between front-line and adjacent back-office staff were tense. In contrast, the knowledge work workflows had high task interdependency, formal and informal relations were blurred, and workers with different but related specialties were integrated at the front line.

Two similarities across the three types of workflows are noteworthy. First, although the knowledge workers were the most dependent on each other for on-the-job learning, the service and sales workers also viewed their co-workers as important sources of learning.[7] Second, the service and sales workers also thought their informal relations with co-workers were important in task activities, despite the individualized task assignments in service work, the competitive nature of sales work, and management disincentives to cooperate in both the service and sales workflows. Though knowledge workers exhibited higher task interdependency, service and sales workers developed communities of coping and partnerships, respectively. Thus, regardless of the level of task interdependency, whether relations among co-workers were positive was important not only in the knowledge work workflows but in the service and sales workflows as well.

Workers' responses to survey questions enable us to explore co-worker relations further. Statistical analysis shows that the service workers valued positive relations with their immediate co-workers significantly more than did the sales or knowledge workers (F $(2,852)$ = 7.71, p < 0.05). Further, the service workers were the most satisfied with these relations (F $(2,855)$ = 10.27, p < 0.001). These findings are surprising in light of what we would expect in B-type organizations and suggest that, despite the informal and "unofficial" nature of co-worker relations in service workflows, peers make an even more important contribution to working life in these bureaucratic compared to knowledge-intensive settings. The lower satisfaction with co-worker relations among the knowledge workers is most likely due to com-

---

[7] Survey responses confirm this observation. Thus, out of seven choices, service employees ranked immediate colleagues as the second most important source of learning and sales workers and knowledge workers ranked immediate colleagues first. There was no significant difference across the three types of workflows on this variable.

munication difficulties stemming from their differences in specialization. These difficulties were less evident, however, in the money market dealers workflow, in which the areas of specialization were less distinct.

We turn now to an analysis of the types of teams we observed in the three types of workflows and their contribution to co-worker relations.

Relations among Co-workers in Teams

Based on the B, E, and KI models, we would expect to find work groups rather than teams in the service workflows, no teams in the sales workflows, and project teams and/or a network design in the knowledge work workflows. According to the hybrid model of work organization, we would expect the knowledge work workflow in Japan to have hierarchically structured project teams but also a more extensive network design than the SD workflows in Australia.

Work Groups in Service Workflows

All of the service workflows had teams, but these assumed the form of work groups. In the words of one employee at MFJSV: *"Each supervisor has a group under them, but not really a cohesive team, more a group of employees who receive info and who people can call on."* Several of the service workplaces also had project teams, analogous to quality circles. These teams were closely supervised but nonetheless important as supports to which workers could turn for help in relieving some of the boredom and stress of telephone work.

At AINSV and MBASV, teams posted members' performance results; and at TELSV, team-level results were posted. In other cases, teams increased the competition among workers in the same team, countering management's rhetoric about teamwork. The rhetoric proved useful, however, when workers wished to cooperate more closely with one another.

In all the service workflows, communication was primarily top down. At MFJSV, where we attended weekly meetings, we literally followed items of information as they were relayed through the hierarchy, from the executive level down to the workers at team meetings. At JBSV, where there were two meetings daily, a supervisor presided over the meetings from the head of a table and relayed information he received from his superiors as well as goals and results for the day. A similar top-down process for relaying information was evident at the other five service workflows. Employees typically asked questions or requested clarification. In sum, team meetings underscored the vertical structure of the service work organizations and were venues for increasing participation, only in a very limited sense.

Working on a team in a service workflow did not mean working together. They were more an important context for learning and coping. In part, teams facilitated peer learning, but mainly they fostered supervisor-led learning, and in the process mitigated this otherwise hierarchical experience. Most supervisors were former customer service representatives, and, except at JBSV, the social distance between them and the workers was narrow. Where team leaders were in separate job grades below supervisors, they were socially even closer to the workers and often functioned more as senior or more experienced workers who had coaching responsibilities. In some workplaces, teams included senior CSRs who had specific duties. At MFJSV, for example, senior CSRs conducted sessions on delivering customer service in English. While preserving the hierarchical element of learning, having supervisors and team leaders with experience as CSRs legitimated the team leaders' authority. This structure also provided an avenue for two-way communication and the development of more personalized relationships between supervisors/coaches and team members.

JBSV was the only workflow that did not have formally designated teams. Further, the supervisor was a male, not a former bond-lady. The most senior bond-lady was appointed team leader (subordinate to the supervisor) and was also expected to take on coaching duties. In this primarily female workplace, the status difference between the male supervisor and the female bond-ladies was substantial. The supervisor's role in learning was mainly to point out errors and in this sense was often indistinguishable from a traditional disciplinary role.

The teams at MFJSV, the other Japanese service site, had many of the same features as the teams at the Australian and American sites—CSRs were recruited as supervisors, team leaders and senior CSRs functioned as coaches, and communication was two way—but in subtle ways, status differences at MFJSV were also present. Thus, unlike the CSRs, three out of four of the supervisors and many senior CSRs at MFJSV wore business suits every day, evidence of the more hierarchical nature of Japanese service organizations.

Partners in Sales

Managers of the sales workflows used team-based language to refer to groups of workers, and there was some interest in using teams to promote sales by creating intergroup competition. Use of the term "teams" was contrary to our expectations. In line with what we expected of an entrepreneurial organization, however, team language was used to encourage competition rather than to facilitate working relationships. Management was ambivalent about teams, fearing they would facilitate the formation of worker alliances that would threaten management's already weak control over sales activities (see chapter 5).

The depth of management's ambivalence about the formation of sales teams was especially evident at ABKS, where two workers had initiated a partnership so they could better cover their sales territory. Management had supported the formation of supervisor-led work groups, which they called teams, as a way to ensure control of sales activity and referral networks. The strategy faltered, however, because managers were not experienced in loan sales and had difficulty supervising the work (see chapter 5). High-performing sales workers had much broader networks and expertise, and they also earned more money through commissions than their salaried supervisors. This tended to delegitimize managers' authority over their work groups' activities.

Outside the team structure, some employees cooperated on a one-to-one basis in some aspects of their sales activities, by exchanging knowledge and rendering assistance in complex cases, for example. The main reasons given for these relationships was to combat social isolation and *"bounce ideas off one another."*

Two experienced sales workers had formed what was in effect a joint venture so they could service their sales applications more effectively; management had even agreed to provide them with additional administrative resources. This made geographical coverage easier (since back-to-back visits could be arranged when one of the workers was in the area), while a more specialized division of labor meant that they had more time with their families. Other experienced salespeople expressed a desire to join the partnership, but management was not keen on this idea. Had these other sales workers joined, the members of this alliance would have collectively represented 25 percent of the workflow's business. Management feared that such a group could become influential and ultimately threaten to leave the organization and take referrers, and hence business, with them.

At MBAS, management also was ambivalent about team working, preferring to use its teams to motivate competition among co-workers. In the Japanese sales workflow, sales workers worked independently of each other, in close communication with their supervisors (see chapter 5).

Project Teams and Networks in Knowledge Work Workflows

In all the SD workflows, the work was accomplished in project teams. The Japanese workflow COMPUJ differed from the Australian SD workflows in that the Japanese workers were primarily organized into sections with a clear hierarchical structure. Project teams were formed out of these sections, and young employees and their immediate supervisors typically belonged to several project teams together. Thus, project teams were overlaid on sections, in keeping with the hybrid organizational model.

Networks were more in evidence in the Japanese workflows than in the Australian. Japanese knowledge workers regularly rotated among workflows and departments every three to five years, and the formation of networks was an important consequence of this practice. Assignments typically lasted long enough for employees to develop close ties with immediate colleagues. The systematic rotation of employees contributed to informal teaming and considerable loosening of the boundaries of project team membership. As a consequence of the rotation system, young engineers especially but also sales staff and supervisory-level employees had networks of previous supervisors and co-workers throughout the organization and regularly contacted them about current project business. These networks were mobilized when problems arose or tasks required more attention or knowledge than was available within the core project team. Most of the engineers' contacts were in product development departments, whereas sales staff had networks throughout the sales divisions. The value of all of these networks was clearly evident in the way COMPUJ employees from outside the workflow communicated with customers at project meetings. In other instances the networks operated more subtly, as, for example, when employees visited or contacted ex-colleagues by phone for advice on how to handle a project-related problem. Networks also extended to regional branches, subsidiary companies, and even customers' organizations.

Another common practice that affected informal networking in the Japanese knowledge work workflows was the mass recruitment of employees at the start of their careers. At COMPUJ, for example, several of the young engineers and sales workers were *doki*, or of the same age. In addition, they had started working at the company on April 1 of the same year and undergone at least part of the month or so of orientation training together. Similar to the practice among other Japanese knowledge workers of building networks as a consequence of rotating, the employees at COMPUJ maintained ties with *doki* elsewhere in the organization and called on these peers to help with project business as needed.

Members of project teams in the Australian SD workflows also rotated throughout the company but with less regularity than at COMPUJ. At TELSD, project positions were advertised internally, and, before hiring from outside, team leaders were compelled to try to hire from a pool of internal candidates. Members of WBSD teams belonged to fixed departments (business unit–level IT or corporate-level IT) and were seconded into projects. Relations in the broker applications project, in which employees knew each other and engaged in similar work, were positive, but the fate of the project depended on the team's ability to work with corporate-level IT staff. During the time of our research, relations broke down over differences in objectives and methodology; there were also communication problems. Similarly, in TELSD, relations among operations staff were amicable, but the project depended on the team members being able to work with design and sub-contracted staff, and the absence of prior personal contact and communications problems handicapped relations across specializations.

Perhaps most telling, team members at the business unit level of WBSD and on the operations side at TELSD generally did not have the autonomy or networks, as the workers at COMPUJ did, to call on colleagues in other parts of the company for help. The formal design of the teams was such that the team members in WBSD were expected to function self-sufficiently, although there and in TELSD, the lack of requisite skills and the complexity of the projects made self-sufficiency a nearly impossible goal. Team members relied on external consultants and subcontractors, adding to the complexity of the project rather than promoting self-sufficiency. In contrast, at COMPUJ, the managers never expected the project teams to be self-sufficient; even young employees were expected to have contacts outside the project team and work group.

In contrast to the SD workflows, WBMM did not have project teams, but in that there was interdependency among co-workers, mainly for the purposes of learning, these teams did not function as teams. The speed with which deals were executed and the breadth of the workers' contextual knowledge made co-workers interdependent and team members highly integrated. As discussed above, the dealers' specializations were not as distinct as in the SD workflows. Front-line team members engaged in similar work, and, as a result of the recruitment process, tended to be hom-ogenous. Further, all new team members went through an initiation period during which co-workers distanced themselves while they judged whether the new recruits would perform well. As one team member remarked, recruits were *"ostracized for three months"* and *"end[ed] up leaving if [they] never [broke] in."*

Based on the homogeneity of the team members, we concluded that these groups functioned more like work teams, in which all the members do the same work; however, based on the level of interdependency among the members and their specialized contextual knowledge, these groups were more like project teams. Also, as discussed in chapter 5, participation at the task level was high. Thus, although not the same as the project teams in the SD workflows, the teams at WBMM also had an integrated division of labor, structured interdependencies among co-workers, and, like the Australian SD workflows, offered workers a relatively high level of participation in decision making.

Types of Teams and Team Cohesion in the Three Types of Workflows

On the whole, our expectations regarding the types of teams we would observe were met. There were, however, several important deviations. First, although the teams in the service workflows were most akin to work groups, they nonetheless provided a context for coping, learning, and the establishment of positive worker-supervisor relations.

Second, contrary to expectations, we saw evidence of team arrangements, essentially work groups, in the sales workflows. In some cases management even supported these groups, while maintaining considerable ambivalence about whether to encourage closer working arrangements. Of more significance was the partnership among co-workers at one sales site.

Third, all of the SD workflows had project teams. As expected, the Japanese workflow differed in that hierarchically structured teams existed within the context of a network design, supported by employee rotation and recruitment practices. One result of this design was considerable blurring of team boundaries. In the Australian money market dealers workflow, a team existed that resembled those in the Australian SD workflows, albeit without the extensive task cooperation required for project work.

This comparison demonstrates that teams take on different forms depending on the complexity of the work (level of interdependency) and management's strategy (participation) regarding work organization. Nonetheless, in all the workflows with teams or other cooperative arrangements, co-worker relations were facilitated.

Survey evidence confirmed the presence of close relations among co-workers in all the workflows. Further, ANOVA showed that there were no statistically significant differences in team cohesion among the service, sales, and knowledge work workflows.[8] Nor was interdependency among co-workers necessarily related to the degree of team cohesion; workflows with both low and high interdependency scored high on this factor. Finally, the presence of teams contributed to improved co-worker relations regardless of the nature of the work involved.

Cross-national comparisons indicate that Japanese workers reported significantly lower team cohesion than their Australian counterparts (F (2,689) = 2.22, p < 0.1). This analysis also pointed to the existence of stronger hierarchical relationships in the Japanese service workplaces and the maintenance of hierarchical supervision in hybrid project teams in knowledge work. This finding suggests that the existence of a hierarchical structure accounts for the differences in the quality of relations among co-workers in team contexts.

In conclusion, despite the high interdependency among co-workers in

---

[8] Note that respondents in the three types of workflows were routed away from the question on team cohesion if they indicated that they spent most of their time working alone. Most workers, especially in the sales workflows, did not answer this question, and we can thus assume a bias among those who considered team members to provide a positive answer to the question about team cohesion.

knowledge work workflows, we found no significant differences in workers' perceptions of the degree of team cohesion in the three types of workflows. We did find significantly lower cohesion in Japanese knowledge work teams, however. Again, our findings run counter to expectations derived from theories of Japanese hybrid work organizations.

In the next section we turn to survey evidence on the relationship between the presence of positive co-worker relations and job satisfaction and learning results.

Co-worker Relations, Job Satisfaction, and Learning Outcomes

So far our analysis has demonstrated the importance of co-worker relations and pointed to several differences in the nature of co-worker relations across the three types of workflows. In this section, we consider whether co-worker relations are of equal importance to workers in the three types of workflows. We will test a number of hypotheses about the relationship between co-worker relations (as indicated by satisfaction with co-workers, lateral trust, and team cohesion) and the quality of working life (job satisfaction and satisfaction with on-the-job learning outcomes).

We begin by considering whether the relationship between co-worker relations and job satisfaction as established in previous research (Hodson 1997) varies across the three types of workflows. Based on our findings, we hypothesize the following variations:

Hypothesis 1: *Higher task interdependency in knowledge work workflows will result in stronger associations between indicators of co-worker relations and job satisfaction than in service and sales workflows.*

Hypothesis 2: *Informal relations among co-workers in service workflows, and the higher value service workers place on friendly co-worker relations, will result in stronger associations between indicators of co-worker relations and job satisfaction than in sales workflows.*

Our qualitative evidence showed that co-worker relations contribute to on-the-job learning. Although this is true regardless of which of the three types of workflows we were studying, inter-workflow comparisons revealed important qualitative differences. Based on these results, we hypothesize the following:

Hypothesis 3: *The positive relationship between co-worker relations and satisfaction with learning will be strongest in knowledge work workflows, where the interdependency among co-workers is highest, and lowest in service workflows, where workers are most dependent on their supervisors.*

Hypothesis 4: *The relationship between co-worker relations and satisfaction with learning will be weakest for sales workers, who are mainly self-reliant with respect to learning, except with regard to adjacent co-workers, in which case we expect indicators to be positively related.*

Finally, our cross-national analyses demonstrated that, regardless of workflow type, Japanese organizations have a more hierarchical structure. This was especially evident in the Japanese knowledge work workflow, in which employees reported significantly higher dependence on supervisors than in the knowledge work workflows in Australia. In these workflows, there was limited qualitative evidence that the presence of a hierarchical structure adversely affected learning. Since the presence of more sharply defined hierarchies is a feature of Japanese work organization in all three types of workflows, we explore cross-national differences in learning outcomes for the entire samples of Japanese, Australian, and U.S. respondents. Based on the qualitative findings, we hypothesize the following:

Hypothesis 5: *Japanese workers will be significantly less satisfied with learning outcomes than Australian or American workers.*

Hypothesis 6: *The association between co-worker relations and satisfaction with learning outcomes will be stronger in the Australian and U.S. workflows than in the Japanese workflows.*

Table 6.2 presents results relevant to hypotheses 1 and 2. Co-worker relations are measured using three indicators: (1) satisfaction with co-workers, an indicator of relations with immediate co-workers; (2) lateral trust, an indicator of relations with adjacent co-workers; and (3) team cohesion.

The correlations in the table show that in the service and knowledge work workflows statistically significant relationships exist between job satisfaction and indicators of co-worker relations. Our hypothesis that the relationship between co-worker relations and job satisfaction would be strongest among knowledge workers was not supported, however. Rather, our evidence points to co-worker relations being of equal importance in service and knowledge work workflows, despite the informal nature of the relations among co-workers and the low interdependency among workers in service settings.

Among the sales workers, there was no statistically significant relationship between their relations with immediate co-workers and their job satisfaction. Job satisfaction was related, however, to relations with adjacent co-workers. This is not surprising given the tensions between front-line workers and back-office staff in sales workflows. Overall, these findings suggest that whether co-worker relations contribute to job satisfaction depends on whether work relations are competitive (true in sales, not true in service and knowledge work), rather than differences in interdependencies.

Table 6.2. Correlations between Co-worker Relations and Job Satisfaction in the Three Types of Workflows

Workflow type	Job satisfaction and satisfaction with co-workers	Job satisfaction and lateral trust	Job satisfaction and team cohesion
Service (n = 575)	0.30*	0.41*	0.28*
Sales (n = 83)	n.s.	0.21†	n.a.
Knowledge (n = 154)	0.32*	0.30*	0.29*

Note: n.a. = not applicable; n.s. = not statistically significant; * $p < 0.05$; † $p < 0.1$.
Source: Employee survey.

Table 6.3. Correlations between Co-worker Relations and Satisfaction with Learning Outcomes in the Three Types of Workflows

Workflow type	Learning outcomes and satisfaction with co-workers	Learning outcomes and lateral trust	Learning outcomes and team cohesion
Service (n = 610)	0.34*	0.40*	0.38*
Sales (n = 86)	n.s.	0.47*	n.s.
Knowledge work (n = 156)	0.37*	0.30*	0.38*

Note: n.s. = not statistically significant; * $p < 0.05$.
Source: Employee survey.

Although there were differences across the three types of workflows, our results on the effect of co-worker relations on job satisfaction are consistent with those reported by Hodson (1997). Nonetheless, we conclude that whether recognized by managers (in knowledge-intensive WOs) or not (in bureaucratic WOs), co-worker relations contribute in important ways to job satisfaction. This contention is explored further in chapter 8.

Table 6.3 presents findings relevant to hypotheses 3 and 4. The indicators of co-worker relations are the same as in table 6.2. The learning results variable is a factor of respondents' reported satisfaction with learning outcomes provided in a number of areas of on-the-job training.

As reported in table 6.3, our findings indicate that, except in the sales workflows, positive co-worker relations contributed to satisfaction with learning outcomes, confirming our hypothesis that positive co-worker relations contribute to on-the-job learning. Our hypothesis that co-worker relations are more important to learning in knowledge work workflows than in service workflows is not supported. Again, our findings indicate that co-worker relations are as important in bureaucratic as in knowledge-intensive settings.

As hypothesized, among sales workers, relations with adjacent co-workers but not with immediate co-workers or team members were significantly correlated with perceptions of learning outcomes. Our qualitative evidence pointed to considerable tensions between sales workers and adjacent workers, yet these findings show a strong relationship between the presence of positive relations between front-line employees and back-office staff and satisfaction with learning.

Our final set of hypotheses (5 and 6) addresses cross-national differences in satisfaction with learning and its relationship to co-worker relations and learning outcomes. In support of hypothesis 5, statistical analysis shows that Japanese workers are significantly less satisfied with their learning outcomes than Australian or U.S. workers. (F $(2,608) = 19.42$, $p < 0.05$). This finding contradicts a broader literature on learning in Japanese organizations (Morishima 1994; Cole 1989, Koike 1995). Contrary to hypothesis 6, however, the relationship between co-worker relations and learning results shows no consistent cross-national differences. This latter finding suggests that in Japan, as in Australia and the United States, the presence of positive co-worker relations leads to satisfaction with learning results. Although this contention needs to be investigated further, we conclude that worker dissatisfaction with the outcomes of on-the-job learning is due to the presence of strong hierarchies in Japanese service and sales workflows and of a hybrid form of organization in Japanese knowledge work settings.

Conclusion

In this chapter we analyzed inter-workflow and cross-national differences in co-worker relations as they relate to interdependencies among co-workers, the emergence of different types of teams, and job satisfaction and satisfaction with learning outcomes. In general, we found that interdependency among co-workers was highest in knowledge work workflows, although there were important deviations among service workers in particular. Thus, though they were relegated to an informal sphere, positive co-worker relations in service work helped alleviate stress and contributed to on-the-job learning. Further, although service teams were really no different from work groups, they mitigated the hierarchical role of supervisors.

Findings regarding knowledge work showed that practice did not accurately reflect the postbureaucratic ideal of network work organizations. Rather than witnessing evidence of highly interactive cooperation across specializations, the relations we observed among specialists tended to be tense, and project teams frequently missed opportunities for learning.

Contrary to what we expected based on the hybrid model of work organization, we did not find evidence of better cooperation across specializations or better learning outcomes in the Japanese knowledge work work-flow. Further, the supervised rather than egalitarian project teams and the more pronounced hierarchies we observed in the Japanese service and sales workflows were associated with significantly lower team cohesion than in comparable workflows in the United States or Australia.

Our analyses of the effects of positive co-worker relations on worker sat-isfaction and learning suggest that in all three types of workflows positive relations contributed to the quality of working life and workers' develop-ment. Based on the KI ideal type, we expected co-worker relations to be especially important to knowledge workers. Instead, we found that positive relations were just as meaningful for workers in bureaucratic and entre-preneurial settings. Our findings suggest that informal relations in service workflows and cooperation in sales workflows have potentially positive effects on WO outcomes, although they go against the logic of the ideal types somewhat and are often contested by supervisors/managers out of concern for time efficiency and service standardization. These effects are explored further in chapter 8.

Our findings are mixed with respect to whether workers fit a more regi-mented or empowered model, as discussed in chapter 1. On the one hand, the formal design of co-worker relations in service and sales settings and the emphasis on lower interdependency among co-workers in favor of stronger dependency on supervisors and the organization approximate the bureaucratic ideal. This favors the image of the regimented worker. In prac-tice, however, workers in all three types of workflows depended on their co-workers, though to varying degrees. The strong finding that relations among co-workers are important to service workers and the association in all three types of workflows and cross-nationally between positive co-worker relations and overall job satisfaction point to a degree of de facto convergence on the postbureaucratic ideals of collaborative relations. In the next chapter we take up another dimension of lateral relations in front-line work organizations: customer-worker relations.

7 *Customer Relations*

F RONT-LINE workers spend much of their workday interacting with customers. This has implications for incumbents of these roles and hence is worthy of close examination. Indeed, this topic has spurred a debate, which is addressed in this chapter, between pessimists, who hold that front-line workers are emotionally emasculated and regimented, and optimists, who view today's workers as having new-found discretion to influence customers. In addition, as William Foote Whyte (1946: 123) has observed, "When workers and customers meet . . . that relationship adds a new dimension to the pattern of human relations in industry." In other words, customer relations also deserve attention because they are a constituent part of work organization.

We shall examine customer relations by comparing the triangular customer-worker-management relationship in the three types of workflows. Just as other aspects of work organization differ systematically among the three ideal types of workflows—B, E, and KI—so we expect to find distinct differences in customer relations and customer-worker-management relations among service, sales, and knowledge work workflows, respectively. Furthermore, we anticipate that such variations will have distinct consequences for workers.

In the first part of this chapter, we describe our expectations of customer relations and the customer-worker-management triangle in the three ideal types of workflows. In the second part, we present data from our workflows, which we compare with the expectations for the ideal types. We found a relatively close but variable correspondence between the empirical evidence and the ideal types. This correspondence is least evident in service workflows, where customer empathy militates against regimentation and associated worker dissatisfaction.

In the third part of this chapter, we test hypotheses concerning the effects of different types of customer relations on outcome variables. In spite of the shorter-term nature of the customer interactions in the service and sales workflows we studied, our data revealed positive correlations between satisfaction with customer relations and discretionary work effort. This was not the case among the knowledge workers. A significant positive relationship between satisfaction with customer relations and job satisfaction existed only for service workers. This runs counter to the assumption that encounters are less satisfying than relationships (Gutek 1995). We argue that sales workers are more instrumental in their attitudes toward customers than service workers and hence are less concerned about the quality of such relations. More generally, we contend that the relatively low impact of customer relations on knowledge workers' discretionary effort and job satisfaction is linked to their more complex, innovative work and employment relations arrangements, which, by and large, are not closely geared to customer responsiveness.

In the final section, we conclude that there is little empirical support for the pessimistic image of the regimented front-line worker. Where the tendency toward regimentation is most pronounced—in service workflows—customer empathy and management practice limit its development, holding out possibilities for greater empowerment. Such empowerment is most apparent in knowledge workers, whose customer relations tend to receive less emphasis than their relations with co-workers and others who are directly involved in solving complex problems.

Customer Relations in Theory

To understand the dynamics of work organization, it is important to examine customer-worker-management relations closely. Leidner (1993) refers to the shifting alliances among these three key actors. We conceptualize these relationships as a triangle in which each of the three actors is dependent on the others. Within this triangle, the parties may have conflicting or complementary interests, so that several potential alliances are possible. For instance, workers and management may be allied *contra* customers. Or there may be relatively harmonious relations between management and workers. Benson's (1986) research on American department stores illustrates the ebb and flow of these alliances over time. Without taking into account customer relations, the nature of control is difficult to comprehend. The same point can be made for co-worker relations. In short, customer relations are central to an explanation of WO. There is thus a good basis for agreeing with Benson (1986: 288) that "taxonomies of management practice derived primarily from manufacturing may not be readily applicable to service industries with their more complicated social reality and greater variability."

Recent political economic change has further emphasized the importance of customer relations. Heightened competition has returned the notion of customer sovereignty from its isolated existence in neoclassical economics to sociology (Abercrombie 1991). Greater customer influence has intensified the impact of customer relations on other aspects of WO. As part of this growing importance, the customer has come to have a role *within* the firm (Lovelock and Young 1979), eliminating the traditional, relatively clear demarcation between the customer and the firm that led to researchers neglecting the customer's role altogether (Hirschhorn 1985).

Concurrently, management has employed an ideology of "customer care" to enhance worker compliance regarding organizational restructuring (Legge 1995: 208–10). In addition, the rhetoric of total quality management assumes that quality is defined as conformance to customer requirements and that these expectations are unquestionable. The heightened importance of management ideologies that refer to customers also invites attention to relations between front-line workers and customers.

Turning to the literature on customer relations, optimistic and pessimistic images emerge. We will use these insights to construct a picture of customer relations in the three ideal types of work organizations.

Mills first drew pessimistic conclusions about customer relations when he suggested that being a front-line worker involved a "sacrifice of one's self" (1951: 182). Hochschild (1983) developed this line of thought by suggesting that managers were increasingly demanding emotional labor from workers. She saw this as having an overwhelmingly negative effect, whereby firms appropriated workers' emotions. Gutek (1995) argues similarly that insofar as recent developments in capitalism encourage firms to deal with customers through superficial *encounters* rather than meaningful *relationships*, the roles of front-line workers are becoming intrinsically less satisfying. Leidner connects these ideas of emotional labor and routine service encounters by suggesting that many firms are seeking to routinize and "standardize the workers' characters, personalities, and habits of thought" (1993: 31). Several other studies have also suggested negative emotional outcomes for workers in front-line roles (Albrecht and Zemke 1985; Mattingly 1977).

Pessimistic images are not restricted to workers engaged in routine work. As noted in chapter 5, there is also reference to the proletarianization of professional workers. Although such claims found little support in our analysis, the growing importance of the customer suggests the possibility that knowledge workers may be becoming not so much subservient to management as subservient to customers.

Other studies suggest a more optimistic image of customer relations, specifically its role in empowering workers. Quinn (1992: 132) even suggests that there may be an inversion of the traditional hierarchy whereby "sufficient professionalism is inculcated in the contact person." Schneider and Bowen (1992) also paint a positive sum picture of customer relations, arguing that there is a strong correlation between customer satisfaction with the quality of service and the satisfaction of front-line workers with the climate of the firm.

Beyond the management literature, Wouters (1989) suggests that emotion management can benefit workers. She argues that Hochschild's approach "hampers understanding of the joy the job [of airline attendant] may bring" (1989: 116). She quotes an airline worker approvingly as follows: "I like to put people at ease and then see how far I can go in building up playful exchanges, using all my imagination. It's enjoyable to find out how one can play together. . . . It cheers everyone up and adorns the situation" (116). Wouters also takes issue with the assumption (shared by Gutek and Leidner) that service encounters are becoming more routinized. She suggests that the demands of emotion management in employment have clearly become more *varied* over the course of the last century. In addition, it is possible to argue that, as the level of workers' knowledge and skill increase—as in the case of professional workers, such as lawyers and psychiatrists—workers have more power over their customers and experience this relationship in more complex ways (Abbott 1988: 122–24).

We are left, then, with contrasting images—that of the lower-skilled worker as a routinized, emotional shell, forced to smile through gritted teeth, against the image of the worker who is able to define and enjoy a variety of ways of interacting with customers. Further, contrasting images abound of knowledge workers becoming increasingly subservient to customers or achieving enhanced autonomy and power based on their specialized knowledge.

An examination and comparison of customer relations in the three types of workflows will help us assess the value of these contrasting images. To do this, we develop conjectures based on the three ideal types. These are shown in table 7.1. Following Benson (1986) and Leidner (1993), customer relations are considered through an inquiry into the nature of the customer-worker-management triangle. Therefore, the table includes dimensions relating to each of the dyads in that triangle as well as a consideration of the triangle.

Bureaucratic Organizations

In the B ideal-type organization, management is able to program and routinize most customer interactions. Management also attempts to routinize customer behavior. Leidner (1993) gives several examples of the way the management of McDonald's, seen by many as the epitome of an organization run with a bureaucratic logic, was successful in routinizing customer behavior. The nature of the interactions between workers and customers involves low interdependence. These interactions are in the form of encoun-

Table 7.1. Customer Relations in the Three Ideal Types of Workflows

Ideal type	Bureaucratic	Entrepreneurial	Knowledge-intensive
Worker-customer relations	Affective neutrality	Affective—instrumental use to warm up "prospect"	Affective to the extent that some empathy is needed to "bond" with customers;
	Encounter* Low worker proactivity; sequential dependence	Quasi-relationship; High worker proactivity; sequential dependence	Relationship High worker proactivity; inter-dependence
Management-customer relations	Customers seen as undifferentiated, amenable to routinization	Customers differentiated into categories; high customer sovereignty acknowledged	Customers seen as highly differentiated
Management-worker relations	Workers used to try and maximize efficiency for standardized service	Contracted worker as agent; management provides infrastructure	Discretion given to professional workers to negotiate service
Customer-worker-management triangle	Management the most powerful party; potential basis for cooperation among all three parties.	Customers the most powerful party; potential basis for cooperation among all three parties.	Ambiguity regarding most powerful party; potential cooperation among all three parties.
Most likely relationships	Two-party alliances between management and workers contra customers	Two-party alliances between management and customer contra workers	Two-party alliances between management and customers

Note: * Following Gutek (1995), encounters exist where repeated interactions between specific workers and specific customers are not likely to occur and workers are interchangeable.

ters rather than relations and are characterized by affective neutrality. As Bauman has argued, albeit in a different context, an "important effect of [the] bureaucratic context of action is the dehumanization of the object of bureaucratic operation" (1989: 102). Under bureaucratic organizational logic, workers come to assume an "ethical indifference" to the dehumanized objects on whom bureaucracies act (103).

The ideal-type bureaucratic organization is primarily producer-oriented, and the customer is essentially treated as an outsider. Thus, there is the potential for an alliance to be formed between management and workers as producers contra the customer as outsider. There is also the potential, however, for the formation of a worker-customer alliance. This may arise if both workers and customers seek to resist the routinizing logic that management asserts on both parties.

Although the producer logic, on the one hand, and the routinizing logic, on the other, often provide conditions for the formation of differing alliances, the potential for cooperation among all three parties should not be neglected. There is likely to be at least surface-level cooperation among the three parties when customers' expectations have been appropriately met within the structure and workers either accommodate to, or embrace, routinization.[1] The strongest party within the triangle is management. Workers have little power, given that they can easily be replaced. The routinizing logic that management displays to customers in the ideal-type B organization clearly suggests limited customer sovereignty and hence implies considerable management power.

Entrepreneurial Organizations

The main goals in the ideal-type E organization are to identify and meet unstable customer requirements. Management does not seek to routinize, therefore, but to set aims to be fulfilled, leaving the ways in which objectives will be attained largely in workers' hands. As chapter 5 argues, these aims are strongly related to measures that reflect customers' attitudes and behavior. Workers must be active, using affectivity instrumentally, to "sell" part of themselves in the process of selling their product (Oakes 1990). Thus, Leidner shows that insurance sales agents use affectivity instrumentally by aiming "to make sales by making friends" (1993: 154). This contrasts with the affective neutrality of workers in B-type organizations.

In the ideal-type E organization, there is a basis for cooperation among the three parties because the workers are satisfied with the level of discretion they are granted by management and because customer satisfaction is based on workers being attentive to customer requirements. Management will also be satisfied since there is an incentive for business to grow under this system. Customers are the strongest party of the three, having been granted considerable sovereignty.[2]

As a result of pressures within the ideal-type E organization, alliances

---

[1] As Leidner has argued (1993), it should not be assumed that workers always seek to resist the routinizing logic of management.

[2] Note that the concept of customer sovereignty as used here means that the customer's expressed interests, rather than their "real" or "objective" interests, dominate. There is considerable scope for expressed interests to differ from objective interests, not least because of the intervention of the firm through advertising and the sales pitches of salespeople.

may form of two parties against the other. The most likely alliance is between management and customers contra the workers. Management places workers in the position of servicing customers' needs and relies on customer data as key elements in its control mechanisms. The organizational logic of the E ideal type means that in disputes between a worker and a customer, management will tend to support the customer.

Knowledge-Intensive Organizations

Our discussion focuses on the typical case in which the customer is an organization rather than an individual. Management cannot routinize worker and customer behavior because the environment is uncertain and complex. Moreover, management often lacks the necessary information to set definitive *aims*. The need to bisociate (Koestler 1970) the two domains of knowledge held by customers and workers means that there is a high level of interdependence between the two parties, who must develop a relationship if adequate communication and problem resolution are to take place. The knowledge worker arrives at the relationship with a considerable body of relatively abstract knowledge, while the customer's knowledge is based on his/her experience in a particular environment. Productive knowledge is created when the two forms of knowledge—theoretical and contextual—are integrated or bisociated. In the KI ideal-type organization, management views customers as highly differentiated, imposes few attempts to routinize customers' behaviors, and grants customers considerable but not absolute sovereignty. Customers are likely to vary in several important respects and are likely to make different demands on the provider. As such, management tends to treat customers as highly differentiated. In effect, management accords greater sovereignty to customers in the KI ideal-type organization than in the B ideal-type organization but not less than in the E type.

In the KI ideal-type organization, there is greater ambiguity than in other types of organizations concerning who is the most powerful party in the triangle. The basis for cooperation among the three parties is also different. In the KI ideal-type organization, cooperation is most likely when the customer requires creative work from employees and such work will generate a profit for management. Given the confluence of interest in controlling and channeling workers' expertise and creativity, the most likely two-party alliance is between management and customers. Two-party alliances are also likely to form between workers and a customer contra management. This could occur if workers wanted to do additional and creative work that would benefit the customer but that was outside the terms of the negotiated customer-management contract. Hence, management would veto such activity.

There is ambiguity over which of the three parties is the most powerful.

Certainly, workers have more power in KI ideal-type organizations than in the ideal-type B or E organization and management has less power in the KI type than in the other two types.

Customer Relations in Practice

In previous chapters we noted the strong parallels between service work and the B ideal-type organization, between sales and the E ideal-type organization, and between knowledge work and the KI ideal-type organization. This section aims to assess how much these parallels hold true with respect to customer relations.

Service Workflows

Our data show that, with regard to important aspects of management-customer relations and management-worker relations, the expectations of the B ideal type were met. There was a significant difference with respect to worker-customer relations, however, in the degree to which affectivity was demanded of workers and the extent to which workers were expected to be proactive.

In only two of the workflows was there relatively stable cooperation among management, workers, and customers. In the other workflows, there was a degree of tension among the three parties in the triangle. Further, there was only one clear instance of a two-party alliance of the form most likely to emerge in the ideal-type B organization.

Worker-customer relations. Commonalties with the B ideal will be described first, followed by an examination of differences. Workers related to customers primarily through encounters rather than via relationships. Thus, individual workers were, in effect, interchangeable. Customer requirements could be met by any of the workers. Further, in the main, workers and customers interacted on an on-off basis in which there was no expectation on either side of resuming this interaction in the future.

Management, however, made several attempts to create the illusion that a relationship existed between the customer and the worker, creating what Gutek (1995) refers to as a "pseudo-relationship." For instance, workers at all the service workflows were instructed to give their first names to customers. Despite such trappings of a relationship, the bureaucratic imperative to deliver efficient, standardized service dominated. This was clear from instances in which the two imperatives—to create a relationship and to deliver efficient, standardized service—clashed. At AINSV, workers were keen to establish some form of relationship with customers—to ensure that when a customer purchased a product, the sale would be credited to the worker involved. Thus, at the end of phone calls, workers were especially keen to remind customers of their names, in the hope that, the next time they called, they would specifically ask to speak to those workers. Management's policy, however, was that a customer was to be transferred to the next available worker rather than to a specific employee. This policy reflected the company's aim of delivering efficient, standardardized service, one element of which was that the time customers spent waiting in the telephone queue—in this case, to speak to particular workers—should be minimized.[3]

The level of sequential interdependence between service workers was relatively low. It had risen in workflows that had recently placed more emphasis on sales but was still relatively low. The majority of customer calls involved requests for information (e.g., the bank balance) or to effect a transaction (e.g., to transfer funds between accounts). Workers also were asked to be problem solvers (see chapter 3). Because the precise nature of the problem was not always apparent to the customer, the worker had to be proactive in seeking relevant information. Similarly, at workflows in which management emphasized sales as well as service, workers were encouraged to be proactive in seeking information that would encourage the customer to purchase particular products.

The clearest break from expectations for the B ideal-type organization was in the area of affectivity. In the ideal type, the worker is ethically and emotionally indifferent toward the object of bureaucratic action. In practice, however, workers were recruited on the basis of their customer empathy, were socialized to identify with customers' interests, and were expected to demonstrate such empathy in interacting with customers.

A range of terms was used to refer to customer empathy, including "customer focus" and "positive customer service attitude." As indicated in chapter 4, this "personality trait" was gaining ground as a key criterion in hiring. As the following examples indicate, firms sought to further socialize/train workers in customer empathy. At AINSV, customer service skills were a central focus of both the content and the process of the training course for new recruits. One of the ways workers were taught to develop customer identification was through role plays, in which the new recruits were placed in the position of customers. In addition, the trainer repeatedly exhorted the recruits to "put [themselves] in the customer's shoes."

Management expected workers to demonstrate customer empathy as a matter of routine in their interactions with customers. As noted in chapter 5, an important management tool for both maintaining control and training was call monitoring, in which a supervisor monitored and subsequently advised on, or reinforced, what were regarded as good customer-worker

---

[3] The Japanese workflow JBSV constituted a deviation from the other service workflows with regard to encounters/relationships. Here, employees had clients whom they regularly serviced in person. Thus, these workers had relationships with their clients, not just encounters.

interactions. Customer empathy was explicitly addressed in these sessions. At MFJSV, for instance, the call monitoring form included not only whether the worker demonstrated "courtesy to customers" (which one would expect even in ideal-type B organizations) but also whether there was evidence that the worker *maintain[ed] rapport with customers."*

Workers' actions and attitudes largely, but not unequivocally, met management's aim of having workers act empathetically toward customers. For example, a worker at AINSV received a call from a person who was phoning on behalf of his recently bereaved mother. The worker acted sympathetically toward the customer, promising that he would make the insurance transaction as simple as possible because the customer's mind was *"quite rightly elsewhere."* At MFJSV, a part-time female worker was particularly adept at handling mothers who wanted to send money to their children studying abroad.

In interviews, workers repeatedly emphasized the satisfaction they gained from *"helping people"* or *"satisfying customers."* This was confirmed by correlating workers' reported ability to satisfy customers (see appendix 2 for details) with their perceived satisfaction with customer relations (a single item). As expected for the service workflows, the two measures were positively and significantly related ($r = 0.25$, $p < 0.05$). A second correlation, between workers' perceived ability to satisfy customers and overall job satisfaction, was also positive and significant ($r = 0.29$, $p < 0.05$). Thus, even though there were no face-to-face relations between workers and customers in call centers, empathy was clearly evident.

Management-customer relations. These relations resembled those in the B ideal type in that management tended to view customers as a relatively undifferentiated mass who were amenable to routinization. For instance, at UB1 and UB2, customers' calls were answered by an automated voice-recording system that gave them instructions. Although this system eliminated a large number of routine calls from the queue, customers nevertheless preferred to speak to an employee.

There were some exceptions to this pattern of treating customers in an undifferentiated way. As indicated in chapter 3, for example, call-center customers were distinguished by the types of products they purchased and by their income categories. These distinctions were a way of socializing customers into a set of expectations as to where and how they would be treated.

Management also sought to routinize customers' behavior in relation to worker interactions. In several workflows, the questions workers were to ask customers were displayed on a screen. As noted elsewhere, management de facto allowed workers to depart from the script, highlighting the difficulties in routinizing front-line encounters down to minute details. At JBSV, management put much less emphasis on routinizing the service encounter, so that the bond-ladies were permitted to visit customers on request.

Management-worker relations. A more comprehensive picture of these relations is given in chapters 4 and 5. Here we focus on those aspects most pertinent to the customer-management-worker triangle.

There were significant commonalties between practice in the service workflows and the expectations of ideal-type B organizations.[4] Management tended to see workers as an instrument in the provision of standardized service, and, hence, workers were subject to considerable routinization and rationalization. In many workflows, actual practice deviated somewhat from this logic.

An example of bureaucratic logic contending with, and ultimately dominating, the aim of instilling customer empathy occurred at MBASV, where management gave workers targets for both average call times and average times to do follow-up work subsequent to calls. Management strengthened the bureaucratic logic in another sense—in an effort to reduce the follow-up time, it relegated the more complex after-call work to a specific group of staff. This strategy also ran counter to the nonbureaucratic aim of instilling customer empathy, since it took away the workers' sense of "ownership" of calls, which management was attempting to instill in order to improve customer service. Management acknowledged this contradiction: *"Ownership is still there in terms of [workers] representing the [firm] and portraying a professional yet empathetic stance. However, the introduction of the Administration Unit has relevance for ownership, when ownership is defined as owning a customer's problem. There is the danger of deflecting the blame onto other departments and shielding [workers] from customers."*

Customer-worker-management triangle. There were several important deviations in the service workflows from the B ideal type. Although management remained powerful, customers wielded increasing power: two of the service workflows experienced relatively stable cooperation among all three parties, while others experienced a degree of tension; in only one instance had a clear two-party alliance formed between workers and management contra customers.

The attempt to shift from being producer-oriented to being customer-oriented meant that customer sovereignty was increasing. This was illustrated at TEL, which was experiencing strong competition after years as a secure monopoly. This encouraged the firm to relinquish its previous producer orientation. Symbolically, this was most obvious in the way that management organized advertising displays in shopping centers (the domain of the customer), in order to win customers back from a competitor.

In our discussion of the B ideal type, we argued that the greatest chance

[4] Again, JBSV was an exception. In keeping with management's only limited emphasis on routinizing customer interaction, workers were given more formal autonomy than other service workers. In practice, however, the bond-ladies were severely constrained by the routinized nature of their product and the relatively unsophisticated customer base.

for cooperation among the three parties was when customer expectations were set appropriately, and could be met within the bureaucratic structure, and workers accepted routinization. These conditions were mostly, but not unambiguously, met in AINSV and UB1 and UB2, where there were relatively few surface tensions within the customer-worker-management triangle.

The element with the greatest potential to undermine cooperation was the way in which workers reacted to routinization. In the cases of AINSV and UB1 and 2, there was evidence that workers both resisted and embraced it. High labor turnover—more than 25 percent—reflected this resistance; and in interviews, it was common for workers to say that after the six or so months it took to learn the job, it essentially became routine. Most workers felt this was a source of dissatisfaction. In addition, according to the survey data on job values, presented in chapter 3, workers in the service workflows valued intrinsically satisfying work.

Workers also saw advantages to routinization. Thus, at AINSV, workers favored placing limitations on their discretion if that contributed to better customer service. Further, although team leaders chaired and guided the quality circles at AINSV, workers had considerable influence over the groups' recommendations. These often included ideas that had the effect of routinizing work and making control systems more pervasive. For instance, workers suggested increasing the amount of call monitoring and formally testing workers before granting them higher levels of discretion in their jobs.

In the other service workflows, there was evidence of greater tension among the three parties. At MBASV, a key element necessary for cooperation had broken down—the ability to meet most customers' demands routinely within the bureaucratic structure. The problem occurred after other departments made a large number of administrative errors, leaving the center faced with many nonstandard requests that could not be dealt with routinely. To solve customers' problems, workers often had to go through a labyrinth of departments, making personal contacts with individual workers and maintaining ongoing dialogues with those workers over several days. Workers were motivated to make this extra effort both by customer empathy and by the desire to engage in more challenging tasks.

The breakdown in the bureaucratic system had several consequences for the triangle of relations. First, a large number of dissatisfied customers were phoning to seek assistance. Second, the demands of many of these customers could not be satisfied immediately. Hence, the proportion of irate customers increased. Third, because so many workers were stepping out of the narrow bounds of designated discretion, individual calls were taking longer, leading to an increase in the length of time customers spent in the telephone queue. This in turn made customers even more dissatisfied. It was the workers who had to face the consequences, even though the cause of the problems lay elsewhere. As one worker put it: *"It's no good. You cop the flak [i.e., suffer the abuse] from the customers and from those lot [pointing upstairs toward senior management] if something goes wrong."* These problems probably contributed to the increase in turnover, which went higher than 30 percent.

Since one of the bases of cooperation was now absent, relationships among the parties in the triangle became antagonistic. Customers antagonized workers; management antagonized workers, because it saw measures of productivity falling; and workers blamed senior management for causing the administrative errors and their own management for limiting their ability to do follow-up work and thereby reimposing routinization of the work process. Notably, the workers expressed very little antagonism toward customers. This was because of the empathy felt toward customers.

At TELSV, an alliance formed between workers and management contra customers. Indeed, throughout the workflow workers and immediate managers made references to customers being "scum" and "scammers." This workflow was an exception, however. Although the front-line workers at other service workflows were required to undertake both service and sales tasks, workers at TELSV were also expected to manage credit. This meant that they had to handle customers who were trying to avoid or evade paying their phone bills. Faced with the possible punitive action of having their phones cut off, these customers occasionally became deceptive. As Hochschild (1983) has shown in her study of credit-management workers, such jobs tend to promote customer antipathy rather than empathy.

Table 7.2 puts the data from our service workflows in the context of the expectations for the B ideal type.

Sales Workflows

In this section we present data showing that customer relations in the sales workflows corresponded closely with the expectations for the E ideal type.

Worker-Customer relations. There were two types of "customer" in the sales workflows—the individual client in search of a mortgage and the referrer. Typically, the referrers at MBAS and ABKS were real estate agents, solicitors, accountants, or financial advisers. The role of the referrer was to furnish the worker with information concerning potential clients. Referrers benefited from passing on this information because clients could more quickly and reliably complete transactions with which the referrers were associated (e.g., house purchases). In the Japanese workflow JBS, in which the workers registered companies' stocks, the main referrers were representatives of banking institutions with which the company had close relations. Overall, there were strong commonalties between customer relations in the sales workflows and the E ideal-type organization.

Table 7.2. Customer Relations in the Bureaucratic Ideal Type and in Service Workflows

	Bureaucratic ideal type	Service workflows
Worker-customer relations	Affective neutrality; encounters; low worker proactivity; sequential dependence	Strong customer empathy; encounters; high worker proactivity; sequential dependence
Management-customer relations	Customers viewed as undifferentiated, amenable to routinization	Routinizing logic with some customization
Management-worker relations	Workers used to maximize efficiency for standardized service	Workers used for same purpose but routinization limited in practice
Customer-worker-management triangle	Management is the most powerful party; potential basis for cooperation among the three parties; two-party alliance between management and workers contra the customers is the most likely	Management powerful but customer power increasing; two workflows experienced relatively stable cooperation, while others experienced tension within the triangle; only one clear instance of an alliance between workers and management contra customers

Customers and workers in the sales workflows related primarily through a form of quasi-relationship involving high worker proactivity and sequential dependence, as well as an instrumental expression of affectivity. These interactions are referred to as quasi-relationships because several meetings were usually necessary to clarify customers' product knowledge and requirements. The period during which these meetings took place was relatively short, however (i.e., between one and three weeks).

Workers were expected to be proactive in two senses—in identifying potential customers and then in interacting with these customers. This requirement was strongest at ABKS, where workers were expected to have active networks of referrers who could be relied upon to pass on information about potential customers. In interacting with customers, workers often had to be proactive both in seeking out information relating to a customer's eligibility for a mortgage and in clarifying customer requirements. For instance, in structuring more complex deals, salespeople needed proactively to seek out more financial information about the client than was required by formal bank policy. At JBS, salesmen (they were all men) used proactive strategies to secure customer business. One salesman even offered to help a client company deal with *sokaiya* (extortionists) should they threaten to disrupt a stockholder meeting.

On average, the level of interdependence between workers and customers was higher in the sales workflows than in the service workflows. In the most straightforward cases, the customer related his/her requirements, the worker related information about available products and procedures, and then both agreed on a loan application. As indicated in chapter 3, sometimes workers had to be both innovators and problem solvers. In such cases, the degree of customer dependence on the worker deepened.

Consistent with the E ideal type, sales workers tended to use more instrumental displays of affectivity toward customers than did workers in the service workflows. This difference reflects the service emphasis in the service workflows and the sales emphasis in the sales workflows. As Oakes (1990) has argued, the sales process involves a commercial idiom. The ultimate concern of sellers is not the product or service for sale but the customer's money. The purpose of sales is to obtain as much of it as possible. The customer is a means to an ends, an instrument in the sales process. Displays of affectivity toward the customer, therefore, are undertaken instrumentally. By contrast, in the service idiom, according to Oakes, the customer is not regarded as a potential antagonist who is manipulated to generate commissions but as a client whose needs are paramount in the transaction. The purpose of the interaction is to meet those needs as fully as possible. The customer is not a means to an end.

We observed several instances in sales workflows of workers who displayed instrumental affectivity toward customers. One worker at ABKS who covered a low-income area stated that *"in the western suburbs, you go down to their level. . . . You pick up their personality very quickly."* Another worker we observed mirrored not only the language but also the posture of a customer during a meeting. Workers were particularly adept at manipulating symbols of empathy. Thus, one worker said, in explaining the importance of accepting a cup of coffee from a customer after a meeting at his house: *"You shift from being a guy from the bank to being a friend."* At another meeting, the worker feigned empathy with the customer by stating that he would make a concession regarding the payment of a particular tax when, in fact, this procedure was standard practice.

Although most of the displays of affectivity we observed appeared to be instrumental in nature, workers also expressed genuine empathy. Several also stated that one of the most satisfying elements of their job was *"helping people fulfill their dream"* (of home ownership). Oakes (1980: 88) explained this divergence between expected and actual behavior by arguing that the simple commercial idiom/service idiom dichotomy is rarely played out as starkly in practice as suggested in theory.

Recapping what was more fully outlined in chapter 2, the MBAS and ABKS workflows contained both entrepreneurial and bureaucratic subsystems. The entrepreneurial element involved salespeople whose job was to proactively search for and sell mortgages to customers. The back office, maintained by credit analysts, was run primarily as a bureaucratic system. The differences in worker-customer relations between the front and back offices were manifested in several ways, including in systematic differences in the way in which the two "sides" of the workflow referred to customers. In correspondence between the front-liners and the back-office people regarding loan applications, the front-liners referred to customers by name and made reference to subjective and potentially affective issues, such as the customer's personality. By contrast, back-office staff referred to customers in more impersonal terms (such as "the client" or "the applicant") and focused on the more "rational" aspects of the loan application.

Front-line workers at MBAS put some stock in the personal integrity and standing of customers and were critical of back-office credit analysts for ignoring personal attributes and playing only by the rules. For example, included in a file was a note from a front-line worker that read: *"From talking to these people I feel they have the utmost integrity, but I find it difficult to convey this to you."* In an effort to clarify relations between front- and back-office workers, the organization ran a survey to determine how these workers' perceived one another and the quality of their relationship. A key finding was that the salespersons were highly critical of the credit analysts for being so disdainful of customers.

Front-line workers also tended to be proactive in their dealings with referrers. At ABKS, salespersons stated that the active creation and maintenance of a good referral base was a key part of the job. There was evidence of empathy between some workers and referrers, sometimes extending to out-of-work friendships. In the main, however, the worker-referrer relationship was instrumental in nature and was becoming more money-oriented. Indeed, one worker spoke of being "squeezed" by referrers: real estate agents would try to play salespersons off against representatives of another company in the pursuit of getting loans approved more quickly.

The instrumental nature of the worker-referrer relationship at ABKS was also clear from an arrangement whereby the referrers would be given financial rewards for successful referrals. MBAS also was introducing this system. Under this arrangement, the workers had to attempt to keep two "customers" satisfied—referrers and individual clients—which occasionally led to conflicts of interest. At a meeting, salespeople suggested that they were more likely to side with the referrers than with the customers.[5] This is not surprising given that the workers relied on the referrers for future business to a greater extent than on individual clients.

Management-customer relations. Management-customer relations were in line with what one would expect to find in E ideal-type organizations. Management tended to view customers as differentiated into broad categories and acknowledged the considerable scope for customer sovereignty. The differentiation of customers into types was primarily by income/wealth.

[5] This meeting was called by the manager at MBAS for the purpose of discussing whether to compensate referrers financially for providing successful leads. No concern was raised that such a move would compromise the interests of individual clients.

Management believed that, given the range of customer types, it was not appropriate to try to routinize customer behavior. This was also consistent with management's acknowledgment that customers had considerable sovereignty. This sovereignty was symbolically manifested in the creation of "mobile" workers who were expected to visit customers in their homes or workplaces rather than demand that they come to the office. Management also expected workers to hand-deliver loan approval letters.

Customer sovereignty was highest in ABKS. The dominant management philosophy was that the referrer was the "boss," and referrers were encouraged to think of workers as their employees. According to the senior manager, if a referrer was dissatisfied with a salesperson's performance, the referrer was to phone him and he would threaten to *"get rid of [the salesperson] the next day."* High customer sovereignty was also evident insofar as performance was based directly on sales (i.e., customer decisions).

Management-worker relations. Again, there were significant commonalties with the ideal-type E organization. Unlike the service workflows, where management gave workers programmed tasks, management in the sales workflows set aims for the workers to fulfill. As in the E ideal type, management was able to define these aims closely. Workers were effectively taken on as quasi-agents who were given targets and the organizational and technological infrastructure to facilitate the completion of those aims. In addition, as discussed in chapter 5, management used customers as part of its control mechanism.

Once management had defined output goals, albeit taking into account differences in individual experience, workers were hired to fulfill those goals. At ABKS, workers were not even provided with desk space in an office. The most important part of the infrastructure was the strong referral base, which salespersons might inherit from an incumbent; salespersons still needed to actively solicit customers, however. Further, as noted in chapter 4, new salespersons were expected to have contacts from previous sales jobs.

Customer-worker-management triangle. The dominant party in the sales workflows was the customer, and although there was a strong basis for cooperation among the parties, there was tension between management and the workers over which party was the more important in relation to the referrers. The picture was further complicated because the sales workflows had two kinds of customers: final clients and referrers. At ABKS, and to a lesser extent at MBAS, it was the referrer "customer" to whom management accorded the greatest influence.

Despite the symbolic power in having workers go to the customer, there were aspects of the worker-referrer relationship that made the individual customer vulnerable to manipulation. Specifically, customers may have trusted the referrer and followed his/her advice regarding mortgage lending in the belief that the advice was proffered with the customers' best interests in mind. This may not have been the case, however. At both MBAS and ABKS, the organization had a sanctioned practice of paying referrers for introductions that led to sales. Thus, it was widely acknowledged that referrers were likely to make introductions with monetary gain, not customer-related objectives, in mind.

The dominance of customers, particularly referrer customers, and management's alliance with the referrers placed the workers in positions of subservience. As female workers commented, in that the referrers were overwhelmingly male, the referrers sometimes also expected gender-based subordination. A female worker at MBAS noted that male customers and referrers talked down to her. At ABKS, a female salesperson stated: *"I don't like socializing with real estate agents—they're highly sexist and are usually revolting to me. I'm there on a business level, not for anything else."* Another female worker, however, claimed that she *"use[d] gender to [her] advantage."* The women's subservient role, played out in gender terms, combined with management siding with customers, was manifest in a case a female worker at ABKS related. She had received pornographic photos from a customer in the mail, but she said that when she recounted the incident to her manager, he *"wasn't sympathetic."*

Although alliances formed in the sales workflows between customers and management, there was also, especially among the more successful workers, a strong basis for cooperation among all three parties. This paralleled the situation in the E ideal type. Thus, workers were satisfied with the discretion they were granted and, in attempting to sustain their relationships with referrers, tended to give the best possible service to customers referred to them. Consequently, customers, by and large, were satisfied with the service. Management also was satisfied in these cases because the system tended to generate business. Given that workers relied more for leads from referrers than from individual clients, the key relationship was with the referrer.

In some cases, management was keen to regulate employees' relations with their referral networks and, in the case of ABKS, even to wrestle control of referral networks from employees. At MBAS, sales workers were required to register the names of referrers with the organization. This was partly so that if the workers left the company, the names could be redistributed to other sales employees. At ABKS, building relations with referrers was a stated goal of corporate strategy, and it was understood to be part of the manager's role.

In turn, sales workers knew their value to the organization depended to a large extent on their referral networks. A sales worker noted that if he had trouble with the company and had to leave, he'd "take the network" with him. This threat seemed credible since these networks were often based on dense interpersonal contacts and sometimes required after-hours socializing and complex exchanges between the sales workers and their referrers.

At ABKS, sales workers managed their networks far more directly than at MBAS, primarily by establishing matching sets of relationships with referral organization hierarchies. Loan salespeople at ABKS would deal with the referrers, managers would establish relationships with the referrers' managers, and senior managers would have contact with the executives of the referrers' organizations. In addition, managers regularly introduced employees' referrers to other ABKS sales employees, with the aim of broadening the dyadic nature of the referrer–sales worker relationship. In one case, a sales worker successfully opposed this strategy because it disrupted his relationship with his contacts outside the organization.

Such disputes over "ownership" of the customer relationship are more common in sales than service settings. Thus, as noted earlier, in service settings management seeks to control the *process* of work, whereas in sales settings management is concerned with *output*. When management has considerable control over the work process, it will structure the customer-worker relationship in a way that makes it clear that the interaction occurs within the dominant rubric of the firm-customer relationship. When management has less control over the work process, it is less able to shape customer-worker interactions and to highlight the firm-customer relationship. This gives workers an opportunity to fill this gap. The result is more frequently conflict with the firm in sales than in service settings.

The Japanese workflow JBS was different in that the referral networks were within the company and associated firms. As a result, there was little threat that if employees left they would take their networks with them. JBS salespeople depended on *shukko* supervisors not only to make introductions but also to lend legitimacy to the company, in that they were employees with more prestigious but closely associated financial institutions. JBS salespeople also depended on their supervisors' connections with these institutions to provide client companies with credit and other financial services. Consequently, compared with the Australian workflows, the Japanese workflow exhibited much less worker-management tension over control of the referrers.

Table 7.3 summarizes the data on customer relations in the sales workflows in the context of the expectations for the E ideal type.

Knowledge Work Workflows

The overall picture that emerges of the knowledge work workflows is that a strong correspondence exists between theory and practice in all but one area—relations in the customer-worker-management triangle. Here, as suggested by the KI ideal type, there was ambiguity in who constituted the most powerful party. Although there is the potential for cooperation within the triangle, at least in the KI ideal type, in practice the level of cooperation varied and two-party alliances formed.

Table 7.3. Customer Relations in the Entrepreneurial Ideal Type and in Sales Workflows

	Entrepreneurial ideal type	Sales workflows
Worker-customer relations	Affective—instrumental use to warm up "prospect"; quasi-relationships; high worker proactivity; sequential dependence	As in the E ideal type
Management-customer relations	Customers differentiated into broad categories; high customer sovereignty	As in the E ideal type, but dominant customer was the referrer rather than the end client
Management-worker relations	Worker as agent; management provides infrastructure	As in the E ideal type
Customer-worker-management triangle	Customers the most powerful party; potential basis for cooperation among all three parties, most likely two-party alliance between management and customer contra workers	Customers were the dominant party; significant basis for cooperation among all parties; alliances between customers and managers contra workers; tension over whether management or workers were the key nexus with referrers

Worker-Customer relations. Worker-customer relations mirrored what one would expect based on our knowledge of the KI ideal type. Workers and customers had relationships, not just encounters; workers and customers both displayed high levels of proactivity; interdependence was high; and the affectivity shown by workers toward customers varied.

Because of their specialized knowledge and skills, workers were not functionally interchangeable. For example, the project manager at WBSD could not be replaced by someone else because, during a series of meetings, team members had acquired shared, tacit knowledge and had established a manner, language for communicating, and trust, all of which would be disrupted if he were replaced. This project manager and certain customer representatives had been attending meetings for more than a year, with the prospect of their relationship extending fairly far into the future. At COMPUJ, the organizational practice of rotating staff through several positions led to problems in this regard. Clients tended to upgrade their systems every five years, and if the staff they dealt with had been rotated elsewhere, knowledge about their systems and concerns had also migrated.

As suggested in the discussion of the KI ideal type, for knowledge work to be executed successfully, the two domains of knowledge—the theoretical and the contextual—must become bisociated, requiring both workers and customers to be proactive. At COMPUJ, the need for this bisociation had become obvious to management only recently. Previously, COMPUJ, a leader in the world of large mainframe solutions, had been able to proceed with relatively little knowledge of the specific customer and to impose, what were in effect, producer-led solutions (Lillrank 1994). Over the last decade, however, the move had been toward providing customized software solutions. As a result, the need to combine theoretical and contextual knowledge became more apparent. This realization led management to undertake a major reorganization of work practices aimed at fostering the deep interdependencies between workers and customers that have been discussed elsewhere (Mankin, Cohen, and Bikson 1996). Management sought to bring those workers with technical expertise into more direct contact with customers at an earlier stage in project work. The argument was that, by asking proactive questions, these technical experts could provide a more complete and accurate picture of customer requirements.

In two of the four knowledge work workflows, workers who were in direct contact with customers were expected to display some customer empathy. In the other two workflows, there were no such expectations. At COMPUJ, the workers were expected to interact with customers occasionally, in social as well as business contexts. For example, workers sometimes socialized with customer representatives after meetings.

Knowledge workers with direct customer contact tended to display empathetic feelings, albeit in an instrumental manner. At WBMM, the policy was to match workers with customers based on their respective personality types. Considerable effort went into identifying the client's personality type and acting accordingly. As the manager stated: *"We deliberately want different types of [workers]. It makes sense to have diversity. We can pick each customer and their life cycle and match them to the characteristics of the dealer. There is a constant strategy to identify real needs of the customer and satisfy them; these needs vary between customers."*

Workers' descriptions of their interactions with clients indicated their use of the commercial idiom, and workers were instrumental in reaping financial rewards from doing so. For instance, a worker mentioned that after drinking and forming a good relationship with a client, the client began to purchase more sophisticated products. The worker concluded his story by saying, *"You need to work out what type of person the customer is,"* revealing the ultimately instrumental nature of their relationship.

Management-customer relations. Management-customer relations in the knowledge work workflows corresponded significantly with such relations in the KI ideal type. Management viewed customers as highly differentiated, made no attempts to routinize customers' behaviors, and granted customers considerable but not absolute sovereignty. As at WBMM, management at TELSD treated customers as discrete entities with specific needs and requirements. Thus, at the time it expressed interest in undertaking a contract with a prospective organization, TELSD would set up a specific "bid team" whose composition would vary depending on the customers' particular requirements.

Overall, management at the knowledge work workflows granted customers considerable authority, or, more accurately, "negotiated sovereignty." There was variation, however, in the degree to which they granted such authority. Customers of WBSD had the least sovereignty. Here, as a number of interviewees (technical experts included) intimated, the project team *"built a solution before [it] knew what the problem was."* As noted in chapter 5, it was at this workflow that the IT corporate group used a customer's project as a vehicle for introducing a new IT architecture. In this case, the customer—the customer services business group—was internal to the organization. Although the formal project plan was structured to show clear customer relevance, the contents were highly subjective and considered of little relevance beyond the approval stage. Furthermore, although the formal language concerning the IT architecture made constant reference to potential benefits for the business, in practice, these benefits were never realized. In effect, all of this negated the notion that the systems developers were serving the business, despite the rhetoric of senior IT management to the contrary.

As noted above, at COMPUJ, management had recently granted customers more influence. This was most evident at a client meeting that we observed. Although representatives of the client firm were openly critical of COMPUJ, they were able to win concessions from COMPUJ's representatives. Customer sovereignty was also displayed symbolically. Thus, on a hot summer day, employees of the client organization took off their jackets, while COMPUJ staffers felt compelled to keep theirs on.

TELSD gave its customers the greatest amount of sovereignty. This was manifested in the negotiation of the original tender agreement between the client organization and TELSD and in subsequent interpretations of that agreement. In the initial stage, for instance, the client organization successfully negotiated with TELSD to hire a specific firm named by the client as a contractor, and the project manager continued to defer to the client as the project was undertaken.

Management-worker relations. Management-worker relations varied considerably, and only some workflows conformed to the KI ideal type. In the ideal type, not only is management unable to program the process of tasks to be completed, it cannot closely specify the aims of such tasks. Thus, management cedes considerable control of the work process to the firm's professional employees and accommodates these employees in establishing project aims. As discussed in chapter 5, management made use of some information on both outputs and behavior to control knowledge workers, and workflows varied regarding workers' influence in goal setting.

At TELSD, the workers had very little voice in determining their objectives. This workflow was organized in such a way that the team of workers who negotiated the contract with the customer differed from the team that actually undertook the work. As such, the goals for the latter group were a fait accompli. At COMPUJ, the workers were not separated in this way. Rather, the same workers played a role in negotiating and executing projects; however, the customers' power to determine the terms of service had also increased.

At WBSD, as noted above, there was considerable ambiguity regarding the precise aim of projects. Consequently, input from knowledge workers was welcomed. This was also true at project meetings, which were participative in nature. The only problem was that many applications experts lacked knowledge of and experience with the object-oriented design technology that was pressed on them by the IT corporate "gurus."

Customer-worker-management triangle. Although our discussion of the KI ideal type suggested a basis for cooperation, in practice there was both disarticulation and cooperation among the parties in the triangle. At WBSD, the relationships between the parties were characterized by their disarticulation. The "religious wars" surrounding the IT architecture, including its application in the broker applications project, effectively left the workers disoriented and subject to changes in direction. Meanwhile, the customer was largely oblivious to these politics. Given the circumstances, the workers tended to distrust both senior IT management and the internal customer (for abrogating control).

At COMPUJ, there had previously been an alliance between management and the workers as producers. Management cemented this alliance by offering the workers employment security and a predictable career path, and, in response, the workers demonstrated a strong commitment to the organization. With the increase in customer sovereignty, this alliance was beginning to crumble. Although the workers still had employment security, management was seeking a major change in the promotion system so as to reward performance rather than seniority. Management was also seeking to establish ways to ensure workers' commitment to the customer as well as to the company.

At WBMM, the strongest alliance was between management and the workers. Customers were treated as "prospects" to be "warmed" to the idea of buying or selling money market products. Both management and the workers discussed customers in instrumental terms (i.e., their susceptibility to manipulation). The management-worker alliance was strong as a result of the close working relationships that had developed and the participative way in which work was organized (see chapter 5). By contrast, there was less management-worker cooperation at TELSD, where it had taken some time to negotiate the terms of service with the client, and, thereafter, the client had adopted a low-trust, opportunis-

Table 7.4. Customer Relations in the Knowledge-Intensive Ideal Type and in Knowledge Work Workflows

	Knowledge-intensive ideal type	Knowledge work workflows
Worker-customer relations	Affective to a degree; relationships; high worker proactivity; considerable interdependence	Some affectivity in two workflows; relationships; proactivity and interdependence as in ideal type
Management-customer relations	Customers viewed as highly differentiated	As in KI ideal type
Management-worker relations	Management gives professional workers discretion to negotiate service	In all but one workflow, knowledge workers negotiated service
Customer-worker-management triangle	Ambiguity regarding who constitutes the most powerful party; potential cooperative relations among all three parties; most likely two-party alliance between management and customers	Ambiguity as in KI ideal type; range of disarticulation and cooperation in the triangle; various alliances.

tic approach to the service provider. This in turn adversely worker-management relations.

Table 7.4 summarizes the nature of customer relations in the knowledge work workflows given the expectations outlined for the KI ideal type.

The empirical examination of customer relations in the three types of workflows revealed many commonalties with the benchmarks for the ideal types. The practice, however, deviated from the theory in several important ways. Most notably, management in the service workflows demanded greater affectivity of workers than expected based on the B ideal type. Further, in the knowledge work workflows, there was greater disarticulation in the customer-worker-management triangle than suggested by the KI ideal type. Having compared customer relations in the three types of workflows, we now examine the effects of these relations on workers' discretionary work effort and job satisfaction.

Customer-Related Outcomes

Several hypotheses regarding the likely effects of variations in workers' satisfaction with customer relations on workers' discretionary work effort and job satisfaction can be derived from the picture of customer relations developed above. These are summarized and then evaluated with the help of employee survey data.

Satisfaction with Customer Relations, Discretionary Work Effort, and Job Satisfaction

Our research showed that workers in the service workflows had the strongest degree of customer empathy. Although management monitored workers on their ability to demonstrate this trait, they were not forced to display it. Rather, many workers in service workflows embraced customer empathy actively. We would therefore expect to find a significant positive correlation between satisfaction with customer relations and discretionary work effort in service workflows.

By contrast, the research showed that the workers in the sales workflows had a more instrumental view of customer empathy. The driving force in their expressing empathy was the operation of the commission-based reward scheme. Given that there is likely to be a correlation between satisfaction with customer relations and higher earnings (in that better customer relations are likely to reflect higher sales and hence higher earnings), we expected to find a positive correlation between satisfaction with customer relations and discretionary work effort.

Finally, in the knowledge work workflows, customer empathy was a much less significant trait, and the relationship between pay and performance in relation to meeting customer expectations was less obvious. We would expect to find little correlation, therefore, between satisfaction with customer relations and discretionary work effort. In sum, we hypothesize the following:

Hypothesis 1a: *In the service workflows, there will be a strong association between satisfaction with customer relations and discretionary work effort.*

Hypothesis 1b: *In the sales workflows, there will be a strong association between satisfaction with customer relations and discretionary work effort.*

Hypothesis 1c: *In the knowledge work workflows, there will not be a strong association between satisfaction with customer relations and discretionary work effort.*

For each type of workflow, a correlation analysis was conducted using as outcome variables workers' satisfaction with customer relations and their discretionary work effort (described in chapter 5). For the service and sales workflows, the correlations were significant—0.30 ($p < 0.05$) and 0.40 ($p < 0.1$) respectively—whereas for the knowledge work workflows, the correlation was not significant. These results confirm the three hypotheses (1a-1c).

Given their high level of customer empathy, we also expected to find a strong positive correlation between satisfaction with customer relations and job satisfaction for the workers in the service and sales workflows. In the latter case, the key mediating link was the commission scheme. Better customer relations will reflect higher sales, which will mean higher income and higher job satisfaction.

For the knowledge work workflows, we expected customer relations to have a much smaller impact on the outcome variables. This is based on a similar logic to that underlying hypothesis 1c above. In sum, the hypotheses are as follows:

Hypothesis 2a: *In the service workflows, there will a strong association between satisfaction with customer relations and job satisfaction.*

Hypothesis 2b: *In the sales workflows, there will be a strong association between satisfaction with customer relations and job satisfaction.*

Hypothesis 2c: *In the knowledge work workflows, there will not be a strong association between satisfaction with customer relations and job satisfaction.*

The results of our correlation analysis support hypotheses 2a and 2c. There is no support for hypothesis 2b, however. Thus, for the service workflows, there is a correlation of 0.40 ($p < 0.05$) between satisfaction with customer relations and job satisfaction, and for the sales and knowledge work workflows, respectively, the correlation between the two variables is insignificant ($p < 0.05$).

One plausible interpretation of the unexpected finding with respect to sales workers is that, as argued earlier, these workers bring a more instrumental perspective to customer relations. Simply having good relations with prospective customers is not enough; these prospects need to be converted into customers, and these customers must fit the lending criteria so that applications can be converted into sales. Thus, by themselves, good customer relations do not lead to sales, and it is the latter that is crucial in determining workers' earnings and job satisfaction.

Incongruence and Other Customer-Related Relationships

The dynamics of the customer-worker-management triangle leads to the possibility that management and customers may impose conflicting demands on workers. Accordingly, we developed a measure of the degree to which workers perceive there to be incongruence between management's and the customer's interests. For the service workflows, we expected to see a significant negative correlation between the degree of perceived incongruence and job satisfaction. Our reasoning was that job satisfaction would be impaired if the worker was pulled one way by management and another way by customers.

For the sales workflows, we expected to see a similar correlation based on slightly different reasoning. Service workers relate to customers based on empathy, whereas sales workers depend on customers to achieve acceptable levels of income. We would therefore expect conflict between customers and management to directly affect sales workers' livelihoods and hence to have an adverse effect on their job satisfaction.

In the knowledge work workflows, the concern wasn't so much that workers could be pulled in conflicting directions but, rather, that they could be placed in the position of negotiating the terms of service with both customers and management. The likely result would be low levels of perceived incongruence, which would have limited impact on job satisfaction.

Based on the above reasoning, we proposed the following four hypotheses:

Hypothesis 3a: *In the service workflows, there will be a strong negative association between perceived incongruence and job satisfaction.*

Hypothesis 3b: *In the sales workflows, there will be a strong negative association between perceived incongruence and job satisfaction.*

Hypothesis 3c: *The level of perceived incongruence will be lower in knowledge work workflows than in the other types of workflows.*

Hypothesis 3d: *In the knowledge work workflows, there will be no correlation between perceived incongruence and job satisfaction.*

Incongruence was measured with an internally reliable three-item factor (see appendix 2 for details), while job satisfaction was measured with an internally reliable seven-item factor (see appendix 2 for details). Correlational analysis provided support for hypotheses 3a, 3b, and 3d. For the service workflows and the sales workflows, the correlation coefficients were -0.22 ($p < 0.05$) and -0.23 ($p < 0.05$) respectively; there was no correlation for the knowledge work workflows.

To assess hypothesis 3c, the levels of perceived incongruence in the three types of workflows were compared with each other using ANOVA. The level of perceived incongruence was found to be significantly lower for knowledge workers than for sales workers or service workers ($F (2,747) = 1.034$; $p < 0.001$). These results provide support for hypothesis 3c.

Two hypotheses related directly to the contrasting images of front-line workers are also relevant. Gutek (1995) sees management's aim of increasing efficiency as underpinning the increasing tendency for relationships to become encounters. In her view, this represents a progressive dehumanization of social relations. Thus, as mentioned earlier, Gutek claims that encounters are considerably less satisfying to workers than relationships. Hence, this hypothesis:

Hypothesis 4: *Customer interactions in the form of encounters will be less satisfying to workers than customer interactions in the form of relationships.*

As noted earlier, customer-worker interactions took the form of encounters in service workflows, quasi-relationships in sales workflows, and relationships in knowledge work workflows. The clearest test of hypothesis 4 would be to compare the level of workers' satisfaction with customer relations in both the service and knowledge work workflows. These levels of satisfaction were compared using ANOVA. No statistically significant difference was found in the level of satisfaction with customer relations in the two workflows: $(F (2,747) = 0.72, p < 0.49)$. Thus, the hypothesis was disconfirmed.

This result suggests problems in Gutek's arguments. In particular, there is a tendency to romanticize the nature of relationships and to denigrate encounters. Potential negative aspects of relationships are ignored. For instance, management may expect the level of affectivity toward customers to be higher in relationships than in encounters. In Hochschild's terms (1983), there is more potential in relationships for the private self to be taken over by the public self. Furthermore, workers are more dependent on customers in relationships than in encounters. If customers use dependence as a tool to manipulate workers, relationships may again have relative disadvantages for employees.

By the same token, Gutek's emphasis on the negative aspects of encounters leads her to overlook the possibility that satisfying customers might provide workers with real satisfaction. Indeed, our research found strong support for this. As noted earlier, in the service workflows, where workers interacted with customers almost exclusively through encounters, time and again workers replied in interviews that "the best part of the job is knowing that you're helping people."

As noted at the beginning of this chapter, several commentators have argued that workers in customer service jobs are increasingly being required to show affectivity in their work and that this trend has important deleterious effects on workers (Mills 1951; Hochschild 1983). This line of argument suggests the following hypothesis:

Hypothesis 5: *The more management demands affectivity from workers, the less satisfied workers will be with customer relations.*

Our research showed variation in the amount of affectivity required of workers. The clearest way to test the hypothesis was to identify and compare satisfaction with customer relations in the two workflows where the most affectivity was expected (WBMM and JBS) and the two where the least was required (WBSD and TELSD). Thus, workers in WBMM and JBS were aggregated and contrasted with workers in WBSD and TELSD (also aggregated) for their levels of satisfaction with customer relations. ANOVA shows no significant differences between the two groups. Thus, the hypothesis was disconfirmed.

The reason for this lack of support probably lies with problems in the arguments advanced by Mills (1951) and Hochschild (1983). These researchers assumed that workers do not wish to display affectivity toward customers and, hence, will report lower levels of satisfaction with customer relations where management demands affectivity. This assumption is probably misplaced. Recall that in many workflows management explicitly sought to recruit workers who possessed a "customer focus" or empathy toward customers.

Given that many respondents to our survey were satisfied with the quality of the customer relations in their workflow, it is likely that they liked displaying affectivity toward customers. This critique echoes that of Wouters (1989), who argued that Hochschild's thesis emphasized the negative aspects of demanding affectivity from workers, a position reached by using a questionable distinction between "real" and "false" selves and emphasizing the costs and ignoring the benefits of emotional labor. In so doing, Hochschild spuriously separated the interests of firm and workers and neglected customer interests. This contrasts with our approach, which has emphasized the importance of moving away from a simple management-labor dichotomy toward an examination of the triangular relationship. Thus, we can find comfort in the lack of support for a hypothesis derived from Hochschild's approach.

Conclusion

We have argued in this chapter that the existing literature on customer relations contains contrasting descriptions of what happens when workers and customers meet. On the one hand, service workers are portrayed as routinized, emotional shells forced to smile through gritted teeth, and knowledge workers are described as becoming increasingly subservient to customers. On the other hand, there is a more optimistic image, associated with empowerment, which points to the emergence of an intrinsically satisfied service worker who is able to define and enjoy a variety of ways of interacting with customers. This image also points to the emergence of knowledge workers whose specialist knowledge confers power and status, enabling these employees to meet clients on nothing short of an equal basis. This chapter has sought to examine these images through theoretical reflection and empirical evidence. We argued, theoretically, that the nature of customer relations would differ systematically and significantly in ideal-type B, E and KI organizations.

With this established, we sought to benchmark our empirical data against expectations for the ideal types. In many respects customer relations in the service workflows corresponded with our expectations of a B-type organization. Customer relations were centrally informed by a routinizing logic, and workers related to customers while undertaking narrow, routine tasks. Management sought to routinize customers and used workers to provide standardized service. Finally, whether there was cooperation or conflict between the parties hinged on how much workers and customers accepted the routinizing logic.

Our data diverged from what we expected in one significant regard, however. This was in the extent of affectivity demanded of, and expressed by, service workers toward customers.

We noted that workers were recruited on the basis of, socialized into, and assessed on the basis of their empathy toward customers. We also showed that in practice workers frequently demonstrated empathy. Clearly, emotional labor is an important issue for workers in service workflows. Indeed, it is with reference to these workers that front-line work has been so pessimistically portrayed. It is hard, however, to match the findings of our research with characterizations of the service worker as inauthentic, disinterested, and emotionally disengaged.

When customer relations were negative, there were important negative consequences for workers—for instance, when customers were irate, workers who generally had empathy for customers were often deeply affected. Moreover, workers became dissatisfied when management's routinizing logic conflicted with the workers' desire to help customers.

Workers found several aspects of customer relations satisfying. In particular, as mentioned earlier, most workers liked helping people and demonstrated customer empathy actively and not artificially. Workers' satisfaction with customer relations were therefore critical to the dynamics of conflict and cooperation within the customer-worker-management triangle.

In the service workflows, the image of the optimistic, empowered front-line worker able to define and enjoy a variety of customer interactions sometimes conflicted with the strong routinizing logic of service workflows. Certainly workers enjoyed interacting with customers, but there were severe limits regarding how much variety was possible in these interactions and the extent to which workers could define the nature of these interactions.

Our findings and our expectations corresponded most closely for the sales workflows. Management was especially concerned with identifying customer requirements, which varied and tended to change over time. Thus, management did not seek to routinize the work process but to set aims to be fulfilled, leaving how these aims were to be met largely up to the workers. In that these aims were strongly related to customers' attitudes and behavior (products purchased), customers had considerable sovereignty. Workers were expected to be proactive and to show affectivity, which, as we noted, was instrumental in nature. The dominant party was the referrer. Although there was a significant basis for cooperation among all parties in several instances, two-party alliances between customers and managers contra the workers tended to prevail.

Little attention has been paid in the literature to sales workers. Again, the image of the regimented worker appears to be well off the mark. Arguments focused on the potentially debilitating effects of emotional labor have little resonance for sales workflows, where workers relate to customers in a primarily instrumental rather than an empathetic manner and workers have considerable autonomy in defining their interactions with customers. Workers may smile at customers, but this is not something management is forcing the workers to do (see Erickson and Wharton 1997). Rather, these workers know that they receive commissions based on customers' purchases, and, for this reason, are not likely to smile at customers through gritted teeth.

The negative aspects of front-line work in sales workflows are more likely to be associated with the increase in customer sovereignty and the consequential increase in subservience to the customer, which, as noted in the case of women, may be reinforced by gender discrimination. In this respect, and by virtue of their pay and employment prospects being so closely tied to performance, sales workers might best be regarded as task empowered rather than empowered more generally.

We found strong commonalties between customer relations in our knowledge work workflows and in the KI ideal type. Knowledge workers acted within an environment of considerable uncertainty and complexity, which discouraged routinizing worker behavior and limited the extent to which aims could be clearly defined. The need to bisociate the two domains of knowledge held by customers and knowledge workers usually resulted in high levels of interdependence between representatives of these groups. Within the discussion of the KI ideal type, it was suggested that, given that customer sovereignty was strong but far from absolute, there would be considerable ambiguity with regard to the main alliances within the customer-worker-management triangle. This, too, was mirrored in our findings.

Overall, our research offers only limited support for the Hochschild-inspired image of front-line workers as regimented automatons. Indeed, we tested and disconfirmed two hypotheses derived from this perspective. Our analysis suggests that although emotional labor is a key element of WO in service workflows, it is best understood by considering customer relations as a triangle of relationships involving the three key parties rather than artificially dichotomizing workers' and management's interests and ignoring the role of customers.

Similarly, the question of whether knowledge workers are becoming more subservient to, or more powerful in relation to, customers cannot be answered without taking the role of management into account. Our research suggests that knowledge workers play a key role in negotiating between customers and management. This is not always the case, but generally the need to bisociate knowledge within the constraints negotiated with management encourages collaboration rather than subservience or attempts to wield power by one party over the other.

Finally, this chapter has made clear that customer relations do matter. In the service and sales workflows, aspects of customer relations were strongly associated with workers' willingness to expend discretionary effort and their job satisfaction. This was not the case for knowledge workers, however, who placed less value on satisfying customers than did service or sales workers.

8 Work Organization: Consequences and Cross-National Comparisons

In previous chapters, we noted at various junctures how Japanese work-flows differed from their Australian and U.S. (hereafter Western) counter-parts. In this chapter, we look more systematically at these differences and examine the consequences or outcomes of these differences in the context of work organization.

The two outcome variables that we will examine in depth are job satis-faction and organizational commitment. We argue that the three types of workflows differ in three key aspects of employee dependence and that these differences determine the relative impact of the various elements of WO—employment relations, control relations, lateral relations, and customer relations—on satisfaction and commitment among the workers in the three types of workflows.

Cross-nationally, we have shown that regardless of the type of workflow one is studying, Japanese workflows tend to be more bureaucratic than Western workflows. From this general conclusion, we derive specific propo-sitions about cross-national differences in terms of patterns of WO and employee job satisfaction and organizational commitment. We argue that institutional factors produce cross-national variations that are workflow-specific but that irrespective of workflow type, Japanese workflows are characterized by stronger gender discrimination and bureaucratic features than their Western counterparts.

We begin the chapter by discussing the meaning and significance of job satisfaction and organizational commitment as outcome variables. This is followed by an examination of the notion of employee dependence as it applies to workers in the three types of workflows. We then summarize five theoretical approaches that have been used to explain satisfaction and com-mitment. Viewed in the context of employee dependence, this helps to gen-erate hypotheses to explain variations in the two outcome variables across the three types of workers/workflows. We then present and discuss our findings.

In the second section, we use the dependence perspective to examine the proposition that Japanese workflows are more bureaucratic than their Western counterparts. We develop and discuss the implications of this proposition as it relates to employee satisfaction and commitment. The chapter concludes with some comments on the implications of these findings as they relate to work organization and cross-national differences.

Concepts and Theories of Job Satisfaction and Organizational Commitment

In chapter 1, we noted that job satisfaction and commitment are consequences or outcomes of work organization and, as such, they comprise the dependent variables in our interworkflow comparisons. Job satisfaction is a widely accepted measure of workers' well-being. Commitment is a concept that encompasses the extent to which the worker is linked to the organization. It is a reflection of management's interest in obtaining maximum support from employees, a condition that is vitally important in competing successfully in highly competitive markets (Ghoshal and Bartlett 1995).

Research has demonstrated that job satisfaction and organizational commitment are related to several indicators of work behavior, including absenteeism, labor turnover, and work effort. More satisfied and committed employees are less likely to quit a company. Low commitment imposes costs on employers in the form of increased recruitment and training and reduced quality and productivity. In addition, low commitment limits an organization's flexibility, since less committed employees are more resistant to change. Industrial sociologists have also invoked commitment to explain differences in economic performance between U.S. and Japanese organizations and in the job performance of British and American workers (Lincoln and Kalleberg 1990). Studies vary, however, in their findings regarding the extent to which satisfaction and commitment contribute to higher motivation to work and better job performance (Morrow 1993; Mowday, Steers, and Porter 1982; Mathieu and Zajac 1990; Cohen and Lowenberg 1990).

Locke defined job satisfaction as "a pleasurable or positive emotional state resulting from the appraisal of one's job or job experiences" (1976: 1300). As this definition indicates, job satisfaction has an affective aspect (do you like your job?) and an evaluative component (compared to your expectations or relative to other people?). Our measure of job satisfaction is adapted from Quinn and Shepard (1974) and is based on three questions that are underscored by a single factor (see appendix 2 for descriptive statistics of these three items). Mowday, Steers, and Porter define commitment as "the relative strength of an individual's identification with, and involvement in, a particular organization" (1982: 27). Our operationalization of the concept is adapted from Mowday, Steers, and Porter. Factor analysis shows that a one-factor structure underlies four indicators (see appendix 2 for operationalizations and descriptive statistics).

Employee Dependence Framework

The concept of employee dependence provides a basis for developing hypotheses pertaining to elements of WO that purport to explain the relative satisfaction and commitment of the three types of workers. Throughout the previous chapters, we have shown that the work organization in service workflows generally resembles the bureaucratic ideal type; sales workflows are more like the entrepreneurial type; and knowledge work workflows are akin to the knowledge-intensive ideal type.

By virtue of their employee status, employees rely on management for the provision of IT, information and knowledge, and the skills required for the sourcing and servicing of customers. The degree of dependence, however, varies among the three types of employees. Bureaucratic WO engenders a higher degree of employee dependence on management than the entrepreneurial and knowledge-intensive ideal types. To the extent that service workflows resemble the bureaucratic type, service employees are likely to be the most dependent and knowledge workers the least dependent on management. Sales employees are likely to occupy the middle ground. Likewise, to the extent that Japanese workflows are more bureaucratic, Japanese employees are more dependent on management for their knowledge and skills, for their use of IT, and in determining the nature of their relations with customers than their Western counterparts.

Work-related knowledge and skills comprise the human capital on which employees depend for task accomplishment and internal and external job opportunities. Where the organization is the primary source of human capital, work-related knowledge and skills are likely to have relatively high degrees of firm specificity; in other words, human capital cannot easily be transferred to other companies. Hence, we may speak of the employees as being highly dependent on the organization. By contrast, if the employees have acquired the human capital of their own volition and/or from industry or publicly provided education and training programs, it is likely to be less firm specific and more portable. Thus, these employees are less dependent on management.

The extensive use of IT in most workplaces has made workers increasingly dependent on their organizations for the provision of technology to execute their work tasks. Because of this technical division of labor, workers differ from each other in the amount of control they can exert over the design of the technology, the specific uses to which it can be put, and whether they can easily reconfigure systems to meet their own needs. The degree of control employees have over technology at work is also closely related to the way management structures WO. Where management adopts a highly specialized division of labor, employees are dependent for their use of the technology on the expertise of their colleagues (typically, technicians and technologists) and management coordination.

Control over how customers are procured and serviced is also determined by the extent to which employees are dependent on management. Where management has greater control, management is likely to structure employee skills and knowledge. By contrast, where employees have some discretion in their choice of customers, employees are able to use knowledge and skills they have developed from sources outside the workplace.

The complexity of the service being provided also shapes employee dependence. When outputs require the expertise of various specialists whose knowledge and skills are likely to change as improvements are made in the technology, management is likely to be less knowledgeable and therefore less capable of determining the kind of human capital that should be acquired. Under such circumstances, management plays a limited, facilitative role in developing workers' skills and knowledge.

Of the three types of employees in our study, service workers were the most dependent on management. As we discussed in chapters 3 and 5, although these workers' task discretion was increasing, their work was still relatively standardized and routinized. Standardization enhanced management's knowledge and measurement of the work process (chapter 5), and service employees relied heavily on their supervisors and on management-structured training courses, manuals, and reference guides for relevant knowledge and information (chapter 6). Further, the pervasive IT system in service workflows was generally designed without much input from employees. The detailed functional division of labor engendered a relatively high level of interdependence between workers in service workflows and adjacent departments. As a result, service employees relied on management coordination for effective task completion. Using the IT system, management structured the speed and nature of customer service. Service employees had little choice in the type of customers they served and the nature of the service they provided.

Sales workers were less dependent on management and their employing organization. As we pointed out in chapter 3, sales workers were expected to have accumulated substantial work experience and referral networks. Unlike service employees, whose knowledge and skills were shaped primarily by management, sales employees acquired their competencies through work experiences. It will be recalled from chapter 7 that sales employees, in pursuit of their sales targets, were also relatively free to choose different types of customers. Thus, sales employees relied far less than service workers on management for the formation of human capital and customer sourcing and servicing. Securing successful deals depended less on management-provided IT than on personal qualities and social skills, such as the ability to establish rapport and trust with customers.

Among the three types of employees, knowledge workers were the least dependent on management. Unlike service employees, knowledge workers depended mainly on their peers for knowledge and skill formation. And, compared with service and sales workers, knowledge workers had more control over technology. Systems developers, for example, were themselves technology designers. This enabled them to both design and reconfigure the technology they worked with to suit their needs and those of their clients. Similarly, the money market dealers were serviced by a highly responsive IT applications team, so that, except in determining the annual budget, they deferred very little to management.

The level of independence the knowledge workers enjoyed is also evident from their more transferable knowledge and skills. In that it was highly customized, their work was less amenable to codification than the work of the service and sales workers we studied (see chapter 3). The sourcing of customers, however, was not generally within the knowledge workers' control. They accepted contracts won by the company for which they worked or, in the case of internal clients, they had to accept the broad requirements of the customer. As we emphasized in chapter 7, however, the effective resolution of technical problems required an ongoing synthesis of the customers' knowledge and that of the knowledge workers and, through this bisociative process, workers were able to influence customers. As long as this did not have major adverse financial implications for the organization, this process normally proceeded with little interference from management.

How these differences in employee dependence on management affect workers' job satisfaction and commitment can now be summarized. To the extent that service employees are more dependent on management, their employment relations (chapter 4) and control relations (chapter 5) are likely to contribute more to their satisfaction and commitment than they do to the satisfaction and commitment of knowledge workers. In that knowledge workers rely on colleagues for learning and task accomplishment, co-worker relations are likely to matter more to these workers (see chapter 6). The individualistic nature of sales work suggests that the effects of co-worker relations on these workers' satisfaction and commitment are likely to be weaker than among service and knowledge workers. Instead, in that employment relations and control relations are commission-based, they are likely to have more pronounced effects on sales employees' job satisfaction and organizational commitment.

Having provided the foundation for comparative analysis, we now develop our hypotheses concerning job satisfaction and commitment.

Five Perspectives on Job Satisfaction and Organizational Commitment

Our five perspectives on job satisfaction and organizational commitment derive from the interplay between extant theories on satisfaction and commitment and reflections on our qualitative data. The discussion and hypotheses are organized around the key elements of work organization—namely, work relations, employment relations, control relations, co-worker relations, and customer relations.

Work relations. The theory of job design emphasizes that a range of work characteristics influences employee attitudes. According to this theory, jobs that offer variety, mental challenge, opportunities for initiative, and autonomy give rise to favorable employee attitudes. Empirical studies have noted that *intrinsically interesting jobs* that offer employees considerable autonomy and discretion enhance satisfaction and organizational commitment (Hackman and Lawler 1980; Mowday, Steers, and Porter 1982; Mathieu and Zajac 1990). Accordingly, we asked the respondents to our survey how satisfied they were with the nature of their work. This gave us our measure of intrinsic work satisfaction (see chapter 3). As we noted in chapter 3, all three types of workers, and especially knowledge workers, valued sources of intrinsic work satisfaction.

We found that knowledge and sales work provided more opportunities for autonomous creativity than service work. Accordingly, we hypothesized the following:

Hypothesis 1a: *The effect of satisfaction with the nature of work on job satisfaction and organizational commitment is likely to be stronger for sales and knowledge workers than for service workers.*

Effectiveness of the technology. The effectiveness of the technology is the second work-related factor highlighted by other researchers (e.g., Adler 1992) and by our research as reported in chapter 3. We noted that technology that was slow, complicated, and inflexible led to employee dissatisfaction. Through its impact on worker motivation, it is also likely to lead to lower levels of commitment. Service workers are highly dependent on technology and, as described in chapter 3, have little control over it. Thus, our next hypothesis is as follows:

Hypothesis 1b: *The perceived effectiveness of technology is likely to have a larger impact on job satisfaction and organizational commitment among service workers than among sales or knowledge workers.*

Employment Relations: Expectations regarding Pay, Promotion, and Job Security

The second approach emphasizes the effects of job expectations on job satisfaction and commitment. To the extent that workers' expectations regarding most aspects of work are met, they are likely to be more satisfied with their jobs. Satisfaction is likely to be stronger if all the expectations regarding the more valued aspects are satisfied. Further, if workers' expectations are met, particularly those that are most important to employees, employee commitment is likely to increase. Since it is impossible to consider all aspects of jobs, we concentrate on the three most salient aspects—pay, promotion opportunities, and job security—discussed in chapter 3. These comprise three of the major elements of employment relations, as discussed in chapter 4.

Satisfaction with pay. Satisfaction with pay has been highlighted as a determinant of job satisfaction and commitment (Cohen and Gattiker 1994). The pay of the sales and knowledge workers in our study, but not the pay of the service workers, varied according to individual job performance. In addition, in absolute dollar amounts, the service employees earned the lowest pay of the three types of workers. To the extent that satisfaction with pay is a function of a job's objective rewards and the value workers place on pay, we postulate the following:

Hypothesis 2a: *For all three types of workers, satisfaction with pay has a significant effect on job satisfaction and commitment.*

Satisfaction with promotion opportunities. Where satisfaction with opportunities for promotion is a salient job value, it is likely to be positively related to job satisfaction (Clark 1996). Satisfaction with promotion opportunities also enhances commitment, as employees come to identify more strongly with the organization in anticipation of continuing in a higher position (Kalleberg and Mastekaasa 1994; Ornstein, Cron, and Slocum 1989; Gallie and White 1993).

In chapter 4, we argued that promotion opportunities were limited for service and sales workers, whereas knowledge workers tended to have career prospects in the occupational labor market. The knowledge and skills of service employees were more firm specific than those of sales and knowledge workers. For service employees, employment outside the organization was therefore likely to be less advantageous (at least in the short term) than employment within the organization. This leads to this hypothesis:

Hypothesis 2b: *Satisfaction with promotion prospects has a larger effect on the job satisfaction and commitment of service workers than of sales and knowledge workers.*

Job security. Organizational restructuring and the growth of nonstandard employment, as outlined in chapter 1, have probably increased the salience of job security as a factor influencing job satisfaction and commitment. The risk of job loss has a negative effect on psychological well-being and increases levels of work stress (Warr 1987; Whelan, Hannan, and Creighton

1991; Gallie, Marsh, and Vogler 1994; Cappelli et al. 1997). We would expect, therefore, that satisfaction with job security would be positively related to job satisfaction and commitment. Given that service and sales workers valued job security more than knowledge workers did, we would expect satisfaction with job security to contribute more to the job satisfaction and commitment of service and sales employees than to the job satisfaction and commitment of knowledge workers. Further, we would expect this to be especially true for sales workers, whose job security depends on consistently reaching sales targets. Hence, we postulate the following:

Hypothesis 2c: *Satisfaction with job security has a stronger effect on the job satisfaction and commitment of service and sales employees than of knowledge workers.*

Control Relations: Fairness and Employee Participation

Our third approach suggests that workers who believe that management is treating them fairly and that there are opportunities to participate in decision making are likely to be more satisfied and more committed to the organization (Fox 1974; Morrow 1993). We focus on three aspects of control relations highlighted in chapter 5: the trustworthiness of senior management, support from immediate supervisors, and the amount of influence in decision making workers exercise above the task level.[1] Differences in the magnitude of the effects of these three variables on employee satisfaction and commitment among the three types of workers are discussed below.

Trustworthiness of senior management. Workers who trust senior management are likely to feel less threatened and hence to be more satisfied. Such trust is also likely to be associated with higher commitment as employees reciprocate management's concern for their well-being. Having more trust in senior management is therefore likely to be associated with higher levels of satisfaction and commitment (Cappelli et al. 1997).

Earlier discussion noted that service employees acquired their firm-specific knowledge and skills primarily through their current employment. This suggests that their employment prospects were likely to reside in the organization rather than in the external labor market. Hence, perceiving senior management as trustworthy is likely to be more important to service workers than to knowledge workers.

In the case of the sales workers, the terms of their employment contracts and their participation in marketing and pricing products led to high levels

---

[1] We did not include satisfaction with the capability and efficiency of management, mentioned in chapter 5, since this variable does not distinguish between the effect of relations with immediate supervisors from those with senior management. These are theoretically distinct aspects that need to be kept separate in empirical analysis.

of dependence on senior management. Thus, control relations were likely to contribute significantly to these workers' satisfaction and commitment. Accordingly, we hypothesize the following:

Hypothesis 3a: *The trustworthiness of senior management will have a stronger effect on the job satisfaction and organizational commitment of service and sales workers than on knowledge workers' job satisfaction and commitment.*

First-line management support. In chapter 5, we characterized the style of supervision the service workers in our study received as facilitative rather than directive. Supervisors provided psychological support and relevant information and knowledge. This reliance on their supervisors strongly suggests that these supervisors' support contributed significantly to these workers' satisfaction and commitment.

We also pointed out in chapter 5 that first-line managers in sales and in knowledge work workflows were less acquainted than supervisors in service workflows with the details of employees' work tasks. This suggests that managers in sales and knowledge work workflows play less central roles in the work lives of sales and knowledge workers. In addition, in that knowledge workers in particular have relatively high levels of portable skills points to a relatively weak attachment to the organization. These differences in the importance of first-line managers in the lives of the three types of workers lead us to make the following conjecture:

Hypothesis 3b: *Having the support of their immediate supervisors has a larger impact on the job satisfaction and commitment of service workers than on the job satisfaction and commitment of sales and knowledge workers.*

Employee participation. Involvement and influence in decision making have been found to have an impact on job satisfaction and, to a lesser extent, on commitment through cognitive and motivational processes (Miller and Monge 1986). The form of participation may also affect satisfaction and commitment (Batt and Appelbaum 1995). Given that influence in decision making above the task level has a broader scope than influence at the task level, the former is included in this analysis, although experimentation with the latter made little difference to the findings. This variable will contribute to satisfaction and commitment, but its effect is likely to vary among the three types of workers.

In chapter 5, we noted that, compared to the service workers, the sales and knowledge workers in our study enjoyed a higher level of influence in decision making at both the task and above-task levels. As we pointed out in chapter 3, the knowledge and sales workers valued this influence more than did the service employees. We would expect, therefore, influence in decision making above the task level, especially in decisions affecting employment conditions, would contribute to the sales workers' satisfaction and commitment. Among the knowledge workers, the ability to shape decisions that affect the resourcing of their work and the work that can be undertaken (e.g., innovative projects) is likely to contribute to their satisfaction and commitment. Accordingly, we postulate the following:

Hypothesis 3c: *Influence in decision making above the task level will have a stronger effect on the job satisfaction and commitment of knowledge and sales workers than of service workers.*

Co-worker Relations: Immediate and Adjacent Colleagues

It has been argued that higher levels of social integration with co-workers lead to greater satisfaction and commitment. Teams are the most common vehicle management used to foster and direct social cohesion into productive activity. Studies reviewed by Guzzo and Shea (1992), Evans and Dion (1991), and Morrow (1993) indicate that team cohesion contributes to group performance and commitment. Teams permit higher levels of knowledge and skills to be applied to problems, promote learning, and are a source of psychological support and sociability, all of which we would expect to foster satisfaction and commitment.

We have argued that the service workers in our study were more dependent on management than were the sales and knowledge workers, but this does not mean that the service workers were less dependent on their colleagues. Indeed, as we discussed in chapter 6, in the service workflows the workers' immediate team members were important sources of support. These teams were likely to contribute to commitment where these substructures were integrated into the organization. This was the case in most of the service workflows, where the teams were administered by management.

Favorable relations among co-workers were equally important in the knowledge work workflows, but for different reasons. These related to the close task interdependence between the co-workers and the need to rely on immediate team members for the development of supplementary skills and expertise. We can, therefore, postulate that team cohesion is likely to have a similar impact on job satisfaction in service and knowledge work workflows.

The generally individualistic way of working in sales workflows means that the notion of team cohesion is not applicable to sales employees. Thus, we postulate the following hypothesis:

Hypothesis 4a: *Team cohesion will have stronger effects on the job satisfaction and commitment of service and knowledge workers than of sales workers.*

In chapter 6, we showed that the levels of trustworthiness and reliability between workers in adjacent departments affected satisfaction and commitment. This was especially true for the service and sales workers, who relied on adjacent departments to process transactions (see chapters 3 and 6). The knowledge workers were more self-reliant and worked in a more self-contained manner. They were oriented toward their own team(s) rather than toward colleagues in adjacent departments. This was most evident in WBMM, which operated as an organizational enclave. Hence, we hypothesize the following:

> Hypothesis 4b: *The level of trustworthiness of adjacent colleagues will have a greater impact on the job satisfaction of sales and service workers than on the job satisfaction of knowledge workers.*

Customer-Worker Relations

The customer-worker relations approach suggests that employees derive considerable satisfaction from interchanges with customers (Schneider and Bowen 1995). Where workers have the support and capacity to satisfy customers, they are more likely to be satisfied (Carlson, Logan, and Moyer 1994). There is also evidence that the more management and employees have a congruent orientation toward customer service, the less role conflict and the more committed workers are likely to be (Randall 1988; Koslowsky 1990).

Since most knowledge workers in our sample did not deal with external customers, hypotheses about customer-worker relations are confined to service and sales employees. In chapter 7, we noted that service and sales workers had different attitudes toward customers: the former were more empathetic, the latter more instrumental. This suggests that having favorable relations with customers has a substantial impact on service employees' satisfaction. We therefore hypothesize the following:

> Hypothesis 5a: *The self-reported ability to satisfy customers has a stronger effect on job satisfaction among service employees than among sales workers.*

We also found that incongruity in the demands of management and customers was negatively related to job satisfaction among both service and sales workers. We did not test this factor for commitment, but our qualitative research showed that service employees had less discretion than did sales workers to choose and vary their interchanges with customers. Hence, incongruity is likely to have a more pronounced impact on service employees than on sales employees. This leads to the following hypothesis:

Hypothesis 5b: *The effect of incongruity in management's and customers' demands will be stronger among sales workers than among service workers.*

Comparative Analysis and Discussion

In the following section, we introduce our analysis and offer some caveats. This introduction is followed by a report and a discussion of our findings vis-à-vis the hypotheses outlined above. We consider the hypotheses pertaining to job satisfaction first, then the hypotheses concerning commitment. The section concludes with an overview of our findings, including consideration of the relationship between satisfaction and commitment.

Ordinary least squares regressions were used to test the hypotheses. This method enabled us to consider the determinants of satisfaction and commitment simultaneously, thereby identifying which factors are more important. In the analysis, we controlled for the effects of relevant demographic variables. Many studies have noted that, for reasons related to cohort, aging, or self-selection, age and job satisfaction are positively related (Clark and Warr 1996; Firebaugh and Harley 1995). Further, men have been shown to be less satisfied with their jobs than women (Clark 1995; Hodson 1996). This may be because men have a greater attachment to wage work and hence higher expectations, which in turn leads to lower levels of job satisfaction. For married employees, nonwork responsibilities related to the household are likely to compete with the work organization for commitment. Employees with higher levels of formal qualifications are likely to have more enhanced employment opportunities and higher career-related aspirations and therefore are less likely to be satisfied with their current jobs or their employing organizations. In the analysis of job satisfaction and commitment, degree holders are contrasted with nondegree holders. We control for company tenure in the analysis of commitment. This is because previous research has found that company tenure is moderately and positively associated with company allegiance (Morrow 1993; Mowday, Steers, and Porter 1982).[2]

Three caveats are necessary before beginning the analysis. First, our approach should be seen as combining inductive and deductive analyses. Our hypotheses were drawn from wider theory and are grounded in our qualitative experience and then were developed and tested.

Second, there is a considerable disparity in the number of survey respondents from each type of workflow: 615 service workers, 91 sales workers, and 161 knowledge workers. The larger the sample size, the more likely

[2] The reasons for this positive association include self-selection (uncommitted employees would have left the company); the accumulation of firm-specific working experience, which may not command a premium market value in the external labor market; and work experience in the company that serves as a socializing influence.

that quantitative results will reach the conventional statistically significant level. The smaller number of sales and knowledge workers is likely to result in less precise estimated coefficients in the multivariate analyses.

Third, the survey data reflect employees' perceptions and evaluations; they represent workers' views of workplace reality. In interpreting these findings, we rely on our qualitative data and our own judgment.

Job Satisfaction

Table 8.1 shows the results of our regression analysis for job satisfaction. Regarding *work relations,* the results show that, for all three types of workers, satisfaction with the nature of the work contributed significantly to job satisfaction. Employees who were satisfied with the variety and challenge of their jobs were also satisfied with their jobs as a whole. These results are consistent with hypothesis 1a for knowledge and sales workers but not for service workers. The findings support job design and systems theory, which asserts the universality of the intrinsic work argument (Hackman and Oldman 1976). According to this argument, workers will not become inured to relatively routinized jobs such as those in service workflows and will value intrinsically rewarding work.

The perceived *effectiveness of technology* was significantly and positively related to job satisfaction only for service workers. It had no statistically significant net effect for sales and knowledge workers. This result accords with hypothesis 1b. Compared with the sales workers, the service workers in our study relied more heavily on IT systems to provide customer service. The knowledge workers were either the designers of the IT systems that they used or had a strong hand in shaping these systems. Thus, compared with the service workers, the knowledge workers had more control over IT. Hence, the effectiveness of technology mattered more to the service workers than to the sales and knowledge workers.

Satisfaction with the three major aspects of *employment relations*—pay, promotion prospects, and job security—contributed to the job satisfaction of service employees. Among sales employees, satisfaction with job security and promotion prospects led to higher levels of job satisfaction; pay satisfaction had no statistically significant effect. Among knowledge workers, only satisfaction with pay and promotion prospects had statistically significant and positive effects. Hypothesis 2a—which postulated a pay satisfaction effect—was supported among the service and knowledge workers but not among the sales workers. In the case of the sales workers, who were especially concerned with job security, the pay satisfaction effect was eclipsed by the effect of their satisfaction with their job security.

In that their human capital is relatively firm-specific, the importance service employees attached to whether they had strong opportunities for

Table 8.1. Unstandardized Regression Coefficients for Job Satisfaction by Workflow Type

Independent variable	Workflow type		
	Service	Sales	Knowledge work
Work Relations			
Satisfaction with nature of work	0.233	0.379	0.223
	(0.03)*	(0.15)[†]	(0.08)[†]
Effectiveness of technology	0.122	−0.033	0.06
	(0.04)[†]	(0.11)	(0.09)
Control Relations			
Senior management's trustworthiness	0.09	0.015	0.071
	(0.03)[†]	(0.13)	(0.09)
Immediate supervisor's support	−0.031	0.178	0.071
	(0.04)	(0.14)	(0.08)
Influence above task level	−0.022	0.104	−0.074
	(0.04)	(0.08)	(0.06)[‡]
Co-worker Relations			
Team cohesion	0.054	n.a.[a]	0.119
	(0.03)		(0.08)
External colleagues' trustworthiness	0.114	−0.149	0.142
	(0.04)[†]	(0.14)	(0.08)[‡]
Employment Relations			
Satisfaction with promotion prospects	0.158	0.320	0.222
	(0.04)*	(0.14)[†]	(0.08)[†]
Satisfaction with pay	0.136	0.158	0.180
	(0.04)[†]	(0.14)	(0.07)[†]
Satisfaction with job security	0.111	0.236	0.09
	(0.04)[†]	(0.14)[‡]	(0.09)
Customer Relations			
Self-assessed ability to satisfy customers	0.11	0.087	n.a.[b]
	(0.03)[†]	(0.11)	
Constant	−2.50	−4.89	−2.479
	(0.23)*	(0.97)*	(0.65)[†]
R²	0.578	0.633	0.469
N	437	71	131

Notes: *p ≤ 0.001; [†] p ≤ 0.05; [‡] p ≤ 0.1 (two-tailed test); n.a. = not applicable; standard errors in parentheses. Controls for demographics (age, marital status, gender, education, and company tenure) are not shown. See appendixes 2, 4, 5, and 6 for descriptive statistics and correlations between variables.
[a] Questions about team cohesion were not applicable to the sales workflows.
[b] Self-assessed ability to satisfy customers was not applicable to a majority of the knowledge workers who did not deal with external customers and hence was excluded from the analysis.

promotion was even more significant (see chapter 3). Insofar as satisfaction with this element of employment relations indicates the extent to which preference for promotions was met, employees who were satisfied with their promotion prospects were also satisfied with their jobs. To the extent that sales employees saw promotions as a means to escape their stressful, insecure jobs (see chapter 3), satisfaction with their prospects of an internal promotion led to increased levels of job satisfaction. This result contradicts hypothesis 2b.

Despite the lower value the knowledge workers placed on their chances of an internal promotion compared with the service and sales workers, the knowledge workers' level of satisfaction with their promotion prospects was still statistically significant. This is likely to be related to the inherent prestige associated with a higher-ranking position. Thus, instead of having a differential impact across the three types of workers as we hypothesized earlier, satisfaction with their prospects for promotion had a statistically significant effect on the job satisfaction of all three types of workers.

In chapter 3, we noted that the service and sales workers placed greater value on job security than did the knowledge workers. Thus, satisfaction with job security contributed to the job satisfaction of these service and sales workers but not to the job satisfaction of the knowledge workers. The knowledge workers' favorable and more transferable human capital enhanced their general job prospects (see chapter 4). Knowledge workers were therefore less concerned with job security and, hence, satisfaction with this aspect of employment relations did not have a statistically significant effect on their levels of job satisfaction. These results confirmed hypothesis 2c.

Regarding *fairness and control relations*, the trustworthiness of senior management contributed significantly to the service workers' job satisfaction but had no net effect on the sales or knowledge workers. These results partially accord with hypothesis 3a concerning service employees but contradict the hypothesis vis-à-vis sales workers. This may be because sales workers believed in their individuality; the way they undertook their role reminded them that *"it's all up to you, it's what you make of it [the job]."*

The effect of immediate supervisors' support was statistically insignificant for all three types of workers. This result confirms hypothesis 3b regarding the sales and knowledge workers but runs counter to the hypothesis with respect to the service workers. A plausible explanation is that immediate supervisors in service workflows had considerable influence in the first six months or so of an employee's employment but much less influence after this major learning period, when the support and assistance of peers substituted for those of the supervisor.

The impact on job satisfaction of participating in decision making above the task level was statistically significant only for knowledge workers. The effect was negative, however, and therefore contradicted hypothesis 3c. The perception among these workers that they had more influence *reduced* rather than increased their level of job satisfaction. One possible explanation is that, in the case of systems designers, having greater involvement above the task level distracted employees from project work and, in the case of money market dealers, from making lucrative deals. Beyond a certain point, workers avoid participating in decision making, although most knowledge workers would like to have the benefits of doing so.

Furthermore, participating in decision making is often stressful—witness the politics around the new architecture at WBSD. We can conclude, therefore, that since senior management tended to make major decisions, knowledge workers might participate in decision making but their influence is limited.

With respect to *co-worker relations*, team cohesion contributed to the job satisfaction of service workers but was statistically insignificant for knowledge workers, a result that partly supports hypothesis 4a. The support members of service worker teams gave each other was crucial in relieving the distress of dealing with irate customers (see chapter 6).

Two reasons may explain the absence of a team cohesion effect among the knowledge workers. First, our measurement of team cohesion tapped the affective rather than the technical competence dimension of working in a team. Knowledge workers are likely to view technically competent co-workers as more valuable than congenial and sociable co-workers. Second, knowledge workers might work together, but they were also intensely competitive. Not only were promotion opportunities and bonuses at stake but status symbols such as control over high-prestige projects (systems developers) and team accolades for winning big deals (money market dealers).

The maintenance of a high level of trust among adjacent co-workers was significantly and positively related to the job satisfaction of both the service workers and the knowledge workers but statistically insignificant for the sales workers. These results support hypothesis 4b regarding service workers but are contrary to the hypothesized effects for sales and knowledge workers. Our qualitative research findings indicate that the service workers had to rely extensively on the services provided by adjacent departments. Delivery problems created by these departments resulted in customer dissatisfaction, which in turn was directed toward service employees and, hence, led to lower levels of job satisfaction.

The nature of teamwork and the level of dependence on adjacent colleagues were different among the knowledge workers than among the service or sales workers. The knowledge workers relied extensively on colleagues from different sections and on their work teams to supplement their skills and expertise (see chapter 6). These teams were formed and dissolved according to the time span of individual projects or specific problems.

In the sales workflows, the workers' adjacent colleagues were mainly credit analysts and financial specialists who processed and approved loans or stock listing applications. Our measure of trustworthiness tapped these co-workers' reliability, which was based on their work proficiency and competence. The level of these attributes among adjacent co-workers affected how easily and efficiently both the service workers and the knowledge workers accomplished their tasks.

In the sales workflows, the credit analysts' skeptical orientation toward loan applications affected the sales workers' employment security and earnings stability. Hence, having trustworthy adjacent colleagues contributed to the job satisfaction of the service and knowledge workers but not of the sales workers.

Finally, regarding *customer-worker relations,* it will be recalled that our results concerning workers' self-assessed ability to satisfy customers applied to the service and sales employees in our study but not to the knowledge workers. These findings support hypothesis 5a. The ability to satisfy customers had a positive and statistically significant effect on the job satisfaction of the service employees but was statistically insignificant for the sales workers. The more instrumental orientation of the sales employees meant that the ability to satisfy customers was associated more closely with pecuniary job rewards and greater job security than with intrinsic work satisfaction. In contrast, the greater degree of customer empathy demonstrated by the service workers meant that their ability to satisfy customers affected these workers' intrinsic levels of job satisfaction (see chapter 7).

These results suggest that our general postulate concerning employee dependence on management and the specific propositions derived from it were better supported among the service workers than among the sales and knowledge workers. We now examine the results for commitment, before assessing our findings in the context of all the hypotheses.

Organizational Commitment

The results concerning the determinants of commitment across the three types of workflows are given in table 8.2. With regard to *work relations,* the finding that satisfaction with the nature of work contributes to the commitment of service and sales workers is consistent with hypothesis 1a. The statistically insignificant result for knowledge workers is contrary to the hypothesis. It can be explained, however, by our employee dependence argument. In short, knowledge workers valued and expected to engage in intrinsically rewarding work but did not see it as emanating from management. Rather, they viewed rewarding work as a feature of their occupation. Consequently, the presence of such work does not evoke strong commitment.

The same argument could be said to apply to sales workers—with one important difference: more intrinsically satisfying work was usually associated with greater sales opportunities (more complex deals) and thus higher extrinsic rewards. Under performance-related pay systems, sales workers tended to associate increased levels of work satisfaction with the organization, and this in turn evoked higher commitment.

The results regarding how workers perceive the effectiveness of technology are in line with hypothesis 1b. Among the service workers, who were

Table 8.2. Unstandardized Regression Coefficients for Organizational Commitment by Workflow Type

Independent variable	Workflow type		
	Service	Sales	Knowledge work
Work Relations			
Satisfaction with nature of work	0.159	0.373	0.097
	(0.042)*	(0.124)[†]	(0.092)
Effectiveness of technology	0.11	−0.036	0.013
	(0.042)[†]	(0.087)	(0.110)
Employment Relations			
Satisfaction with promotion prospects	0.095	0.121	0.079
	(0.046)[†]	(0.114)	(0.094)
Satisfaction with pay	0.037	0.149	0.097
	(0.044)	(0.118)	(0.086)
Satisfaction with job security	0.120	0.126	0.117
	(0.052)[†]	(0.116)	(0.103)
Control Relations			
Senior management's trustworthiness	0.205	0.160	0.221
	(0.042)*	(0.098)	(0.101)[†]
Immediate supervisor's support	−0.020	−0.079	−0.067
	(0.043)	(0.114)	(0.086)
Influence above task level	−0.154	0.085	0.082
	(0.052)[†]	(0.067)	(0.062)
Co-worker Relations			
Team cohesion	0.203	n.a.[a]	0.191
	(0.041)[‡]		(0.084)[†]
External colleagues' trustworthiness	—	−0.028	—
		(0.109)	
Customer Relations			
Incongruence between management's and customers' interests	−0.163	−0.009	n.a.[b]
	(0.039)*	(0.103)	
Constant	−1.596	−2.62	−0.794
	(0.250)*	(0.673)*	(0.649)
R²	0.399	0.532	0.273
N	460	75	135

Notes: *p ≤ 0.001; [†] p ≤ 0.05; [‡] p ≤ 0.1 (two-tailed test); n.a. = not applicable; standard errors in parentheses. Controls for demographics (age, marital status, gender, education, and company tenure) are not shown. See appendixes 2, 4, 5, and 6 for descriptive statistics and correlations between variables.

[a] Questions about team cohesion were not applicable to the sales workflows.

[b] Self-assessed ability to satisfy customers was not applicable to a majority of the knowledge workers who did not deal with external customers and hence was excluded from the analysis.

highly dependent on technology and relied on management for its provision, the higher the perceived effectiveness of technology, the higher their level of commitment. This factor was statistically insignificant for the sales and knowledge workers for the reasons mentioned earlier.

Moving to the relationships between aspects of *employment relations* and commitment, pay satisfaction was statistically insignificant across all three types of workers. This result is the opposite of what we hypothesized in 4a, which posited that this relationship would be both positive and statistically significant.

Satisfaction with promotion prospects was statistically significant only for the service employees, which is in line with hypothesis 4b. Satisfaction with job security was statistically significant for the service employees but not for the sales and knowledge workers. The results for the service and knowledge workers support hypothesis 4c but are contrary to our expectations for the sales workers.

We pointed out earlier in this chapter and in chapter 7 that sales workers were relatively independent of management. Hence, it was likely that they attributed their job security to their own sales efforts rather than to management's employment policies. This helps to explain the absence of the expected job security satisfaction effect on sales workers' levels of organizational commitment.

Hypothesis 3a, regarding the impact of the variable trustworthiness of management on service workers' commitment, was not borne out by our empirical findings. Instead, trustworthiness of management enhanced the commitment of service and knowledge workers. This is explained by the positive effect that trustworthy senior management had on the so-called psychological contract between workers and management. Employees who considered management to be reliable, trustworthy, and caring reciprocated by showing greater commitment to the organization.

The effect on workers' commitment of receiving support from their immediate supervisors was statistically insignificant for all three types of employees. This is consistent with our expectations regarding the sales and knowledge workers but inconsistent with regard to the service workers, as stated in hypothesis 3b. The reason for the insignificance in the case of the service workers echoes what was said earlier with regard to job satisfaction—that is, supervisors lost their importance once service workers become familiar with the job. Thereafter, other factors played more important roles in determining commitment. These include pay, the intrinsic properties of the work, and promotion opportunities.

Contrary to hypothesis 3c, regarding the impact of employee participation on commitment, the amount of involvement and influence workers had in decision making above the task level was statistically significant for the service employees but not for the sales and knowledge workers. Moreover, in the case of the service workers, the effect was negative; in other words, having more perceived influence led to lower commitment. This can be explained by the nature of the participation above the task level, involving mainly off-line project work. The workers submitted reports and suggestions to management, but with little discernible effect. Moreover, the workers did not receive additional pay for this more complex work.

Hence, such participation was negatively related to the service workers' commitment.

The sales workers had more influence, but it was insufficient to encourage commitment. In the case of knowledge workers, the higher costs of participation, referred to in our discussion of job satisfaction, account for the lack of statistically significant influence on commitment.

Regarding *co-worker relations,* the relationship between team cohesion and commitment was positive for both the service and knowledge workers but not for the sales workers. These results are consistent with hypothesis 4a. Support from team members fostered a sense of community among the service employees (see chapter 6), which contributed to job satisfaction, thereby enhancing commitment.

Among the knowledge workers, teams had norm-enforcing and learning roles, which meant that team cohesion was likely to contribute to commitment. The sales workers were relatively isolated, so that team cohesion was less relevant.

With respect to *customer-worker relations,* our results support hypothesis 5b. The perceived ability to satisfy customers had a more pronounced negative effect on the service workers' levels of commitment than on those of the sales workers.

Overview

Table 8.3 summarizes the findings for each of the hypotheses that have been addressed. The results show that employee satisfaction with the intrinsic nature of the work was an important factor in workers' overall job satisfaction and commitment to the organization. Satisfaction with the intrinsic nature of the work contributed to the job satisfaction of all three types of employees and to the commitment of the service and sales employees. The perceived effectiveness of the technology was statistically significant only for the service employees.

With respect to the three aspects of control relations, perceiving that senior management was trustworthy invariably led to higher levels of commitment among service and knowledge employees but was only statistically significant with respect to job satisfaction among the service employees. The perceived level of support workers received from immediate supervisors had no statistically significant effect on any of the three groups of employees, in relation to job satisfaction or commitment. The amount of influence on decision making above the task level was statistically significant only in relation to the job satisfaction of the knowledge workers, and to the organizational commitment of service workers.

Favorable relations with co-workers, as evident by team cohesion and the perceived trustworthiness of adjacent colleagues, had a similarly important influence on the service and the knowledge workers' satisfaction and com-

Table 8.3. Summary of Regression Results for Job Satisfaction and Organizational Commitment

Hypothesis	Job satisfaction	Organizational commitment
1a The effect of satisfaction with the nature of work on job satisfaction and organizatonal commitment is likely to be stronger for sales and knowledge workers than for service workers.	s,+ for all three types of workers	s,+ for service and sales workers only
1b The perceived effectiveness of technology is likely to have a larger impact on job satisfaction and organizational commitment among service workers, than among sales or knowledge workers.	s,+ for service workers only	s,+ for service workers only
2a For all three types of workers, satisfaction with pay has a significant effect on job satisfaction and commitments.	s,+ for service and knowledge worker	n.s. for all three types of worker
2b Satisfaction with promotion prospects has a larger effect on the job satisfaction and commitment of service workers than of sales and knowledge workers.	s,+ for all three types of worker	s,+ for service workers only
2c Satisfaction with job security has a stronger effect on the job satisfaction and commitment of service and sales employees than of knowledge workers.	s,+ for service and sales workers	s,+ for service workers only
3a The trustworthiness of senior management will have a stronger effect on the job satisfaction and organizational commitment of service and sales workers than on knowledge workers' job satisfaction and commitment.	s,+ for service workers	s,+ for service and knowledge workers
3b Having the support of their immediate supervisors has a larger impact on the job satisfaction and commitment of service workers than of sales and knowledge workers.	n.s. for all three types of workers	n.s. for all three types of workers

Table 8.3. Continued

Hypothesis	Job satisfaction	Organizational commitment
3c Influence in decision making above the task level will have a stronger effect on the job satisfaction and commitment of knowledge and sales workers than of service workers.	s,– for knowledge workers only	s,– for service workers only
4a Team cohesion will have stronger effects on the job satisfaction and commitment of service and knowledge workers than of sales workers.	n.s. for service and knowledge workers	s,+ for service and knowledge workers
4b The level of trustworthiness of adjacent colleagues will have a greater impact on the job satisfaction of sales and service workers than of knowledge workers.	s,+ for service workers only	n.s. for sales workers only
5a The level or trustworthiness of adjacent colleagues will have a greater impact on the job satisfaction of sales and service workers than of knowledge workers.	s,+ for service workers only	n.a.
5b The effect of incongruity in management's and customers' demands will be stronger among sales workers, than among service workers.	n.a.	s,– for service workers only

Note: n.a. = not applicable, s = significant, n.s. = insignificant, + = positive, – = negative.

mitment. We noted earlier that the service workers' job satisfaction and commitment were more closely related to the emotional and social support these workers received, whereas for knowledge workers, their job satisfaction and commitment were more influenced by their co-workers' technical competence and expertise.

Our hypotheses regarding the relative effects of satisfaction with key aspects of employment relations (i.e., pay, promotion prospects, job security) received greater empirical support among the service employees than among the sales or knowledge workers. The results for the service employees accorded with the postulate that, compared with the sales and knowledge workers, the service employees depended considerably on management. Thus, satisfaction with job security and with their prospects for promotion contributed to the service workers' job satisfaction and commitment. The same influences had less pronounced effects on the sales and knowledge workers.

With respect to customer-worker relations, the results were in line with our general argument that the service employees we observed were more dependent on management than the sales workers for the sourcing of customers and the acquisition of the skills and knowledge needed to service customers. From this finding, we concluded that management mediated the relationship between customers and workers much more heavily in service workflows than in sales workflows. This reasoning underscored the statistically significant impact of the perceived ability of workers to satisfy customers, and the level of incongruence between management's and the workers' demands, on the satisfaction and commitment of the service workers. The same two variables had no statistically significant effect on the job satisfaction and organizational commitment of sales workers.

Overall, our findings support the employee dependence perspective that we developed and the specific hypotheses derived from it for service workers. Our data provide less support for our hypotheses concerning sales and knowledge workers. Although the sales workers in our study relied on management less than the service employees, the sales workers' satisfaction with their prospects for promotions within the company contributed to their job satisfaction. Likewise, despite the knowledge workers' lower level of dependence on management, their trust of senior management led to their demonstrating higher levels of commitment. Favorable co-worker relations were similarly statistically significant for the service and knowledge workers. The implications of these results are that, even though service employees were more reliant on management than knowledge workers, management-employee relations had not eclipsed the role favorable co-worker relations played in the day-to-day working lives of service employees. Clearly, the social support service workers received from their co-workers, be they members of their immediate teams or colleagues in adjacent departments, was still important. By contrast, the individualism and entrepreneurialism that were characteristic of sales workers had led to aspects of employment relations having a statistically significant impact on the job satisfaction of these workers.

One final piece of empirical evidence supports the usefulness of our concept of employee dependence. This concerns the relationship between the two dependent variables, job satisfaction and commitment. Although these two concepts are distinct, we would expect more satisfied employees to identify with and be more committed to their employing organizations. We also might expect management to treat these employees more favorably and hence for them to be more satisfied. Should we expect the magnitude of these relationships to vary between the three types of workers? The answer is yes, and our argument is based on the concept of employee dependence. It goes as follows. The higher the level of dependence on management, the more likely workers are to ascribe their job satisfaction to management and hence the more likely they are to identify with management and hence to report having higher levels of commitment to their organization. Insofar as service workers are most dependent on management, we would expect the relationship between satisfaction and commitment to be strongest for these workers. We would expect the relationship to be less strong for sales workers and weakest for knowledge workers, who, as we have argued, were the least dependent on management. Results of the correlation tests supported this hypothesis. The correlation between satisfaction and commitment was strongest in the service workflows ($r = 0.61$, $n = 578$, $p < 0.001$, followed by the sales workflows ($r = 0.58$, $n = 82$, $p < 0.001$), and weakest in the knowledge work workflows ($r = 0.43$, $n = 155$, $p < 0.001$).

Cross-National Comparisons of Work Organization and Its Consequences

In the analyses that follow, we compare the work organization in service workflows in Australia, the United States, and Japan. With regard to the sales and knowledge work workflows, we had no data on U.S. companies operating at home and therefore restricted our comparisons to Australian and Japanese workflows; however, data on U.S. companies operating in Australia are included.

In discussing service workflows, we compare U.S. and Australian workflows with those in Japan. This is based on the proposition that the United States and Australia are more similar to each other than either is to Japan.[3]

Studies of comparative WOs generally focus on the uniqueness of Japanese companies vis-à-vis their Western counterparts, typically U.S. organizations. In reviewing various theories of WO, Lincoln and Kalleberg (1990: 258) argued that Japanese WOs are characterized by "an extraordinary

---

[3] There are at least two good reasons to combine Australia and the United States. First, these two countries have broadly similar cultures and political-economic systems. Both are essentially Christian and have a British colonial heritage overlaid by the influence of European and Asian immigrants. Both countries are liberal democracies with limited government coordination. Second, although Australian industry and labor were regulated in the past, currently there are relatively open markets and decentralized labor relations arrangements in which unions, as in the United States, are relatively weak. By contrast, Japan has an essentially Confucian heritage and a relatively homogeneous population. The Japanese political economy is characterized by corporatist arrangements involving close collaboration between large enterprise groups and the government.

reliance on diffuse, personalistic network relations of commitment, trust, and obligation in conducting administrative and economic affairs." This is manifested by the presence of internal labor markets, a feature of Japanese work life that is applicable to permanent male employees in large corporations. One of the important outcomes of this internal labor market and of Japan's long-term employment practices is that there is substantial company investment in employee training (Morishima 1996; Cole 1979). This firm-specific human capital, accumulated through many years of experience in a single company, gives rise to considerable employee dependence on the organization. This internal labor market model applies to our Japanese sales and knowledge workers but not to females in companies such as JB.

As we have noted, Japanese companies tend to discriminate against women (Brinton 1993; Wakisaka 1997) in spite of the Equal Employment Opportunities Law, enacted in 1985. Chapter 4 noted that the bond-ladies in JBSV received little training and had limited job prospects. The other Japanese service workflow we studied, MFJSV, was different, since it was controlled by a foreign multinational whose HR policies and practices reflected the influence of the parent company.

In the Japanese sales workflows, the *keiretsu* groupings (Gerlach 1992) ensured that associated companies were customers, and management referred workers to these customers more than in Australia. As we pointed out in chapters 6 and 7, in the JBS workflow, supervisors played important roles in customer-worker relations. By contrast, in Australia, salespersons relied on referral networks that they developed themselves.

In yet another variation, employees in COMPUJ, who were rotated regularly from one project to another, often had little experience working on clients' computer systems. Consequently, they had to rely on their managers, or employees who had prior experience with the client, for relevant knowledge and information.

Notwithstanding differences in the reasons why Japanese employees are more dependent on management, our general postulate is as follows: regardless of workflow type, compared with their Western counterparts, Japanese workflows more closely resemble the bureaucratic ideal type.[4] To the extent that bureaucratic WOs run counter to employee requirements for intrinsic satisfaction and create conditions for labor substitutability, thereby engendering job insecurity, these WOs will tend to create employee dissatisfaction and low commitment (see studies reviewed by Mowday,

[4] Support for this proposition comes from data in previous chapters. For example, in chapter 4 we noted the gendered nature of WO in Japanese service workflows and in chapter 6 that supervisors were more dominant in JBS than in the Australian sales workflows. The same chapter also examined the importance in COMPUJ of learning from both supervisors and co-workers. We demonstrated that this workflow combined elements of bureaucratic and knowledge-intensive WO. Note that we are referring specifically to a conception of bureaucracy that applies to work organization rather than the conventional notion that focuses on the organization more generally.

Steers, and Porter 1982 and Morrow 1993). Consequently, Japanese workers are likely to be more dissatisfied and to report lower levels of commitment to their organizations than their counterparts in comparable workflows. A contrary view also merits attention, however. The emphasis here is that the welfarist tendency in Japanese WOs, toward lifetime employment, training, and relatively generous pay and company benefits, encourages higher levels of commitment than in comparable Western organizations (Dore 1973; Lincoln and Kalleberg 1990).

In attempting to adjudicate these contrasting arguments, we shall examine the proposition that Japanese workflows are more bureaucratic than their Western counterparts. With this in mind, the next section discusses aspects of WO mentioned in previous chapters.

Work Organization in Japanese, U.S. and Australian Workflows

The proposition that Japanese WOs are more bureaucratic than their Western counterparts can be tested by examining the relevant aspects of WO canvassed in our employee survey. For the purpose of achieving parity in the sizes of our samples, we focus on specific service workflows in Australia and the United States. These are UB1 in the United States, MBASV in Australia, and JBSV and MFJSV in Japan.[5] Of the knowledge work workflows, we compared WBSD with its Japanese counterpart, COMPUJ. The nature of the work tasks in the latter more closely resembled those in WBSD than WBMM. This restriction enabled us to control more stringently for levels of task complexity (for details, see table 2.3).

An important caveat to the following analysis is that the limited number of workflows studied makes it impossible to ascertain precisely whether cross-national differences or similarities reflect national variations or company-specific elements. Being acquainted with other firms in the industries concerned, and corroborating this knowledge with what is known from the existing literature, we believe that most of the variations reflect country- rather than company-specific factors. In contrast to the three-country comparison for service workers, our analysis of sales and knowledge workers is restricted to two countries: Australia (including U.S. subsidiaries) and Japan. Companies whose headquarters lie outside a particular country may export some foreign practices into a subsidiary located in another country. This is likely to moderate but not eliminate national differences. Table 8.4 reports the results for each workflow type.

The first panel in table 8.4 gives the results for selected aspects of employment relations. As we pointed out in chapter 4, Japanese sales and knowledge workers were regulated by an organizational employment relations

[5] The sample we chose here is larger than that used in the analysis of cross-national comparisons in chapter 4. This is to ascertain the generalizability of findings reported in that chapter.

Table 8.4. Work Organization, Job Satisfaction, and Organizational Commitment in Japanese Workflows versus Australian and American Workflows

Features of work organization*	Workflow type		
	Service[†]	Sales	Knowledge work[‡]
Internal Labor Market			
Average percentage of working time spent on receiving training	U.S.: 27; Australia: 18; Japan: 15	n.s.[§]	n.s.[‖]
Percentage of employees saying their career prospects were best with current employer[§]	U.S.: 70; Australia: 61; Japan: 43**	Australia: 50; Japan: 75	Australia: 70; Japan: 85
Control Relations			
Amount of influence in task level decision making	Japan less than U.S.	n.s.	n.s.
Amount of influence in above task level decision-making	n.s.	n.s.	Japan less than Australia
Supervisor's knowledge of employees' work process	n.s.	n.s.	n.s.
Co-worker Relations			
Adjacent co-worker interdependence	Japan lower than U.S. or Australia	Japan lower than Australia	Japan lower than Australia
Customer Relations			
Incongruence between management's and customers' interests	Japan lower than Australia; U.S. lower than Australia	Japan lower than Australia	n.a.[††]
Work Attitude			
Job satisfaction	Japanese less satisfied than Australians or U.S. workers	Japanese more satisfied than Australian workers	Japanese less satisfied than Australian workers
Organizational commitment	Japanese less committed than Australian or U.S. workers	n.s.	Japanese less committed than Australian workers

Notes: n.s. = insignificant differences between Japan and Australia or America; * All analyses were conducted using one-way ANOVA. [†] N for Japan = 44; for Australia = 67; for U.S. = 60. [‡] WBMM was excluded from the analysis, and there were no U.S. cases in the knowledge work workflow types. N for Australia = 105; for Japan = 26. [§] The averages for Japan and Australia are 8 percent and 5.8 percent respectively. [‖] The averages for Japan and Australia are 8 percent and 7.8 percent respectively. ** The percentages of American service respondents answering the option "my career prospects are very limited" and "I am not interested in a career" were 5 percent and 7 percent respectively. The figures for Australian service workers were 12 percent and 13 percent; for Japan, 27 percent and 12 percent. [††] Not applicable, since a majority of the Australian respondents did not serve external customers and were not routed to answer questions related to incongruence between management's and customers' demands.

system characterized by the presence of internal labor markets. Relevant indicators are the average proportion of working time spent receiving training and workers' perceptions of their career prospects—whether these are focused on the current employer or outside the firm.[6]

In the service workflows, Japanese employees received less training and were less likely to say their career prospects lay with their current employers. Evidence for this includes management's orientation toward the JBSV bond-ladies, who received limited training and were assigned to noncareer employment tracks (see chapter 4). Similarly, in MFJSV, the bilingual skills employees brought to their jobs meant that their career prospects were not tied to the firm's internal labor market (see chapter 3).

By contrast, Japanese sales and knowledge workers resembled employees of a conventional internal labor market. Compared with their Australian counterparts, a greater proportion reported that their career prospects lay with their current employers rather than with other employers. They did not differ, however, from the Australian sales or knowledge workers in the amount of training they received. Except for induction training for new recruits, salespersons at JBS were not generally given formal ongoing training. They relied primarily on on-the-job training and self-study for external certification. The situation was similar in the Australian sales workflows, where management believed that the best way to train salespersons was by enabling them to learn from experience.

In bureaucratic WOs, the centralization of decision making and the hierarchical authority structure imply that employees have limited influence. In their review of comparative studies of Japanese and U.S. WOs, Lincoln and Kalleberg (1990: 177) concluded that, "in general, there is wide agreement that Japanese decision-making is group and consensus oriented and involves low delegation of formal authority to positions held by individuals." Agreeing with other scholars, they noted that in Japanese WOs, there is a de facto decentralization of task performance to the lower level without decentralization of formal authority. These authors concluded that the participatory, decentralized aspect of Japanese decision making was more form than substance. To the extent that these general observations and our comparative proposition apply to our cases, we would expect that, compared with their Western counterparts, the Japanese employees in our study would report similar amounts of influence on decision making at the task level but less influence above the task level.

The second panel in table 8.4 indicates that empirical support for this proposition varies between the three types of workflows. Service workers in JBSV and MFJSV enjoyed less influence at the task level but did not differ significantly from their Western counterparts with respect to above-task-

---

[6] There were two other precoded choices to this question: "my career prospects are limited," and "I am not interested in a career." Results for these two questions were not reported, since they are not directly relevant to the issue of the presence of an internal labor market.

level influence. This can be explained by the secondary status of JBSV and JBS workers (see chapters 4 and 6).

Japanese and Australian sales workers did not differ significantly in the two types of influence they exerted. As chapter 5 pointed out, the Australian salespersons in our study had little influence regarding the terms of their employment. As we argued in chapter 7, in the sales workflows, customers were the dominant party in the triangular relationship that included management, customers, and workers. Salespersons earned task-level discretion and autonomy primarily through reaching or exceeding their sales targets. Otherwise, they had little influence over workplace decisions.

Salespersons in JBS relied on their immediate supervisors, who acted as customer referrers. Together with the hierarchical authority structure, this meant that the amount of influence a salesperson had at and above the task level was as limited as it was in MBAS and ABKS.

In the knowledge work workflows, employees at COMPUJ reported having similar task-level influence as their counterparts at WBSD in Australia but significantly less above-task-level influence. This is in line with the hypothesis advanced above.

The bureaucratic principles of job specialization and a strictly defined division of labor imply that where WOs resemble the bureaucratic ideal type, supervisors are, in theory, better informed about employees' work processes. To the extent that the Japanese workflows were more bureaucratic, we would expect Japanese employees to rate their immediate supervisors higher for their knowledge of the work process than Australian or U.S. employees. In fact, across all three types of workflows, Japanese employees did not rate their supervisors significantly higher. The reasons vary by workflow type.

As we pointed out in chapters 5 and 6, in JBSV work was organized in a gendered manner and male supervisors treated the bond-ladies disrespectfully. It is not surprising, therefore, that the bond-ladies did not think highly of their supervisors.

Chapter 6 noted that salespersons in JBS relied for information and knowledge on personal networks that they built up through their previous rotation experience. This is likely to have eclipsed the importance of their immediate supervisors as information providers, although supervisors played an important role and acted as referrers in the salespersons' relations with clients. Moreover, given the long-term process necessary to cultivate contacts, it was difficult for supervisors to measure performance and progress objectively.[7] For these reasons, the salespersons at JBS rated their supervisors' knowledge of the work process lower than did their counterparts in Australia.

---

[7] Supervisors held periodic meetings with individual salesmen, who were required to discuss their customer prospects and give clear self-evaluations of their progress. They were also required to articulate their short-term goals.

Chapters 5 and 6 pointed out that employees at COMPUJ preferred to seek advice from their peers rather than from their supervisors. Combined with management's emphasis on self-learning, this pattern of behavior underlies why the system developers at COMPUJ and their counterparts in Australia gave their immediate supervisors similar ratings for their knowledge of the work process.

Yet another indicator of the level of bureaucratization is the interdependence between workflows and other functional departments. The clearly demarcated division of labor in bureaucratic WOs necessitates a relatively high degree of interdependency and coordination among functional departments. Lincoln and Kalleberg (1990), for example, have observed a relatively greater proliferation of collective subunits in Japanese WOs. To the extent that this observation applies to our cases and that the Japanese workflows in our study were more bureaucratic than the workflows we observed in Australia and the United States, we would expect Japanese employees to report a higher level of interdependence between themselves and members of adjacent departments.

As shown in the third panel of table 8.4, our results contradict this proposition for all three types of workflows. Japanese employees reported a significantly lower level of interdependence with other departments compared with their Western counterparts. Again, the explanation for this varies for each type of workflow.

Chapter 6 noted that management at JBSV did not practice job rotation. Consequently, the bond-ladies had no ties to employees in other divisions, thereby reducing interdepartmental interdependencies. In the sales section and the specialist division, the workers also reported a lower level of interdependence compared with their Australian counterparts.

In the Australian knowledge work workflow WBSD, there was extensive discussion between the corporate systems development team and the IT personnel responsible for servicing particular business units. This engendered a high degree of interdependence.

We noted in chapter 6 that in COMPUJ tension between the engineers and salespeople escalated when management attempted to integrate product development engineers into a sales department. Salespersons increasingly relied on the engineers' systems development knowledge in making sales, while the engineers believed that they had nothing to gain from working with salespeople (see chapter 6). The result was a one-sided reliance rather than interdependence. Thus, compared with the system developers at WBSD, the engineers at COMPUJ reported a lower level of interdependence between themselves and members of adjacent departments.

Chapter 7 pointed out that in the bureaucratic ideal type, service provision is producer-oriented rather than customer-oriented. Employees tend to be indifferent toward customers and to follow management directives closely. This implies that, to the extent that our Japanese workflows were more bureaucratic than their Western counterparts, service and sales employees will experience lower levels of incongruence between management's and customers' demands. Our findings, given in the fourth panel of table 8.4, support this proposition. JB salespersons, JB bond-ladies, and MFJSV service workers all reported a significantly lower level of incongruence than their Western counterparts.

Job Satisfaction and Organizational Commitment

We postulated earlier that, to the extent that the Japanese workflows we studied were more bureaucratic, we would expect Japanese employees to be less satisfied with their jobs and to be less committed to their work organizations. A contrary proposition is offered by the argument that the welfarist tendency in Japanese WOs maximizes employees' organizational commitment. The final panel of table 8.4 gives the results for job satisfaction and commitment. As we can see, Japanese service and knowledge workers were less satisfied with their jobs. On the contrary, JB salespersons were more satisfied than their Australian counterparts. Japanese service and knowledge workers reported less commitment than their Australian counterparts, but Japanese sales workers did not differ significantly.

In the most detailed comparison to date of Japanese and U.S. manufacturing workers, Lincoln and Kalleberg (1990: 78) showed that Japanese employees were less satisfied and more committed than their U.S. counterparts. Our findings from the service sector support their conclusions regarding satisfaction but contradict their findings on commitment. This is possibly because of recent changes in the permanent employment system and internal labor market practices (Lincoln and Nakata 1997; Berggren and Nomura 1997; Morishima 1996). Whether these changes are permanent or merely transient responses to Japan's economic recession is a contentious issue. Nevertheless, these changes may have shaken the traditional allegiance of Japanese employees to their organizations.

Using the concept of employee dependence and insights from our qualitative research, we now seek to understand and explain differences in job satisfaction and commitment.

Service employees. The lower level of job satisfaction of Japanese service employees can be explained by the gender discrimination practiced by management at JB and the hierarchical control at MFJ, which left few opportunities for team interaction. At MFJ, both regular employees and those employed by the contracting company had limited prospects for internal advancement. This led to lower levels of job satisfaction. The final reason has to do with the team arrangement in our Australian and U.S. service workflows. Team working provided a basis for conviviality and psychological support and a medium for co-worker learning (see chapter 6). In addition, supervisors and team leaders were more supportive than their

Japanese equivalents, and there were more opportunities for internal promotion. Both management and the workers regarded the American service workflow included in our comparative analysis as a major source of training for workers destined to fill positions in other parts of the organization.[8] All these differences contributed to the lower level of job satisfaction and commitment of the Japanese service workers compared with their Western counterparts.

Salespersons. At MBAS and ABKS, salespersons were constrained by the decisions of the firms' bureaucratic credit analysts (see chapter 5). Lack of control over loan approvals threatened to jeopardize the salespersons' attainment of performance targets and to have adverse effects on their earnings and employment security. Together with the competitive nature of coworker relations, this led to relatively higher job dissatisfaction than at JBS. At the latter workflow, a commission reward system was not used, and employees enjoyed greater employment security. Both the relative earnings stability and the higher level of job security contributed to the relatively higher level of satisfaction of these sales workers compared with the sales employees in Australia.

Knowledge workers. As chapter 6 pointed out, at COMPUJ the young systems developers were wary of becoming too involved in sales activities, which these employees regarded as interfering with their pursuit of careers in engineering. This work tension was likely to be a source of job dissatisfaction and lower levels of commitment. Another source of dissatisfaction and lower commitment was the employees' hierarchical relations with their supervisors, which inhibited workplace learning (see chapter 6). Finally, customer sovereignty was increasing. It will be recalled that management increasingly emphasized sales in performance evaluations. As described in chapter 7, this also led to dissatisfaction.

The changes that the management at COMPUJ introduced in the promotion system also bred dissatisfaction and lower commitment. Under the new system, promotions were based on performance, not seniority. In chapter 4, we noted that at COMPUJ performance evaluations were increasingly based on evidence of self-development through training and sales. The latter was an area from which systems engineers tried to distance themselves. Reflecting a more general trend, these changes deviated from the conventional employment system, under which employees were guaranteed promotion after working for a company for an average of seven years (see chapter 4). COMPUJ's systems developers had been employed for an average of eight years. Thus, uncertainties about employment

---

[8] It is difficult to determine how much UB1 workers' higher expectations of internal promotions represent a company-specific rather than a wider, culturally based finding. This finding may well reflect a tendency for U.S. workers and management, more than their Australian counterparts, to emphasize individualism and achievement.

prospects gave rise to negative psychological effects, thereby leading to job dissatisfaction and lower levels of commitment.

In contrast to COMPUJ, which was under intense international competition and struggling to maintain its market share, WB was considered one of the most successful companies in the Australian financial sector. Industry survey data indicate that the level of pay was above average for the sector. As noted in chapters 4 and 5, considerable autonomy and decision-making authority, including decision making on HR matters, was devolved to line management and teams. The systems developers at WBSD also enjoyed a higher level of task discretion than their counterparts at COMPUJ. As a result, the systems developers at WBSD had comparatively higher scores on job satisfaction and commitment than their COMPUJ colleagues.

Overview. Based on the above results, there is substantial, though not unqualified, support for the proposition that Japanese workflows are more bureaucratic than their Western counterparts. The Japanese workflows in our study, particularly the service type, were notable for the presence of such bureaucratic features as limited employee influence and a producer-oriented ethos. Work setting-specific factors, such as gender discrimination, contributed to the lower levels of employee satisfaction and commitment.

In the sales workflows, the legal restriction on stock sales (see chapter 6), interfirm relationships, and the presence of internal labor markets contributed to the differences between our findings for JBS and for the two sales workflows in Australia. In COMPUJ, management's attempt to combine features of bureaucratic and knowledge-intensive WOs resulted in tensions among closely related employees. Further, changes in the promotion policies led to concerns about long-term job prospects within the organization. These factors led to lower levels of job satisfaction and organizational commitment among these knowledge workers than among their counterparts in Australia.

Conclusion

In this chapter, we analyzed employee job satisfaction and organizational commitment as outcomes of WO. Using insights developed from previous chapters and the bureaucratic ideal type as a benchmark, we explored the concept of employee dependence on management. Together with our qualitative findings, this concept was then used to derive both general and specific propositions regarding the determinants of job satisfaction and commitment for the three types of workflows. We argued that, to the extent that service workflows more closely resemble the bureaucratic ideal type than do sales or knowledge workflows, service employees are more dependent on management for accomplishing work tasks and expanding their employment prospects. In the case of service workers, management was more influential in mediating relations with customers. This led to the proposition that vertical relations (employment and control relations) would be a relatively more important influence on job satisfaction and commitment to the organization among service employees than among knowledge workers, who are less dependent on management.

We had the opposite expectations for sales workers. On the one hand, we noted that aspects of employment relations, such as pay and employment security, were strongly related to performance and determined by management. Hence, we expected that variations in these elements would affect sales workers' satisfaction and commitment significantly. On the other hand, the arm's-length relationship between entrepreneurial sales workers and their first-line managers suggested that these elements would not have a statistically significant impact on the two dependent variables.

Among the knowledge workers, there was a relatively high level of co-worker interdependence and reliance on colleagues for supplementary skills. This suggested that, compared to sales and service workers, the quality of these relations would have a more pronounced effect on knowledge workers' job satisfaction and commitment.

Our analyses indicated that although satisfaction with key aspects of employment relations and control relations contributed to both the job satisfaction and commitment of service employees, their effects in the case of sales and knowledge workers were either limited to job satisfaction or statistically insignificant. For sales workers, we noted that satisfaction with promotion prospects, with job security, and with the intrinsic nature of their work were important determinants of job satisfaction and commitment. We argued that the uncertain employment conditions of sales employees were more fundamental than the quality of management-employee relations in affecting these employees' satisfaction and commitment.

Although knowledge workers need to rely on management for work-related resources, their knowledge and skills are highly transferable. Thus, we found that, as for service workers, the quality of management-employee relations (as indicated by the trustworthiness of senior management and satisfaction with aspects of employment relations) and of relations with coworkers (trustworthiness of adjacent coworkers) contributed significantly to knowledge workers' job satisfaction and organizational commitment.

Our cross-national comparisons showed that institutions matter in shaping both the way work is organized and employees' attitudinal responses. Studies of Japanese manufacturing WOs indicate that lifetime employment, internal labor markets, and welfarist personnel policies combine to make Japanese employees more dependent on management for knowledge, skills, and careers than their Western counterparts. This proposition, however, underestimates the heterogeneity of various work settings, as indicated in our analysis.

We have also drawn attention to the need for contextualized explanations of cross-national differences. Our findings show that, contrary to the welfare corporatist argument (based on large manufacturing companies), the Japanese service workers in our study, many of whom were women, were *less* committed to their organizations than their Western counterparts. Chief among the reasons for the dissatisfaction and lower levels of commitment was the gender discrimination these women experienced. This resulted in their receiving limited job training and being offered limited opportunities for internal promotions.

In the case of the sales workflows, the Japanese employees faced less precarious employment conditions than their Australian counterparts; however, the levels of commitment of the Japanese employees were not comparably higher. In the case of the knowledge workers, one explanation was that recent employment relations changes introduced by COMPUJ management weakened the psychological bond between the employees and the organization. The adverse effects on staff were accentuated by the fact that core Japanese male employees rely heavily on their employing organizations for employment security and career progress. Hence, the Japanese knowledge workers had lower levels of job satisfaction and commitment than their Australian counterparts. These results suggest that more complex work can be arranged in a bureaucratic manner, but the cost is lower levels of employee satisfaction and organizational commitment.

9   Conclusion

In this book we have described and analyzed various forms of work organization among front-line workers. We have also attempted to explain some of the consequences of variations in these forms. We began by agreeing with arguments that emphasize the rise and significance of services in the postindustrial informational economy. In emphasizing the importance of theoretical knowledge and IT respectively, theorists such as Daniel Bell (1974) and Emmanuel Castells (1996) ignored a significant tendency: the rise of customer sovereignty in the context of a more competitive, globalized economy. It is this feature that led us to focus on the front-line worker, whose distinguishing feature is regular contact with prospective or actual customers.

We noted that the significance of front-line workers has been increasing more rapidly than that of front-line support and back-office workers, while, concomitantly, front-line workers are undertaking more diverse tasks. These range from relatively low-skill through paraprofessional activities to highly knowledge-intensive professional jobs. To reflect this diversity, we selected workers undertaking front-line work of differing levels of complexity. At the low end were mass customized service workers; in the middle were workers who sold home loans and shares in companies; and at the high end were knowledge workers—systems developers and money market dealers. Our sample was restricted to major service-oriented industries—financial services, telecommunications, and computers—and to large, successful firms. In other words, our aim was to understand the nature of work organization in the heartland of advanced economies.[1]

[1] Studies of work organization need to be extended to other economic areas, particularly those that are growing most rapidly. Smaller high-technology companies in computing and biotechnology are a prime example. It is quite possible that the work organization of these firms more closely resembles that of the knowledge-intensive ideal type. There are other pos-

Our approach to the study of work organization—described in chapters
1 and 2—was informed by a perspective that acknowledges the dialectics
of structure and agency in explaining social phenomena. Our theoretical
strategy was to employ two kinds of foils. The first was a developmental
perspective that emphasized emergent types of work organization; the
second was an ideal-type framework crafted to enhance the comparative
analysis of front-line workers across different kinds of workflows.

At the center of both schemas is the idea, suggested by our research, that
work is becoming more complex rather than more routinized. Whether this
leads to a departure from the image of the regimented worker is an empirical question. One can assume, however, that work will be organized in
ways that at the very least will compromise bureaucracy and quite possibly transcend this form.

The first perspective noted above, labeled work organization imagery,
offers a pessimistic, regimented model that essentially assumes continuity
of the bureaucratic form while accommodating to new circumstances that,
nevertheless, do not substantially improve employees' well-being. Thus, any
loosening of bureaucratic controls, as might be envisaged where work is
becoming more complex and workers are increasingly expected to respond
to customer requirements, is offset by increasing electronic surveillance and
more stringent performance requirements. The result is an adaptive contemporary form of bureaucracy—which we labeled the *regimented work
organization*—in which there are few significant departures from the traditional bureaucracy but less coercion and formalization (Adler and Borys
1996).

By contrast, the more optimistic perspective posits an *empowered work
organization* whose level of formalization is lower than its regimented counterpart and that is enabling rather than coercive in character. Thus, there
is more reliance on lateral relations, common norms, and trust. This
network form is usually favored for its effectiveness (its flexibility and
capacity to innovate) and equity (as a source of more intrinsically and
socially satisfying work).

Although these images are important for policy purposes (either to avoid
or to pursue) and hence recur throughout this book, they offer stark alternatives and hence are less suitable for detailed comparative analysis. In
addition, they are value laden—bureaucracies are viewed as bad, and networks are viewed as good—which is inappropriate for use in analytical
research. Thus, the focus in this volume has been on the notion of work

---

sibilities as well. For example, the work of some front-line computer technicians may lend
itself to individualized, remote working. Such workers may work alone but have strong on-
line connections with their colleagues. Similarly, some front-line sales work, such as telemar-
keting, may be undertaken from home under conditions that resemble the entrepreneurial
ideal type.

organizations as composed of two principal dimensions—a vertical and a lateral—and five primary elements—work relations, employment relations, control relations, co-worker relations, and customer relations. Specific configurations of these elements constitute the three ideal types to which we have consistently referred—the *bureaucratic, entrepreneurial,* and *knowledge intensive.* These ideal types formed the basis for our comparison of work organizations across the three types of workflows. These ideal types also enabled us to explore some of the consequences or outcomes of different forms of work organization and to assess Japanese versus Western (Australian and U.S.) differences.

Our empirical findings regarding each of the five elements of work organization, and some of their consequences, are reported in previous chapters. Here our intention is to synthesize these findings by attempting to answer three questions. First, to what extent does our empirical evidence support or contradict either of the images of work organization alluded to above and sketched in more detail in chapter 1? Second, do we need to adjust our conclusions on this point to account for cross-national differences, particularly between Japanese organizations and those in the West? And third, since work organizations are dynamic, how are they likely to change over time? The remainder of this chapter addresses each of these three questions in turn.

Imagery versus Evidence

The pessimistic image of work organizations as regimented and routinized and its opposite, the optimistic, empowered vision, are detailed in table 1.4. These perspectives can be summarized as follows. In the case of regimented work, the assumption is that the work is more interesting but more difficult than in the past. Management views employees as replaceable resources. Constant surveillance and high performance standards are reinforced by programmed learning and strict discipline. Customer contact involves emotional labor that results in inadequate additional compensation. Work is consequently experienced as coercive and enervating, although acceptable where there is the threat of unemployment.

The alternative image is based on the notion that work is intrinsically rewarding and that HR systems provide skill- and knowledge-enhancing competencies that assist employees in developing their careers. Workers identify with management goals and undertake initiatives consistent with these objectives. Relationships with co-workers are mutually beneficial, particularly with regard to learning, and customer relations contribute to workers' job satisfaction. In sum, work is experienced as enabling, competency enhancing, and socially satisfying.

Our analysis points to substantial differences in work organization in the three types of workflows. It is necessary, therefore, to examine each in turn. We can then draw more general conclusions about whether either the positive or the negative image outlined above accurately reflects work organization in these workflows.

Service Work

As we have shown, work organization in the service workflow tends to be regimented. The work is relatively routinized, training is oriented mainly to ensuring job proficiency rather than employee development, workers' career opportunities are limited, and there is considerable emphasis on numerical flexibility (i.e., adjusting employment numbers and working hours to changes in demand). Teams, such as they are, are controlled by management. Employees are expected to spend much more of their time interacting with customers than with colleagues. Service workers recognize the contradiction inherent in management's demand that they provide high-quality service and answer the requisite number of calls in the time available. Consequently, as we noted in chapter 3, the service workers in our study derived significantly lower intrinsic satisfaction from their work than did the sales and knowledge workers. Satisfaction with the intrinsic elements of their work contributed more to the service workers' overall job satisfaction, however, than it did for the sales and knowledge workers.

That service work provides opportunities, though limited, to pursue challenges and express creativity runs counter to the image of the regimented service worker. Thus, aspects of service work are intrinsically satisfying—for example, working with various products and assisting customers with their queries. Further, supervision tends to be more facilitative than directive, management tends to have a high tolerance for shortfalls in productivity, and relations with co-workers are generally positive. These enabling elements suggest that the image of the service organization as regimented is overdrawn and therefore invalid.

Sales Work

We have shown in previous chapters that sales work tends to be neither regimented nor empowering. Rather, it resembles the entrepreneurial ideal type. Thus, the salesperson is part businessperson, part employee, dependent on the market but also on his/her own aptitude and determination, as well as on the quality of the product and marketing of the organization.

Salespeople work mainly individually and rely less on IT and more on their social skills than do service or knowledge workers, although this may change in the future. Sales workers enjoy a high level of autonomy and feel a strong sense of achievement when sales targets are met.

Pay and employment security are strongly linked to sales workers' performance. In good times pay is high, but there is no organizational cushion. They receive little training, and opportunities for promotions are limited. Sales workers do not work in teams, and their relations with their immediate colleagues are mainly competitive or, in the case of colleagues responsible for authorizing loan applications, conflictual. Sales workers develop strong ties with other professionals who can refer customers to them. Relationships with the latter are mainly instrumental, although we noted some empathy with customers.

Overall, salespeople experience work in much the way small business owners do—as a challenge—and success depends largely on their taking initiative. As evident during our research, in bad times, or in periods of increasing competition, salespeople experience their work as stressful and requiring relentless pitching—persuading referrers to refer customers, persuading customers to buy, and persuading credit analysts to approve loan applications.

Knowledge Work

The knowledge worker comes closest to working under conditions that resemble our knowledge-intensive ideal type or in a value-laden sense, the empowered work organization. But even in knowledge work workflows, there is some deviation. The work is intrinsically satisfying; technology promotes task effectiveness, and, more so than sales or service workers, knowledge workers maintain control of their work. Although knowledge work is accompanied by on-the-job learning, as we pointed out, the process whereby this takes place is less systematic than it might be. Further, the work is stressful, significantly more so than for service workers. Complex problems need to be solved, both to suit customers and to maintain professional standards, and the work has to be completed within agreed-upon timelines and on budget.

On the one hand, employers attempt to retain valued knowledge workers by offering them valuable learning opportunities and challenging assignments and, especially, by providing them with favorable compensation. On the other hand, career opportunities are often restricted in the employing organization so that knowledge workers feel compelled to seek more satisfying work in the external market.

Management allows knowledge workers considerable discretion, which extends to collaborative projects. As we have seen, however, an absence of structure and control can lead to technical conflicts that can undermine collaborative efforts, leaving workers with a sense of anomie. Indeed, as we argued, the importance accorded the lateral dimension in knowledge work can have the effect of making such conflicts likely. One problem with knowledge work is that it tends to foster workplace politics as powerful individuals and groups seek to persuade others of the correctness of their strategies.

Knowledge workers relate to both external and internal customers. In each case, the relationships are complex, enduring over relatively long time periods and involving the continuous exchange of information and knowledge. This process assists in the development of shared perspectives and consistent approaches to problem solving. There is no doubt that knowledge work is experienced as enabling and competency enhancing. It is also competitive, so that social relations are less satisfying than suggested by the image of the empowered work organization.

Overview

Having briefly reviewed the evidence, our answer to the first question is that neither image reflects our findings accurately. On the one hand, service work represents a significant adaptation that we have labeled a mass customized bureaucracy (Frenkel et al. 1998). This term captures its similarity to the bureaucracy, including coercive elements associated with that form. On the other hand, because of the customizing aspect of service work, it requires creativity and hence discretion, which implies the need for learning more than just routinized patterns of behavior. Thus, service work organizations can be characterized as bureaucracies, but embedded within them are aspects of work organization more associated with knowledge work settings.

As noted earlier, in their market responsiveness, sales organizations diverge from both our images. From a historical standpoint, they signify a return to unregulated market forces, which, in difficult times, can have devastating effects on workers and their families.

Finally, with some important qualifications, knowledge work organizations can be characterized as empowered. The nature of the work is more complex, however, than depicted in the conventional imagery.

Japanese versus Western Work Organization

Having compared workflows in Japan with those in the United States and Australia, we conclude that Japanese WO tends to be more bureaucratic. In the service workflows, vertical relations overshadowed the lateral aspects, and the gendered organization of employment relations precluded the tendency, found in the American and Australian workflows, toward the empowerment model. Lower levels of customization and less investment in information technology meant that front-line Japanese service work was more routinized and managers tended to rely more on direct, personal, rather than info-normative, control and supervision. Japanese service workers were also less satisfied and reported that they were less committed to their organizations than their Western counterparts. In other words, the service workflows in Japan departed less from the bureaucratic ideal type than did the service workplaces in the United States and Australia.

The tendency toward bureaucratic WO was also evident in Japanese sales and knowledge work workflows. Specifically, the differences between sales and knowledge work workflows, especially with respect to employment relations, were less evident in Japan than in the United States or Australia. In both types of workflows, management relied on internal labor markets and used similar evaluation and remuneration systems.

The Japanese sales and knowledge workers we observed were less autonomous than their Australian counterparts, although the Japanese workers also enjoyed some task-level participation. Australian workers in these two categories, and especially knowledge workers, tended to be empowered, whereas opportunities for co-worker learning and cooperation in Japan, particularly in the knowledge work workflows, were far more limited.

Management influence on workers' relations with customers was also stronger in Japan. If customers needed to be persuaded, managers were integral to this process, a practice that reflected the more hierarchical Japanese culture.

In both sales and knowledge work, however, rotation practices enabled Japanese employees to develop networks of co-workers throughout their companies. This practice introduced an element of lateral relations that was less developed in Australia. In this sense, work organization in Japan was more complex than the imagery associated with the bureaucratic organization. Several changes contribute to this complexity. For example, appraisal and reward systems were being revised to encourage stronger employee performance, and promotions were becoming more competitive.

To summarize, even in the knowledge work workflows, where the empowered Japanese worker was somewhat in evidence, bureaucratic elements were much more apparent than in the United States or Australia. Interworkflow differences in the Japanese cases were thus less pronounced, and the tendency to empower workers was less strong than in comparable American and Australian workflows.

The Present versus the Future

Our third question concerns the likely shape of work organizations in the future. In chapter 1, we noted three perspectives on this issue: the convergence view, which suggests the universal ascendancy of the network form of work organization; the continuity view, which argues that change will not break the mold of bureaucracy, so that new ways of organizing will be contained within this form; and the postmodern patternless perspective, which asserts that the elements that constitute work organization are likely to be mixed and matched in many different ways.

Because our research is essentially cross-sectional rather than longitudinal, we cannot claim to provide an authoritative view of the changes ahead. This requires a more longitudinal perspective. We were, however, able to identify processes rooted in the recent past that were being emphasized in the present and that are likely to be significant in the future. This, together with information provided in interviews with managers and workers and assessments based on secondary sources, provides the basis for our conjectures on future tendencies. This term is used instead of trends since the evidence suggests there will be considerable variation. This is underlined by the absence of evidence that management will pursue any best practice or high-performance concept universally.

Tendencies in Service Work

Our analysis points to service work becoming more complex. Greater product variety and more frequent policy and procedural changes suggest that service workers will require increasingly better access to information, which they will need to be able to readily convert to usable knowledge. Simultaneously, workers will be required to possess more higher-order contextual knowledge (i.e., about industry and market developments) to deal with more complex customer queries and to demonstrate more persuasive selling techniques. The greater emphasis on sales will also necessitate higher-level social skills.

To encourage selling and relationship building, service workers are likely to be given more authority (within strict limits) in dealing with exceptional cases. As a result of this devolution of responsibility, we are likely to see an increase in workers' stress levels but also in a feature these workers particularly value—satisfaction with the intrinsic nature of their work.

The way in which more complex service work will be organized depends on technological developments. Smart technology, in the form of computer-integrated performance support (Winslow and Bramer 1994), could result in the realization of the empowered front-line workforce. This is unlikely, however, if past experience is any guide, except in a small number of firms with special characteristics. A more common tendency will be for novices to continue to be differentiated from experienced specialists and experienced generalists. In other words, workers in settings such as call centers are likely to see their internal career paths slightly extended and formalized. Experienced generalists will constitute a growing elite resembling empowerment in its ideal form. By contrast, if technology is able to provide adequate support, the work complexity of their more numerous specialist colleagues is not likely to change very significantly.

Employment and control relations are likely to develop along one of two paths, although these are not mutually exclusive.[2] The first route is notable for its continuity. Employment relations can be described as following a truncated bureaucratic form characterized by a combination of info-normative control that includes facilitative management. Performance-related rewards are emphasized.

Workers who travel this conventional pathway are likely to be reminded of the contradictions between the greater demands being placed on front-line service employees and their limited pay, training, and career opportunities. Management's traditional solution to this problem has been to employ more women (Baran 1987; Appelbaum and Albin 1989), but this approach will not be considered efficacious in cultures that emphasize gender equality at work.

The alternative is to change the vertical relations systems so as to bring them into closer alignment with the growing complexity of service work. This would result in an employment relations system that resembles the hybrid knowledge work pattern but with more emphasis on its bureaucratic aspects. Similarly, with respect to control relations, we would expect to see more emphasis on learning and task interdependence, particularly among more experienced workers, who might act as network nodes for novices and experienced specialists.

A final point to bear in mind is that our prognosis is confined to technologically intensive service work in large corporations. Where business units are disaggregated—a more common tendency—service work may be outsourced and "dumbed down." In these workplaces, a low-knowledge/low-skill strategy may be pursued, enabling these specialist agencies to deal effectively with the work of various companies through insourcing. Reliance on technology will increase in order to standardize work as much as possible. In these specialist companies, the Taylorization of front-line work is likely to take either of two paths: increasing union representation and collective regulation or increasing atomization and high labor turnover where home-based teleworking is attempted as an operational strategy.

Tendencies in Sales Work

If home loan sales is broadly representative of most specialized direct sales work, our evidence suggests that management will more closely integrate the business units responsible for this work with other units in the organization, leading to a more widespread entrepreneurial spirit. Work organization will tend to become more bureaucratic, as the hybrid model of vertical relations, associated with knowledge workers, is applied to sales

---

[2] The behavior of novice and experienced specialists may be motivated and regulated by vertical relations arrangements similar to those that currently exist, while experienced generalists may benefit from a hybrid system more characteristic of knowledge work.

personnel. These employees will welcome the training and even limited promotion opportunities. As management expects its sales workers to engage in a wider range of transactions (e.g., foreign exchange), some of which will require developing relationships with workers outside sales units, management is likely to encourage the formation of teams for the purpose of learning and mutual support.

As in the case of service work, the changes in sales work are predicated on the work increasing in complexity. In addition to wider ranges of products, we can expect rapid changes in products as consumers are persuaded or attracted to alternatives. Accordingly, sales workers will need to master more contextual knowledge and have the necessary skills to offer the right products to the right customers at the right time. In the case of financial product sales workers, more reliance on IT software is likely to reduce the amount of routine, contextual knowledge-gathering work, freeing workers to concentrate on analyzing and presenting the advantages of more complex products to customers. Concomitantly, sales workers will be expected to provide even more professional and more personalized service, consistent with the increasing sophistication associated with more highly educated and more knowledgeable customers.

There are four ways in which IT will reduce the need for routine work and enable salespeople to pursue work that is more skilled and creative. First, databases will provide information and contextual knowledge so that sales workers will not need to spend time learning the details of their products. Product, policy, and process information will be at salespeople's fingertips. This will include customer information (if the person is already a customer) and market and trend analyses.

Second, the use of Internet-based information and applications by prospective customers will reduce the amount of routine sales tasks. Similarly, more extensive use of IT will virtually eliminate time-consuming paperwork and speed up loan processing.

Third, expert systems will enable sales workers to approve or reject relatively straightforward applications on the basis of information requested, supplied, and checked by on-line credit agencies. This will reduce the conflict with credit analysts (or their equivalents), who will continue to be responsible for more complex loan requests.

Fourth, instead of simply referring potential customers to salespeople, referrers, with the assistance of IT, will conduct preliminary loan assessments and then transfer this information to the sales workers on-line. Thus, referrers will act more as agent/brokers, for which they will receive fees.

This review suggests that as sales work becomes more complex, it will require more analytical skills and afford more possibilities to use techniques of persuasion. Computer skills will be mandatory.

This tendency for sales work to become similar to knowledge work is likely to be paralleled by the emergence of knowledge-intensive elements in sales, particularly opportunities for promotion and learning, and closer co-worker relations. As we shall see, the risk of losing well-trained, strongly integrated sales workers could become more acute, however.

Overlaying elements of a KI work organization on E-type sales workers could have negative or positive consequences. On the one hand, morale and sales performance may improve as management attempts to mitigate the individualistic, performance-based, contract arrangement. In this case, sales workers would become even more committed and productive. On the other hand, if the overlay is too strong, it could suffocate the entrepreneurial spirit. In this case, sales workers would be more disposed either to quit or to act collectively in opposing management's plans. Conflict could result in lower performance. Much will depend on management's communication and negotiating skills.

Tendencies in Knowledge Work

Because knowledge work is undertaken in diverse settings and is novel and customized, it is difficult to discern tendencies and to assert their generalizability. Nevertheless, we will make several observations.

First, globalization is contributing to an atmosphere of more intense competition and more discerning customers. A strong customer focus and technology to speed up innovation are paramount. Concurrently, work is becoming more complex. Thus, new systems and legacy systems are continuously being integrated, and, in the case of money market dealing, markets for fixed-interest and longer-term financial instruments are overlapping as clients operate across various markets and demand to transact all their business with single dealers (in accordance with the one-stop shopping principle). This increasing complexity is likely to encourage greater reliance on co-workers in executing work, for learning, and for psychological support in coping with uncertainty. This tendency partly accounts for the emphasis on teamwork. It also underlines another organizational preoccupation: the concern with learning and knowledge management.

Successful project performance requires the application of relevant knowledge to new problems. The presence of strong co-worker relations encourages this transfer on an individual level. Such transfers are often unsystematic, however, and depend on personal contacts with current and past colleagues. In the case of multinationals, which aim to extend their networks globally, there is increasing reliance on Internet technology, particularly intranets.

Knowledge repositories also need to be developed for proprietary use. How to structure these appropriately so that there are incentives to elicit, transfer, and appropriate relevant knowledge constitutes a major management challenge. IT is already available to facilitate knowledge sharing and learning. More intractable is the development and maintenance of employment and control systems that foster the use of these processes among employees whose financial stake in the enterprise is limited.

The growing importance of lateral relations will also be evident in new ways of thinking about the selection and retention of knowledge workers. The focus will be less on identifying employees who will contribute as individuals and more on assessing their likely effectiveness in teams. The increasing involvement of clients in project and product design and development implies that knowledge workers will need to focus more attention on such social skills as listening, presenting, persuading, and negotiating, especially as they deal with more knowledgeable customers (typically representatives of client organizations).

Knowledge work in the future is likely to be characterized by paradoxical and experimental elements. On the one hand, management will emphasize the lateral dimensions of organizations. On the other hand, management will be pressured by the market and clients to secure timely and profitable investments, which will encourage close oversight of work processes. The result is likely to be a shift in accountability and rewards to teams. Thus, teams will develop their own norms for ensuring that work is accomplished within parameters agreed upon by senior management. The processes for successful execution will often be improvised and experimental and influenced by managers.

The term "manager" will become less meaningful as leadership assumes increasing importance. Leaders' responsibilities will include greater emphasis on interpreting and conveying corporate and business unit values and norms to knowledge workers and communicating the latter's views to senior management. But leaders will not simply act as go-betweens. They will also be expected to embody the entrepreneurial spirit by seeking out and seizing innovative opportunities for their teams to exploit. Leaders will also be responsible for coordinating workers, including selecting and integrating project teams across business units. Using a metaphor appropriated from a money market manager, tribes (teams) will need to be kept unified and dissuaded both from destroying other tribes and from deserting their territories in search of more lucrative hunting grounds. In short, if centrifugal forces are to be countered effectively, tomorrow's leaders will have to make the nation (business unit) mean something to knowledge workers. They are likely to do this by implementing carefully designed, flexible, employment relations systems that emphasize company or project ownership more strongly than today.

Conclusion

In general, work in all three types of workflows appears to be becoming more complex. This suggests that in time service and sales work will resemble knowledge work, which in a hybrid organizational form combines weak vertical relations with strong lateral relations. This broad tendency toward the knowledge-intensive or network work organization does not tell the whole story, however. As we argued above, work in the future will depend crucially on management's employment relations and technology strategy. Thus, the future is relatively open. This is less true of sales work. In this case, management will seek to integrate the work more closely into the overall organization and, with rising work complexity coupled with greater reliance on IT, there will be more emphasis on training and collaboration with co-workers. Nevertheless, performance-related commissions that represent a relatively large proportion of total compensation will continue to encourage individual competition. Thus, sales work will constitute a hybrid consisting of elements of all three ideal types: entrepreneurial, bureaucratic, and knowledge-intensive.

With regard to knowledge work, we have argued that the tendency toward the knowledge-intensive ideal type or network form will be reflected in considerable experimentation with team working, project execution, and organizational learning. Paradoxically, knowledge work will increasingly emphasize both lateral and vertical relations. The former tendency has its roots in the shift toward increasing work complexity, whereas the latter reflects the highly competitive, globalized market context in which problem solving must occur within agreed-upon time and cost limitations.

In Japan, the pressures of deregulation and globalization will also result in an increase in the complexity of front-line work. This will counter some of the tendency toward the perpetuation of bureaucracies; however, whether change occurs quickly will be influenced by progress made in granting more equality to women workers. A new equal opportunity law is scheduled to be introduced in 1999. On the one hand, this legislation is more progressive than the current law and hence may encourage the eradication of the more routine work currently undertaken mainly by women in bureaucratic settings. On the other hand, the proposed legislation does not include meaningful sanctions against employers who continue to discriminate against women (Shire and Ota 1997).

In male-dominated Japanese workplaces, the job-rotation system points to the importance of co-workers as a basis of network-type organizations. The preservation of managerial hierarchies has interfered, however, with the development of more autonomous and collaborative co-worker relations. Attempts to introduce more meritocratic elements into performance evaluations and to reduce the number of middle managers, transforming them into experts rather than supervisors, may reduce the strength of this hierarchy in the future. This may not be enough of a change, however, since a deeper cultural shift away from the centrality of vertical relations is also necessary.

To return to the questions posed earlier: Are work organizations converging on the network model? Or are we more likely to see a continuation of the bureaucratic model? Or will the future be devoid of any clear pattern? Our argument suggests that these three options are not mutually exclusive. There is relative openness in organizational choice. We anticipate initially a process of adaptation and subsequently one of hybridization. In short, for the foreseeable future, we are likely to see work organizations that combine features of two or more ideal types.

Finally, we would like to reaffirm the importance of basic research. We see our work as laying a foundation for applied research. Such work might usefully contrast alternative models of work organization, focusing more specifically on the consequences of various forms of organization and highlighting adverse aspects that need to be eliminated or minimized. Such research should also form the basis of public policies that hasten the diffusion of more beneficial forms of work organization and limit the spread of less desirable alternatives. In this regard, such measures should form part of a broader strategy designed to regulate economic globalization through international cooperation, reduce unemployment, spread work more evenly across the workforce, and limit wealth and earnings inequality arising from gender and occupational disparities. Work organization is an instrument for improving efficiency and equity. As such, public policy should regulate its direction, while management and employees, in consultation with customer representatives, should be responsible for its detailed design.

Appendixes

Appendix 1. Results of Discriminant Analysis

A. Results of Discriminant Analysis in Three Types of Workflow

Function	Eigen value	Percentage of variance	Canonical correlation	Significance level of F
1	0.8410	91.83	0.676	0.000
2	0.0749	8.17	0.263	0.000

Source: Employee survey.

B. Significant Discriminating Variables

Variable	Wilks' lambda	Significance level
Interpersonal skills	0.819	0.00
Knowledge of company policies, systems, and procedures	0.710	0.00
Knowledge of market and other trends in the industry	0.659	0.00
Knowledge of principles and techniques specific to occupation	0.591	0.00
Level of creativity	0.554	0.00
Self-management skills	0.533	0.00
Analytical skills	0.523	0.00
Knowledge of individual customers' needs	0.513	0.00
Knowledge of competitors' products or services	0.505	0.00

Source: Employee survey.

Appendix 2. Definition of Factors, Descriptive Statistics, and Cronbach Alpha Coefficients of Factors

Factor	Definition (mean, standard deviation)	Cronbach's alpha coefficient
Effectiveness of technology	The technology I usually work with (1 = strongly disagree to 5 = strongly agree) —enables me to do my job effectively (4.25, 0.91) —is not user-friendly (e.g., is too slow, programs are too complex, etc.) [reverse coded] (2.83, 1.23) —restricts my ability to satisfy customers' needs [reverse coded] (3.37, 1.24) —is flexible enough for me to make adjustments to suit my needs (3.03, 1.10) —enables me to contact my colleagues easily when I need to (3.03, 1.10)	0.65
Enabling capacity of technology	The technology I usually work with (1 = strongly disagree to 5 = strongly agree) —controls the way I work [reverse coded] (2.20, 1.13) —makes me feel too reliant on the technology [reverse coded] (2.87, 1.21)	0.55
Creativity	In your work, how often do you (1 = never to 5 = very often) —try out new ways to solve problems (3.64, 0.95) —come up with new ideas and ways of doing things (3.45, 0.99) —deal with nonroutine or unique problems (3.62, 0.99)	0.82
Trustworthiness of adjacent colleagues	Thinking about people outside your section or department, how much do you agree or disagree with each of the following statements? (1 = strongly disagree to 5 = strongly agree) —If I get into difficulties at work, I know other people in this company will try to help me. (3.84, 1.04) —If I need assistance at work, I can trust other people in this company to help me. (3.83, 1.01) —I can rely on other people in this company not to make my job more difficult by careless work. (3.01, 1.08)	0.70
Interdependence among colleagues	Thinking about people outside your section or department, how much do you agree or disagree with each of the following statements? (1 = strongly disagree to 5 = strongly agree) —Doing my job well depends on other people in this company doing their jobs well. (3.92, 1.10) —The way I do my work affects the quality of other people's work in this company. (4.13, 0.96)	0.65

Appendix 2. Continued

Factor	Definition (mean, standard deviation)	Cronbach's alpha coefficient
Team cohesion	Considering the team in which you spend most of your working time, how much do you (1 = none at all to 5 = very much) —feel that you are part of your work team (4.24, 0.87) —look forward to working with your team members every day (4.04, 0.91) —socialize with your team members outside work (2.71, 1.12)	0.67
Knowledgeability of immediate supervisor	How much do you agree or disagree that your immediate supervisor (1 = strongly disagree to 5 = strongly agree) —knows little about the tasks you do [reverse coded] (3.94, 1.21) —knows little about the procedures you follow [reverse coded] (3.97, 1.18) —is good at his or her own job (4.11, 0.97)	0.79
Immediate supervisor support	How much do you agree or disagree that your immediate supervisor (1 = strongly disagree to 5 = strongly agree) —helps you develop your skills (3.34, 1.17) —gives recognition for a job well done (3.89, 1.07) —keeps you informed (3.85, 1.07) —encourages you to participate in important decisions (3.49, 1.18)	0.86
Trustworthiness of senior management	Thinking about the senior management here, how much do you agree or disagree with each of the following? (1 = strongly disagree to 5 = strongly agree) —They are sincere in dealing with employees' problems [reverse coded] (3.32, 1.08) —They cannot be trusted to do what they say [reverse coded] (3.34, 1.10) —They cannot be relied upon to make good decisions [reverse coded] (3.42, 1.09)	0.73
Amount of influence at task level	How much direct influence and involvement do you have in each of the following? (1 = none at all to 5 = a lot) —Deciding how to do your job and organize the work (3.71, 1.19) —Deciding what training is needed for people in your team or section (2.23, 1.14) —Setting work schedules, including breaks, overtime, and time off (2.52, 1.46)	0.80

Appendix 2. Continued

Factor	Definition (mean, standard deviation)	Cronbach's alpha coefficient
	—Setting goals for your team or section (2.27, 1.26) —Deciding how to work with new equipment or software if that's ever been needed (1.88, 1.21)	
Amount of influence above task level	How much direct influence and involvement do you have in each of the following? (1 = none at all to 5 = a lot) —Deciding about replacement of equipment you work with or new technology (1.77, 1.11) —Developing new products or services (1.78, 1.17) —Promotion decisions (1.46, 0.92) —Hiring decisions (1.39, 0.92)	0.83
Incongruence between management's and customers' interests	In providing customer service or in selling company products/services, how often do you (1 = never to 5 = very often) —have to bend company rules in order to satisfy customers (2.86, 0.84) —receive incompatible requests from customers and management (2.55, 1.05) —do things that are acceptable to management but not acceptable to customers (2.49, 1.01)	0.70
Self-assessed ability to satisfy customers	How often do you feel that (1 = never to 5 = very often) —you cannot satisfy customers' requirements [reversed coded] (3.18, 0.85) —you are not confident about your ability to satisfy customers [reverse coded] (3.83, 0.90) —you are not making customers happy [reverse coded] (3.70, 0.77)	0.718
Discretionary effort	In doing your work, how often do you do each of the following? (1 = never to 5 = very often) —Go beyond the scope of your duties when necessary (3.75, 0.97) —Put in extra effort (4.01, 0.85) —Do more than the acceptable level (3.85, 0.91)	0.883
Job satisfaction	All in all, how satisfied are you with your job? (1 = very dissatisfied to 5 = very satisfied) —If you were free to go into any type of job you wanted, what would your choice be? 1 = I want the job I have now. 2 = I want to retire and not work at all.	0.685

Appendix 2. Continued

Factor	Definition (mean, standard deviation)	Cronbach's alpha coefficient
	3 = I prefer some other job to the job I have now. [The above precoded choices were recoded.] —If a good friend of yours told you he or she was interested in working in a job like yours for your employer, what would you tell him or her? 1 = I would strongly recommend it. 2 = I would have doubts recommending it. 3 = I would advise the friend against it. [The above precoded choices were recoded.]	
Work stress	Thinking of the past three months or so, how often has your job made you feel like each of the following? (1 = never to 5 = very often) —After I leave my work, I keep worrying about job problems (2.82, 1.17) —I find it difficult to unwind at the end of a workday (2.79, 1.15) —I feel used up at the end of a workday (3.17, 1.12)	0.837
Organizational commitment	Thinking about this company, how much do you agree or disagree with each of the following? (1 = strongly disagree to 5 = strongly agree) —I am willing to work harder than I have to in order to help this company succeed (3.72, 0.89) —I am proud to tell others that I work for this company (4.00, 0.88) —I feel very little loyalty to this company [reverse coded] (3.59, 1.20) —I would turn down a job at comparable pay and prospects in another company to stay with this company (3.48, 1.23)	0.651

Source: Employee survey.

Appendix 3. Gender, Supervision, and Perceived Effectiveness of Service Workers

	Mean weighted factor score		Number of respondents (according to gender of supervisors)
	Male supervisor	Female supervisor	
Supervisor's knowledge*	3.30	3.46	Male = 238 Female = 369
Supervisor's supportiveness*	3.07	3.26	Male = 237 Female = 370
Team effectiveness*	3.21	3.33	Male = 202 Female = 309
Team cohesion*	2.88	3.00	Male = 199 Female = 301
Satisfaction with management*,†	3.11	3.38	Male = 236 Female = 370

Note: * Difference between the groups is significant ($p < 0.05$); † not a factor.
Source: Employee survey.

Appendix 4. Means, Standard Deviations (S.D.), and Correlations of Independent Variables Used in Service Workflow Regressions

Variable	Mean	S.D.	1	2	3	4	5	6	7	8	9	10
Dependent variables												
Job satisfaction	0.09	0.93										
Organizational commitment	0.025	1.007										
Independent variables												
1. Satisfaction with nature of work	3.327	1.080	—									
2. Effectiveness of technology	-0.131	0.959	0.22**	—								
3. Senior management's trustworthiness	0.090	1.011	0.33**	0.21**	—							
4. Immediate supervisor's support	0.146	0.966	0.30**	0.13**	0.32**	—						
5. Influence above task level	-0.180	0.738	0.10**	0.09**	0.03	0.003	—					
6. Team cohesion	0.050	1.010	0.25**	0.09**	0.24**	0.38**	0.02	—				
7. External colleagues' trustworthiness	0.090	0.976	0.27**	0.35**	0.35**	0.31**	0.06*	0.27**	—			
8. Satisfaction with pay	3.396	0.989	0.27**	0.33**	0.23**	0.15**	-0.04	0.16**	0.24**	—		
9. Satisfaction with promotion prospects	3.057	1.044	0.50**	0.20**	0.33**	0.33**	0.08*	0.28**	0.26**	0.44**	—	
10. Satisfaction with job security	4.021	0.814	0.25**	0.28**	0.20**	0.18**	0.00	0.24**	0.22**	0.38**	0.30**	—
11. Self-assessed ability to satisfy customers	0.011	0.963	0.22**	0.17**	0.20**	0.12**	0.05	0.15**	0.26**	0.09**	0.22**	0.13**
12. Incongruence between customers' and management's demands	-0.004	0.969	-0.24**	-0.13**	-0.27**	-0.12**	-0.03	-0.04	-0.19**	-0.14**	-0.20**	-0.03

Note: * $p < 0.1$ level; ** $p < 0.05$ level.
Source: Employee survey.

Appendix 5. Means, Standard Deviations (S.D.), and Correlations of Independent Variables Used in Sales Workflow Regressions

Variable	Mean	S.D.	1	2	3	4	5	6	7	8	9	10
Dependent variable												
Job satisfaction	−0.337	1.17										
Organizational commitment	−0.204	0.94										
Independent variable												
1. Satisfaction with nature of work	3.813	0.865	—									
2. Effectiveness of technology	−0.202	1.278	0.28*	—								
3. Senior management's trustworthiness	−0.505	1.040	0.36*	0.39*	—							
4. Immediate supervisor's support	−0.305	0.947	0.34*	0.20†	0.42*	—						
5. Influence above task level	0.194	1.524	0.06	0.12	0.19†	0.12	—					
6. External colleagues' trustworthiness			0.48*	0.65*	0.33*	0.28*	0.04	—				
7. Satisfaction with pay	2.560	1.165	0.14	0.28*	0.35*	0.34*	0.34*	0.24*	—			
8. Satisfaction with promotion prospects	2.693	1.039	0.20†	0.27*	0.30*	0.22*	0.36*	0.14	0.62*	—		
9. Satisfaction with job security	2.933	1.119	0.27*	0.26*	0.50*	0.28*	0.10	0.20*	0.58*	0.57*	—	
10. Self-assessed ability to satisfy customers	−0.19	1.09	0.16†	0.33*	0.30*	0.18†	−0.08	0.40*	−0.01	−0.02	0.22*	—
11. Incongruence between customers' and management's demands	0.24	1.04	−0.11	−0.21†	−0.30*	−0.19†	−0.06	−0.13	0.08	0.08	−0.12	−0.44†

Note: $* p < 0.05$ level; $† p < 0.1$ level.
Source: Employee survey.

Appendix 6. Mean, Standard Deviations (S.D.), and Correlations of Independent Variables Used in Knowledge Work Workflow Regressions

Variable	Mean	S.D.	1	2	3	4	5	6	7	8	9	10
Dependent variable												
Job satisfaction	0.09	0.95										
Organizational commitment	0.19	0.95										
Independent variable												
1. Satisfaction with nature of work	3.956	0.897	—									
2. Effectiveness of technology	0.591	0.783	0.17*	—								
3. Senior management's trustworthiness	−0.031	0.882	0.18*	0.33*	—							
4. Immediate supervisor's support	−0.116	1.008	0.04	0.24*	0.31*	—						
5. Influence above task level	0.667	1.296	0.11	0.06	0.14†	0.06	—					
6. Team cohesion	−0.171	1.045	0.26*	0.09	0.18*	0.42*	0.19*	—				
7. External colleagues' trustworthiness	−0.171	0.996	−0.05	0.35*	0.35*	0.27*	−0.11†	0.04	—			
8. Satisfaction with pay	3.467	1.013	0.31*	0.25*	0.25*	0.12*	0.08	0.19*	0.1	—		
9. Satisfaction with promotion prospects	3.141	0.963	0.24*	0.30*	0.31*	0.21*	0.19*	0.11	0.16*	0.44*	—	
10. Satisfaction with job security	3.741	0.855	0.10	0.38*	0.36*	0.28*	0.06	0.22*	0.31*	0.19*	0.34*	—

Note: * p < 0.05 level; † p < 0.1 level.
Source: Employee survey.

References

Abbott, A. 1988. *The System of Professions: An Essay on the Division of Expert Labor.* Chicago: University of Chicago Press.

——. 1991. "The Future of Professions: Occupation and Expertise in the Age of Organization." *Research in the Sociology of Organizations* 8: 17–42.

Abercrombie, N. 1991. "The Privilege of the Producer." In *Enterprise Culture*, edited by R. Keat and N. Abercrombie, 171–85. London: Routledge.

Ackroyd, S. 1996. "Organization contra Organizations: Professionals and Organizational Change in the United Kingdom." *Organization Studies* 17(4): 599–622.

Adler, P. S. 1992. *Technology and the Future of Work.* New York: Oxford University Press.

Adler, P. S., and B. Borys. 1996. "Two Types of Bureaucracy: Enabling and Coercive." *Administrative Science Quarterly* 41: 61–89.

Albrecht, K., and R. Zemke. 1985. *Service America! Doing Business in the New Economy.* Homewood, Ill.: Dow Jones-Irwin.

Alvesson, M. 1995. *Management of Knowledge-Intensive Companies.* Berlin: de Gruyter.

Aoki, M. 1988. *Information, Incentives, and Bargaining in the Japanese Economy.* Cambridge, U.K.: Cambridge University Press.

Appelbaum, E. 1993. "New Technology and Work Organisations: The Role of Gender Relations." In *Work, Gender, and Technology*, edited by B. Probert and B. W. Wilson, 60–84. Carlton, Aust.: Melbourne University Press.

Appelbaum, E., and P. Albin. 1989. "Computer Rationalisation and the Transformation of Work: Lessons from the Insurance Industry." In *The Transformation of Work: Skill, Flexibility, and the Labour Process*, edited by S. Wood, 247–65. London: Unwin Hyman.

Appelbaum, E., and R. Batt. 1994. *The New American Workplace.* Ithaca, N.Y.: ILR Press.

Applegate, L. 1994. "Managing in an Information Age: Transforming the Organisation for the 1990s." In *Transforming Organisations with Information Technology: Proceedings of the IFIP WG8.2 Working Conference*, edited by R. Baskerville et al., 15–94. Amsterdam: Elsevier Science B.V.

——. 1996. "In Search of a New Organizational Model: Lessons from the Field."

In *Communication Technology and Organization Forms*, edited by G. DeSanctis and J. Fulk. Newbury Park, Calif.: Sage Publications.

Atkinson, J. 1984. *Flexibility, Uncertainty, and Manpower Management.* IMS Report no. 89. Brighton, U.K.: Institute of Manpower Studies.

Australian Bureau of Statistics. 1996a. *Australian Economic Indicators.* Cat. no. 1350.0. Canberra: Australian Government Publishing Service.

——. 1996b. "Hours Worked." *Labour Force, Australia.* Cat. no. 6203.0. Canberra: Australian Government Publishing Service.

——. 1996c. *Labour Force, Australia, 1978–1995.* Canberra: Australian Government Publishing Service.

——. 1996d. *Trade Union Members Survey.* Cat. no. 6325.0. Canberra: Australian Government Publishing Service.

Austrin, T. 1980. "The 'Lump' in the UK Construction Industry." In *Capital and Labour: Studies in the Capitalist Labour Process*, edited by T. Nichols, 302–15. London: Fontana.

——. 1991. "Flexibility, Surveillance and Hype in New Zealand Financial Retailing." *Work, Employment, and Society* 5(2): 201–21.

Bacharach, S. B., P. Bamberger, and S. C. Conley. 1991. "Negotiating the 'See-Saw' of Managerial Strategy: A Resurrection of the Study of Professionals in Organizational Theory." In *Research in the Sociology of Organizations* 9: 217–38.

Bailey, T. 1993. "Discretionary Effort and the Organization of Work: Employee Participation and Work Reform since Hawthorne." Columbia University working paper.

Baldamus, W. 1961. *Efficiency and Effort.* London: Tavistock Publications.

Bamber, G. J., M. Shadur, and D. Simmons. 1997. "Australia." In *Telecommunications: Restructuring Work and Employment Relations Worldwide*, edited by H. C. Katz, 122–52. Ithaca, N.Y.: Cornell University Press.

Baran, B. 1987. "The Technological Transformation of White-Collar Work: A Case Study of the Insurance Industry." In *Computer Chips and Paper Clips: Technology and Women's Employment*, edited by H. I. Hartmann, 25–62. Washington, D.C.: National Academy Press.

Barley, S. R. 1993. *What Do Technicians Do?* Philadelphia: National Center on the Educational Quality of the Workforce.

Barley, S. R., and J. E. Orr. 1997. "Introduction: The Neglected Workforce." In *Between Craft and Science: Technical Work in U.S. Settings*, edited by S. R. Barley and J. E. Orr, 1–19. Ithaca, N.Y.: Cornell University Press.

Baron, J. N., A. Davis-Blake, and W. T. Bielby. 1986. "The Structure of Opportunity: How Promotion Ladders Vary within and among Organizations." *Administrative Science Quarterly* 31(2): 248–73.

Baron, J. N., and J. Pfeffer. 1994. "The Social Psychology of Organizations and Inequality." *Social Psychology Quarterly* 57(3): 190–209.

Baron, R., and D. Kenny. 1986. "The Moderator-Mediator Variable Distinction in Social Psychological Research." *Journal of Personality and Social Psychology* 51(6): 1173–82.

Batt, R. 1996. "From Bureaucracy to Enterprise? The Changing Jobs and Careers of Managers in the Telecommunications Service." In *Broken Ladders: Managerial Careers in the New Economy*, edited by P. Osterman, 55–80. Oxford: Oxford University Press.

Batt, R., and E. Appelbaum. 1995. "Worker Participation in Diverse Settings: Does the Form Affect the Outcome, and If So, Who Benefits?" *British Journal of Industrial Relations* 33(3): 353–78.

Batt, R., and J. Keefe. 1996. "Human Resource and Employment Practices in Telecommunications Services, 1980–1997." Report to the New American Realities Committee, National Planning Association.

Bauman, Z. 1989. *Modernity and the Holocaust.* Cambridge, Mass.: Polity Press.

Becker, H. S. 1963. *Outsiders.* New York: Free Press.

Beirne, M., H. Ramsay, and A. Panteli. 1998. "Developments in Computing Work: Control and Contradiction in the Computing Labour Process." In *Workplaces of the Future*, edited by P. Thompson and C. Warhurst, 142–62. Basingstoke, U.K.: Macmillan.

Bell, D. 1974. *The Coming of Post-Industrial Society: A Venture in Social Forecasting.* London: Heinemann.

Beninger, J. R. 1986. *The Control Revolution: Technological and Economic Origins of the Information Society.* Cambridge, Mass.: Harvard University Press.

Benson, S. 1986. *Counter Cultures.* Chicago: University of Illinois Press.

Berggren, C., and M. Nomura. 1997. *The Resilience of Corporate Japan: New Competitive Strategies and Personnel Practices.* London: Paul Chapman.

Biggart, N. W. 1987. *Charismatic Capitalism.* Chicago: University of Chicago Press.

Blackler, F. 1995. "Knowledge, Knowledge Work and Organizations: An Overview and Interpretation." *Organization Studies* 16(6): 1021–46.

Block, F. 1990. *Post Industrial Possibilities.* Berkeley: University of California Press.

Bowen, D., and E. E. Lawler, III. 1995. "Empowering Service Employees." *Sloan Management Review* 36(4): 73–84.

Boyer, R. 1997. "How Does a New Production System Emerge?" In *After Fordism*, by R. Boyer and J.-P. Durand, 1–63. Houndmills, U.K.: Macmillan.

Brewer, L. 1996. "Bureaucratic Organization of Professional Labour." *Australian and New Zealand Journal of Sociology* 32(3): 21–38.

Brint, S. 1994. *In an Age of Experts: The Changing Role of Professionals in Politics and Public Life.* Princeton, N.J.: Princeton University Press.

Brinton, M. C. 1993. *Women and the Economic Miracle: Gender and Work in Postwar Japan.* Berkeley: University of California Press.

Brown, J. S., and P. Duguid. 1991. "Organizational Learning and Communities of Practice: Toward a Unified View of Working, Learning and Innovation." *Organization Science* 2: 40–57.

Burawoy, M. 1979. *Manufacturing Consent: Changes in the Labor Process under Monopoly Capitalism.* Chicago: University of Chicago Press.

———. 1983. "Between the Labor Process and the State: The Changing Face of Factory Regimes under Advanced Capitalism." *American Sociological Review* 48 (October): 587–605.

Burns, T., and G. M. Stalker. 1961. *Management of Innovation.* London: Tavistock Publications.

Cappelli, P. 1997. "The Effects of Restructuring on Employees." In *Change at Work*, edited by P. E. Cappelli, 173–204. New York: Oxford University Press.

Cappelli, P., and K. C. O'Shaughnessey. 1995. *Changes in Skill and Wage Structures in Corporate Headquarters, 1986–1992.* Philadelphia: National Center on the Educational Quality of the Workforce.

Cappelli, P., et al., eds. 1997. *Change at Work.* New York: Oxford University Press.

Carlson, P., J. K. Logan, and J. Moyer. 1994. "Does Employee Satisfaction Lead to Customer Satisfaction?" Citibank working paper, Washington, D.C.

Carlzon, J. 1987. *Moments of Truth*. Sydney: Harper and Row.

Casey, C. 1995. *Work, Self, and Society: After Industrialism*. London: Routledge.

Castells, M. 1996. *The Information Age: Economy, Society, and Culture*, vol. 1, *The Rise of the Network Society*. Oxford: Blackwell.

Castells, M., and Y. Aoyama. 1994. "Paths towards the Informational Society: Employment Structure in G-7 Countries, 1920–90." *International Labour Review* 133(1): 5–33.

Cattell, R. B., and H. J. Bucher. 1968. *The Prediction of Achievement and Creativity*. New York: Bobbs-Merrill.

Child, J., and R. Loveridge. 1990. *Information Technology in European Services: Towards a Microelectronic Future*. Oxford: Blackwell.

Clark, A. E. 1995. *Job Satisfaction and Gender: Why Are Women So Happy at Work?* Report no. 95–10. DELTA.

———. 1996. "Job Satisfaction in Britain." *British Journal of Industrial Relations* 34(2): 189–217.

Clark, A. E., and P. B. Warr. 1996. "Is Job Satisfaction U-Shaped in Age?" *Journal of Occupational and Organizational Psychology* 69: 88–101.

Clawson, D. 1980. *Bureaucracy and the Labor Process: The Transformation of U.S. Industry, 1860–1920*. New York: Monthly Review Press.

Cohen, A., and U. E. Gattiker. 1994. "Rewards and Organizational Commitment across Structural Characteristics: A Meta-Analysis." *Journal of Business and Psychology* 9(2): 137–57.

Cohen, A., and G. Lowenberg. 1990. "A Re-examination of the Side-Bet Theory as Applied to Organizational Commitment: A Meta-Analysis." *Human Relations* 43: 1015–50.

Cohen, S. G. 1993. "New Approaches to Teams and Teamwork." In *Organizing for the Future: The New Logic for Managing Complex Organizations*, edited by J. R. Galbraith and E. E. Lawler III, 194–224. San Francisco: Jossey-Bass.

Cohen, S. S., and J. Zysman. 1987. *Manufacturing Matters: The Myth of the Post-Industrial Economy*. New York: Basic Books.

Cole, R. E. 1979. *Work, Mobility, and Participation. A Comparative Study of American and Japanese Industry*. Berkeley: University of California Press.

———. 1989. *Strategies for Learning: Small-Group Activities in American, Japanese and Swedish Industry*. Berkeley: University of California Press.

Cole, R. E., ed. 1995. *The Death and Life of the American Quality Movement*. New York: Oxford University Press.

Collier, D. 1991. "The Comparative Method: Two Decades of Change." In *Comparative Political Dynamics: Global Research Perspectives*, edited by D. A. Rustow and K. P. Erickson, 7–31. New York: HarperCollins.

Commission on the Future of Worker Management Relations. 1994. *Fact Finding Report*. Washington, D.C.: U.S. Departments of Commerce and Labor.

Cooke, W. N. 1994. "Employee Participation Programs, Group-Based Incentives and Company Performance: A Union-Non-Union Comparison." *Industrial and Labor Relations Review* 47: 594–609.

Crook, S., J. Pakulski, and M. Waters, 1992. *Postmodernization: Change in Advanced Society*. London: Sage.

Cunningham, I., J. Hyman, and C. Baldry. 1996. "Empowerment: The Power to Do What?" *Industrial Relations Journal* 27(2): 143–54.

Daft, R. L. 1982. "Bureaucratic versus Nonbureaucratic Structure and the Process of Innovation and Change." *Research in the Sociology of Organizations* 1: 129–66.

Daft, R. L., and A. Y. Lewin. 1993. "Where Are the Theories for the 'New' Organizational Forms?: An Editorial Essay." *Organization Science* 4(4): ii–vi.

Davidow, W. H., and M. S. Malone. 1992. *The Virtual Corporation*. New York: HarperCollins.

Davidow, W. H., and B. Uttal. 1989. *Total Customer Service: The Ultimate Weapon*. New York: Harper and Row.

Davis, L. E., and J. C. Taylor. 1976. "Technology, Organization and Job Structure." In *Handbook of Work, Organization, and Society*, edited by R. Dubin, 379–419. Chicago: Rand McNally.

Deery, S., D. Plowman, and J. Walsh. 1997. *Industrial Relations: A Contemporary Analysis*. Sydney: McGraw Hill.

Department of Employment and Training. 1991. *Australia's Workforce in the Year 2001*. Canberra: Australian Government Publishing Service.

Department of Industrial Relations. 1995. *Enterprise Bargaining in Australia. Annual Report 1994*. Canberra: Australian Government Publishing Service.

——. 1996. *Enterprise Bargaining in Australia. Annual Report 1995*. Canberra: Australian Government Publishing Service.

Derber, C. 1982. *Professionals as Workers*. Boston: Hall.

Derber, C., W. A. Schwartz, and Y. Magrass. 1990. *Power in the Highest Degree: Professionals and the Rise of a New Mandarin Order*. New York: Oxford University Press.

DiMaggio, P. J., and W. W. Powell. 1991. *The New Institutionalism in Organizational Analysis*. Chicago: University of Chicago Press.

Donnellon, A., and M. Scully. 1994. "Teams, Performance, and Rewards: Will the Post-Bureaucratic Organization Be a Post-Meritocratic Organization?" In *The Post-Bureaucratic Organization: New Perspectives on Organisational Change*, edited by C. Heckscher and A. Donnellon, 63–90. Thousand Oaks, Calif.: Sage.

Dore, R. 1973. *British Factory–Japanese Factory: The Origins of National Diversity in Industrial Relations*. London: Allen & Unwin.

——. 1987. *Taking Japan Seriously: A Confucian Perspective on Leading Economic Issues*. Stanford, Calif.: Stanford University Press.

Drucker, P. 1993. *The Post-Capitalist Society*. New York: HarperCollins.

Du Gay, P. 1996. *Consumption and Identity at Work*. London: Sage.

Du Gay, P., and G. Salaman. 1992. "The Cult[ure] of the Customer." *Journal of Management Studies* 29(5): 615–33.

Dun and Bradstreet (Australia) Pty Ltd. 1996–97. *Australia's Top 500 Companies*. Crows Nest: Riddell.

Dunphy, D., and B. Bryant. 1996. "Teams: Panaceas or Prescriptions for Improved Performance?" *Human Relations* 49(5): 677–99.

Durand, J.-P. 1997. "Is a New Production System Really Emerging?" In *After Fordism*, by R. Boyer and J.-P. Durand, 65–144. Houndmills, U.K.: Macmillan.

Eccles, R. G., and D. B. Crane. 1988. *Doing Deals: Investment Banks at Work*. Cambridge, Mass.: Harvard Business School Press.

Eccles, R. G., and N. Nohria. 1992. *The Post-Structuralist Organization*. Report no. 92–035. Cambridge, Mass.: Harvard Business School Press.

Edwards, P. K. 1986. *Conflict at Work: A Materialist Analysis of Workplace Relations*. Oxford: Blackwell.

Edwards, P. K., and H. Scullion. 1982. *The Social Organization of Industrial Conflict: Control and Resistance in the Workplace*. Oxford: Blackwell.

Edwards, R. 1979. *Contested Terrain: The Transformation of the Workplace in the Twentieth Century*. London: Heinemann.

Eisenhardt, K. 1985. "Control: Organizational and Economic Approaches." *Management Science* 31(2): 134–49.

Elger, T., and C. Smith, eds. 1994. *Global Japanisation? The Transnational Transformation of the Labour Process.* London: Routledge.

Endo, K. 1994. "Satei (Personal Assessment) and Inter-Worker Competition in Japanese Firms." *Industrial Relations* 33(1): 70–82.

Erickson, R. J., and A. S. Wharton. 1997. "Inauthenticity and Depression: Assessing the Consequences of Interactive Service Work." *Work and Occupations* 24(2): 188–213.

Etzioni, A. 1961. *A Comparative Analysis of Organizations.* New York: Free Press.

Evans, C. R., and K. L. Dion. 1991. "Group Cohesion and Performance: A Meta-Analysis." *Small Group Research* 22: 175–86.

Fantasia, R. 1988. *Cultures of Solidarity: Consciousness, Action, and Contemporary American Workers.* Berkeley: University of California Press.

"Fatal Attraction." 1997. *Asiaweek,* May 23, 18.

Filby, M. 1992. "The Figures, the Personality and the 'Bums': Service Work and Sexuality." *Work, Employment and Society* 6(1): 23–42.

Fincham, R. 1994. "Computing Occupations: Organizational Power, Work Transition and Collective Mobility." *New Technology, Work and Employment* 9(1): 43–53.

Fincham, R., et al. 1994. *Expertise and Innovation: Information Technology Strategies in the Financial Services Sector.* Oxford: Clarendon Press.

Firebaugh, G., and B. Harley. 1995. "Trends in Job Satisfaction in the United States by Race, Gender and Type of Occupation." *Research in the Sociology of Work,* 87–104.

"The Fortune 500." 1996. *Fortune,* April 29, F1–F68.

"The Fortune Global 500." 1996. *Fortune,* April 29, 60–98.

Foucault, M. 1977. *Discipline and Punish: The Birth of the Prison.* London: Penguin.

Fox, A. 1974. *Beyond Contract: Work, Power, and Trust Relations.* London: Faber.

Freeman, R. B. 1978. "Job Satisfaction as an Economic Variable." *American Economic Review* 68: 135–41.

Freeman, R. B., and J. L. Medoff. 1984. *What Do Unions Do?* New York: Basic Books.

Frenkel, S., and A. Coolican. 1984. *Unions against Capitalism?: A Sociological Comparison of the Australian Building and Metal Workers' Unions.* Sydney: Allen and Unwin.

Frenkel, S., and D. Peetz. 1990. "Enterprise Bargaining: The Business Council of Australia's Report on Industrial Relations Reform." *Journal of Industrial Relations* 32(1): 69–99.

Frenkel, S., and C. Royal. 1997. "Globalization and Employment Relations." *Research in the Sociology of Work* 7: 1–39.

Frenkel, S., et al. 1995. "Re-constituting Work: Trends towards Knowledge Work and Info-Normative Control." *Work, Employment and Society* 9(4): 773–96.

——. 1998. "Beyond Bureaucracy? Work Organization in Call Centres." *International Journal of Human Resource Management* 9(6): 958–79.

Friedman, A. L. 1977. *Industry and Labour: Class Struggle at Work and Monopoly Capitalism.* London: Macmillan.

Friedson, E. 1986. *Professional Powers.* Chicago: University of Chicago Press.

Fuller, J. B., et al. 1996. "A Closer Look at Select Cognitive Precursors to Organizational Turnover: What Has Been Missed and Why." *Psychological Reports* 78: 1331–52.

Fuller, L., and V. Smith. 1991. "Consumers' Reports: Management by Customers in a Changing Economy." *Work, Employment and Society* 5(1): 1–16.

Gallie, D. 1996. "Skill, Gender and the Quality of Employment." In *Changing Forms of Employment: Organisations, Skills, and Gender*, edited by R. Crompton, D. Gallie, and K. Purcell, 133–59. London: Routledge.

Gallie, D., C. Marsh, and C. Vogler. 1994. *Social Change and the Experience of Unemployment*. Oxford: Oxford University Press.

Gallie, D., and M. White. 1993. *Employee Commitment and the Skills Revolution: First Findings From the Employment in Britain Survey*. London: Policy Studies Institute.

Garson, B. 1988. *The Electronic Sweatshop: How Computers Are Transforming the Office of the Future into the Factory of the Past*. New York: Simon and Schuster.

Gerlach, M. L. 1992. *Alliance Capitalism: Tthe Social Organization of Japanese Business*. Berkeley: University of California Press.

Ghoshal, S., and C. Bartlett. 1995. "Building the Entrepreneurial Corporation: New Organizational Processes, New Managerial Tasks." *European Management Journal* 13(2): 139–55.

Giddens, A. 1976. *New Rules of Sociological Method: A Positive Critique of Interpretative Sociologies*. London: Hutchinson.

Glazer, N. Y. 1984. "Servants to Capital." *Review of Radical Political Economics* 16: 67–87.

Gordon, D. M., R. Edwards, and M. Reich. 1982. *Segmented Work, Divided Workers: The Historical Transformation of Labor in the United States*. Cambridge, U.K.: Cambridge University Press.

Graham, J., and J. Brandon. 1995. "Reinventing the Psychological Contract." Paper presented at the 1995 Human Resource Planning Society Research Symposium, Cornell University, Ithaca, N.Y.

Graham, L. 1995. *On the Line at Subaru-Isuzu: The Japanese Model and the American Worker*. Ithaca, N.Y.: Cornell University Press.

Granovetter, M. 1992. "The Sociological and Economic Approaches to Labor Market Analysis: A Social Structural View." In *The Sociology of Economic Life*, edited by M. Granovetter and R. Swedberg, 233–63. Boulder, Colo.: Westview Press.

Greider, W. 1997. *One World, Ready or Not: The Manic Logic of Global Capitalism*. New York: Simon and Schuster.

Gutek, B. A. 1995. *The Dynamics of Service*. San Francisco: Jossey-Bass.

Guzzo, R. A., and G. P. Shea. 1992. "Group Performance and Intergroup Relations in Organisations." In *Handbook of Industrial and Organizational Psychology*, edited by M. D. Dunnette and L. M. Hough, 269–313. Palo Alto, Calif.: Consulting Psychology Press.

Hackman, J. R., and E. Lawler. 1971. "Employee Reactions to Job Characteristics." *Journal of Applied Psychology*, Monograph no. 55, 259–86.

Hackman, J. R., and G. R. Oldham. 1980. *Work Redesign*. Reading, Mass.: Addison-Wesley.

Hage, J., and C. H. Powers. 1992. *Post-Industrial Lives*. Newbury Park, Calif.: Sage.

Hakim, C. 1991. "Grateful Slaves and Self-Made Women: Fact and Fantasy in Women's Work Orientations." *European Sociological Review* 7: 101–21.

Halal, W. E. 1994. "From Hierarchy to Enterprise: Internal Markets Are the New Foundation in Management." *Academy of Management Executive* 8(4): 69–82.

——. 1996. "The Rise of the Knowledge Entrepreneur." *Futurist* 30(6): 13–16.

Heckscher, C. 1994. "Defining the Post-Bureaucratic Type." In *The Post-Bureaucratic Organization: New Perspectives on Organizational Change.* Thousand Oaks, Calif.: Sage.

Heckscher, C. 1995. *White Collar Blues: Management Loyalties in an Age of Corporate Restructuring.* New York: Basic Books.

Heckscher, C., and L. M. Applegate. 1994. "Introduction." In *The Post-Bureaucratic Organization: New Perspectives on Organizational Change*, edited by C. Heckscher and A. Donnellon, 1–13. Thousand Oaks, Calif.: Sage.

Heckscher, C., and A. Donnellon, eds. 1994. *The Post-Bureaucratic Organization: New Perspectives on Organizational Change.* Thousand Oaks, Calif.: Sage.

Heery, E. 1993. "Industrial Relations and the Customer." *Industrial Relations Journal* 24(4): 284–95.

Hennessey, B. A., and T. M. Amabile. 1988. "The Conditions of Creativity." In *The Nature of Creativity: Contemporary Psychological Perspectives*, edited by R. J. Sternberg, 11–38. New York: Cambridge University Press.

Hepworth, M. 1990. *Geography of the Information Economy.* New York: Guilford Press.

Herzenberg, S., J. Alic, and H. Wial. 1998. *New Rules for a New Economy.* Ithaca, N.Y.: Cornell University Press.

Hickson, D. J., and D. S. Pugh. 1995. *Management Worldwide. The Impact of Societal Culture on Organizations around the Globe.* Harmondsworth, U.K.: Penguin Books.

Hirsch, P. M., and M. Stanley. 1996. "The Rhetoric of Boundaryless or, How the Newly Empowered Managerial Class Bought into Its Own Marginalization." In *The Boundaryless Career: A New Employment Principle for a New Organizational Era*, edited by M. B. Arthur and D. M. Rousseau, 218–33. Oxford: Oxford University Press.

Hirschhorn, L. 1985. "Information Technology and the New Services Game." In *High Technology, Space, and Society*, edited by M. Castells. Newbury Park, Calif.: Sage.

Hochschild, A. 1983. *The Managed Heart: Commercialization of Human Feeling.* Berkeley: University of California Press.

Hodson, R. 1996. "Dignity in the Workplace under Participative Management: Alienation and Freedom Revisited." *American Sociological Review* 61: 719–38.

——. 1997. "Individual Voice on the Shop Floor: The Role of Unions." *Social Forces* 75(4): 1183–1212.

Houseman, S. N. 1995. "Part-Time Employment in Europe and Japan." *Journal of Labor Research* 16(3): 249–92.

Hughes, E. C. 1959. "The Study of Occupations." In *Sociology Today: Problems and Prospects*, edited by R. K. Merton, L. Broom, and S. L. Cottrell, 442–58. New York: Basic Books.

Hyman, R., and I. Brough. 1975. *Social Values and Industrial Relations. A Study of Fairness and Inequality.* Oxford: Basil Blackwell.

Hyman, R., and W. Streeck, eds. 1988. *New Technology and Industrial Relations.* Oxford: Blackwell.

Ibarra, H. 1992. "Structural Alignments, Individual Strategies, and Managerial Action: Elements toward a Network Theory of Getting Things Done." In *Networks and Organizations: Structure, Form, and Action*, edited by N. Nohria and R. G. Eccles, 165–88. Boston: Harvard Business School Press.

Ichniowski, C., et al. 1996. "What Works at Work: Overview and Assessment." *Industrial Relations* 35(3): 299–333.

Inglehart, R. 1977. *The Silent Revolution*. Princeton, N.J.: Princeton University Press.

Inglehart, R., and P. R. Abramson. 1995. *Value Change in Global Perspective*. Ann Arbor, Mich.: University of Michigan Press.

International Labour Organization. 1996. *World Employment 1996–97*. Geneva.

International Survey Research Center Corporation. 1996. *Perceptions of U.S. Employees: A Historical View*. <http://www.isrsurvey.com>

Jacoby, S. M. 1985. *Employing Bureaucracy*. New York: Columbia University Press.

Jowell, R. E. A., ed. 1993. *International Social Attitudes*. Aldershot, U.K.: Dartmouth.

Kalleberg, A. L. 1977. "Work Values and Job Rewards: A Theory of Job Satisfaction." *American Sociological Review* 42: 124–43.

Kalleberg, A. L., and K. A. Losocco. 1983. "Aging, Values, and Rewards: Explaining Age Differences in Job Satisfaction." *American Sociological Review* 42: 124–43.

Kalleberg, A. L., and A. Mastekaasa. 1994. "Firm Internal Labour Markets and Organisational Commitment in Norway and the United States." *Acta Sociologica* 37: 269–86.

Kalleberg, A. L., et al., eds. 1996. *Organizations in America: Analyzing Their Structures and Human Resource Practices*. Thousand Oaks, Calif.: Sage.

Kanter, R. M. 1976. "The Impact of Hierarchical Structures on the Work Behaviour of Women and Men." *Social Problems* 23: 415–30.

Karasek, R., and T. Theorell. 1990. *Healthy Work: Stress, Productivity, and the Reconstruction of Working Life*. New York: Basic Books.

Katz, H. C. 1997a. "Downsizing and Employment Insecurity." In *Change at Work*, edited by P. E. Cappelli, 66–88. New York: Oxford University Press.

———. 1997b. "Introduction and Comparative Overview." In *Telecommunications: Restructuring Work and Employment Relations Worldwide*, edited by H. C. Katz, 1–30. Ithaca, N.Y.: Cornell University Press.

———. 1997c. *Telecommunications: Restructuring Work and Employment Relations Worldwide*. Ithaca, N.Y.: Cornell University Press.

Kawakita, T. 1997. "Corporate Strategy and Human Resource Management." In *Japanese Labour and Management in Transition: Diversity, Flexibility, and Participation*, edited by M. Sako and H. Sato, 79–103. London: Routledge.

Keefe, J. H., and R. Batt. 1997. "United States." In *Telecommunications: Restructuring Work and Employment Relations Worldwide*, edited by H. C. Katz, 31–88. Ithaca, N.Y.: Cornell University Press.

Kidwell, R. E., Jr., and N. Bennett. 1994. "Employee Reactions to Electronic Control Systems." *Group and Organization Management* 19(2): 203–18.

Kirsch, L. J. 1996. "The Management of Complex Tasks in Organizations: Controlling the Systems Development Process." *Organization Science* 7(1): 1–21.

Klecka, W. R. 1980. *Discriminant Analysis*. Beverly Hills, Calif.: Sage.

Knights, D. 1990. "Subjectivity, Power and the Labour Process," In *Labour Process Theory*, edited by D. Knights and H. Willmott, 297–335. London: Macmillan.

Knights, D., and A. Sturdy. 1990. "New Technology and the Self-Disciplined Worker in Insurance." In *Deciphering Science and Technology*, edited by M. McNeil, I. Varcoe, and S. Yearly, 126–54. Basingstoke, U.K.: Macmillan.

Knoop, R. 1994. "The Relationship between Importance and Achievement of Work Values and Job Satisfaction." *Perceptual and Motor Skills* 79: 595–605.

Kochan, T. A., H. C. Katz, and R. B. McKersie. 1986. *The Transformation of American Industrial Relations*. New York: Basic Books. Reprint, Ithaca, N.Y.: ILR Press, 1994.

Kochan, T. A., and P. Osterman. 1994. *The Mutual Gains Enterprise: Forging a Winning Partnership among Labor, Management, and Government*. Boston: Harvard Business School Press.

Koestler, A. 1970. *The Act of Creation*. London: Picador.

Kohn, M., and C. Schooler. 1983. "Job Conditions and Personality: A Longitudinal Assessment of Their Reciprocal Effects." In *Work and Personality: An Inquiry into the Impact of Social Stratification*, 125–53. Norwood, N.J.: Ablex.

Koike, K. 1995. *The Economics of Work in Japan*. Tokyo: LTCB International Library Foundation.

Korczynski, M., et al. 1996. "Frontline Work in the 'New Model of Service Firm': Australian and Japanese Comparisons." *Human Resource Management Journal* 6(2): 72–87.

Korczynski, M., S. Frenkel, and M. Tam. in press. "When Customers and Workers Meet: Customer-Worker Relations in Service and Sales Work." *Work and Occupations*.

Kosaka, K., ed. 1994. *Social Stratification in Contemporary Japan*. London: Kegan Paul.

Koslowsky, M. 1990. "Staff/Line Distinctions in Job and Organizational Commitment." *Journal of Occupational Psychology* 63: 167–73.

KPMG. 1996. *Financial Institution Performance Survey*. Sydney: Peat Marwick Hungerfords.

Krugman, P. 1996. *Pop Internationalism*. Cambridge, Mass.: MIT Press.

Kumar, K. 1978. *Prophecy and Progress: The Sociology of Industrial and Post-Industrial Society*. Harmondsworth, U.K.: Penguin.

——. 1995. *From Post-Industrial to Post-Modern Society: New Theories of the Contemporary World*. Oxford: Blackwell.

Kunda, G. 1992. *Engineering Culture*. Philadelphia: Temple University Press.

Lam, A. 1996. "Engineers, Management and Work Organization: A Comparative Analysis of Engineers' Work Roles in British and Japanese Electronics Firms." *Journal of Management Studies* 33(2): 183–212.

Lash, S., and J. Urry. 1987. *The End of Organized Capitalism*. Cambridge, Mass.: Polity Press.

——. 1994. *Economies of Signs and Space*. Thousand Oaks, Calif.: Sage.

Lave, J., and E. Wenger. 1991. *Situated Learning: Legitimate Peripheral Participation*. Cambridge, U.K.: Cambridge University Press.

Lawler, E. E., III. 1992. *The Ultimate Advantage: Creating the High-Involvement Organization*. San Francisco: Jossey-Bass.

——. 1994. "From Job-Based to Competency-Based Organizations." *Journal of Organizational Behavior* 15: 3–15.

Lee, E. 1996. "Globalization and Employment: Is Anxiety Justified?" *International Labour Review* 135(5): 485–97.

Legge, K. 1995. *Human Resource Management*. London: Macmillan.

298 | *References*

Leidner, R. 1991. "Selling Hamburgers and Selling Insurance: Gender, Work, and Identity in Interactive Service Jobs." *Gender and Society* 5(2): 154–177.

———. 1993. *Fast Food, Fast Talk: Service Work and the Routinization of Everyday Life.* Berkeley: University of California Press.

Lette, L., and J. Schor. 1994. "Assessing the Time-Squeeze Hypothesis: Hours Worked in the United States, 1969–89." *Industrial Relations* 33 (1): 25–43.

Lieberson, S. 1991. "Small N's and Big Conclusions: An Examination of the Reasoning in Comparative Studies Based on a Small Number of Cases." *Social Forces* 70(2): 307–20.

Lillrank, P. 1994. *The Software Society: Japan's Software Industry and Its Role in the Information Society.* Working Paper no. 14. Stockholm: European Institute of Japanese Studies.

Lincoln, J. R. 1982. "Intra- (and Inter-) Organizational Networks." In *Research in the Sociology of Organizations* 1: 1–38.

Lincoln, J. R., and A. Kalleberg. 1990. *Culture, Control, and Commitment: A Study of Work Organization and Work Attitudes in the United States and Japan.* Cambridge, U.K. and Mass.: Cambridge University Press.

Lincoln, J. R., and Y. Nakata. 1997. "The Transformation of the Japanese Employment System." *Work and Occupations* 24(1): 33–55.

Lipietz, A. 1995. "Capital-Labour Relations at the Dawn of the Twenty-First Century." In *Capital, the State, and Labour: A Global Perspective*, edited by J. Schor and J.-I. You, 345–72. Aldershot, U.K.: Edward Elgar.

Littler, C. R. 1982. *The Development of the Labour Process in Capitalist Societies: A Comparative Study of the Transformation of Work Organization in Britain, Japan, and the USA.* London: Heinemann.

Littler, C. R., T. Bramble, R. Dunford, and A. Hede. 1997. "The Dynamics of Downsizing in Australia and New Zealand." *Asia Pacific Journal of Human Resources* 35(1): 65–79.

Locke, E. A. 1976. *Handbook of Industrial and Organizational Psychology.* Chicago: Rand-McNally.

Locke, R., T. Kochan, and M. Piore. 1995. "Reconceptualizing Comparative Industrial Relations: Lessons from International Research." *International Labour Review* 134(2): 139–61.

Lopez, H. 1996. "The Politics of Service Production: Routine Sales Work in the Potato-Chip Industry." In *Working in the Service Society*, edited by C. MacDonald and C. Sirianni. Philadelphia: Temple University Press.

Lovelock, C. H., and R. Young. 1979. "Look to Customers to Increase Productivity." *Harvard Business Review* 57(May-June): 168–78.

Macdonald, K. M. 1995. *The Sociology of Professions.* London: Sage.

MacDuffie, J. P. 1995. "Human Resource Bundles and Manufacturing Performance: Organizational Logical and Flexible Production Systems in the World Auto Industry." *Industrial and Labor Relations Review* 48: 197–221.

MacDuffie, J. P., and F. K. Pil. 1997. "Changes in Auto Industry Employment Practices: An International Overview." In *After Lean Production: Evolving Employment Practices in the World Auto Industry*, edited by T. A. Kochan, R. D. Lansbury, and J. P. MacDuffie. 9–42. Ithaca, N.Y.: Cornell University Press.

MacKinnon, D. W. 1962. "The Nature and Nurture of Creative Talent." *American Psychologist* 17: 484–95.

Mankin, D., S. Cohen, and T. Bikson. 1996. *Teams and Technology: Fulfilling the Promise of the New Organization.* Boston: Harvard Business School Press.

Maslach, C. 1977 "The Burn-Out Syndrome in the Day Care Setting." *Child Care Quarterly* 6(2): 100–13.

Maslach, C., and S. E. Jackson. 1985. "The Role of Sex and Family Variables in Burnout." *Sex Roles* 12: 837–51.

Mathews, J. 1994. *Catching the Wave: Workplace Reform in Australia.* Ithaca, N.Y.: ILR Press.

Mathieu, J. E., and D. M. Zajac. 1990. "A Review and Meta-analysis of the Antecedents, Correlates and Consequences of Organisational Commitment." *Psychological Bulletin* 108: 171–94.

Mattingly, M. A. 1977. "Sources of Stress and Burn-Out in Professional Child Care Work." *Child Care Quarterly* 6: 127–37.

Menzies, H. 1996. *Whose Brave New World?: The Information Superhighway and the New Economy.* Toronto: Between the Lines.

Miles, I., and J. Gershuny. 1987. "The Social Economics of Information Technology." In *Information Technology: Social Issues*, edited by R. Finnegan, G. Salaman, and K. Thompson. London: Hodder & Stoughton/Open University.

Milgram, R. M. 1990. "Creativity: An Idea Whose Time Has Come and Gone?" In *Theories of Creativity*, edited by M. A. Runco and R. S. Albert, 215–33. Newbury Park, Calif.: Sage.

Miller, K. I., and P. R. Monge. 1986. "Participation, Satisfaction, and Productivity: A Meta-Analytic Review." *Academy of Management Journal* 29(4): 727–53.

Mills, C. Wright. 1951. *White Collar.* New York: Oxford University Press.

Mintzberg, H. 1983. *Structure in Fives: Designing Effective Organizations.* Englewood Cliffs, N.J.: Prentice-Hall.

——. 1996. "Some Surprising Things about Collaboration—Knowing How People Connect Makes It Work Better." *Organizational Dynamics* 24(4): 60–71.

Mintzberg, H., J. B. Quinn, and J. Voyer. 1996. *The Strategy Process: Concepts, Contexts, and Cases*, 3d ed. Upper Saddle River, N.J.: Prentice Hall.

Mohrman, S. A., A. M. Mohrman, Jr., and S. G. Cohen. 1995. "Organizing Knowledge Work Systems." *Advances in Interdisciplinary Studies of Work Teams* 2: 61–91.

Moorehead, A., et al. 1997. *Changes at Work: The 1995 Australian Workplace Industrial Relations Survey (AWIRS).* Melbourne: Longman.

Morishima, M. 1994. "The Japanese Human Resource Management System: A Learning Bureaucracy." In *Human Resource Management in the Pacific Rim: Institutions, Practices, and Values*, edited by L. Moore and J. D. Jennings, 119–50. Berlin: de Gruyter.

——. 1995. "Embedding HRM in a Social Context." *British Journal of Industrial Relations* 33(4): 617–40.

——. 1996. "The Evolution of White-Collar Human Resource Management in Japan." *Advances in Industrial and Labor Relations* 7: 145–76.

Morrill, C., and G. A. Fine. 1997. "Ethnographic Contributions to Organizational Sociology." *Sociological Methods and Research* 25(4): 424–51.

Morris, J. A., and D. C. Feldman. 1996 "The Dimensions, Antecedents, and Consequences of Emotional Labor." *Academy of Management Review* 21(4): 986–1010.

Morrow, P. C. 1993. *The Theory and Measurement of Work Commitment*. Greenwich, Conn.: JAI Press.

Mowday, R. T., R. M. Steers, and L. W. Porter. 1982. *Employee-Organization Linkages: The Psychology of Commitment, Abseneteeism, and Turnover*. New York: Academic Press.

Nakamura, K., and S. Hiraki. 1997. "Japan." In *Telecommunications: Restructuring Work and Employment Relations Worldwide*, edited by H. C. Katz, 228–62. Ithaca, N.Y.: Cornell University Press.

National Research Council. 1994. *Information Technology in the Service Society*. Washington: National Academy Press.

Neuman, W. L. 1997. *Social Research Methods: Qualitative and Quantitative Approaches*, 3d ed. Boston: Allyn and Bacon.

Nohria, N., and J. D. Berkley. 1994. "The Virtual Organization: Bureaucracy, Technology, and the Implosion of Control." In *The Post-Bureaucratic Organization: New Perspectives on Organizational Change*, edited by C. Heckscher and A. Donnellon, 108–28. Thousand Oaks, Calif.: Sage.

Nonaka, I. 1988. "Toward Middle-Up-Down Management: Accelerating Information Creation." *Sloan Management Review* 29(3): 9–18.

Nonaka, I., and H. Takeuchi. 1995. *The Knowledge Creating Company*. New York: Oxford University Press.

——. 1996. "A Theory of Organizational Knowledge Creation." *International Journal of Technology Management* 11: 833–45.

Noon, M., and P. Blyton. 1997. *The Realities of Work*. Basingstoke, U.K.: Macmillan.

"Not Quite Magic." 1997. *Economist*, February 22, 73–74, 81.

Oakes, G. 1990. *The Soul of the Salesman: The Moral Ethos of Personal Sales*. Atlantic Heights, N.J.: Humanities Press.

Oravec, J. A. 1996. *Virtual Individuals, Virtual Groups: Human Dimensions of Groupware and Computer Networking*. Cambridge, U.K.: Cambridge University Press.

Organ, D. W., and K. Ryan. 1995. "A Meta-Analytic Review of Attitudinal and Dispositional Predictors of Organisational Citizenship Behaviour." *Personnel Psychology* 48: 775–802.

Organization for Economic Cooperation and Development. 1996a. *Employment Outlook*. Paris.

——. 1996b. *Labour Force Statistics, 1974–1994*. Paris.

——. 1996c. *Main Economic Indicators*. Paris.

——. 1997a. *OECD Economic Surveys: Japan*. Paris.

——. 1997b. *OECD Economic Surveys: United States*. Paris.

——. 1998. *OECD Economic Surveys: Australia*. Paris.

Ornstein, S., W. L. Cron, and J. W. Slocum. 1989. "Life Stage versus Career Stage: A Comparative Test of the Theories of Levinson and Super." *Journal of Organizational Behavior* 10: 117–33.

Orr, J. E. 1996. *Talking about Machines: An Ethnology of a Modern Job*. Ithaca, N.Y.: Cornell University.

Osterman, P. 1984. "White-Collar Internal Labor Markets." In *Internal Labor Markets*, edited by P. Osterman, 163–89. Cambridge, Mass.: MIT Press.

——. 1987. "Choice of Employment Systems in Internal Labor Markets." *Industrial Relations* 26(1): 46–67.

———. 1988. *Employment Futures: Reorganization, Dislocation, and Public Policy.* New York: Oxford University Press.

———. 1996. *Broken Ladders: Managerial Careers in the New Economy.* Oxford: Oxford University Press.

———. 1997. "Work Organization." In *Change at Work*, edited by P. E. Cappelli, 89–121. New York: Oxford University Press.

Ouchi, M. 1979. "A Conceptual Framework for the Design of Organizational Control Mechanisms." *Management Science* 25(9): 833–48.

———. 1981. *Theory Z: How American Business Can Meet the Japanese Challenge.* Reading, Mass.: Addison-Wesley.

Parcel, T. L., and R. L. Kaufman. 1993. "Mental Piecework: Explaining Occupational Variation in Work Attitudes in a High-End Service Sector Firm." *Research in the Sociology of Organizations* 11: 151–94.

Parsons, T. 1951. *The Social System.* New York: Free Press.

Partnoy, F. 1997. *F.I.A.S.C.O.: Blood in the Water on Wall Street.* New York: Norton.

Pava, C. 1983. *Managing New Office Technology: An Organizational Strategy.* New York: Free Press.

Pfeffer, J. 1998. "Seven Practices of Successful Organizations." *California Management Review* 40(2): 96–123.

Pinchot, G., and E. Pinchot. 1993. *The End of Bureaucracy and the Rise of the Intelligent Organization.* San Francisco: Berrett-Koehler.

Pine, J. 1993. *Mass Customization: The New Frontier in Business Competition.* Boston: Harvard Business School Press.

Piore, M. 1995. *Beyond Individualism.* Cambridge, Mass.: Harvard University Press.

Piore, M., and C. Sabel. 1984. *The Second Industrial Divide: Possibilities for Prosperity.* New York: Basic Books.

Piore, M., et al. 1994. "The Organisation of Product Development." *Industrial and Corporate Change* 3(2): 405–34.

"Please Hold." 1997. *Economist,* February 22, 74.

Poole, M. 1975. *Workers' Participation in Industry.* London: Routledge.

Porat, M. 1977. *The Information Economy.* Washington, D.C.: Office of Telecommunications/U.S. Government Printing Office.

Powell, W. W. 1990. "Neither Market nor Hierarchy: Network Forms of Organization." *Research in Organizational Behavior* 12: 295–336.

Prus, R. C. 1989. *Making Sales: Influence as Interpersonal Accomplishment.* Newbury Park, Calif.: Sage.

Quinn, J. B. 1992. *Intelligent Enterprise: A Knowledge and Service- Based Paradigm for Industry.* New York: Free Press.

Quinn, J. B., P. Anderson, and S. Finkelstein. 1996. "Managing Professional Intellect: Making the Most of the Best." *Harvard Business Review*, March-April, 71–80.

Quinn, R. P., and L. J. Shepard. 1974. *The 1972–1973 Quality of Employment Survey: Descriptive Statistics with Comparison Data from the 1969–1970 Survey of Working Conditions.* Ann Arbor, Mich.: Institute for Social Research.

Raelin, J. A. 1986. *The Clash of Cultures: Managers and Professionals.* Boston: Harvard Business School Press.

Ragin, C. C. 1987. *The Comparative Method: Moving beyond Qualitative and Quantitative Strategies.* Berkeley: University of California Press.

Ramsay, H., N. Panteli, and M. Beirne. 1998. "Challenging the Blueprint Approach to Software Quality." Typescript.

Randall, D. M. 1988. "Multiple Roles and Organizational Commitment." *Journal of Organizational Behavior* 9: 309–17.

Reich, R. 1991. *The Work of Nations*. New York: Knopf.

Ritzer, G. 1993. *The McDonaldization of Society: An Investigation into the Changing Character of Contemporary Life*. Newbury Park, Calif.: Pine Forge Press.

Rockart, J. F., and J. E. Short. 1991. "The Networked Organization and the Management of Interdependence." In *The Corporation of the 1990s: Information Technology and Organizational Transformation*, edited by M. S. Scott Morton, 189–219. New York: Oxford University Press.

Roethlisberger, F. J., and W. J. Dickson. 1939. *Management and the Worker: An Account of a Research Program Conducted by the Western Electric Company*. Cambridge, Mass.: Harvard University Press.

Roy, D. 1952. "Quota Restriction and Goldbricking in a Machine Shop." *American Journal of Sociology* 57: 427–42.

——. 1953. "Work Satisfaction and Social Reward in Quota Achievement." *American Sociological Review* 18: 507–14.

Sako, M., and H. Sato, eds. 1997. *Japanese Labour and Management in Transition: Diversity, Flexibility, and Participation*. London: Routledge.

Sato, H. 1997. "Human Resource Management Systems in Large Firms: The Case of White-Collar Graduate Employees." In *Japanese Labour and Management in Transisition: Diversity, Flexibility, and Participation*, edited by M. Sako and H. Sato, 104–30. London: Routledge.

Schlesinger, L. A., and J. L. Heskett. 1992. "De-industrializing the Service Sector: A New Model for Service Firms." In *Advances in Services Marketing and Management: Research and Practice*, edited by T. Swartz, D. Bowen, and S. Brown, 159–76. Greenwich, Conn.: JAI Press.

Schneider, B., and D. E. Bowen. 1995. *Winning the Service Game*. Boston: Harvard Business School Press.

Schneider, B., J. K. Wheeler, and J. F. Cox. 1992. "A Passion for Service: Using Content Analysis to Explicate Service Climate Themes." *Journal of Applied Psychology* 77(5): 705–16.

Sewell, G., and B. Wilkinson. 1992. "'Someone to Watch over Me': Surveillance, Discipline and the Just-in-Time Labour Process." *Sociology* 26(2): 271–90.

Shapira, P., ed. 1995. *The R&D Workers: Managing Innovation in Britain, Germany, Japan, and the United States*. Westport, Conn.: Quorum Books.

Shire, K., and M. Ota. 1997. "The First Decade of Equal Employment Opportunities in Japan: A Review of Research." *Journal of Social Science* 36: 51–63.

Smith, V. 1994. "Institutionalizing Flexibility in a Service Firm: Multiple Contingencies and Hidden Hierarchies." *Work and Occupations* 21(3): 284–307.

Sorge, A., and W. Streeck. 1988. "Industrial Relations and Technical Change: The Case for an Extended Perspective." In *New Technology and Industrial Relations*, edited by R. Hyman and R. Streeck, 19–47. Oxford: Basil Blackwell.

Spector, P. E. 1986. "Perceived Control by Employees: A Meta-Analysis of Studies concerning Autonomy and Participation at Work." *Human Relations* 39(11): 1005–16.

Standing, G. 1992. "Do Unions Impede or Accelerate Structural Adjustment? Industrial Versus Company Unions in an Industrializing Labour Market." *Cambridge Journal of Economics* 16(3): 327–54.

Statistics Bureau. Management and Coordination Agency. 1996. *Japan Statistical Yearbook 1997.* Tokyo.

——. 1997. *Labour Force Survey, January 1997.*Tokyo.

Stinchcombe, A. 1990. *Information and Organizations.* Berkeley: University of California Press.

Strauss, G. 1982. "Workers Participation in Management: An International Perspective." *Research in Organizational Behavior* 4: 173–265.

——. 1990. "Toward the Study of Human Resources Policy." In *Reflections on the Transformation of Industrial Relations*, edited by J. A. Chelius, 73–95. Metuchen, N.J.: IMLR Press /Scarecrow Press.

——. 1998. "Comparative International Industrial Relations." In *Researching the World of Work: Strategies and Methods in Studying Industrial Relations*, edited by K. Whitfield and G. Strauss, 175–92. Ithaca, N.Y.: Cornell University Press.

Szafran, R. F. 1996. "The Effect of Occupational Growth on Labor Force Task Characteristics." *Work and Occupations* 23(1): 54–86.

Tam, M., S. Frenkel, and M. Korczynski. 1999. "Conflict or Adaptation? An Examination of the Occupational and Organizational Commitment of Knowledge Workers in Large Corporations." Centre for Corporate Change Working paper, Australian Graduate School of Management.

Tam, M., S. J. Frenkel, and M. Korczynski. 1999. "The Relationship between Work Values, Job Characteristics and Contextual Factors in Three Advanced Service Settings." Centre for Corporate Change Working paper, Australian Graduate School of Management.

Tapscott, D. 1996. *The Digital Economy: Promise and Peril in the Age of Networked Intelligence.* New York: McGraw-Hill.

Taylor, S. 1998. "Emotional Labour and the New Workplace." In *Future Work*, edited by C. Warhurst and P. Thompson. London: Macmillan.

Thompson, J. D. 1967. *Organizations in Action: Social Science Bases of Administrative Theory.* New York: McGraw-Hill.

Thompson, P. 1989. *The Nature of Work.* London: Macmillan.

——. 1990. "Crawling from the Wreckage: The Labour Process and the Politics of Production." In *Labour Process Theory*, edited by D. Knights and H. Willmott, 95–124. Basingstoke, U.K.: Macmillan.

Thurow, L. 1996. *The Future of Capitalism: How Today's Economic Forces Will Shape Tomorrow's World.* New York: William Morrow.

Torrance, E. P. 1988. "The Nature of Creativity as Manifest in Its Testing." In *The Nature of Creativity: Contemporary Psychological Perspectives*, edited by R. Sternberg, 43–75. Cambridge, U.K.: Cambridge University Press.

Tran, M. 1997. "The Geek Shall Inherit the Earth." *Guardian Weekly*, March 30, 19.

U.S. Bureau of the Census. 1996. *Statistical Abstract of the United States: 1996.* Washington, D.C.

U.S. Bureau of Labor Statistics. 1995. *Monthly Labor Statistics.* Washington, D.C.

——. 1996. "Projected Employment Change in Services Industries, 1994–2005." Washington, D.C.

U.S. Department of Labor. Employment and Training Administration. 1991. *Dictionary of Occupational Titles.* 4th ed. Indianapolis, Ind.: JIST Works.

Useem, M., and P. Cappelli. 1997. "The Pressures to Restructure Employment." In *Change at Work*, edited by P. E. Cappelli, 15–65. New York: Oxford University Press.

Van Maanen, J. 1991. "The Smile Factory: Work at Disneyland." In *Reframing Organizational Culture*, edited by P. J. Frost et al., 58–76. Newbury Park, Calif.: Sage.

Wakisaka, A. 1997. "Women at Work." In *Japanese Labour and Management in Transition: Diversity, Flexibility, and Participation*, edited by M. Sako and H. Sato, 131–50. London: Routledge.

Warr, P. 1987. *Work, Unemployment, and Mental Health*. Oxford: Clarendon Press.

Weick, C. 1969. *The Social Psychology of Organizing*. Reading, Mass.: Addison-Wesley.

Wertheimer, M. 1945. *Productive Thinking*. New York: Harper.

Wharton, A. 1996. "Service with a Smile: Understanding the Consequences of Emotional Labor." In *Working in the Service Society*, edited by C. L. Macdonald and C. Sirianni, 91–112. Philadelphia: Temple University Press.

Whelan, C., D. F. Hannan, and S. Creighton. 1991. *Unemployment, Poverty, and Psychological Distress*. Dublin: Economic and Social Research Institute.

Whyte, W. F. 1946. "When Workers and Customers Meet." In *Industry and Society*, edited by W. F. Whyte, 123–47. New York: McGraw-Hill.

Willmott, H. 1990. "Subjectivity and the Dialectics of Praxis: Opening Up the Core of Labour Process Analysis." In *Labour Process Theory*, edited by D. Knights and H. Willmott, 336–78. London: Macmillan.

Winslow, C. D., and W. L. Bramer. 1994. *Futurework*. New York: Free Press.

Womack, J. P., D. T. Jones, and D. Roos. 1990. *The Machine That Changed the World*. New York: Rawson Associates.

Wouters, C. 1989. "The Sociology of Emotions and Flight Attendants." *Theory, Culture and Society* 6: 95–123.

Wriston, W. B. 1992. *The Twilight of Sovereignty: How the Information Revolution Is Transforming Our World*. New York: Macmillan International.

Yankelovitch, E. A. 1983. *Work and Human Values: An International Report on Jobs in the 1980s and 1990s*. New York: Aspen Institute for Humanistic Studies.

Zabusky, S. E., and S. R. Barley. 1996. "Redefining Success: Ethnographic Observations on the Careers of Technicians." In *Broken Ladders: Managerial Careers in the New Economy*, edited by P. Osterman, 185–214. New York: Oxford University Press.

Zuboff, S. 1988. *In the Age of the Smart Machine: The Future of Work and Power*. New York: Basic Books.

Authors

Stephen J. Frenkel is a professor of management in the Australian Graduate School of Management at the University of New South Wales. E-mail address: S. Frenkel@agsm.edu.au

Marek Korczynski is a lecturer in employment relations at Loughborough University in the United Kingdom.

Karen A. Shire is an associate professor of comparative sociology and Japanese studies at the Gerhard Mercator University Duisburg in Germany.

May Tam is a research fellow in the Department of Sociology at the University of Hong Kong. E-mail address: mymtam@hkucc.hku.hk

Index

Page numbers in italic denote locations of tables.

job satisfaction, 241, 260, 264; and part-time work, 10; and service work tendencies, 273
Generalizability of research, 58–59
Germany, 2n.1, 37
Giddens, A., 24
Globalization, 9, 15, 49, 275
Gordon, D. M., 16
Great Britain, 37
Gutek, B. A., 200, 205, 224–25
Guzzo, R. A., 239

Hage, J., 18
Heckscher, C., 27, 170n.1
Hegemonic despotism, 15
Herzenberg, S., 21, 23
Heterogeneity effect, 80–81
High-skill autonomous work systems, 21–22
High-technology companies, small, 265n.1
Hiring. *See* Recruitment
Hirschhorn, L., 65
HLCs. *See* Home loan consultants
Hochschild, A., 200, 201, 210, 225–26, 228
Hodson, R., 195
Home loan consultants (HLCs), 51–52, 55, 71–74, 108–9, 110–11; procedural rules for, 145–46. *See also* Entrepreneurial model; Sales workflows
"Horizontal hierarchy," 171n.2
Human capital: in Japan, 254; transferability of, 232, 233–34, 242–43
Hybrid model, 19, 168, 171–72, 196–97; employment relations in, 94, 101, 116, 119; interdependencies in, 167, 185–86; teamwork in, 192–93; tendency toward, 273, 277–78
"Hypertext organization," 19

Immediate co-worker relations, 24–25, 169, 170; in sales workflows, 178–80, 185, 186, 194, 196; in service workflows, 174–77, 185, 186, 239. *See also* Co-worker relations
Industrial era, 62
Industrial production model, 37
Industrial relations researchers, 20–23
Info-normative control, 139–42, 154, 163, 164–65, 273; and call monitoring, 141, 142–44; defined, 134; and facilitative supervision, 144–45
Informal co-worker relations, 170–71; in sales workflows, 178, 185, 186; in service workflows, 174, 175–76, 186, 193

Information technology (IT), 4n.5, 6, 37, 38, 147, 154
changes in, 47, 74–75, 76
cost advantage of, 97–98
and co-worker relations, 174, 175, 176
and employee dependence, 232–33, 234
as key work medium, 62
and management control in the ideal types, 137, 138–39
and money market dealers, 80
satisfaction with, 61, 86–88, 242, 246–47, 249; hypotheses regarding, 83, 235
and strategic practices, 157
and types of management control, 135–36
and workflow tendencies, 272, 274
See also Info-normative control
Information technology systems developers. *See* Systems developers
Initiative, employee, 102, 103
Instrumental affectivity, 211, 212, 213, 222, 228; and entrepreneurial ideal type, 203; in knowledge work workflows, 218. *See also* Emotional labor
Insurance salespeople, 17
Intellective skills. *See* Analytical skills
Interdependencies, 166–67, 169–70, 173–74, 259
and job satisfaction, 193–96
in knowledge work workflows, 38–40, 181–85, 191, 239; and other workflows compared, 185–87
in sales workflows, 38, 39, 178–81, 185–86
in service workflows, 39, 174–77, 185, 186–87
and teamwork, 192–93
Internet, 274, 275
Interpretive microsociologists, 23–24
Intrinsic satisfaction, 61, 82–84, 85–86, 88–89, 90–92; and organizational commitment, 246, 247, 250; and overall job satisfaction, 235, 242, 249, 250, 268; and service work tendencies, 272
IT. *See* Information technology
Italy, 20

Japan, 11, 12, 20, 22n.23
control relations in, 257–58
co-worker relations in, 171–72, 173, 259, 271, 277; and job satisfaction, 194, 196; in knowledge work workflows, 182–84, 185–86, 189–90, 192; in sales workflows, 178–81; teamwork, 188, 189–90, 192